AF207082

THE PREACHER'S HEBREW/GREEK COMPANION SERIES

General Editor / Old Testament Editor

Jonathan G. Kline, PhD
Senior Editor
Hendrickson Publishers

New Testament Editor

Sean M. McDonough, PhD
Professor of New Testament
Gordon-Conwell Theological Seminary

Deuteronomy

THE PREACHER'S HEBREW COMPANION TO

Deuteronomy

A Selective Commentary for
Meditation and Sermon Preparation

Ryan P. O'Dowd

HENDRICKSON
ACADEMIC

an imprint of Hendrickson Publishing Group

**The Preacher's Hebrew Companion to Deuteronomy:
A Selective Commentary for Meditation and Sermon Preparation**

© 2024 by Hendrickson Publishers

Published by Hendrickson Academic
P. O. Box 3473
Peabody, Massachusetts 01961-3473
www.hendricksonpublishers.com

ISBN 978-1-68307-349-9

Printed in the United States of America

First Printing — December 2024

Library of Congress Control Number: 2024941422

CONTENTS

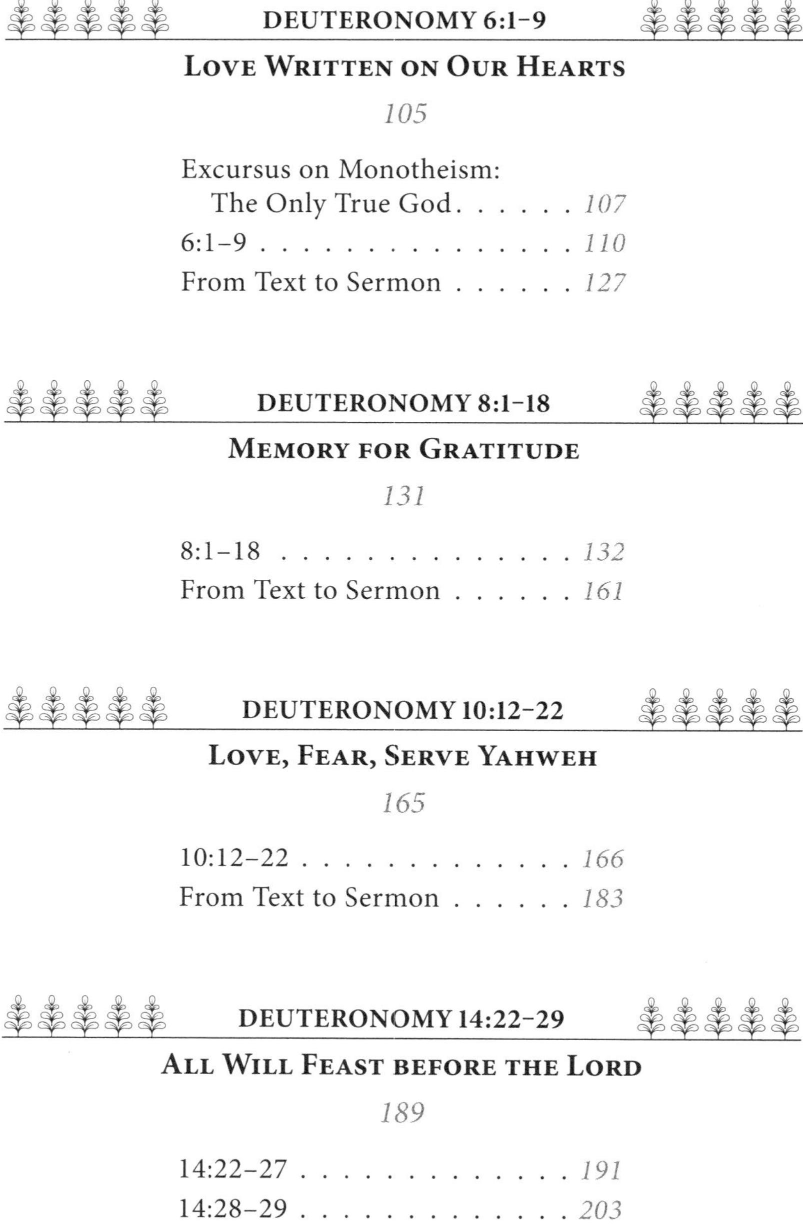

DEUTERONOMY 6:1–9

LOVE WRITTEN ON OUR HEARTS

105

DEUTERONOMY 8:1–18

MEMORY FOR GRATITUDE

131

DEUTERONOMY 10:12–22

LOVE, FEAR, SERVE YAHWEH

165

DEUTERONOMY 14:22–29

ALL WILL FEAST BEFORE THE LORD

189

SERIES EDITORS' PREFACE

Overview

Like many preachers, you may wish you could use the biblical languages in your sermon preparation, but the task seems daunting. Perhaps you lack confidence in your language skills—especially if it's been a long time since you studied Greek or Hebrew—and when you turn to technical commentaries, you feel overwhelmed. Or perhaps you simply don't have the time to do the laborious work of digging into the original-language texts. To help you overcome these challenges, we designed this series, the Preacher's Hebrew Companion (as well as its New Testament counterpart series, the Preacher's Greek Companion). In collaboration with the series authors, our goal as series editors is to gently guide you, the busy preacher, through the Hebrew text of select biblical passages in a way that will empower you to integrate original-language exegesis and homiletics. Our prayer is that you will find this book and the other volumes in this series spiritually and intellectually encouraging as well as pleasant to use. We hope your use of the series will make your sermon preparation a more profound and satisfying process and will invigorate your preaching.

Structure

Each volume in this series includes the following three features for a given biblical book (or portion of a book):

- ❧ **a curated selection of passages** we believe many preachers would likely choose to preach on from the biblical book (or portion of the book) in question; **or, for shorter biblical books, the entire book**, broken up into manageable passages

- ❧ all the basic **lexical and grammatical tools** you need (whatever your Hebrew skill level may be) **to work through and meditate on the Hebrew text** of these passages in a way that strengthens your sermon preparation and empowers you to preach more effectively

- ❧ **succinct, select comments** intended to help you responsibly and effectively bridge the gap between reading the Hebrew text and delivering a sermon on it

The Preacher's Hebrew Companion is not a traditional commentary series, as is reflected in its title and subtitle: "*Companion*" (not "Commentary") and "*Selected* Passages for *Meditation* and *Sermon Preparation*." That is, we conceived this series as a *supplement* to the wealth of fine commentaries that already exist, not as a replacement for any of them. We recommend using this series alongside traditional commentaries, which by design include helpful information that is not covered in ours.

The Selection of Passages

Each volume in the Preacher's Hebrew Companion series provides the Hebrew text of **approximately ten to twelve passages** from a particular biblical book (or portion thereof):

- In addition to having expertise in Hebrew and exegesis, our series authors typically have extensive preaching experience or are full-time preachers by vocation. Unless the biblical book in question is short enough to be included in full, they chose **passages** they think **preachers would most likely desire to preach**. In order to encourage preaching through the biblical book in an "expository" rather than a thematic manner, these passages are presented in canonical order. That said, for longer books (such as Isaiah or Matthew), we encouraged authors to choose passages that highlight or represent important themes found in the book; for such books, however, the chosen passages are still presented in canonical order. The curated, limited number of passages in each series volume allows you, if you wish, to use the passages as the basis for a "ready-made" sermon series of whatever length suits your schedule (e.g., for a series consisting of, say, four, seven, ten, or twelve sermons). Alternatively, you might choose to preach a series using some of the passages in a volume and then supplement these with passages from the biblical book in question that are not found in the volume.

- The aims of the series guided our decisions about passage length. On the one hand, we encouraged authors to choose **passages that are not too long**, so that the portions of text won't be daunting to you if your Hebrew skills are rudimentary; nor do we want you to be overwhelmed by wading through dozens of verses in Hebrew. For this reason, our ideal length for most passages has been approximately ten verses. On the other hand, in order to do justice to the natural boundaries of longer passages, we have taken care not to artificially truncate such texts. Consider, for example, the account of the crossing of the Red Sea (Exod 14–15) or the story of the raising of Lazarus (John 11). Although these texts are far too long to be included in full in a volume in this series, each constituent part of these texts is vital to understanding their narrative development and message. For such passages, we asked authors to focus—as a preacher might typically do when delivering a sermon on a lengthy passage—on what they consider to be the most salient verses from the passage. Accordingly, we have provided the Hebrew text for only these verses, with the author summarizing the other verses (in English).

🌱 Finally, when authors deemed it helpful (especially for longer biblical books), they have indicated, on the first page devoted to each passage, the **larger literary unit to which the passage belongs**,[1] thus helping you see the passage in question as part of a larger whole rather than as an isolated pericope. In cases where this larger literary context is indicated, we encourage you to pick up a Bible and read and dwell on this context while using this volume to work through the passage.

The Presentation of Each Passage

This volume helps you work through each passage it contains by presenting the Hebrew text of the passage along with the lexical and grammatical information you need in order to dig into this original-language text. Designed to be highly accessible, this format is intended (1) to enable you to work through the text in manageable chunks and according to your abilities, regardless of your skill level in Hebrew; (2) to simultaneously facilitate both study and devotion; and (3) in conjunction with the author's commentary, to help you bridge the gap, as easily and seamlessly as possible, between the original-language text and preaching.

More specifically, this volume contains the following five sections for each passage:

🌱 A **brief introduction** to the passage—typically comprising only a few sentences—is included in order to set the stage for the passage and highlight its important themes.

🌱 For ease of reading and to encourage you to slow down and contemplate the text, the passage is typically divided into subunits. For each of these subunits, we provide the **Hebrew text** of each clause or phrase, along

---

1. Occasionally, such a literary unit is coterminous with the passage itself.

with **transliteration** (as a pronunciation help for those whose Hebrew is at a rudimentary level) and the author's **translation**.[2]

 Next, each clause or phrase from the subunit is presented in an interlinear fashion, notably with **a contextual gloss (or multiple contextual glosses) and parsing for each word**.[3] For example:

1a	בְּרֵאשִׁית בָּרָא אֱלֹהִים		
	In the beginning, God created		
בְּרֵאשִׁית *bə·rē·šît*	in beginning of/ when . . . began	CST W/ PREP בְּ	noun
בָּרָא *bā·rāʾ*	(he) created	QAL PF 3MS	verb
אֱלֹהִים *ʾĕ·lō·hîm*	God	ABS	noun

This formatting allows you to easily analyze each word in the clause or phrase (by helping you on the level of semantics and morphology) and to perceive how the words work together as a whole (by helping you on the level of syntax).

A key feature of each volume in this series is the inclusion of **concise comments** to accompany some clauses and phrases. These have two primary goals: (1) to enable you to understand and exegete the text more deeply than might be possible from reading it in English, and (2) to equip

---

2. The Hebrew text used in this series has been taken from the Michigan-Claremont-Westminster Electronic Hebrew Bible, a popular electronic version based on the BHS that has been revised by its creators on the basis of comparison with the Leningrad Codex. This electronic text is in the public domain and has been made available courtesy of the J. Alan Groves Center for Advanced Biblical Research. For simplicity's sake, whenever there is a *ketiv-qere*, only the *qere* has been presented (without being marked as such). Interested readers should feel free to consult critical editions, such as the BHS, to see where instances of *ketiv-qere* or other text-critical issues occur.

3. The glosses are the author's own and intentionally err on the "literal" end of the spectrum, in order to help you apprehend the basic meaning(s) of each word in context. The parsings have been supplied by the team at Hendrickson. Naturally, some words can plausibly be parsed more than one way in context; in such cases, the parsing provided is the one we deemed to make the most sense, but other parsings could have been listed instead.

you with insights into the original-language text that will be of direct value for your preaching. To help you focus and not become overwhelmed with too much information, we encouraged our authors to comment only on those clauses and phrases for which they thought doing so would accomplish these two goals. In addition, because the volumes in this series are not only language aids but—ultimately and more importantly—preaching aids, we asked authors to highlight those features in the Hebrew text that bring out key themes, rhetorical and theological emphasis, narrative development, character development, connections with other biblical texts, and the like. Although noting various other features in the Hebrew text may have been intrinsically interesting from a grammatical perspective or helpful for strengthening your language skills, authors have generally refrained from commenting on such features when doing so would not be likely to aid you in moving from text to sermon in any substantial way.[4] In short, an author's brief, select comments are intended—in conjunction with the volume's language aids—to provide you both with *focus* and with *space* to slow down, meditate, wonder, and mature in your understanding and experience of the text, as you form your own judgments on it and prepare to proclaim the divine word to your hearers. The author's comments are not intended to circumscribe the possible interpretive options with one single answer (especially for texts whose interpretation is the particular subject of debate among Christian believers). Rather, they are meant to stimulate your thinking, to help you see features of the text (and connections with other texts) that you may not have perceived before, and to prompt you to ask questions that may not have previously occurred to you.

 Each passage ends with a brief section titled **"From Text to Sermon,"** in which our authors, building on their comments, suggest ways you can move from working through the Hebrew text to the task of homiletics, highlighting potential points of emphasis or particular insights you may wish to share with your audience. In this way, the authors provide you with possible ways to bring the text to life for your audience (e.g., types

---

4. Another way we have kept the presentation streamlined and uncluttered, so that you can achieve maximum focus, is by intentionally keeping source citations to a minimum. Authors' comments on a given passage are the fruit of their scholarly research on the passage, their personal reflection on it, and their experience preaching and teaching it. They cite secondary sources only when they draw a specific insight from one particular source or wish to point you to a particularly helpful resource for further reading. As stated above, we naturally encourage you to also use traditional commentaries (which typically provide more documentation) in your study and sermon preparation.

of illustrations you might use). Because individual preachers (and each of our series authors) bring their own particular skills, perspectives, backgrounds, and oratorial approaches to bear on the homiletical task, and because every biblical text has its own unique features, we encouraged our authors to structure the "From Text to Sermon" section as a free-form series of short paragraphs whose content and emphases are guided by their own personal judgment about what is most helpful for a variety of preachers in different places, cultures, and times. The remarks in this section are always grouped according to rubrics (in the form of inline headers); but rather than restrict authors with a "one-size-fits-all" set of rubrics, we allowed them to create their own rubrics and even, if helpful, to vary these rubrics across passages within their volume in light of the unique features and emphases of each passage.[5] We view the resulting diversity of approaches and emphases across this series (and even within a given volume) as a strength, and we hope this aspect of the series will encourage you to use your own judgment about how to preach each passage in a way that best suits you and your listeners, being sensitive to the promptings and guidance of the Spirit of God.

Audience and Theological Perspective

Since our hope is that many different kinds of people will find the volumes in this series useful, we have designed the Preacher's Hebrew Companion to be helpful to a broad spectrum of Christian preachers:

 Our intention is that the series will be **useful and accessible to a large and diverse group of preachers serving a variety of communities throughout the world**. For this reason, we encouraged authors to exercise sensitivity and broad-mindedness in their comments and particularly when writing the "From Text to Sermon" section, in which they could run the risk of being too culturally specific. In particular, we asked authors that any sermon illustrations they included in this section generally be as universal as possible or that, instead of providing specific illustrations, they point to themes from the passage you may wish to illustrate in one way or another. That said, because specificity is essential for good communication, we also allowed authors to suggest—when they deemed

---

5. That said, we suggested the following possible rubrics to authors as starting points to consider: theological themes, themes for application and illustration, integrating the broader historical and literary context, learning from the language, and (as deemed helpful and not reductionistic) "the big idea" of the passage.

it particularly helpful—concrete, culturally specific examples as springboards to help you think about examples that will be relevant for your own context.

- We asked our authors to express any **theological perspectives** in a way that is **consistent with the beliefs stated in the Apostles' Creed**. Because this series aims to meet the needs of Christian preachers of various theological viewpoints, we encouraged a diversity of theological perspectives within these bounds across the volumes in the series. In addition, because the series has a joint focus on exegesis (close attention to what a specific text says) and homiletics (how to preach said text), we advised authors when making any theological comments to let these flow naturally from the text at hand, rather than using the text as a springboard to discuss issues that would more properly fall under the rubric of systematic theology. Although we asked authors to avoid reading any given passage through the lens of a theological system grounded in other biblical texts, we also strongly encouraged them to discuss allusions to other biblical passages or other innerbiblical literary connections if they felt that doing so would help you understand the message of the text at hand and know how to preach it more effectively.

Acknowledgments

We would like to offer our heartfelt gratitude to the following individuals, who have played a central role in the creation of this series:

- Arley Kangas, Marco Resendes, and Tyler Comer, for their excellent work on various aspects of the making of these volumes, especially transliterating, proofreading, and generating the indexes.

- Phil Frank, for his expert typesetting and for patiently working with us, in our capacity as series editors, to achieve the desired formatting and aesthetic for these volumes.

- The series authors, for joining us in this unique project and for sharing our vision and lending their considerable skills to the task. These volumes are the result of a fruitful collaboration between the Hendrickson team and the series authors (with both parties contributing to the content). We are truly grateful for the opportunity to have worked on this project together.

All of us—the series editors, the series authors, and the team at Hendrickson—pray that the volume you now hold in your hands will empower and encourage you to work through the Hebrew text of the Bible in order to deepen your sermon preparation and strengthen your proclamation of the word of God. We nurture a deep respect and appreciation for the challenging work that you as a preacher do on the "front lines," and we recognize the many challenges (logistical, mental, emotional, spiritual, and more) that you encounter on a weekly, indeed a daily, basis. We are honored to come alongside you and support you in your important labors, and we pray that your use of this book will bear much fruit for the kingdom of God.

Jonathan G. Kline
Sean M. McDonough

Overview

While the first two sermon selections below (Deut 1:1–8 and 4:1–14) provide most of the introductory and background information that the reader or preacher requires. It will be helpful to add a few summarizing notes here at the start.

Deuteronomy is as foundational to the Bible as Genesis and Exodus even though the latter are more popular among readers. That is a controversial claim, but just consider this: Deuteronomy is the backdrop for the rest of what has significantly been called the "Deuteronomistic history" that runs from Joshua through 2 Kings. The book is also the substance of what is described as the "law," or תּוֹרָה, in Psalms, especially in the great hymns to the law in Pss 1, 19, and 119. Furthermore, Deuteronomy's covenant is a major source for most of the prophets, especially Jeremiah, Ezekiel, and Hosea. Above all, the New Testament cites Deuteronomy more than any other book, and Jesus himself refers to Deuteronomy more than any other book. In short, if Jesus is to be discovered and known in Scripture, this is a book that must be read and preached.

Authorship

Until the last two centuries, Moses was viewed as the author of Deuteronomy. The debate has become increasingly tense in some circles and made more complicated by archaeological and social-historical studies. There are a few brief things to bear in mind when comparing commentaries and evaluating arguments.

First, while most scholars now date the book to the six or seventh century BC, it is generally recognized that much of the material in Deuteronomy arose in earlier centuries. When exactly these laws and stories were written and just how much Moses said or wrote simply cannot be known with any degree of certainty. As such, arguments *for* Mosaic authorship of Deuteronomy should not be dismissed simply because they are out of fashion today. But neither should the insights of scholars assigning a later date be overlooked given the careful historical analysis they provide.

Second, one must remember that both fashion and politics can play significant roles in academic publishing. Dating Deuteronomy later, for example, is often a way of signaling one's academic sophistication and religious neutrality. In addition, Mosaic authorship of Deuteronomy has been at the center of major debates about

Israel's claim to the land of Palestine and the corresponding displacement of Palestinians. If Moses' existence can be discredited, Israel's claim to their land might be questioned. A wise preacher will tread this ground lightly, not saying more about Moses or Israel than is necessary to proclaim God's inspired word to the church.

Third, Deuteronomy begins and ends with the voice of an anonymous narrator. This has earned Deuteronomy a significant place in academic research, and I refer curious readers to works by Sonnet (1997), McConville (2002), and Olson (1994) for more on the "omniscient narrator" in Deuteronomy. The bottom line is this: someone other than Moses is telling this story and has likely put the book into its final shape. And this leads us to the next point.

"The Book within the Book"

This clever title of Jean-Pierre Sonnet's (1997) study of Deuteronomy captures the subtle genius of this ancient text. One writer is telling us about Moses the writer. There is indeed a sense that Deuteronomy is as much a story about Moses—and by Moses—as it is a story about writing and reading books and laws: the narrator writes, God writes, Moses writes, families write, the king writes, and future generations like yours and mine read and write. Reading and writing come to symbolize true and faithful obedience to God and his commands and the tradition that carries that into future generations. If we get caught up on arguments about Moses' authorship and fail to ingest and live by these words, we will have gotten the book precisely upside down.

A Covenant of Love

Deuteronomy 6:4–5 contains the famous passage known as the Shema, "Hear, O Israel," and with it, the great command to love God with all of our heart, soul, and strength. Deuteronomy simultaneously situates our love *for* God inside the covenant initiated by God out of his great love *for* Israel, its ancestors, and its descendants (7:6–11). The individual laws as well as the ceremonies that commit Israel to keeping these laws are not merely legal or political measures; they are the key to wise living rooted in the great and perfect source of all love. It is a love we receive from God, give back to God, and share with our neighbor (10:12–20).

Not Your Ordinary Law

It will become clear below that biblical law is not like modern legislative law. Biblical law comes from God, not from human institutions. It is also situated in narratives. Often it is poetic in its repetitive, casuistic *if-then* form (e.g., "If there is a dispute between men and they present themselves for judgment . . . then you shall . . ." [25:1–2]). And it frequently targets the heart: "do not harden your heart" and "be careful lest you have a wicked thought in your heart . . . and you look meanly at your brother" (15:7, 9). The paradigms in the law thus serve as storied and easily memorized moral principles for deliberating situations and carrying out actions. The legal scholar Bernard Jackson (2006) has called these "wisdom-laws" since their purpose is less one of legislation than of informing and shaping moral reasoning. In this way, the laws are very much like proverbs, since no single law or proverb tells us what to do in a given situation (see Prov 26:4–5). Rather, it is in the collection of the laws and proverbs that we come to discover a sense of the comprehensive moral order of our world. Laws concerning, for example, the sanctity of life and marriage, moral purity, the proper use of material goods, work and rest, and human need and humanitarian aid offer us a picture of the whole. This panorama provides the order we need to deliberate and make moral decisions that fit in the structure of God's righteous ways. Given the universal and generic scope of wisdom, Paul Fiddes (2013:333) helpfully describes torah as "a reduction of the vastness of wisdom to boundaries that can be grasped. The boundless text of the world is condensed, as it were, into one text with universal application." As we know from the psalms, the law "makes wise" (Pss 19:7; 119:98) and bestows "understanding" (Ps 119:99, 104).

How to Use This Book

The Preacher's Hebrew Companion series is designed to *accompany* other commentaries. New Deuteronomy commentaries are always being published, but, if affordable to the reader, I recommend the works by Gordon McConville, Christopher Wright, Patrick Miller, and Richard Nelson. More advanced volumes worth reading include the works of Georg Braulik, Jean Pierre Sonnet, Moshe Weinfeld, Mark Glanville, Jeffries Hamilton, Dennis Olson, and Oliver O'Donovan.

As I wrote this companion, I was aware that readers may not have any of these books and that some readers may have no commentaries at all (or have difficulty accessing them). For that reason, I have provided sufficient preaching guidance and discussion so that my suggestions will be conceptually and theologically clear. I have also sometimes drawn on theological or cultural ideas that I have not found in other commentaries (e.g., theologies of love, time, and place). So there is a degree to which this volume, though brief, can stand on its own.

When it comes to guidance for preaching, this volume intentionally does not provide a cut-and-paste, connect-the-dots guide for preachers. I have been preaching for the better part of twenty years. In some of those years I have preached a sermon almost every week. That adds up to nearly a thousand sermons. I have also made homiletics an area of careful study, evaluating others' sermons and receiving feedback on my own. While preaching styles vary, I have found that there are some very basic practices that work well. Above all, the sermon must be the preacher's own, crafted from personal study of the text and the associated labor that goes into shaping, editing, rehearsing, and delivering a message at a particular time and place. For this, I recommend a very basic threefold approach.

First, read the text closely and often, giving patient attention to the original language. Look and listen for patterns, surprising elements, major themes, or important questions. Begin to think about how this text relates to other parts of the canon. This first stage will require concentration, patience, imagination, and a humble and yielding spirit of prayer.

Second, reflect hermeneutically. What themes and ideas require further analysis? What questions have been raised that must be answered? What cannot be answered? What themes speak directly into our moment in time? Here it is proper to draw upon research in cultural studies, philosophy, ethics, and psychology to probe more deeply into these passages and understand how they might speak into our moment in time.

Finally, apply the text theologically in preaching. At this stage, make use of any background reading and reflection that would help you put the biblical text into a format that nurtures, challenges, and strengthens the church. This will demand cutting, narrowing, and ordering of your ideas. Strive to be succinct (contrary to common habits, there is no biblical virtue in a longer sermon). Above all, labor to seek the face of God as you study the text, allowing the sermon to bring the congregation alongside you so that that the scriptures illumine more of God and more of our life in this world.

Gratitude

I end with a note of thanks. Above all to God for his goodness, lovingkindness, and mercy. To Jonathan Kline, who invited me to contribute this volume. For many years now, Jonathan has encouraged me in my research and writing projects and has always found delight in new questions I want to answer. I'm so very glad to finally have the chance to partner with him. Both Jonathan and Karen D. Lavery provided countless helpful editorial comments.

My wife, Amy, is a constant reminder of God's boundless generosity. For all the ways she loves me, encourages me, listens to me, challenges me, cautions me back from error, and pushes me forward to read, write, and teach, I am grateful.

And, finally, to the people at Chesterton House at Cornell and Bread of Life Anglican Church in Ithaca, who have, for over a decade, pushed me to pursue my academic disciplines alongside a pastoral calling. This book is dedicated with thanks to staff, students, parishioners, and friends, past and present.

LIST OF ABBREVIATIONS

1	first person	indef	indefinite
2	second person	INF	infinitive
3	third person	INTERR/interr	interrogative
ABS	absolute	JUSS	jussive
adj	adjective	M	masculine
adv	adverb	NIPH	Niphal
ATTR	attributive	P	plural
C	common	PASS	passive
COHORT	cohortative	PF	perfect
CONJ/conj	conjunction	PRED	predicative
CST	construct	PREP/prep	preposition
DEF. ART.	definite article	PRON/pron	pronoun
demonstr	demonstrative	PTCP	participle
F	feminine	S	singular
HIPH	Hiphil	SUBST	substantive
HITH	Hithpael	SX	suffix
HOPH	Hophal	w/	with
IMPF	imperfect	WAYY	wayyiqtol
IMPV	imperative		

NOTE: All verse numbers in this volume refer to the Hebrew text; when the English verse numbering differs, it is listed in brackets following the Hebrew numbering.

A BOOK ABOUT A PREACHER FOR PREACHERS

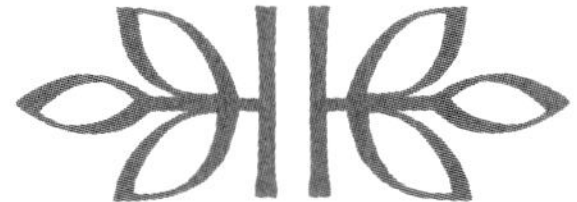

Deuteronomy is *the* book of Moses. In it we hear his sermons, his exhortation, and his mindset during what appear to be the last days of his life. To put this in perspective, pan out to the broader context of the Pentateuch from Genesis to Deuteronomy:

Genesis tells the story of the creation of the world, Israel's election, and their migration to Egypt.

Exodus recounts God's salvation from Egypt, the giving of the law, and the building of the tabernacle.

Numbers overviews the journey in the desert.

Leviticus stipulates the rules for becoming a people holy to the Lord.

Notice especially how these last two books both begin: "And Yahweh called Moses" (Lev 1:1); "And Yahweh spoke to Moses" (Num 1:1). These books emphasize words from God.

But Deuteronomy closes in on the heart and mind of Israel's greatest prophet and preacher with its striking opening: "These are the words that Moses spoke" (1:1). In fact, Deuteronomy reports speech more than any book in the Pentateuch.

So we are led to ask: what will Moses say to God's chosen nation as they prepare to enter the promised land? For those who preach week in and week out, Deuteronomy is a unique gift of sermons on the last day of a preacher's life, reminding us of the urgency and responsibility of declaring the word of God to his people.

LARGER LITERARY CONTEXT ▸ 1:1–3:29

1a

אֵ֣לֶּה הַדְּבָרִ֗ים אֲשֶׁ֨ר דִּבֶּ֤ר מֹשֶׁה֙ אֶל־כָּל־יִשְׂרָאֵ֔ל

ʾēlle haddəvārîm ʾăšer dibber mōše el-kol-yiśrāʾēl

These are the words that Moses spoke to all Israel

1b

בְּעֵ֖בֶר הַיַּרְדֵּ֑ן בַּמִּדְבָּ֡ר בָּֽעֲרָבָה֩ מ֨וֹל ס֜וּף

bəʿēver hayyardēn bammidbār bāʿărāvâ môl sûf

across the Jordan, in the desert, in the Arabah opposite Suph,

1c

בֵּֽין־פָּארָ֨ן וּבֵֽין־תֹּ֜פֶל וְלָבָ֤ן וַחֲצֵרֹת֙ וְדִ֣י זָהָֽב׃

bên-pāʾrān ûvên-tōfel wəlāvān waḥăṣērōt wədî zāhāv.

between Paran and Tophel and Laban and Hazeroth and Dizahab.

2a

אַחַ֣ד עָשָׂ֥ר יוֹם֙

ʾaḥad ʿāśār yôm

It is eleven days

2b

מֵחֹרֵ֔ב דֶּ֖רֶךְ הַר־שֵׂעִ֑יר עַ֖ד קָדֵ֥שׁ בַּרְנֵֽעַ׃

mēḥōrēv derek har-śēʿîr ʿad qādēš barnēaʿ.

from Horeb by the way of Mount Seir to Kadesh Barnea.

3a

וַיְהִי֙ בְּאַרְבָּעִ֣ים שָׁנָ֔ה

wayəhî bəʾarbāʿîm šānâ

It was in the fortieth year,

3b

בְּעַשְׁתֵּֽי־עָשָׂ֥ר חֹ֖דֶשׁ בְּאֶחָ֣ד לַחֹ֑דֶשׁ

bəʿaštê-ʿāśār ḥōdeš bəʾeḥād laḥōdeš

on the first day of the eleventh month,

3c

דִּבֶּ֤ר מֹשֶׁה֙ אֶל־בְּנֵ֣י יִשְׂרָאֵ֔ל כְּכֹ֛ל אֲשֶׁ֥ר צִוָּ֥ה יְהוָ֖ה אֹת֥וֹ אֲלֵהֶֽם׃

dibber mōše ʾel-bənê yiśrāʾēl kəkōl ʾăšer ṣiwwâ YHWH ʾōtô ʾălēhem.

**that Moses spoke to the children of Israel
all that Yahweh commanded him concerning them.**

4a   אַחֲרֵי הַכֹּתוֹ

’aḥărê hakkōtô

After he defeated

4b   אֵת סִיחֹן מֶלֶךְ הָאֱמֹרִי אֲשֶׁר יוֹשֵׁב בְּחֶשְׁבּוֹן

’ēt sîḥōn melek̠ hā’ĕmōrî ’ăšer yôšēv bəḥešbôn

וְאֵת עוֹג מֶלֶךְ הַבָּשָׁן אֲשֶׁר־יוֹשֵׁב בְּעַשְׁתָּרֹת בְּאֶדְרֶעִי׃

wə’ēt ‘ôg melek̠ habbāšān ’ăšer yôšēv bə‘aštārōt bə’edre‘î.

**Sihon, king of the Amorites, who lived in Heshbon,
and Og, the king of Bashan, who lived at Ashtaroth and at Edrei,**

5a   בְּעֵבֶר הַיַּרְדֵּן בְּאֶרֶץ מוֹאָב

bə‘ēver hayyardēn bə’ereṣ mô’āv

across the Jordan in the land of Moab,

5b   הוֹאִיל מֹשֶׁה בֵּאֵר אֶת־הַתּוֹרָה הַזֹּאת לֵאמֹר׃

hô’îl mōše bē’ēr ’et-hattôrâ hazzō’t lē’mōr.

Moses began to explain this torah, saying,

❧⊹❧

1a	אֵלֶּה הַדְּבָרִים אֲשֶׁר דִּבֶּר מֹשֶׁה אֶל־כָּל־יִשְׂרָאֵל		

These are the words that Moses spoke to all Israel

אֵלֶּה	these	---		demonstr
’ēl·le				pron
הַדְּבָרִים	the words	ABS		noun
had·də·vā·rîm		W/ DEF. ART.		
אֲשֶׁר	that/which	---		relative
’ă·šer				pron
דִּבֶּר	(he) said/spoke	PIEL PF 3MS		verb
dib·ber				
מֹשֶׁה	Moses	ABS		noun
mō·še				

אֶל־	to	---	prep
אֶל *'el-*			
כָּל־	all	CST	noun
כֹּל *kol-*			
יִשְׂרָאֵל	Israel	ABS	noun
יִשְׂרָאֵל *yiś·rā·'ēl*			

The combination of "the words" (הַדְּבָרִים) and "spoke" (דִּבֶּר) are anything but incidental here. They anticipate sophisticated wordplay in Deuteronomy that moves from the "words" of Moses' sermons to God's covenant (בְּרִית) with Israel and his theophanic revelation on Mount Horeb (5:2, 4), to the words of a book (סֵפֶר) that Moses writes for the king (17:18) and all future generations to read and copy (6:6–9; 30:10; 31:9–13, 24). Words and speech are also always keywords for the revelation from God in nature and in the law (Pss 19:4; 119:9, 16, 17, etc.), and Deuteronomy has more reported speech—mainly of God and Moses—than any other book in the Pentateuch.

This is typical language in the Pentateuch, weaving Deuteronomy into the narratives that precede it.

1b	בְּעֵבֶר הַיַּרְדֵּן בַּמִּדְבָּר בָּעֲרָבָה מוֹל סוּף

across the Jordan, in the desert, in the Arabah opposite Suph,

בְּעֵבֶר	beyond/across	CST W/ PREP בְּ	noun
עֵבֶר *bə·'ē·ver*			
הַיַּרְדֵּן	the Jordan	ABS W/ DEF. ART.	noun
יַרְדֵּן *hay·yar·dēn*			
בַּמִּדְבָּר	in the desert	ABS W/ PREP בְּ + DEF. ART.	noun
מִדְבָּר *bam·mid·bār*			
בָּעֲרָבָה	in the Arabah	ABS W/ PREP בְּ + DEF. ART.	noun
עֲרָבָה *bā·'ă·rā·bâ*			
מוֹל	opposite/in front of	---	prep
מוֹל *môl*			
סוּף	Suph	ABS	noun
סוּף *sûf*			

Deuteronomy takes us quickly to scenes at particular times and places. These memories will add force to the new times and places where this story is told and lived out, including our own.

1c	בֵּין־פָּארָן וּבֵין־תֹּפֶל וְלָבָן וַחֲצֵרֹת וְדִי זָהָב:		
	between Paran and Tophel and Laban and Hazeroth and Dizahab.		

בֵּין־	between	---	prep
בֵּין	*bên-*		
פָּארָן	Paran	ABS	noun
פָּארָן	*pā'·rān*		
וּבֵין־	and between	---	prep
בֵּין	*û·vên-*	W/ CONJ וְ	
תֹּפֶל	Tophel	ABS	noun
תֹּפֶל	*tō·fel*		
וְלָבָן	and Laban	ABS	noun
לָבָן	*wə·lā·vān*	W/ CONJ וְ	
וַחֲצֵרֹת	and Hazeroth	ABS	noun
חֲצֵרֹות	*wa·ḥă·ṣē·rōt*	W/ CONJ וְ	
וְדִי זָהָב:	and Di-Zahab	ABS	noun
דִי זָהָב	*wə·dî zā·hāv*	W/ CONJ וְ	

While most of these locations are unknown today, it seems likely that they move backwards chronologically, taking Israel from Moab back to Horeb and the initiation of their covenant on the mountain.

2a	אַחַד עָשָׂר יֹום		
	It is eleven days		

אַחַד עָשָׂר	eleven	ABS	cardinal number
אֶחָד עָשָׂר	*'a·ḥad 'ā·śār*		
יֹום	day	ABS	noun
יֹום	*yôm*		

Notice the precise time here, a common trait in covenants and annals of kings in the ancient Near East. Every day counts in the telling of God's history and in the days we seek to live before God, starting with today (see "Today if you hear his voice" in Ps 95:7). Israel also remembers that their ancestors could have entered the promised land very soon after leaving Horeb if they had only trusted God in their day.

2b מֵחֹרֵב דֶּרֶךְ הַר־שֵׂעִיר עַד קָדֵשׁ בַּרְנֵעַ׃

from Horeb by the way of Mount Seir to Kadesh Barnea.

מֵחֹרֵב חֹרֵב	from Horeb *mē·ḥō·rēv*	ABS W/ PREP מִן	noun
דֶּרֶךְ דֶּרֶךְ	(the) way of *de·rek*	CST	noun
הַר־ הַר	mount *har-*	CST	noun
שֵׂעִיר שֵׂעִיר	Seir *śē·ʿîr*	ABS	noun
עַד עַד	to *ʿad*	---	prep
קָדֵשׁ בַּרְנֵעַ׃ קָדֵשׁ בַּרְנֵעַ	Kadesh Barnea *qā·dēš bar·nē·aʿ*	ABS	noun

Horeb is the region of Mount Sinai where the covenant was established. At Kadesh Barnea, Israel rebelled against Yahweh and Moses (Num 13). These first and last locations remind Israel that God has generously given them the gift of a covenant and a land, but that the previous generation had rejected that gift. Though tied to their past, Israel is in a new moment, a new place, and a new opportunity before the Lord.

3a וַיְהִי בְּאַרְבָּעִים שָׁנָה

It was in the fortieth year,

וַיְהִי הָיָה	and it was *wa·yə·hî*	QAL WAYY 3MS	verb
בְּאַרְבָּעִים אַרְבָּעִים	in forty *bə·ʾar·bā·ʾîm*	ABS W/ PREP בְּ	cardinal number

| שָׁנָה | year | | ABS | noun |
| שָׁנָה | *šā·nâ* | | | |

Making the date more precise, Israel knows that it has come to the end of their judgment of forty years of wandering, one year for each day the spies journeyed in the promised land (Num 14:33–34).

3b בְּעַשְׁתֵּי־עָשָׂר חֹדֶשׁ בְּאֶחָד לַחֹדֶשׁ

on the first day of the eleventh month,

בְּעַשְׁתֵּי־עָשָׂר	in (the) eleventh		ABS	cardinal
עַשְׁתֵּי עָשָׂר	*bə·ʿaš·tê·ʾā·śār*		W/ PREP בְּ	number
חֹדֶשׁ	month		ABS	noun
חֹדֶשׁ	*ḥō·deš*			
בְּאֶחָד	on (the) first		ABS	cardinal
אֶחָד	*bə·ʾe·ḥād*		W/ PREP בְּ	number
לַחֹדֶשׁ	of the month		ABS	noun
חֹדֶשׁ	*la·ḥō·deš*		W/ PREP לְ + DEF. ART.	

This is the only precise date listed in the book, perhaps pointing to the day of Moses' death (34:5) and thus the beginning of these sermons and the book that captures them.

3c דִּבֶּר מֹשֶׁה אֶל־בְּנֵי יִשְׂרָאֵל כְּכֹל אֲשֶׁר צִוָּה יְהוָה אֹתוֹ אֲלֵהֶם׃

that Moses spoke to the children of Israel
all that Yahweh commanded him concerning them.

דִּבֶּר	(he) spoke/said		PIEL PF 3MS	verb
דבר	*dib·ber*			
מֹשֶׁה	Moses		ABS	noun
מֹשֶׁה	*mō·še*			
אֶל־	to		---	prep
אֶל	*ʾel-*			
בְּנֵי	(the) sons/children of		CST	noun
בֵּן	*bə·nê*			

Hebrew	Gloss	Parsing	Part of speech
יִשְׂרָאֵ֖ל יִשְׂרָאֵל *yiś·rā·ʾēl*	Israel	ABS	noun
כְּכֹ֕ל כֹּל *kə·kōl*	according to all	ABS W/ PREP כְּ	noun
אֲשֶׁ֥ר אֲשֶׁר *ʾă·šer*	that/which	- - -	relative pron
צִוָּ֧ה צוה *ṣiw·wâ*	(he) commanded	PIEL PF 3MS	verb
יְהוָ֛ה יהוה *YHWH*	Yahweh	ABS	noun
אֹת֖וֹ אֵת *ʾō·tô*	him	- - - W/ 3MS SX	particle
אֲלֵהֶֽם׃ אֶל *ʾă·lē·hem*	concerning them	- - - W/ 3MP SX	prep

This is a partial repetition from 1a–b, with additional information provided in 3d and 5b.

Some translate the final phrase, "to speak to them." In either case, these are not just Moses' words but the revelation from God for a new time and place.

4a	אַחֲרֵי הַכֹּתוֹ

After he defeated

Hebrew	Gloss	Parsing	Part of speech
אַחֲרֵי אַחֲרֵי *ʾa·ḥă·rê*	after	- - -	prep
הַכֹּתוֹ נכה *hak·kō·tô*	he struck/defeated	HIPH INF CST W/ 3MS SX	verb

אֶת סִיחֹן מֶלֶךְ הָאֱמֹרִי אֲשֶׁר יוֹשֵׁב בְּחֶשְׁבּוֹן
וְאֵת עוֹג מֶלֶךְ הַבָּשָׁן אֲשֶׁר־יוֹשֵׁב בְּעַשְׁתָּרֹת בְּאֶדְרֶעִי:

Sihon, king of the Amorites, who lived in Heshbon,
and Og, the king of Bashan, who lived at Ashtaroth and at Edrei,

אֶת אֶת	(direct object marker) 'ēt	---	particle
סִיחֹן סִיחוֹן	Sihon sî·ḥōn	ABS	noun
מֶלֶךְ מֶלֶךְ	king of me·leḵ	CST	noun
הָאֱמֹרִי אֱמֹרִי	the Amorites hā·'ĕ·mō·rî	MS SUBST W/ DEF. ART.	adj
אֲשֶׁר אֲשֶׁר	who 'ă·šer	---	relative pron
יוֹשֵׁב יָשַׁב	(one) living/dwelling yô·šēv	QAL PTCP MS	verb
בְּחֶשְׁבּוֹן חֶשְׁבּוֹן	in/at Heshbon bə·ḥeš·bôn	ABS W/ PREP בְּ	noun
וְאֵת אֵת	and (+ direct object marker) wə·'ēt	--- W/ CONJ וְ	particle
עוֹג עוֹג	Og ôg	ABS	noun
מֶלֶךְ מֶלֶךְ	king of me·leḵ	CST	noun
הַבָּשָׁן בָּשָׁן	Bashan hab·bā·šān	ABS W/ DEF. ART.	noun
אֲשֶׁר־ אֲשֶׁר	who 'ă·šer	---	relative pron
יוֹשֵׁב יָשַׁב	(one) living/dwelling yô·šēv	QAL PTCP MS	verb
בְּעַשְׁתָּרֹת עַשְׁתָּרוֹת	in/at Ashtaroth bə·'aš·tā·rōt	ABS W/ PREP בְּ	noun
בְּאֶדְרֶעִי: אֶדְרֶעִי	in/at Edrei bə·'ed·re·î	ABS W/ PREP בְּ	noun

See Num 21:21–25 and Deut 2:24–3:11. Deuteronomy weaves its telling of the law into the earlier stories of Moses in the Pentateuch, notably God's gift of victory.

<table>
<tr><td>5a</td><td colspan="3" align="center">בְּעֵבֶר הַיַּרְדֵּן בְּאֶרֶץ מוֹאָב</td></tr>
<tr><td></td><td colspan="3" align="center">across the Jordan in the land of Moab,</td></tr>
<tr><td>בְּעֵבֶר
עֵבֶר</td><td>beyond/across
bə·ʿē·ver</td><td>CST
W/ PREP בְּ</td><td>noun</td></tr>
<tr><td>הַיַּרְדֵּן
יַרְדֵּן</td><td>the Jordan
hay·yar·dēn</td><td>ABS
W/ DEF. ART.</td><td>noun</td></tr>
<tr><td>בְּאֶרֶץ
אֶרֶץ</td><td>in (the) land of
bə·ʾe·reṣ</td><td>CST
W/ PREP בְּ</td><td>noun</td></tr>
<tr><td>מוֹאָב
מוֹאָב</td><td>Moab
mô·ʾāv</td><td>ABS</td><td>noun</td></tr>
</table>

<table>
<tr><td>5b</td><td colspan="3" align="center">הוֹאִיל מֹשֶׁה בֵּאֵר אֶת־הַתּוֹרָה הַזֹּאת לֵאמֹר:</td></tr>
<tr><td></td><td colspan="3" align="center">Moses began to explain this torah, saying,</td></tr>
<tr><td>הוֹאִיל
יאל</td><td>(he) prepared/was willing/
began
hô·ʾîl</td><td>HIPH PF 3MS</td><td>verb</td></tr>
<tr><td>מֹשֶׁה
מֹשֶׁה</td><td>Moses
mō·še</td><td>ABS</td><td>noun</td></tr>
<tr><td>בֵּאֵר
באר</td><td>(he) explained/wrote down
bē·ʾēr</td><td>PIEL PF 3MS</td><td>verb</td></tr>
<tr><td>אֶת־
אֵת</td><td>(direct object marker)
ʾet-</td><td>---</td><td>particle</td></tr>
<tr><td>הַתּוֹרָה
תּוֹרָה</td><td>(the) torah/law
hat·tô·râ</td><td>ABS
W/ DEF. ART.</td><td>noun</td></tr>
<tr><td>הַזֹּאת
זֹאת</td><td>(the) this
haz·zōʾt</td><td>---
W/ DEF. ART.</td><td>demonstr
pron</td></tr>
<tr><td>לֵאמֹר:
אמר</td><td>saying/to say
lē·mōr</td><td>QAL INF CST
W/ PREP לְ</td><td>verb</td></tr>
</table>

בָּאַר means to "explain" or "clarify." Meanwhile, תּוֹרָה is much broader than our English word "law," and often means something like "instruction" (Ps 1:2; Prov 1:8). The sermons that lie ahead of us are, as such, more than a mere recitation of legal precepts like the ones we find in Exod 21–24. Rather, this will be Moses' authoritative interpretation and application at a new time and place. The close reading of the text by Moses here foreshadows the reading of the king in the presence of the Levitical priests (Deut 17:18), and our own reading as well (see 32:47).

As Deuteronomy opens, it introduces the final sermons, or "words," of Moses (1:1). His "words" are explained (1:5) and eventually written in a book for future generations to teach, read, write, and remember (6:7–9; 17:18; 31:34).

We must not rush by these verses and miss the hand of the author telling us this story (see 1:1–5; 34:1–12). In a broader perspective, Deuteronomy is *a book about a book*. This frame-narrative structure is central to two major tenets of Israelite religion and western society. First, the themes of speaking and writing in Deuteronomy come to shape the idea of a "canon" of Scripture that sits at the heart of Jewish, Christian, and Muslim faiths (see 4:2; 12:32). The longevity and relative doctrinal uniformity within these faiths owe much to a concrete body of divine revelation.

Second, with its strong emphasis on acts of speaking, listening, writing, and reading, Deuteronomy's covenant takes the shape of a constitution for Israel, which becomes the foundation of modern western politics. As readers, we are challenged to read, listen, and write as a way of expressing our loyalty to Yahweh, our divine king and savior.

6a
יְהֹוָה אֱלֹהֵינוּ דִּבֶּר אֵלֵינוּ בְּחֹרֵב

YHWH ʾĕlōhênû dibber ʾēlênû bəḥōrēv

"Yahweh our God spoke to us at Horeb,

6b
לֵאמֹר רַב־לָכֶם שֶׁבֶת בָּהָר הַזֶּה:

lēʾmōr rav-lākem ševet bāhār hazze.

saying, ʻYou have stayed long enough at this mountain.

7a
פְּנוּ | וּסְעוּ לָכֶם וּבֹאוּ הַר הָאֱמֹרִי וְאֶל־כָּל־שְׁכֵנָיו בָּעֲרָבָה

pənû ûsəʻû lākem ûvōʾû har hāʾĕmōrî wəʾel-kol-šəkēnāyw bāʻărābâ

**Turn and make your way to come to the hill country of the Amorites
and to all their neighbors in the Arabah**

7b
בָּהָר וּבַשְּׁפֵלָה וּבַנֶּגֶב וּבְחוֹף הַיָּם אֶרֶץ הַכְּנַעֲנִי

vāhār ûvaššəfēlâ ûvannegev ûvəḥôf hayyām ereṣ hakkənaʻănî

וְהַלְּבָנוֹן עַד־הַנָּהָר הַגָּדֹל נְהַר־פְּרָת:

wəhalləvānôn ʻad-hannāhār haggādōl nəhar-pərāt.

**in the hill country and the Shephelah and the Negeb
and the coastlands of the sea, the land of the Canaanites
and Lebanon as far as the great river, the Euphrates.**

8a
רְאֵה נָתַתִּי לִפְנֵיכֶם אֶת־הָאָרֶץ

rəʾē nātattî lifnêkem ʾet-hāʾāreṣ

See, I have set the land before you.

8b
בֹּאוּ וּרְשׁוּ אֶת־הָאָרֶץ אֲשֶׁר נִשְׁבַּע יְהוָה לַאֲבֹתֵיכֶם

bōʾû ûrəšû et-hāʾāreṣ ʾăšer nišbaʻ YHWH laʾăvōtêkem

Go and possess the land that Yahweh swore to your ancestors—

8c
לְאַבְרָהָם לְיִצְחָק וּלְיַעֲקֹב

ləʾavrāhām ləyiṣḥaq ûləyaʻăqōv

to Abraham, Isaac, and Jacob—

לָתֵת לָהֶם וּלְזַרְעָם אַחֲרֵיהֶם׃

lātēt lāhem ûləzarʿām ʾaḥărêhem.

to give to them and their descendants after them.'"

6a	יְהוָה אֱלֹהֵינוּ דִּבֶּר אֵלֵינוּ בְּחֹרֵב

"Yahweh our God spoke to us at Horeb,

יְהוָה	Yahweh	ABS	noun
יהוה	*YHWH*		
אֱלֹהֵינוּ	our God	CST	noun
אֱלֹהִים	*ʾĕ·lō·hê·nû*	W/ 1CP SX	
דִּבֶּר	(he) spoke	PIEL PF 3MS	verb
דבר	*dib·ber*		
אֵלֵינוּ	to us	---	prep
אל	*ʾē·lê·nû*	W/ 1CP SX	
בְּחֹרֵב	at Horeb	ABS	noun
חֹרֵב	*bə·ḥō·rēv*	W/ PREP בְּ	

Moses' first sermon begins here. With the narrator's frame in place in vv. 1–5, God's words and commands blend into all that God has commanded Moses to speak on his own (see v. 3). Moses' words and God's words become indistinguishable.

6b	לֵאמֹר רַב־לָכֶם שֶׁבֶת בָּהָר הַזֶּה׃

saying, 'You have stayed long enough at this mountain.

לֵאמֹר	saying/to say	QAL INF CST	verb
אמר	*lē·mōr*	W/ PREP לְ	
רַב־	many/great/enough	MS PRED	adj
רַב	*rav-*		
לָכֶם	to/of you	---	prep
לְ	*lā·kem*	W/ 2MP SX	

Hebrew / Root	Transliteration	Gloss	Parsing	Part of speech
שֶׁבֶת / יֵשֵׁב	še·vet	to stay	QAL INF CST	verb
בָּהָר / הַר	bā·hār	at (the) mountain	ABS — W/ PREP בְּ + DEF. ART.	noun
הַזֶּה: / זֶה	haz·ze	(the) this	--- W/ DEF. ART.	demonstr pron

<table>
<tr><td>7a</td><td dir="rtl">פְּנוּ | וּסְעוּ לָכֶם וּבֹאוּ הַר הָאֱמֹרִי וְאֶל־כָּל־שְׁכֵנָיו בָּעֲרָבָה</td></tr>
</table>

Turn and make your way to come to the hill country of the Amorites and to all their neighbors in the Arabah

Hebrew / Root	Transliteration	Gloss	Parsing	Part of speech
פְּנוּ	/ פנה	pə·nû	turn	QAL IMPV MP	verb
וּסְעוּ / נסע	û·sə·'û	and set out/pull out	QAL IMPV MP W/ CONJ וְ	verb
לָכֶם / לְ	lā·ḵem	to/for yourselves/yourselves	--- W/ 2MP SX	prep
וּבֹאוּ / בוא	û·vō·'û	and go	QAL IMPV MP W/ CONJ וְ	verb
הַר / הַר	har	(the) mountain of	CST	noun
הָאֱמֹרִי / אֱמֹרִי	hā·'ĕ·mō·rî	the Amorites	MS SUBST W/ DEF. ART.	adj
וְאֶל־ / אֶל	wə·'el-	and to	--- W/ CONJ וְ	prep
כָּל־ / כֹּל	kol-	all	CST	noun
שְׁכֵנָיו / שָׁכֵן	šə·ḵē·nāyw	(ones) living/dwelling	MP SUBST W/ 3MS SX	adj
בָּעֲרָבָה / עֲרָבָה	bā·'ă·rā·bâ	in the Arabah	ABS W/ PREP בְּ + DEF. ART.	noun

Deuteronomy recalls Israel's last days at Mount Horeb, when God called the people from their homes to a path ahead, crossing borders, mountains, and valleys, walking before the Lord in the way he leads. The verse is both a command and a reminder of the gift that God seeks to give his covenant people.

7b

בָּהָר וּבַשְּׁפֵלָה וּבַנֶּגֶב וּבְחוֹף הַיָּם אֶרֶץ הַכְּנַעֲנִי
וְהַלְּבָנוֹן עַד־הַנָּהָר הַגָּדֹל נְהַר־פְּרָת׃

in the hill country and the Shephelah and the Negeb
and the coastlands of the sea, the land of the Canaanites
and Lebanon as far as the great river, the Euphrates.

בָּהָר הַר	in the mountain/hill country *vā·hār*	ABS W/ PREP בְּ + DEF. ART.	noun
וּבַשְּׁפֵלָה שְׁפֵלָה	and in the Shephelah/ lowlands *û·vaš·šə·fē·lâ*	ABS W/ CONJ וְ + PREP בְּ AND DEF. ART.	noun
וּבַנֶּגֶב נֶגֶב	and in the Negeb/ south country *û·van·ne·gev*	ABS W/ CONJ וְ + PREP בְּ AND DEF. ART.	noun
וּבְחוֹף חוֹף	and at (the) shore/coast of *û·və·ḥôf*	CST W/ CONJ וְ + PREP בְּ	noun
הַיָּם יָם	the sea *hay·yām*	ABS W/ DEF. ART.	noun
אֶרֶץ אֶרֶץ	(the) land of *ʾe·reṣ*	CST	noun
הַכְּנַעֲנִי כְּנַעֲנִי	the Canaanites *hak·kə·na·ʿă·nî*	MS SUBST W/ DEF. ART.	adj
וְהַלְּבָנוֹן לְבָנוֹן	and (the) Lebanon *wə·hal·lə·vā·nôn*	ABS W/ CONJ וְ + DEF. ART.	noun
עַד־ עַד	to *ʿad-*	---	prep
הַנָּהָר נָהָר	the river *han·nā·hār*	ABS W/ DEF. ART.	noun
הַגָּדֹל גָּדוֹל	(the) great *hag·gā·dōl*	MS ATTR W/ DEF. ART.	adj
נְהַר־ נָהָר	(the) river of *nə·har-*	CST	noun

פְּרָת׃	(the) Euphrates	ABS	noun
פְּרָת	pə·rāt		

שְׁפֵלָה is sometimes translated "lowlands" or "upper lowlands."

<table>
<tr><td>8a</td><td colspan="3" align="center">נָתַתִּי לִפְנֵיכֶם אֶת־הָאָרֶץ</td></tr>
<tr><td></td><td colspan="3" align="center">See, I have set the land before you.</td></tr>
</table>

רְאֵה	see/look	QAL IMPV MS	verb
ראה	rə·'ē		
נָתַתִּי	I give/set	QAL PF 1CS	verb
נתן	nā·tat·tî		
לִפְנֵיכֶם	before you	---	prep
לִפְנֵי	lif·nê·ḵem	W/ 2MP SX	
אֶת־	(direct object marker)	---	particle
אֵת	'et-		
הָאָרֶץ	the land	ABS	noun
אֶרֶץ	hā·'ā·reṣ	W/ DEF. ART.	

The command רְאֵה ("see" or "look") is a common rhetorical tool Moses will use to heighten the urgency in his sermons (see 1:21). In this case, Moses states the central truth of Israel's covenant with God: the land is a gift. Israel would have no life or future apart from God gifting them with the means to live and multiply (see 8:11–20).

<table>
<tr><td>8b</td><td colspan="3" align="center">בֹּאוּ וּרְשׁוּ אֶת־הָאָרֶץ אֲשֶׁר נִשְׁבַּע יְהוָה לַאֲבֹתֵיכֶם</td></tr>
<tr><td></td><td colspan="3" align="center">Go and possess the land that Yahweh swore to your ancestors—</td></tr>
</table>

בֹּאוּ	go	QAL IMPV MP	verb
בוא	bō·'û		
וּרְשׁוּ	and possess/inherit/dispossess	QAL IMPV MP	verb
ירשׁ	û·rə·šû	W/ CONJ וְ	
אֶת־	(direct object marker)	---	particle
אֵת	'et-		
הָאָרֶץ	the land	ABS	noun
אֶרֶץ	hā·'ā·reṣ	W/ DEF. ART.	

אֲשֶׁר	that/which	---	relative pron
אֲשֶׁר	'ă·šer		
נִשְׁבַּע	(he) swore	NIPH PF 3MS	verb
שׁבע	niš·baʿ		
יְהוָה	Yahweh	ABS	noun
יהוה	YHWH		
לַאֲבֹתֵיכֶם	to your ancestors	CST W/ PREP לְ + 2MP SX	noun
אָב	la·ʾă·vō·tê·kem		

Verse 8 is an outworking of the original promise made to Abraham in Gen 12:1–3 and repeated to Isaac and Jacob. נִשְׁבַּע ("he swore" or "he promised") points us to the theological relationship between divine promise and human hope. The Jewish and Christian faiths are deeply grounded in hope (see "From Text to Sermon" below). I translate אֲבֹתֵיכם as "ancestors," but these promises in 8b are made specifically to the three patriarchal "fathers" who received God's promises and stand as exemplars of faith for Israel in future generations.

8c לְאַבְרָהָם לְיִצְחָק וּלְיַעֲקֹב

to Abraham, Isaac, and Jacob—

לְאַבְרָהָם	to Abraham	ABS W/ PREP לְ	noun
אַבְרָהָם	lə·ʾav·rā·hām		
לְיִצְחָק	to Isaac	ABS W/ PREP לְ	noun
יִצְחָק	lə·yiṣ·ḥaq		
וּלְיַעֲקֹב	and to Jacob	ABS W/ CONJ וְ + PREP לְ	noun
יַעֲקֹב	û·lə·ya·ʿă·qōv		

8d לָתֵת לָהֶם וּלְזַרְעָם אַחֲרֵיהֶם:

to give to them and their descendants after them.' "

לָתֵת	to give	QAL INF CST W/ PREP לְ	verb
נתן	lā·tēt		
לָהֶם	to them	--- W/ 3MP SX	prep
לְ	lā·hem		

וּלְזַרְעָם	and to their seed/offspring	CST	noun
זֶרַע	*û·lə·zar·ʿām*	W/ CONJ וּ + PREP לְ + 3MP SX	
אַחֲרֵיהֶם:	after them	---	prep
אַחֲרֵי	*ʾa·ḥă·rê·hem*	W/ 3MP SX	

As Deuteronomy unfolds, readers like us are included in וּלְזַרְעָם אַחֲרֵיהֶם, "and to their seed after them." First, the second generation hears a call to move forward in obedience. Those of us later readers discover ourselves as the recipients of the original promise to the patriarchs. God has given us a new opportunity to demonstrate our faithfulness on the road he has set before us.

 *The Word: Here and Now.* At its core, Deuteronomy is a book of sermons that draws us in with the power of its vision and its carefully constructed admonitions: "Hear!" "Today!" "See!" "Turn," "Go," "And now!" The sermons are also the final words of Moses. Humans throughout history have always shown a natural interest in the "last words" of their prominent figures, so it should not be difficult for us to imagine how important this book was for ancient Israel. Israel's greatest prophet had one final chance to offer the next generation a "here is what you need to know" address as they ventured into the hopes and uncertainties of the future. Notice how the book describes the contents: "Moses began to explain this תּוֹרָה." This greatly expands our common understandings of תּוֹרָה, typically translated as "law," to something that consists of interpretation, exhortation, command, and catechism all in one. Here are three possible ideas for sermons or three points for a sermon.

 *Time, Place, and Liminality.* Anthropologists use the word "liminal" to describe the boundary between times and places: a kind of waiting space between here and there and today and tomorrow. Liminality thus describes our move over the thresholds from one stage to the next: birth, graduation, marriage, parenthood, singleness, and death. Notice how powerfully this liminal journey metaphor appeals to our imagination in this chapter: "Turn and make your way!" (1:7) as Moses describes it. In fact, the journey through the wilderness becomes the imagery for Israel to live each day, inspiring Israel to remember God's provision and care (cf. 8:1–20). The New Testament similarly appeals to the way we "walk" as disciples, and "take up our cross" to follow Jesus. Life is, in a manner of speaking, always a journey into new times and spaces.

Time and place also communicate the deep mysteries of our *fit* and thus our *identity* in this world. The philosopher Edward Casey once said that "A thing is not merely *in* a place . . . but *a thing constitutes its (own) place*" (1993:16, emphasis original). One could ask people to imagine a shelf in their home with a piece of pottery or a picture. Or perhaps a painting on a favorite wall. Those things give those places identity by their sheer presence. They are not just in that place, but they make up the meaning of that place. The same is true for us in the time and spaces in which we live. Our identity is defined by our place and vice versa.

Time is a more difficult concept and it's interesting to see that humans have always understood time using metaphors of place. We look "back" to the past and "forward" to the future. As we can surely appreciate, time and place together are essential to finding our sense of meaning and identity and the way forward in life. The question "Who am I?" can only be answered if we know the where and when of our lives and where they are headed.

Israel's wandering in the desert was precisely a liminal space of longing to find a firm sense of time and place. The "now" (4:1; 5:25; 10:12) and "today" (4:4; 5:1) of entering the promised land will give them their meaning and settle them with a new identity after a time of wandering in the wilderness and waiting for the promise (see Heb 3–4). The land ahead will also be a home for the Israelites to dwell in and encounter God together—where God chooses to "place his name" (Deut 12:5; 26:2). The place will be constituted—made what it is—more than anything by God's dwelling in it.

In an increasingly mobile world, we are prone to forget our present time and place in our community, neighborhood, and home. We come to think less and less of the needs of the moment and the shared rights and responsibilities we have with the fellow human beings who live around us. Symbols like the local parade, town hall, market, country fair, and city monuments, which seem increasingly irrelevant and outdated, speak powerfully to this collective sense of belonging and ownership—even for those who journey and move from place to place (see O'Donovan 2004:296–320). As humans, we constitute this place not just by having a house but also by the way we nurture, observe, and share the things we have with those around us.

This truth will become central to Israel's ethical outlook in chapters ahead, for this land that is gifted to them will be characterized not only by what it produces in its soil, but by how Israel will use the land and its resources to build communities (16:1–17; 26:12), honor God (8:1–20; 12:5), and share with the most needy in their midst (15:1–19; 16:16–17; 24:19–22).

By naming Kadesh Barnea at the outset (1:2, 19–23), Moses leads Israel to remember its failings and to look forward to a time and place of obedience. As McConville and Millar put it, the sermons name the *places of failure* and *the road to success*" (McConville and Millar 1994:23, emphasis original). And so, as Israel crosses these thresholds of time and place, it enters a new possibility of identity.

We should naturally see this promise of future rest fulfilled in the death and resurrection of Jesus. Our salvation is not merely some spiritual and disembodied experience, but a promise for God's kingdom to "come" and for his will to be "done on earth as it is in heaven" (Matt 6:10). The inbreaking of God's kingdom institutes a transformation of the places in which we live, from lands of war, division, hoarding, and poverty to places of peace, sharing, and community. In an increasingly rootless world, the need to take notice of place is all the more important. The Samaritan who noticed the injured traveler faced the temptation to leave an anonymous man to the nameless, liminal space of a roadside. By caring for his needs, the Samaritan restores dignity to the man in need. And he transforms the place by marking it with his presence and compassion (O'Donovan 2004:317).

Above all, the boundary crossing brings about urgency in the Christian message. "Now!" "Today!" and "Hear, O Israel!" are but a few of dozens of highly charged appeals that Moses makes to the nation. A new threshold is a time for renewing our faith and our resolve to follow God's ways.

🌱 *Canon, Constitution, and Community.* Recall the progression we pointed to above that moves from Moses' דְּבָרִים, "words" (v. 1), to God's having "commanded" (צִוָּה) Moses to speak (v. 3), to Moses "explaining" (וּבֵאֵר) the torah (v. 5). There is something inescapably living and revealing about this unfolding set of sermons. It is a word from God and yet also a word interpreted and applied to the new contexts in which we find ourselves. Moses has taken a sacred tradition and made it fresh and accessible for us here and now.

We should see above all that there is an addition to what was given to a previous generation that departed Egypt (see 4:45). This does not mean that the laws in Exodus, Leviticus, and Numbers were deficient or irrelevant for the Israelites crossing into the land. Rather, for Deuteronomy, God's word given in the ancient past always has the power to come to life in every new present moment.

A preacher could turn to an important and well-recognized relationship between Deuteronomy and the Psalter. Psalms, it should be remembered, is divided into five books, mirroring the five books of the Pentateuch. More importantly, Psalms also begins with a vision of the one who "walks," "stands," "sits," and "meditates on the torah day and night" (Ps 1), just as the individual "walks," "stands," and "sits," as she places these words on her "heart" (Deut 6:6–9). So too, the king on his throne in Deut 17 is commanded to write a copy of this torah for himself and read it "all the days of his life" (vv. 18–20; cf. Josh 1:7–8). The meditative, devotional focus on words permeates both books.

Further, based on the placement of Pss 1–2, and their parallels in Pss 19 and 119, Clinton McCann has observed that "torah" and kingship are the two foundational themes of the Psalter (1993:25–50).

Patrick Miller (1999:3–18) and Jamie Grant (2004) also pick up on many important echoes between Deuteronomy and Psalms. Both books play out the intense dialogue that takes place between us and God. God's commands, blessings, and warnings give way to prayers, oaths, arguments, complaints, and thanksgivings (Miller 1999:10). Miller claims, in fact, that "for the Psalter, the law is Deuteronomy" (1999:11). In other words, the psalms mimic the themes of conversation with God and a growing tradition among the people in Deuteronomy's laws. In this light we can see how these books give Israel a means to sustain their sense of a communal identity. They have a "law book" to guide the people towards moral and social order, and "a song book" that lifts the law and its story back to God in prayer (Miller 1999:13, 15). In what way does our Christian prayer and song arise from the stories and words of Scripture?

As we will see in Deut 4:2 (and 12:32), this law book becomes fixed into a canon: "You shall not add to it or take from it." One only has to imagine how inconceivable it is to exist as a nation without a form of law or follow a religion for long without a sacred revelation; each requires a common sourcebook to which we may appeal and in which we find our life and way of life. Sean McBride argues that Deuteronomy's book of laws was unique in this way in the ancient Near East (1993:62–77). Although ancient law codes did exist, the individual responsibility and the social structures laid out in Deuteronomy form an unparalleled way of organizing the people under a single set of laws. As we noted above, Deuteronomy eventually laid the foundation for our modern ideas of constitutional government.

Deuteronomy as a community law book for Israel is taken up in many places in the New Testament and used to guide the church and explain the revelation in and through Jesus Christ (e.g. Matt 4:4; 5–7; John 1:1, 21; Acts 3:22; 7:37; Rev 22:18). Jesus is the λόγος, "word" (John 1:1, 17–18), the "image of the invisible God," and the one through whom God speaks a new revelation of himself (Col 1:15–20; Heb 1:1–4). All that has gone before in the laws, poetry, prophets, and stories of Israel comes to its fullness in the word and life of the Son.

 ***Promise, Gift, and Hope.*** One could preach a sermon about the way the promise of a future gift inspires hope in the receiver.

"Go in and possess the land Yahweh swore to your fathers" (Deut 1:8). Israel's whole life in the Pentateuch follows this promise of a gift of אֶרֶץ, "land/portion of earth." Few of us in the developed world are dependent on any more than a place to eat and sleep and charge our phones. In Israel's ancient context, however, land could be easily equated with life, family, survival, and nationhood. Just consider how the laws in 19:14 and 27:17 prohibit moving a neighbor's "landmark" or "boundary," which shows just how necessary good land was to sustain life and just how tempting it was to squeeze out a little more property from my neighbor to ensure greater yields and to feed my livestock.

It's also important to understand the rhetorical force of anticipation in Deuteronomy and how, in the narrative, the land is always yet to come. It has been "sworn" (נִשְׁבַּע), which, in Deuteronomy, is a legally weighted term for a promise made in God's covenant with Israel. God has committed himself to blessings that lie ahead of us. Moreover, Israel is being given a land it did not own and did not earn (8:17–18). The land is a gift of gratuitous love that was set on the patriarchs when God gave them his promise (7:6–8).

We can thus appreciate the way Deuteronomy is carried along by the hope of the future promises, and we will see the call for hope arise often throughout the book. Here, in our opening verses (1:1–8), Israel is reminded that they have waited a long time for this day—as emphasized by the details of the journeys these last forty years—and that, by their rebellion, they nearly lost the gift altogether. Only by God's grace and his faithfulness as a keeper of promises does Israel have a chance to go, enter, and possess.

We should also be alert as we read Deuteronomy to the way Moses seeks to inculcate the paired virtues of hope and gratitude. Hope is one of the three major virtues that are mentioned in the New Testament alongside faith and love (1 Cor 13:13; Col 1:4; 1 Thess 1:3; 5:8). Stated in theological language, hope is *faith at work in time*. Or one could say that it is faith that grounds our identity in Christ, love that acts in the present, and hope that reaches out to what lies ahead. Hope puts faith and love into action, as Paul indicates in Col 1:3–5.

Theological hope should be clearly distinguished from natural hope, or passions, emotions, and optimism: "I hope it's nice weather for the parade" (Pinches 2014:349–68). Theological hope is a gift from God—a gift based on a promise that we take up as our own virtue to be practiced in community. (The Christian tradition going back to at least Augustine adopted the "cardinal" virtues of courage, temperance, prudence, and justice, adding to them the theological virtues of faith, love, and hope. These latter virtues are gifts of God's grace, and necessary for sinful humans to grow in the cardinal virtues (see Westberg 2015:141–271).

Paul tells the Ephesians that they were once "without hope" (Eph 2:12), but now in Christ they have been called to "one body" and "one hope" (4:4). This is not too different than what Moses is telling Israel, and, like Paul, Moses will institute practices to renew their hope throughout future chapters.

Every audience should hear God's promises anew, finding ourselves on the cusp of a new moment of God's work in this world "today" (Ps 95:7; Heb 3:7–8; 4:7).

WISDOM, UNDERSTANDING, AND DIVINE PRESENCE

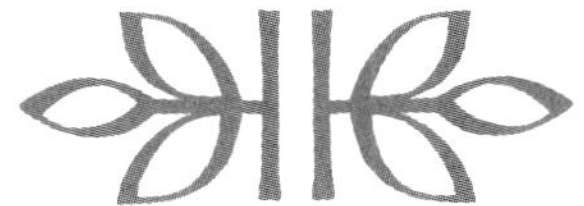

After three long chapters of historical background (chs. 1–3), Moses issues his rhetorically heightened appeals to his audience: עַתָּה, "now," and שְׁמַע, "hear!" There is urgency in this very moment. In fact, the section unfolds in a cascading sequence of impassioned appeals to Israel. Preaching, we might observe, is more than just giving commands and telling stories; rather, it is an event in which the preacher brings the audience before the face of God in the moment. Notice also that Moses offers Israel the possibility of "life" (תִּחְיוּ, "so that you may live"). Moses is going to die, so this is no small promise. *I have failed*, he has just reminded them (3:23–29), and *I will die here outside the land*. Israel thus is given a remarkable opportunity not afforded to its leader. But, more than that, what lies ahead of them is the very opposite of what happens to Moses; his service and dying have given way to Israel's chance to live again. *It is a better gift than we deserve, and we have God and others to thank for bringing us here.*

LARGER LITERARY CONTEXT ▸ 4:1–49

1a

וְעַתָּה יִשְׂרָאֵל

wə'attâ yiśrā'ēl

"And now, O Israel,

1b

שְׁמַע אֶל־הַחֻקִּים וְאֶל־הַמִּשְׁפָּטִים

šəma' 'el-hāḥuqqîm wə'el-hammišpāṭîm

hear the statutes and the ordinances

1c

אֲשֶׁר אָנֹכִי מְלַמֵּד אֶתְכֶם לַעֲשׂוֹת

'ăšer 'ānōḵî məlammēd 'etḵem la'ăśôt

that I am teaching you to do,

1d

לְמַעַן תִּחְיוּ וּבָאתֶם וִירִשְׁתֶּם אֶת־הָאָרֶץ

ləma'an tiḥyû ûvā'tem wîrištem 'et-hā'āreṣ

in order that you may live and go in and possess the land

1e

אֲשֶׁר יְהוָה אֱלֹהֵי אֲבֹתֵכֶם נֹתֵן לָכֶם:

'ăšer YHWH 'ĕlōhê 'ăvōtêḵem nōtēn lāḵem.

that Yahweh the God of your ancestors is giving to you.

2a

לֹא תֹסִפוּ עַל־הַדָּבָר אֲשֶׁר אָנֹכִי מְצַוֶּה אֶתְכֶם

lō' tōsīfû 'al-haddāvār 'ăšer 'ānōḵî məṣawwɛ 'etḵem

You shall not add to the word that I am commanding you,

2b

וְלֹא תִגְרְעוּ מִמֶּנּוּ

wəlō' tigrə'û mimmennû

and you shall not take from it,

2c

לִשְׁמֹר אֶת־מִצְוֺת יְהוָה אֱלֹהֵיכֶם אֲשֶׁר אָנֹכִי מְצַוֶּה אֶתְכֶם:

lišmōr 'et-miṣwōt YHWH 'ĕlōhêḵem 'ăšer 'ānōḵî nōtēn lāḵem.

that you may keep the commandments of Yahweh your God,
which I am commanding you.

עֵינֵיכֶם֙ הָרֹאֹ֔ת אֵ֛ת אֲשֶׁר־עָשָׂ֥ה יְהוָ֖ה בְּבַ֣עַל פְּעֹ֑ור

ʿênêkem hārōʾt ʾēt ʾăšer-ʿāśâ YHWH bəvaʿal pəʾôr

Your eyes saw what Yahweh did at Baal of Peor,

כִּ֣י כָל־הָאִ֗ישׁ אֲשֶׁ֤ר הָלַךְ֙ אַחֲרֵ֣י בַֽעַל־פְּעֹ֔ור

kî kol-hāʾîš ʾăšer hālak ʾaḥărê vaʿal-pəʾôr

that every man who followed after Baal-Peor

הִשְׁמִיד֛וֹ יְהוָ֥ה אֱלֹהֶ֖יךָ מִקִּרְבֶּֽךָ׃

hišmîdû YHWH ʾĕlōhêkā miqqirbekā.

Yahweh your God wiped out from among you.

וְאַתֶּם֙ הַדְּבֵקִ֔ים בַּיהוָ֖ה אֱלֹהֵיכֶ֑ם חַיִּ֥ים כֻּלְּכֶ֖ם הַיּֽוֹם׃

wəʾattem haddəvēqîm baYHWH ʾĕlōhêkem ḥayyîm kulləkem hayyôm.

But you who clung to Yahweh your God,
all of you are alive to this day.

רְאֵ֣ה׀ לִמַּ֣דְתִּי אֶתְכֶ֗ם חֻקִּים֙ וּמִשְׁפָּטִ֔ים

rəʾē limmadtî ʾetkem ḥuqqîm ûmišpāṭîm

Look, I teach you statutes and ordinances,

כַּאֲשֶׁ֥ר צִוַּ֖נִי יְהוָ֣ה אֱלֹהָ֑י

kaʾăšer ṣiwwanî YHWH ʾĕlōhay

as Yahweh my God commanded me,

לַעֲשֹׂ֣ות כֵּ֔ן בְּקֶ֣רֶב הָאָ֔רֶץ אֲשֶׁ֥ר אַתֶּ֛ם בָּאִ֥ים שָׁ֖מָּה לְרִשְׁתָּֽהּ׃

laʿăśôt kēn bəqerev hāʾāreṣ ʾăšer ʾattem bāʾîm šāmmâ lərištāh.

for you to do them in the midst of the land
you are going in to possess.

וּשְׁמַרְתֶּם֙ וַעֲשִׂיתֶ֔ם

ûšəmartem waʿăśîtem

Keep them and do them,

6b כִּי הִוא חָכְמַתְכֶם וּבִינַתְכֶם לְעֵינֵי הָעַמִּים

kî hî' ḥokmatkem ûvînatkem lə'ênê hā'ammîm

**for that will be your wisdom and your discernment
in the eyes of the peoples**

6c אֲשֶׁר יִשְׁמְעוּן אֵת כָּל־הַחֻקִּים הָאֵלֶּה

'ăšer yišmə'ûn 'ēt kol-haḥuqqîm hā'ēlle

who hear all these statutes.

6d וְאָמְרוּ רַק עַם־חָכָם וְנָבוֹן הַגּוֹי הַגָּדוֹל הַזֶּה׃

wə'āmərû raq 'am ḥākām wənāvôn haggôy haggādôl hazze.

**And they will say, 'Surely this foremost nation
is a wise and discerning people!'**

7a כִּי מִי־גוֹי גָּדוֹל אֲשֶׁר־לוֹ אֱלֹהִים קְרֹבִים אֵלָיו

kî mî gôy gādôl 'ăšer-lô 'ĕlōhîm qərōvîm 'ēlāyw

For what nation is so superior that has a God so near to it

7b כַּיהוָה אֱלֹהֵינוּ בְּכָל־קָרְאֵנוּ אֵלָיו׃

kaYHWH 'ĕlōhênû bəkkol-qārə'ēnû 'ēlāyw.

as Yahweh our God is whenever we call upon him?

8a וּמִי גּוֹי גָּדוֹל אֲשֶׁר־לוֹ חֻקִּים וּמִשְׁפָּטִים צַדִּיקִם

ûmî gôy gādôl 'ăšer-lô ḥuqqîm ûmišpāṭîm ṣaddîqîm

**And what nation is so superior that has statutes
and ordinances so righteous**

8b כְּכֹל הַתּוֹרָה הַזֹּאת אֲשֶׁר אָנֹכִי נֹתֵן לִפְנֵיכֶם הַיּוֹם׃

kəkōl hattôrâ hazzō't 'ăšer 'ānōkî nōtēn lifnêkem hayyôm.

as this whole law that I am setting before you today?"

<table>
<tr><td>1a</td><td align="center">וְעַתָּה יִשְׂרָאֵל</td></tr>
</table>

"And now, O Israel,

וְעַתָּה עַתָּה	and/but now *wə·ʿat·tâ*	--- W/ CONJ וְ	adv
יִשְׂרָאֵל יִשְׂרָאֵל	Israel *yiś·rā·ʾēl*	ABS	noun

וְעַתָּה ("and now") is repeated often (2:13; 5:25; 10:12; 12:9; 26:10; 31:19; 32:39) and supplements the repetition of "today" (הַיּוֹם) to bring moral urgency to each new moment this book is read and heard.

<table>
<tr><td>1b</td><td align="center">שְׁמַע אֶל־הַחֻקִּים וְאֶל־הַמִּשְׁפָּטִים</td></tr>
</table>

hear the statutes and the ordinances

שְׁמַע שׁמע	listen/hear/obey *šə·maʿ*	QAL IMPV MS	verb
אֶל־ אל	to *ʾel-*	---	prep
הַחֻקִּים חֹק	the statutes/regulations *hā·ḥuq·qîm*	ABS W/ DEF. ART.	noun
וְאֶל־ אל	and to *wə·ʾel-*	--- W/ CONJ וְ	prep
הַמִּשְׁפָּטִים מִשְׁפָּט	the judgments/ordinances *ham·miš·pā·ṭîm*	ABS W/ DEF. ART.	noun

This is the first use of חֻקִּים וּמִשְׁפָּטִים ("statutes and ordinances"), a phrase that will appear again several times through 26:16. As we will see below, this word pair knits the appeals in the sermons to the Decalogue (5:1) and the expanded rules and stipulations in chs. 4–26.

This is also the first of eleven times that שׁמע ("hear") appears in this chapter (vv. 1, 10, 12, 28, 30 and twice each in vv. 32, 33, 36). The verb ראה ("see") appears almost as much: beginning in v. 3, it appears nine times in this chapter (vv. 3, 5, 9, 12, 15, 19, 28, 35, 36). No other chapter uses these two words more often. Both words serve to raise the urgency in Moses' message. The "seeing" communicates the objective clarity of God's mighty works in the past and the plain claims of the message. To "hear" is to listen and obey.

<table>
<tr><td>1c</td><td colspan="3" align="center">אֲשֶׁר אָנֹכִי מְלַמֵּד אֶתְכֶם לַעֲשׂוֹת</td></tr>
<tr><td></td><td colspan="3" align="center">that I am teaching you to do,</td></tr>
<tr><td>אֲשֶׁר
ʾă·šer</td><td>that/which</td><td>---</td><td>relative pron</td></tr>
<tr><td>אָנֹכִי
ʾā·nō·ḵî</td><td>I</td><td>---</td><td>personal pron</td></tr>
<tr><td>מְלַמֵּד
mə·lam·mēd</td><td>(am) teaching</td><td>PIEL PTCP MS</td><td>verb</td></tr>
<tr><td>אֶתְכֶם
אֵת ʾet·ḵem</td><td>you</td><td>W/ 2MP SX</td><td>particle</td></tr>
<tr><td>לַעֲשׂוֹת
עשׂה la·ʿă·śôt</td><td>to do</td><td>QAL INF CST
W/ PREP לְ</td><td>verb</td></tr>
</table>

Notice the plural form אֶתְכֶם ("you"), which appears again in vv. 3 and 5. The singular, meanwhile, enters in vv. 9–10, and a pattern of switching back and forth between singular and plural becomes regular throughout these early chapters. The idea that this switching indicated two earlier textual layers has largely been abandoned. We will address this briefly in Text to Sermon below.

"Teach/learn," למד, is a keyword in Deuteronomy and one that, significantly, appears nowhere else in the Pentateuch. About 25 percent of Deuteronomy's uses of למד appear in ch. 4 alone (4:1, 5, 10, 14; 5:1, 31; etc.). We will address this further under "From Text to Sermon" below. For now, it bears mentioning that the present Piel participle here stands alongside a Piel perfect in v. 5 and Qal imperfect and Piel imperfect in v. 10. Past and present teaching from Moses become future teaching and learning in each Israelite home.

<table>
<tr><td>1d</td><td colspan="3" align="center">לְמַעַן תִּחְיוּ וּבָאתֶם וִירִשְׁתֶּם אֶת־הָאָרֶץ</td></tr>
<tr><td></td><td colspan="3" align="center">in order that you may live and go in and possess the land</td></tr>
<tr><td>לְמַעַן
lə·ma·ʿan</td><td>so that/in order that</td><td>---</td><td>prep</td></tr>
<tr><td>תִּחְיוּ
חיה tiḥ·yû</td><td>you will live</td><td>QAL IMPF 2MP</td><td>verb</td></tr>
<tr><td>וּבָאתֶם
בוא û·vā·ʾtem</td><td>and enter</td><td>QAL WEQATAL 2MP</td><td>verb</td></tr>
</table>

וִירִשְׁתֶּם	and possess/dispossess	QAL WEQATAL 2MP	verb
יָרַשׁ	*wî·riš·**tem***		
אֶת־	(direct object marker)	- - -	particle
אֵת	*'et-*		
הָאָרֶץ	the land	ABS	noun
אֶרֶץ	*hā·'ā·reṣ*	W/ DEF. ART.	

See the opening comments on the gifts of life (תִּחְיוּ) and land (הָאָרֶץ) above.

<table>
<tr><td>1e</td><td colspan="2" align="center">אֲשֶׁר יְהוָה אֱלֹהֵי אֲבֹתֵיכֶם נֹתֵן לָכֶם:</td></tr>
<tr><td></td><td colspan="2">that Yahweh the God of your ancestors is giving to you.</td></tr>
</table>

אֲשֶׁר	that/which	- - -	relative pron
אֲשֶׁר	*'ă·šer*		
יְהוָה	Yahweh	ABS	noun
יהוה	*YHWH*		
אֱלֹהֵי	(the) God of	CST	noun
אֱלֹהִים	*'ĕ·lō·hê*		
אֲבֹתֵיכֶם	your ancestors	CST W/ 2MP SX	noun
אָב	*'ă·vō·tê·kem*		
נֹתֵן	is giving	QAL PTCP MS	verb
נתן	*nō·tēn*		
לָכֶם:	to you	- - -	prep
ל	*lā·kem*	W/ 2MP SX	

<table>
<tr><td>2a</td><td colspan="2" align="center">לֹא תֹסִפוּ עַל־הַדָּבָר אֲשֶׁר אָנֹכִי מְצַוֶּה אֶתְכֶם</td></tr>
<tr><td></td><td colspan="2">You shall not add to the word that I am commanding you,</td></tr>
</table>

לֹא	do not	- - -	particle
לֹא	*lō'*		
תֹסִפוּ	add/increase	HIPH IMPF 2MP	verb
יסף	*tō·sī·fû*		
עַל־	to	- - -	prep
עַל	*'al-*		

הַדָּבָר֙	the word	ABS	noun
דָּבָר	*had·dā·vār*	W/ DEF. ART.	
אֲשֶׁר	that/which	---	relative
אֲשֶׁר	*'ă·šer*		pron
אָנֹכִי֙	I	---	personal
אָנֹכִי	*'ā·nō·ḵî*		pron
מְצַוֶּה	(am) commanding	PIEL PTCP MS	verb
צוה	*mə·ṣaw·wê*		
אֶתְכֶֽם	you	---	particle
אֵת	*'et·ḵem*	W/ 2MP SX	

It might occur to us that Deuteronomy is already adding to (יסף) or supplementing earlier laws in the Pentateuch. One must avoid a kind of overly literal reading of Deuteronomy as a collection of commands that have to be followed to the letter. Deuteronomy has a nuanced way of setting down a fixed canon of law, such that the people are encouraged and required to apply that law wisely and faithfully to the unfolding events in their history (see Rev 22:18–19).

2b   וְלֹא תִגְרְעוּ מִמֶּנּוּ

and you shall not take from it,

וְלֹא	and do not	---	particle
לֹא	*wə·lō'*	W/ CONJ וְ	
תִגְרְעוּ	cut/trim/take away	QAL IMPF 2MP	verb
גרע	*tig·rə·'û*		
מִמֶּנּוּ	from it	---	prep
מִן	*mim·men·nû*	W/ 3MS SX	

2c   לִשְׁמֹר אֶת־מִצְוֺת יְהוָה אֱלֹהֵיכֶם אֲשֶׁר אָנֹכִי מְצַוֶּה אֶתְכֶם:

that you may keep the commandments of Yahweh your God,
which I am commanding you.

| לִשְׁמֹר | to keep | QAL INF CST | verb |
| שׁמר | *liš·mōr* | W/ PREP לְ | |

Hebrew / Transliteration	Gloss	Parsing	Category
אֶת־ 'et-	(direct object marker)	---	particle
מִצְוֺת֙ miṣ·wōt	(the) commandments of	CST	noun
יְהוָ֣ה YHWH	Yahweh	ABS	noun
אֱלֹהֵיכֶ֔ם 'ĕ·lō·hê·ḵem	your God	CST W/ 2MP SX	noun
אֲשֶׁ֛ר 'ă·šer	that/which	---	relative pron
אָנֹכִ֥י 'ā·nō·ḵî	I	---	personal pron
מְצַוֶּ֖ה nō·tēn	(am) commanding	PIEL PTCP MS	verb
אֶתְכֶֽם׃ lā·ḵem	you	--- W/ 2MP SX	particle

צוה means "promulgate" or "put into legal force." As far as we can tell, most law codes in the ancient Near East were never promulgated to all the people, but rather were written down and stored for use by classes of priests, nobles, and kings. Deuteronomy, on the other hand, is public law (see more on 30:11–14 below).

3a עֵינֵיכֶם֙ הָרֹאֹ֔ת אֵ֚ת אֲשֶׁר־עָשָׂ֣ה יְהוָ֔ה בְּבַ֖עַל פְּעֽוֹר

Your eyes saw what Yahweh did at Baal of Peor,

Hebrew / Transliteration	Gloss	Parsing	Category
עֵינֵיכֶם֙ 'ê·nê·ḵem	your eyes	CST W/ 2MP SX	noun
הָרֹאֹ֔ת hā·rō't	(they) saw/have seen	HIPH INF CST	verb
אֵ֚ת 'ēt	(direct object marker)	---	particle
אֲשֶׁר־ 'ă·šer-	that/which	---	relative pron
עָשָׂ֣ה 'ā·śâ	(he) did	QAL PF 3MS	verb

<table>
<tr><td>יְהוָה
יהוה</td><td>Yahweh
YHWH</td><td>ABS</td><td>noun</td></tr>
<tr><td>בְּבַעַל פְּעֹור
בַּעַל פְּעֹור</td><td>at/to Baal of Peor
bə·va·ʿal pə·ʿôr</td><td>ABS
W/ PREP בְּ</td><td>noun</td></tr>
</table>

See v. 1b for the emphasis on sight.

<table>
<tr><td>3b</td><td colspan="3" align="center">כִּי כָל־הָאִישׁ אֲשֶׁר הָלַךְ אַחֲרֵי בַעַל־פְּעֹור</td></tr>
<tr><td></td><td colspan="3" align="center">that every man who followed after Baal-Peor</td></tr>
</table>

כִּי כִּי	that/for/because *kî*	---	conj
כָל־ כֹּל	each *kol-*	CST	noun
הָאִישׁ אִישׁ	(the) man/person *hā·ʾîš*	ABS W/ DEF. ART.	noun
אֲשֶׁר אֲשֶׁר	who *ʾă·šer*	---	relative pron
הָלַךְ הלך	(he) walks/follows *hā·lak*	QAL PF 3MS	verb
אַחֲרֵי אַחֲרֵי	after *ʾa·ḥă·rê*	---	prep
בַעַל־פְּעֹור בַּעַל פְּעֹור	Baal of Peor *va·ʿal-pə·ʿôr*	ABS	noun

<table>
<tr><td>3c</td><td colspan="3" align="center">הִשְׁמִידֹו יְהוָה אֱלֹהֶיךָ מִקִּרְבֶּךָ׃</td></tr>
<tr><td></td><td colspan="3" align="center">Yahweh your God wiped out from among you.</td></tr>
</table>

הִשְׁמִידֹו שׁמד	(he) destroyed/wiped out *hiš·mî·dû*	HIPH PF 3MS W/ 3MS SX	verb
יְהוָה יהוה	Yahweh *YHWH*	ABS	noun
אֱלֹהֶיךָ אֱלֹהִים	your God *ʾĕ·lō·hê·kā*	CST W/ 2MS SX	noun

Hebrew	Translation	Parsing	Part of speech
מִקִּרְבֶּֽךָ׃ קֶרֶב *miq·qir·**be**·kā*	from your midst/within you	CST W/ PREP מִן + 2MS SX	noun

4 וְאַתֶּם֙ הַדְּבֵקִים֙ בַּיהוָ֣ה אֱלֹהֵיכֶ֔ם חַיִּ֥ים כֻּלְּכֶ֖ם הַיּֽוֹם׃

But you who clung to Yahweh your God,
all of you are alive to this day.

Hebrew	Translation	Parsing	Part of speech
וְאַתֶּם֙ אַתֶּם *wə·'at·**tem***	and/but you	--- W/ CONJ וְ	personal pron
הַדְּבֵקִים֙ דָּבֵק *had·də·vē·**qîm***	the (ones) clinging/ holding fast	MP PRED W/ DEF. ART.	adj
בַּיהוָ֣ה יהוה *ba·YHWH*	to Yahweh	ABS W/ PREP בְּ	noun
אֱלֹהֵיכֶ֔ם אֱלֹהִים *'ĕ·lō·**hê**·ḵem*	your God	CST W/ 2MP SX	noun
חַיִּ֥ים חַיִּים *ḥay·**yîm***	living/alive	MP PRED	adj
כֻּלְּכֶ֖ם כֹּל *kul·lə·**ḵem***	all of you	CST W/ 2MP SX	noun
הַיּֽוֹם׃ יוֹם *hay·**yôm***	today/this day	ABS W/ DEF. ART.	noun

5a רְאֵ֣ה | לִמַּ֣דְתִּי אֶתְכֶ֗ם חֻקִּים֙ וּמִשְׁפָּטִ֔ים

Look, I teach you statutes and ordinances,

Hebrew	Translation	Parsing	Part of speech
רְאֵ֣ה | ראה *rə·**'ē***	see/look	QAL IMPV MS	verb
לִמַּ֣דְתִּי למד *lim·**mad**·tî*	(I) teach	PIEL PF 1CS	verb
אֶתְכֶ֗ם אֵת *'et·**ḵem***	you	--- W/ 2MP SX	particle
חֻקִּים֙ חֹק *ḥuq·**qîm***	statutes/regulations	ABS	noun

| וּמִשְׁפָּטִים
מִשְׁפָּט | and judgments/ordinances
û·miš·pā·ṭîm | ABS
W/ CONJ וְ | noun |

as Yahweh my God commanded me,

כַּאֲשֶׁר אֲשֶׁר	as/when/according *ka·ʾă·šer*	--- W/ PREP כְּ	relative pron
צִוַּנִי צוה	(he) commanded me *ṣiw·wa·nî*	PIEL PF 3MS W/ 1CS SX	verb
יְהוָה יהוה	Yahweh *YHWH*	ABS	noun
אֱלֹהָי אֱלֹהִים	my God *ʾĕ·lō·hay*	CST W/ 1CS SX	noun

**for you to do them in the midst of the land
you are going in to possess.**

לַעֲשׂוֹת עשׂה	to do *la·ʿă·śôt*	QAL INF CST W/ PREP לְ	verb
כֵּן כֵּן	thus/so *kēn*	---	adv
בְּקֶרֶב קֶרֶב	in the midst of *bə·qe·rev*	CST W/ PREP בְּ	noun
הָאָרֶץ אֶרֶץ	the land *hā·ʾā·reṣ*	ABS W/ DEF. ART.	noun
אֲשֶׁר אֲשֶׁר	that/which *ʾă·šer*	---	relative pron
אַתֶּם אַתֶּם	you *ʾat·tem*	---	personal pron
בָּאִים בוא	(are) going/coming *bā·ʾîm*	QAL PTCP MP	verb

שָׁמָּה	there	---	adv
שָׁם	*šām·mâ*	W/ LOCATIVE ה	
לְרִשְׁתָּהּ׃	to possess/dispossess it	QAL INF CST	verb
יָרַשׁ	*lə·riš·tāh*	W/ PREP לְ + 3FS SX	

<table>
<tr><td>6a</td><td colspan="3" align="center">וּשְׁמַרְתֶּם וַעֲשִׂיתֶם</td></tr>
</table>

Keep them and do them,

וּשְׁמַרְתֶּם	and (you) keep/observe/obey	QAL WEQATAL 2MP	verb
שָׁמַר	*û·šə·mar·tem*		
וַעֲשִׂיתֶם	and (you) do	QAL WEQATAL 2MP	verb
עָשָׂה	*wa·ʿă·śî·tem*		

<table>
<tr><td>6b</td><td colspan="3" align="center">כִּי הִוא חָכְמַתְכֶם וּבִינַתְכֶם לְעֵינֵי הָעַמִּים</td></tr>
</table>

for that will be your wisdom and your discernment
in the eyes of the peoples

כִּי	for/because/that	---	conj
כִּי	*kî*		
הִוא	it	---	personal pron
הִיא	*hîʾ*		
חָכְמַתְכֶם	your wisdom	CST	noun
חָכְמָה	*ḥok·mat·kem*	W/ 2MP SX	
וּבִינַתְכֶם	and your understanding	CST	noun
בִּינָה	*û·vî·nat·kem*	W/ 2MP SX	
לְעֵינֵי	to/in (the) eyes of	CST	noun
עַיִן	*lə·ʿê·nê*	W/ PREP לְ	
הָעַמִּים	the peoples	ABS	noun
עַם	*hā·ʿam·mîm*	W/ DEF. ART.	

Deuteronomy is the only book in the Pentateuch to pair the terms חָכְמָה ("wisdom") and בִּינָה ("understanding"). See also the use of this word pair in the qualifications for leaders in 1:13, 15.

who hear all these statutes.

אֲשֶׁר אֲשֶׁר	that/which *ʾă·šer*	---	relative pron
יִשְׁמְע֔וּן שׁמע	(they) hear *yiš·mə·ʿûn*	QAL IMPF 3MP W/ PARAGOGIC ן	verb
אֵת אֵת	(direct object marker) *ʾēt*	---	particle
כָּל־ כֹּל	all *kol-*	CST	noun
הַחֻקִּים חֹק	(the) statutes/regulations *ha·ḥuq·qîm*	ABS W/ DEF. ART.	noun
הָאֵלֶּה אֵלֶּה	(the) these *hā·ʾēl·le*	--- W/ DEF. ART.	demonstr pron

And they will say, 'Surely this foremost nation
is a wise and discerning people!'

וְאָמְר֗וּ אמר	and they say *wə·ʾā·mə·rû*	QAL WEQATAL 3CP	verb
רַק רַק	only/still/but *raq*	---	adv
עַם־ עַם	people *ʿam*	ABS	noun
חָכָם חָכָם	wise/skillful *ḥā·ḵām*	MS ATTR	adj
וְנָבוֹן בין	and understanding *wə·nā·vôn*	NIPH PTCP MS W/ CONJ ן	verb
הַגּוֹי גּוֹי	(the) nation *hag·gôy*	ABS W/ DEF. ART.	noun
הַגָּדוֹל גָּדוֹל	(the) great *hag·gā·dôl*	MS ATTR W/ DEF. ART.	adj
הַזֶּה׃ זֶה	(the) this *haz·ze*	--- W/ DEF. ART.	demonstr pron

The phrase הַגּוֹי הַגָּדוֹל ("the great nation"), which is repeated in v. 7a, is a direct echo of God's promise to Abram in Gen 12:2 that he would make his seed into a "great nation." "Foremost" or "superior" is a better sense of what גָּדוֹל means in the context of comparison to other nations (see also Gen 17:5–6, 16; 18:18; 28:14; 35:1; 46:3; Weinfeld 1991:202). This law, when lived out conscientiously, shines a light of witness to the nations that neighbor the Israelites. It also reminds Israel not to be jealous of Egypt, Babylon, or other "great" nations in their context.

<table>
<tr><td>7a</td><td colspan="3" align="center">כִּי מִי־גוֹי גָּדוֹל אֲשֶׁר־לוֹ אֱלֹהִים קְרֹבִים אֵלָיו</td></tr>
<tr><td></td><td colspan="3" align="center">For what nation is so superior that has a God so near to it</td></tr>
</table>

כִּי	for/because	---	conj
כִּי	*kî*		
מִי־	what/who/whichever	---	interr pron
מִי	*mî*		
גוֹי	nation	ABS	noun
גּוֹי	*gôy*		
גָּדוֹל	great	MS ATTR	adj
גָּדוֹל	*gā·dôl*		
אֲשֶׁר־	that/which	---	relative pron
אֲשֶׁר	*ʾă·šer-*		
לוֹ	to it/him	---	prep
לְ	*lô*	W/ 3MS SX	
אֱלֹהִים	god(s)	ABS	noun
אֱלֹהִים	*ʾĕ·lō·hîm*		
קְרֹבִים	near/close	MP PRED	adj
קָרוֹב	*qə·rō·vîm*		
אֵלָיו	to it	---	prep
אֶל	*ʾē·lāyw*	W/ 3MS SX	

The questions in vv. 7 and 8 are raised again in vv. 32–35, once again pointing to Israel's unique status, but even more to the one and only true God who chose them, saved them, and gave them this law.

כִּיהוָה אֱלֹהֵינוּ בְּכָל־קָרְאֵנוּ אֵלָיו׃

as Yahweh our God is whenever we call upon him?

כַּיהוָה	as/that Yahweh	ABS	noun
יהוה	*ka·YHWH*	W/ PREP כְּ	
אֱלֹהֵינוּ	our God	CST	noun
אֱלֹהִים	*ʾĕ·lō·hê·nû*	W/ 1CP SX	
בְּכָל־	in all/whenever	CST	noun
כֹּל	*bək·kol-*	W/ PREP בְּ	
קָרְאֵנוּ	we call	QAL INF CST	verb
קרא	*qā·rə·ʾē·nû*	W/ 1CP SX	
אֵלָיו׃	upon/to him	---	prep
אֶל	*ʾē·lāyw*	W/ 3MS SX	

וּמִי גּוֹי גָּדוֹל אֲשֶׁר־לוֹ חֻקִּים וּמִשְׁפָּטִים צַדִּיקִם

And what nation is so superior that has statutes
and ordinances so righteous

וּמִי	and what/who/whichever	---	interr
מִי	*û·mî*	W/ CONJ וְ	pron
גּוֹי	nation	ABS	noun
גּוֹי	*gôy*		
גָּדוֹל	great	MS ATTR	adj
גָּדוֹל	*gā·dôl*		
אֲשֶׁר־	that/which	---	relative
אֲשֶׁר	*ʾă·šer-*		pron
לוֹ	to it	---	prep
לְ	*lô*	W/ 3MS SX	
חֻקִּים	statutes/regulations	ABS	noun
חֹק	*ḥuq·qîm*		
וּמִשְׁפָּטִים	and judgments/ordinances	ABS	noun
מִשְׁפָּט	*û·miš·pā·ṭîm*	W/ CONJ וְ	
צַדִּיקִם	right/righteous/just	MP ATTR	adj
צַדִּיק	*ṣad·dî·qîm*		

as this whole law that I am setting before you today?"

כְּכֹל כֹּל	as/according to all *kə·ḵōl*	CST W/ PREP כְּ	noun
הַתּוֹרָה תּוֹרָה	(the) law *hat·tô·râ*	ABS W/ DEF. ART.	noun
הַזֹּאת זֹאת	(the) this *haz·zō't*	--- W/ DEF. ART.	demonstr pron
אֲשֶׁר אֲשֶׁר	that/which *ă·šer*	---	relative pron
אָנֹכִי אָנֹכִי	I *'ā·nō·ḵî*	---	personal pron
נֹתֵן נתן	(am) giving/setting *nō·tēn*	QAL PTCP MS	verb
לִפְנֵיכֶם לִפְנֵי	before you *lif·nê·ḵem*	--- W/ 2MP SX	prep
הַיּוֹם: יוֹם	today/this day *hay·yôm*	ABS W/ DEF. ART.	noun

This opening salvo in Moses' first sermon ushers his audience on a journey through time:

present → past → present → future

This way of moving through time weighs down the present with a sense of urgency and hope. These commandments come today, in the shadow of your past failures at Baal of Peor, and God is giving you a new opportunity to "keep them and do them" today (v. 6). If you do, it will transform your nation into a people unparalleled in the ancient world. Israel will shine forth as a people of wisdom, understanding, and righteousness—a people loved by the One True God who dwells very near to them. But you *must* keep this law.

9a

רַ֣ק הִשָּׁ֣מֶר לְךָ֩ וּשְׁמֹ֨ר נַפְשְׁךָ֜ מְאֹד

raq hiššāmer ləkā ûšəmōr nafšəkā mə'ōd

"Only you shall be very careful to guard your life,

9b

פֶּן־תִּשְׁכַּ֣ח אֶת־הַדְּבָרִ֗ים אֲשֶׁר־רָא֣וּ עֵינֶ֗יךָ

pen-tiškāḥ 'et-haddəvārîm 'ăšer-rā'û 'ênêkā

lest you forget the things your eyes have seen,

9c

וּפֶן־יָס֙וּרוּ֙ מִלְּבָבְךָ֔ כֹּ֖ל יְמֵ֣י חַיֶּ֑יךָ

ûfen-yāsûrû milləvavkā kōl yəmê ḥayyêkā

and lest your hearts turn away all the days of your life.

9d

וְהוֹדַעְתָּ֥ם לְבָנֶ֖יךָ וְלִבְנֵ֥י בָנֶֽיךָ׃

wəhôda'tām ləvānêkem wəlivnê vānêkā.

**You shall make them known to your children
and your children's children—**

10a

י֗וֹם אֲשֶׁ֨ר עָמַ֜דְתָּ לִפְנֵ֨י יְהוָ֤ה אֱלֹהֶ֙יךָ֙ בְּחֹרֵ֔ב

yôm 'ăšer 'āmadtā lifnê YHWH 'ĕlōhêkā bəḥōrēv

the day that you stood before Yahweh your God at Horeb,

10b

בֶּאֱמֹ֨ר יְהוָ֤ה אֵלַי֙

be'ĕmōr YHWH 'ēlay

when Yahweh spoke to me,

10c

הַקְהֶל־לִי֙ אֶת־הָעָ֔ם

haqhel-lî 'et-hā'ām

'Gather the people to me,

10d

וְאַשְׁמִעֵ֖ם אֶת־דְּבָרָ֑י אֲשֶׁ֤ר יִלְמְד֙וּן֙

wə'ašmi'ēm 'et-dəvārāy 'ăšer yilmədûn

and I will make them hear my words, that they may learn

10e

לְיִרְאָ֣ה אֹתִ֗י כָּל־הַיָּמִים֙ אֲשֶׁ֨ר הֵ֤ם חַיִּים֙ עַל־הָ֣אֲדָמָ֔ה

ləyir'â 'ōtî kol-hayyāmîm 'ăšer hēm ḥayyîm 'al hā'ădāmâ

to fear me all the days that they live on the land

10f

וְאֶת־בְּנֵיהֶ֖ם יְלַמֵּדֽוּן׃

wə'et-bənêhem yəlammēdûn.

and that they may teach their children.'

11a

וַתִּקְרְב֥וּן וַתַּֽעַמְד֖וּן תַּ֣חַת הָהָ֑ר

wattiqrəvûn watta'amdûn taḥat hāhār

And you drew near and stood under the mountain,

11b

וְהָהָ֞ר בֹּעֵ֤ר בָּאֵשׁ֙ עַד־לֵ֣ב הַשָּׁמַ֔יִם

wəhāhār bō'ēr bā'ēš 'ad-lēv haššāmayim

and the mountain burned with fire from the heart of the heavens:

11c

חֹ֖שֶׁךְ עָנָ֥ן וַעֲרָפֶֽל׃

ḥōšek 'ānān wa'ărāfel.

darkness, cloud, and deep gloom.

12a

וַיְדַבֵּ֧ר יְהוָ֛ה אֲלֵיכֶ֖ם מִתּ֣וֹךְ הָאֵ֑שׁ

wayyədabbēr YHWH 'ălêkem mittôk hā'ēš

And Yahweh spoke to you from the midst of the fire.

12b

ק֤וֹל דְּבָרִים֙ אַתֶּ֣ם שֹׁמְעִ֔ים

qôl dəvārîm 'attem šōmə'îm

The sound of words you heard,

12c

וּתְמוּנָ֛ה אֵינְכֶ֥ם רֹאִ֖ים

ûtəmûnâ 'ênəkem rō'îm

but you saw no form,

12d

זוּלָתִ֥י קֽוֹל׃

zûlātî qôl.

only a voice.

13a וַיַּגֵּד לָכֶם אֶת־בְּרִיתוֹ אֲשֶׁר צִוָּה אֶתְכֶם לַעֲשׂוֹת

wayyagēd lākem ʾet-bərîtô ʾăšer ṣiwwâ ʾetkem laʿăśôt

And he declared to you his covenant,
which he commanded you to do,

13b עֲשֶׂרֶת הַדְּבָרִים

ʿăśeret haddəvārîm

the ten words.

13c וַיִּכְתְּבֵם עַל־שְׁנֵי לֻחוֹת אֲבָנִים׃

wayyiktəvēm ʿal-šənê luḥôt ʾăvānîm.

And he wrote them on two tablets of stone

14a וְאֹתִי צִוָּה יְהוָה בָּעֵת הַהִוא

wəʾōtî ṣiwwâ YHWH bāʿēt hahîʾ

And Yahweh commanded me at that time

14b לְלַמֵּד אֶתְכֶם חֻקִּים וּמִשְׁפָּטִים

ləlammēd ʾetkem ḥuqqîm ûmišpāṭîm

to teach you the statutes and ordinances,

14c לַעֲשֹׂתְכֶם אֹתָם בָּאָרֶץ אֲשֶׁר אַתֶּם עֹבְרִים שָׁמָּה לְרִשְׁתָּהּ׃

laʿăśōtkem ʾōtām bāʾāreṣ ʾăšer ʾattem ʿōvərîm šāmmâ lərištāh.

that you might do them in the land
that you are crossing over to possess.”

9a רַק הִשָּׁמֶר לְךָ וּשְׁמֹר נַפְשְׁךָ מְאֹד

“Only you shall be very careful to guard your life,

רַק	only/still/but	adv
raq		

הִשָּׁמֶר שׁמר	take heed *hiš·šā·mer*	NIPH IMPV MS	verb
לְךָ לְ	to yourself *lə·ḵā*	--- W/ 2MS SX	prep
וּשְׁמֹר שׁמר	and keep/guard/observe *û·šə·mōr*	QAL IMPV MS W/ CONJ וְ	verb
נַפְשְׁךָ נֶפֶשׁ	your life/soul *naf·šə·ḵā*	CST W/ 2MS SX	noun
מְאֹד מְאֹד	very/diligently *mə·ʾōd*	---	adv

שׁמר ("keep, guard") appears twice in this verse and is a keyword throughout Deuteronomy. Notice especially that שׁמר begins the Sabbath command in 5:12 in place of the word "remember" (זכר) in the same command in the Decalogue in Exod 20:8. In fact, some form of the word שׁמר occurs over seventy times in Deuteronomy, which is over three times more than any other book in the Pentateuch. Braulik has argued that the term is better understood as an intellectual sense of persistent attention, rather than keeping simply by obeying (Braulik 2019:91).

9b	פֶּן־תִּשְׁכַּח אֶת־הַדְּבָרִים אֲשֶׁר־רָאוּ עֵינֶיךָ

lest you forget the things your eyes have seen,

פֶּן־ פֶּן	lest/so that not *pen-*	---	conj
תִּשְׁכַּח שׁכח	you forget *tiš·kāḥ*	QAL IMPF 2MS	verb
אֶת־ אֵת	(direct object marker) *ʾet-*	---	particle
הַדְּבָרִים דָּבָר	the words *had·də·vā·rîm*	ABS W/ DEF. ART.	noun
אֲשֶׁר־ אֲשֶׁר	that/which *ʾă·šer-*	---	relative pron
רָאוּ ראה	(they) see *rā·ʾû*	QAL PF 3CP	verb
עֵינֶיךָ עַיִן	your eyes *ʿê·nɛ̂·ḵā*	CST W/ 2MS SX	noun

Forgetting (שׁכח) is another common danger warned against in Moses' sermons, especially in ch. 8. As we will see, forgetting is not the loss of information but the loss and abandoning of values and a way of life.

| 9c | וּפֶן־יָסֹ֙וּרוּ֙ מִלְּבָ֣בְךָ֔ כֹּ֖ל יְמֵ֣י חַיֶּ֑יךָ |

and lest your hearts turn away all the days of your life.

וּפֶן־	and lest/so that not	---	conj
פֶּן	*û·fen-*	W/ CONJ וְ	
יָסֹ֙וּרוּ֙	(they) turn/turn aside	QAL IMPF 3MP	verb
סוּר	*yā·sû·rû*		
מִלְּבָ֣בְךָ֔	from your heart	CST	noun
לֵבָב	*mil·lə·vav·ḵā*	W/ PREP מִן + 2MS SX	
כֹּ֖ל	all	CST	noun
כֹּל	*kōl*		
יְמֵ֣י	(the) days of	CST	noun
יוֹם	*yə·mê*		
חַיֶּ֑יךָ	your life	CST	noun
חַיִּים	*ḥāy·yê·ḵā*	W/ 2MS SX	

| 9d | וְהוֹדַעְתָּ֥ם לְבָנֶ֖יךָ וְלִבְנֵ֥י בָנֶֽיךָ׃ |

You shall make them known to your children
and your children's children—

וְהוֹדַעְתָּ֥ם	and you shall make them known	HIPH WEQATAL 2MS	verb
ידע	*wə·hô·da'·tām*	W/ 3MP SX	
לְבָנֶ֖יךָ	to your children	CST	noun
בֵּן	*lə·vā·nê·ḵem*	W/ PREP לְ + 2MS SX	
וְלִבְנֵ֥י	and to (the) children of	CST	noun
בֵּן	*wə·liv·nê*	W/ CONJ וְ + PREP לְ	
בָנֶֽיךָ׃	your children	CST	noun
בֵּן	*vā·nê·ḵā*	W/ 2MS SX	

יוֹם אֲשֶׁר עָמַדְתָּ לִפְנֵי יְהוָה אֱלֹהֶיךָ בְּחֹרֵב

the day that you stood before Yahweh your God at Horeb,

יוֹם / יוֹם	(the) day / *yôm*	ABS	noun
אֲשֶׁר / אֲשֶׁר	that/which / *'ă·šer*	---	relative pron
עָמַדְתָּ / עמד	you stand / *'ā·mad·tā*	QAL PF 2MS	verb
לִפְנֵי / לִפְנֵי	before / *lif·nê*	---	prep
יְהוָה / יהוה	Yahweh / *YHWH*	ABS	noun
אֱלֹהֶיךָ / אֱלֹהִים	your God / *'ĕ·lō·hê·ḵā*	CST W/ 2MS SX	noun
בְּחֹרֵב / חֹרֵב	at/on Horeb / *bə·ḥō·rēv*	ABS W/ PREP בְּ	noun

Time works playfully in Deuteronomy. Notice that few who were in Moses' original audience at Horeb forty years earlier would still be alive to be counted among the "you." That's particularly significant when we think of Deuteronomy as a book intended to be read by countless future generations. In fact, in 5:3 Moses describes the second generation as those with whom God made his covenant at Horeb. I agree with scholars who believe that Deuteronomy wants us to think as if the witness of previous generations is true of us every time we read this story (e.g., McConville 2002:106–7). And that is what we will see in the following verses.

בֶּאֱמֹר יְהוָה אֵלַי

when Yahweh spoke to me,

בֶּאֱמֹר / אמר	in saying/speaking / *be·'ĕ·mōr*	QAL INF CST W/ PREP בְּ	verb
יְהוָה / יהוה	Yahweh / *YHWH*	ABS	noun
אֵלַי / אֶל	to me / *'ē·lay*	--- W/ 1CS SX	prep

Moses' role as intermediary is constantly reinforced in Deuteronomy. Moses' command (4:2) is therefore also God's command (1:3).

10c הַקְהֶל־לִי אֶת־הָעָ֔ם

'Gather the people to me,

הַקְהֶל־ קהל	gather/assemble/summon *haq·hel-*	HIPH IMPV MS	verb
לִי לְ	to me *lî*	--- W/ 1CS SX	prep
אֶת־ אֵת	(direct object marker) *'et-*	---	particle
הָעָ֔ם עַם	the people *hā·'ām*	ABS W/ DEF. ART.	noun

10d וְאַשְׁמִעֵם אֶת־דְּבָרַי אֲשֶׁר יִלְמְדוּן

and I will make them hear my words, that they may learn

וְאַשְׁמִעֵם שמע	and I will make them hear/ obey/listen to *wə·'aš·mi·'ēm*	CS W/ CONJ וְ + 3MP SX	verb
אֶת־ אֵת	(direct object marker) *'et-*	---	particle
דְּבָרַי דָּבָר	my words *də·vā·ray*	CST W/ 1CS SX	noun
אֲשֶׁר אֲשֶׁר	that/which *'ă·šer*	---	relative pron
יִלְמְדוּן למד	they will learn *yil·mə·dûn*	QAL IMPF 3MP W/ PARAGOGIC ן	verb

<table>
<tr><td>10e</td><td style="text-align:center">לְיִרְאָ֣ה אֹתִ֗י כָּל־הַיָּמִים֙ אֲשֶׁ֨ר הֵ֤ם חַיִּים֙ עַל־הָ֣אֲדָמָ֔ה</td></tr>
</table>

to fear me all the days that they live on the land

לְיִרְאָ֣ה	to fear	QAL INF CST	verb
ירא	lə·yir·'â	W/ PREP לְ	
אֹתִ֗י	(direct object marker +) me	---	particle
אֵת	'ō·tî	W/ 1CS SX	
כָּל־	all	CST	noun
כֹּל	kol-		
הַיָּמִים֙	the days of	ABS	noun
יוֹם	hay·yā·mîm	W/ DEF. ART.	
אֲשֶׁ֨ר	that/which	---	relative pron
אֲשֶׁר	'ă·šer		
הֵ֤ם	they	---	personal pron
הֵם	hēm		
חַיִּים֙	(are) alive/living	MP PRED	adj
חַיִּים	ḥay·yîm		
עַל־	on/upon	---	prep
עַל	'al		
הָ֣אֲדָמָ֔ה	the land/earth	ABS	noun
אֲדָמָה	hā·'ă·dā·mâ	W/ DEF. ART.	

"Fear" (יִרְאָה) is semi-synonymous with other rhetorical vocabulary that calls for consciousness or wakefulness (see 10:12).

<table>
<tr><td>10f</td><td style="text-align:center">וְאֶת־בְּנֵיהֶ֖ם יְלַמֵּדֽוּן׃</td></tr>
</table>

and that they may teach their children.'

וְאֶת־	and (+ direct object marker)	---	particle
אֵת	wə·'et-	W/ CONJ וְ	
בְּנֵיהֶ֖ם	their children	CST	noun
בֵּן	bə·nê·hem	W/ 3MP SX	
יְלַמֵּדֽוּן׃	they teach	PIEL IMPF 3MP	verb
למד	yə·lam·mē·dûn	W/ PARAGOGIC ן	

11a

וַתִּקְרְבוּן וַתַּעַמְדוּן תַּחַת הָהָר

And you drew near and stood under the mountain,

וַתִּקְרְבוּן קרב	and you came/drew near *wat·tiq·rə·vûn*	QAL WAYY 2MP W/ PARAGOGIC ן	verb
וַתַּעַמְדוּן עמד	and you stood *wat·ta·ʿam·dûn*	QAL WAYY 2MP W/ PARAGOGIC ן	verb
תַּחַת תַּחַת	below/under *ta·ḥat*	- - -	prep
הָהָר הַר	the mountain *hā·hār*	ABS W/ DEF. ART.	noun

11b

וְהָהָר בֹּעֵר בָּאֵשׁ עַד־לֵב הַשָּׁמַיִם

and the mountain burned with fire from the heart of the heavens:

וְהָהָר הַר	and the mountain *wə·hā·hār*	ABS W/ CONJ ן + DEF. ART.	noun
בֹּעֵר בער	burning *bō·ʿēr*	QAL PTCP MS	verb
בָּאֵשׁ אֵשׁ	in/with fire *bā·ʾēš*	ABS W/ PREP בְּ + DEF. ART.	noun
עַד־ עַד	until/as far as *ʿad-*	- - -	prep
לֵב לֵב	(the) heart of *lēv*	CST	noun
הַשָּׁמַיִם שָׁמַיִם	the heavens/skies *haš·šā·ma·yim*	ABS W/ DEF. ART.	noun

11c

חֹשֶׁךְ עָנָן וַעֲרָפֶל׃

darkness, cloud, and deep gloom.

חֹשֶׁךְ חֹשֶׁךְ	darkness *ḥō·šek*	ABS	noun

| עָנָן
עָנָן | cloud/clouds
'ā·nān | ABS | noun |
| וַעֲרָפֶל:
עֲרָפֶל | and thick darkness
*wa·'ă·rā·**fel*** | ABS
W/ CONJ וְ | noun |

There is a strong echo here of the primordial world at the start of creation in Gen 1. In fact, just after our passage in vv. 15–19, Moses clearly alludes to the creatures and objects of creation in the Genesis account. The law, as seems clear from vv. 5–8, is meant to connect us to the cosmic order of creation and God's moral and judicial designs for human life.

12a וַיְדַבֵּר יְהוָה אֲלֵיכֶם מִתּוֹךְ הָאֵשׁ

And Yahweh spoke to you from the midst of the fire.

וַיְדַבֵּר דבר	and (he) spoke *way·yə·dab·**bēr***	PIEL WAYY 3MS	verb
יְהוָה יהוה	Yahweh *YHWH*	ABS	noun
אֲלֵיכֶם אל	to you *'ă·lê·**kem***	--- W/ 2MP SX	prep
מִתּוֹךְ מתוך	from (the) midst/middle/ center of *mit·**tôḵ***	---	prep
הָאֵשׁ אש	the fire *hā·**'ēš***	ABS W/ DEF. ART.	noun

Note a transformation of something seen, הָאֵשׁ ("the fire"), into speech and words here and through the rest of v. 12.

12b קוֹל דְּבָרִים אַתֶּם שֹׁמְעִים

The sound of words you heard,

| קוֹל
קוֹל | (the) voice/sound of
qôl | CST | noun |
| דְּבָרִים
דָּבָר | words/things
*də·vā·**rîm*** | ABS | noun |

אַתֶּם	you	---	personal
אַתֶּם	'at·**tem**		pron
שֹׁמְעִים	hearing	QAL PTCP MP	verb
שׁמע	šō·mə·**'îm**		

<table>
<tr><td>12c</td><td colspan="3" align="center">וּתְמוּנָה אֵינְכֶם רֹאִים</td><td align="right">4:1–14</td></tr>
</table>

but you saw no form,

וּתְמוּנָה	and/but form/appearance	ABS	noun
תְּמוּנָה	û·tə·mû·**nâ**	W/ CONJ וְ	
אֵינְכֶם	you not	---	particle
אֵין	'ê·nə·**kem**	W/ 2MP SX	
רֹאִים	seeing	QAL PTCP MP	verb
ראה	rō·**'îm**		

<table>
<tr><td>12d</td><td align="center">זוּלָתִי קוֹל:</td></tr>
</table>

only a voice.

זוּלָתִי	only/except	---	prep
זוּלָה	zû·lā·**tî**		
קוֹל:	voice/sound	ABS	noun
קוֹל	**qôl**		

The word זוּלָה ("only"), usually understood as a conjunction or adverb (see the other use in 1:36), is rare. Here it confirms that God's revelation at Horeb was not in the things (fire, cloud, darkness) but in the words. See further the "From Text to Sermon" section below.

And he declared to you his covenant,
which he commanded you to do,

וַיַּגֵּד נגד	and he declared *way·ya·gēd*	HIPH WAYY 3MS	verb
לָכֶם לְ	to you *lā·ḵem*	--- W/ 2MP SX	prep
אֶת־ אֵת	(direct object marker) *'et-*	---	particle
בְּרִיתוֹ בְּרִית	his covenant *bə·rî·tô*	CST W/ 3MS SX	noun
אֲשֶׁר אֲשֶׁר	that/which *'ă·šer*	---	relative pron
צִוָּה צוה	he commanded *ṣiw·wâ*	PIEL PF 3MS	verb
אֶתְכֶם אֵת	you *'et·ḵem*	--- W/ 2MP SX	particle
לַעֲשׂוֹת עשה	to do *la·ʻă·śôt*	QAL INF CST W/ PREP לְ	verb

the ten words.

עֲשֶׂרֶת עֶשֶׂר	ten *ʻă·śe·ret*	CST	ordinal number
הַדְּבָרִים דָּבָר	the words *had·də·vā·rîm*	ABS W/ DEF. ART.	noun

The Decalogue is never called the "Ten Commandments" in the Old Testament. We will comment further on this in our discussion of Deut 5:1–21.

וַיִּכְתְּבֵם עַל־שְׁנֵי לֻחוֹת אֲבָנִים׃

And he wrote them on two tablets of stone

וַיִּכְתְּבֵם כתב	and he wrote/inscribed them *way·yiḵ·tə·vēm*	QAL WAYY 3MS W/ 3MP SX	verb
עַל־ עַל	on *ʿal-*	---	prep
שְׁנֵי שְׁנַיִם	two *šə·nê*	CST	cardinal number
לֻחוֹת לוּחַ	plates/tablets of *lu·ḥôt*	CST	noun
אֲבָנִים׃ אֶבֶן	stones *ʾă·vā·nîm*	ABS	noun

The specific mention of "two tablets" (שְׁנֵי לֻחוֹת) has provoked a great variety of interpretations (see also 5:22; Exod 24:12). Why are there two, rather than one? Some have argued that the tables represent the vertical commands about God (1–3) and the horizontal commands about society (5–10) with command 4 or 5 as a bridge. But there are several objections to this command, chief among those is that all of the commands represent obedience and honor to God (Block 2012:1–27).

The remains of Aramaic decrees from the seventh century BCE suggest that legal tablets were about one foot by one foot in measurement, easily able to contain the full list of laws on one side of stone (Tigay 1996:48). So it has been increasingly assumed that the two stones represented two legal copies of the law, one for God and one for Israel. Both were placed in the ark of the covenant that rested in the holy of holies (cf. Deut 10:1–5; 1 Kgs 8:6)—the place where Israel's concrete world intersected with the infinite, transcendent, and eternal (Kline 1960).

וְאֹתִי צִוָּה יְהוָה בָּעֵת הַהִוא

And Yahweh commanded me at that time

וְאֹתִי אֵת	and (+ *direct object marker* +) me *wə·ʾō·tî*	W/ CONJ וְ + 1CS SX	particle
צִוָּה צוה	(he) commanded *ṣiw·wâ*	PIEL PF 3MS	verb

יְהֹוָה	Yahweh	ABS	noun
יהוה	*YHWH*		
בָּעֵת	at (the) time	ABS	noun
עֵת	*bā·'ēt*	W/ PREP בְּ + DEF. ART.	
הַהִוא	(the) that	---	demonstr
הִיא	*ha·hī'*	W/ DEF. ART.	pron

We must not forget that this law is *commanded*—that is, a publicly declared mandate for the people to follow. In legal terms, it is "promulgated."

14b לְלַמֵּד אֶתְכֶם חֻקִּים וּמִשְׁפָּטִים

to teach you the statutes and ordinances,

לְלַמֵּד	to teach	PIEL INF CST	verb
למד	*lə·lam·mēd*	W/ PREP לְ	
אֶתְכֶם	you	---	particle
אֵת	*'et·kem*	W/ 2MP SX	
חֻקִּים	(the) statutes/regulations	ABS	noun
חֹק	*ḥuq·qîm*		
וּמִשְׁפָּטִים	and judgments/ordinances	ABS	noun
מִשְׁפָּט	*û·miš·pā·ṭîm*	W/ CONJ וְ	

14c לַעֲשֹׂתְכֶם אֹתָם בָּאָרֶץ אֲשֶׁר אַתֶּם עֹבְרִים שָׁמָּה לְרִשְׁתָּהּ׃

that you might do them in the land
that you are crossing over to possess."

לַעֲשֹׂתְכֶם	for you (all) to do/that you (all) may do	Q INF CST	verb
עשׂה	*la·'ă·śōt·kem*	W/ PREP לְ + 2MP SX	
אֹתָם	them (object marker)	---	particle
אֵת	*'ō·tām*	W/ 3MP SX	
בָּאָרֶץ	in the land	ABS	noun
אֶרֶץ	*bā·'ā·reṣ*	W/ PREP בְּ + DEF. ART.	
אֲשֶׁר	that/which	---	relative
אֲשֶׁר	*'ă·šer*		pron

אַתֶּם אַתֶּם ʾat·tem	you	---	personal pron
עֹבְרִים עבר ʿō·və·rîm	(are) passing through/ passing over/crossing	Q PTCP MP	verb
שָׁמָּה שָׁם šām·mâ	(to) there	--- W/ LOCATIVE ה	adv
לְרִשְׁתָּהּ׃ ירש lə·riš·tāh	to possess/to dispossess it	QAL INF CST W/ PREP לְ + 3FS SX	verb

The significance of ch. 4 can hardly be overstated. Supported by other scholars, Gordon McConville describes the chapter as "an anticipation, or even a summation, of the scope and themes of the whole book" (McConville 2002:102; see also Olson 1994:30). And so, as we think about preaching this section of ch. 4, it will do us good to look closely at the structure of the material within the larger context of the book.

Opening of Chs. 1–4	1:1–5	
Prologue	4:1–8	
Main Body	4:9–31	Prologue to the laws
Epilogue	4:32–40	
Ending of Chs. 1–4	4:41–49	

Chapter 4 has a cohesive structure in 4:1–40, after which it turns to third-person narrative in 4:41–49. This ties us back to the third-person narrative that opened the book in 1:1–5, closing four introductory chapters that set up the laws in chs. 5–26. Such framing of the law is likely meant to render Deuteronomy in the form of prominent ancient Near Eastern treaties and law codes, particularly that of Hammurabi, which has a distinct prologue and epilogue around the main body of laws.

Here is a more elaborate outline of the prologue and the way its themes echo throughout Deuteronomy.

1	עַתָּה (present time reference; "now")	
	חֻקִּים וּמִשְׁפָּטִים	4:14, 45; 5:31; 6:1; 12:1; 26:16
5	חֻקִּים וּמִשְׁפָּטִים	4:14, 45; 5:31; 6:1; 12:1; 26:16
8	חֻקִּים וּמִשְׁפָּטִים	4:14, 45; 5:31; 6:1; 12:1; 26:16
	הַיּוֹם (present time reference; "today")	

First, notice how Moses draws upon *time* and *history* to give the law a sense of immediacy for anyone reading the book (4:1, 3–4, 8). The events of the past and the hope of the future place us among the succeeding generations of those have been called to follow God. Today is the day to act.

Second, scholars have also documented the repetition of key terms in Deuteronomy (Braulik 2006:77–109; Strawn 2003). Of particular note, the word pair חֻקִּים וּמִשְׁפָּטִים ("statutes and ordinances") in 4:1, 14, etc., is repeated seven times in total, ending at 26:16. This encloses all of the laws in chs. 4–26 and, as will see below, establishes a relationship between the general commands in the Decalogue (5:6–21) and the particular applications of law in chs. 12–26.

With this overview in mind, let's look at several approaches to preaching ch. 4.

 You, You All, and Us. Moses' address in Deut 4 (and later chapters) alternates conspicuously between second-person singular—you—and second-person plural—you all (see vv. 1, 5, 8, 9). This alternation was once believed to be evidence of diverse fragments being brought together to form the book. By and large, most scholars now acknowledge that the changes are a rhetorical strategy designed to draw us both individually and corporately into this message (McConville 2002:100–2).

As we will see in the chapters to follow, individual responsibility to write the law on our hearts is joined to the corporate responsibility to teach it to the next generation (4:9–10; 6:6–9). In an age when Western cultures imagine faith and religion as purely individual ventures—and church attendance as a matter of *my needs* on any given day—Deuteronomy binds me to my neighbor. A preacher can tie these themes to teachings on the church as a body in places like Rom 12:3–13; 1 Cor 12–13, and Eph 4:1–12, where our gifts, talents, and dispositions are given for the sake of the "common good" and "building up of the body."

Another way to address this topic is through the two major conciliar creeds:

Apostles' Creed	I believe in . . . the holy catholic Church; the communion of saints
Nicene Creed	And we believe in one holy catholic and apostolic Church

The early church understood well the spiritual bonds created by the Holy Spirit that brought us into union with Christ. As Paul puts it in Ephesians, "There is one body and one Spirit—just as you were called to the one hope that belongs to your call—one Lord, one faith, one baptism, one God and Father of all, who is over all and through all and in all" (Eph 4:4–6; see Williams 2007:104–33).

In these early chapters of Deuteronomy, a theology of community leads Israel to hold one another up in loving God and remaining faithful to his law. In Deut 14–16, these bonds give way to liturgical practices that celebrate Israel's unity and care for those who are marginalized economically or socially.

 ***Teach the Next Generation.*** One may choose to address the topic of teaching here or in a sermon on Deut 6:1–9 or 8:1–16. The alternation of second person singular and plural pronouns addressed above appears alongside vocabulary that combines teaching, learning, and doing (4:1, 5, 9, 10), resulting in a progressive sequence of images: Yahweh reveals himself on the mountain, Israel learns and does the law in the camp, and one generation teaches the law to the next in the home and at festivals.

Above all, ch. 4 uses teaching in a way that ties it to the second command against making images in the form of God. Israel is told that their ancestors saw only clouds, darkness, and fire but not a form or image of God. Instead, God's theophany, or appearing to Israel, is transformed into the aural realm of words (Sonnet 1997). The theophany is not only about what your ancestors *saw* during those forty days but also what they *heard* from the divine voice that came from heaven. God's transcendent and infinite nature may come to each generation of Israel through the practices of teaching in the home, gathering at the gates, and regularly shared tithes and festivals.

We already noted the creation imagery throughout this chapter which reinforces the link between the creation coming into existence by its response to the voice of God (Gen 1:1–31) and Israel's becoming God's people by obeying the words of the law at Horeb. One might pair this passage with Pss 1, 19, and 119. See especially Clinton McCann's (1993) brief treatment of the relationship between the divine order in creation and תּוֹרָה ("law") in Ps 19: just as the sun runs its proper course (19:4–5), so the laws of the Lord guide humanity (19:7–8).

As noted above, Deuteronomy is the only book in the Pentateuch that mentions "teaching" (Piel of למד), which occurs three times in 4:1–14 alone. Understood in the broader context of creation in ch. 4, teaching is more than simply a guide to catechesis for children. The vision for teaching this law is one that brings the whole nation into the shape and way of life God has designed for it within the moral order of the universe. It is also a shape, as we will see in the final preaching theme, that gives Israel its witness to the nations around it. No other nation has a law or a God like this.

The Voice, The Incarnation, and the Ends of the Law. Can anyone see God and live? Exodus 33:20 says, "no." Deut 5:24 complicates the matter when the Israelites say: "this day we have seen that God speaks to man and he lives."

We can appreciate why these texts about seeing God are so powerful: visual sight offers us a sense of recognition and confirmation that we
instinctually crave. This is partly because seeing has a uniquely first-person
quality, which is why Thomas is slow to believe until he sees the risen Jesus
(John 20:24–29). The narrative in the Bible nurtures and fulfills this deep
human longing within us.

In Exodus 33–34 we get a vague sense that Moses is continually ex-
posed to God's glory on the mountain and in the tent of meeting. It's less
clear whether that glory is visibly seen by Moses. Indeed, God orchestrates
a way to cover Moses' face so that Moses only sees God's back when he
passes by him in his appearing (33:20–23). The ambiguity surrounding
this scene entices us to wonder what Moses saw and what God must look
like to human eyes. In all this, Exodus refuses to consent to the ancient
practice of making an idol to fill in the gaps for the Israelites.

Deuteronomy 4 plays on the tension between seeing and not seeing
God to transform the desire for visual sight into hearing the words of
the law (4:10–12). The passage is closely tied to the first two commands
of the Decalogue in 5:6–10. In the ancient world, gods became present
to a people when their idols were consecrated and set in holy places.
In sharp contrast, this God cannot be reduced to physical or meteoro-
logical manifestations (4:10–12, 15–20). God is above, apart from, and
before his creation. In a world dominated by what it saw in the skies
or in religious temples, Israel is trained to orient itself to what it has
heard and believed about God and his actions. Contrary to most other
ancient temples, Israel's tabernacle never depicts God visually. At the
center of the holy of holies Israel was to place the ark of the covenant
that housed the two tablets of the Decalogue (cf. Deut 10:1–5; 1 Kgs
8:6). If you want to know what God is like, you must *look* to his law
and his mighty works.

The gospel of John makes an unambiguous connection between the
God of creation, the word (λόγος), and the notion of seeing or not seeing God (John 1:1–18). The Synoptic Gospels give us something closer to
a narrative development of God's image that follows what we see in the
Pentateuch. In a way, the elusive power of God's spirit over the waters
anticipates the power of the Holy Spirit to bring us face to face with the
Son of God in our own human form
(Matt 1:18). The barrier between God and our material life in this
world was decisively crossed in Mary and her child.

 *Law, Wisdom, and the Nearness of God.* Deuteronomy 4:5–8 boasts of the
incomparable desirability of this law from Moses. It will be "your wisdom

and discernment" in the opinion of surrounding nations. Keeping the law will also emphasize the uniqueness of Israel's God who is "so near" as well as their law, which is superbly "righteous." We may expand on the judicial, revelatory, and missional superiority of this law.

First, Israel's law is a *judicially superior ancient law code*. Whenever Deuteronomy was written, Israelites would have likely known by reputation if not in detail the widespread fame of the Code of Hammurabi—probably other laws as well (Weinfeld 1991:202). There are often important parallels between these laws, yet Deuteronomy clearly reflects the most humanitarian vision.

Deuteronomy makes numerous provisions to love and protect the foreigner, widow, and orphan (24:17–22); provides protections for livestock (5:12–25); makes a practice of relieving debts of bondservants or "slaves" (15:1–18); protects involuntary manslaughter against the avenger of blood (19:1–13); protects against discrimination against women (15:12; 22:13–19); does not allow the death penalty for economic crimes; establishes the first known tax that is applied to social welfare (14:22–29); and recognizes the right of the individual before the law (see Baker 2009; Braulik 1994c:131–50). In Israel's ancient context, these laws stood alone in their ennobling and protection not only of the creation but especially of all who bear God's image.

Second, the nations will marvel at the *revelatory* power of this law. In most ancient religions, gods were tied to specific idols and often to local places. This led to a plurality of tribal deities, such that the applicable worship and laws were dependent upon where you lived or traveled. In Israel's religion, not only is there only one God, but he is not bounded by geography or temples. He is near whenever his people call upon him (4:7).

This one true God also centralizes all the laws around his sole authority, and the implications are enormous. Justice and social order would not be subject to local custom or the whims of the ruler in power but ordered around the one Creator and his righteous decrees (4:8).

This leads us, thirdly, to the *missional* dimension of the law. This comes through in the "wisdom and discernment" (חָכְמַתְכֶם וּבִינַתְכֶם) that the nations will attribute to Israel when they keep all this law (4:6 [twice]). These two terms are also paired in 1:13 and 1:15, and wisdom language appears elsewhere in 16:19; 32:4, 9. Specifically, the adjective "wise" (4:6; 34:9) and noun "wisdom" (1:13, 15; 4:6; 16:19; 32:6) occur seven times in the book (along with dozens of other key terms that are each used seven times). If we compare this to the seven superscriptions in the book of Proverbs (1:1; 10:1; 22:17; 24:23; 25:1; 30:1; 31:1) and seven pillars of Woman Wisdom's house in Prov 9:1, we can see that wisdom shapes both the language and the style of Deuteronomy. Why does wisdom language appear so prominently in Deuteronomy? The question has provoked an intense debate for the last few decades (Weinfeld 1992; Braulik 1994a; Schipper and Teeter 2013).

We begin by noting that these same terms and themes of wisdom, law, righteousness, rule, and the witness to the nations are found rather famously together in the succession narrative of Solomon in 1 Kgs 3–10 and the prophesy in Isa 11:1–9. This is not a new theme but an underlying thread in the biblical narrative.

The language of comparison (a "superior nation") in 4:6 signifies God's work through Israel to reveal his glory to the world. Later, in Deut 26:19, Moses will speak of the "fame and honor" God intends for Israel among the nations. "Wisdom and discernment" reflect the wisdom tradition in Israel, Proverbs in particular. Such folk wisdom sayings were common and shared across cultures, giving the law its international and comparative appeal. If Israel obeys, the nations will see the superiority of the law, liturgies and, above all, the God of Israel.

Unlike the church, Israel was not sent out on a mission to proclaim the gospel to the world. Instead, its life under Yahweh and his law act as salt and light that *attracted* the nations *to* God: "The motivation for God's people to live by God's law is ultimately to bless the nations. As so often in the Old Testament, mission and ethics are inseparable" (Wright 1996:49). Jesus certainly had Israel's global mission in mind in his call to be "salt" and "light" so that the glory of God might be made known to the world (Matt 5:13–16). Like Israel, the church's works of love and justice attract the eyes of the nations to behold our God.

THE TEN WORDS: LAW OF THE COVENANT

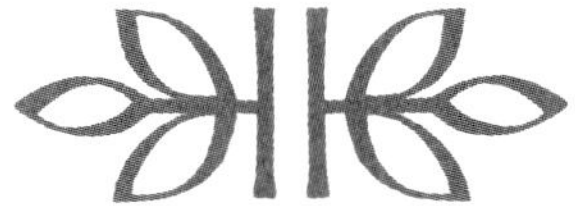

This is probably the most recognized passage in the Old Testament, having shaped cultures around the world for thousands of years.

As we saw in ch. 4, the Decalogue is carefully woven into the flow of the book (see 4:13). In Exodus and Deuteronomy, this list is called the "ten words," never the "ten commands." Both books center the law around God's theophany (appearance) at Mount Horeb (Sinai), representing God's covenant with Israel (Exod 19:5; Deut 5:2). These are not presented as universal laws but as the stipulations of a covenant with a particular people in a particular time and place. We will return to the universal implications of the law below.

LARGER LITERARY CONTEXT ▸ 5:1–33

EXCURSUS ON THE DECALOGUE

Given the significance of the Decalogue in Scripture and history, this extended excursus provides background that teachers and preachers will need to cover this material well.

To start, it is difficult to date the books of the Pentateuch. We can point to several significant additions in the Deuteronomic Decalogue that—when compared to the Decalogue in Exodus—seem to hint at Deuteronomy's later provenance, certainly that it was meant to be read as later. As Georg Braulik argues, these changes are critical to understanding the theology of Deuteronomy and its unique humanitarian aims (2019:82–99). These are the major differences:

Two changes in the Sabbath law. First, Deuteronomy's motivation is no longer based on the seven-day pattern of the creation in Exodus 20:11, but on the remembrance of God's redemption from Egypt (Deut 5:15). The central meaning shifts from a universal law of creation to Israel's indebtedness for redemption, though the two are interconnected. Second, and directly related, Israel extends the rest for "livestock" in Exodus to one's שׁוֹר ("ox") and חֲמוֹר ("donkey"), while adding כָּל ("all") (5:14) to encapsulate the full scope of this law: *every sphere of creation* must rest.

Two additions to the law to honor parents. One, the clause "as Yahweh your God commanded you," ties this law and those that follow it to the same phrase in the Sabbath law. Two, the phrase "that it may go well for you in the land," reinforces the sermonic force of the law and the promise of flourishing for covenant obedience (Miller 2018:171). We should also notice that the phrase "the land Yahweh your God is giving you," which appears in both versions of the Decalogue, also appears frequently in laws for Israel's priests, judges, kings, and prophets in Deut 16:18–18:22. This ties the authority and responsibility of parents to the authority and responsibility of Israel's leaders.

The use of שָׁוְא ("falsely") in the ninth commandment—"And you shall not answer falsely (שָׁוְא) against your neighbor" (Deut 5:20)—to parallel its use in the third commandment: "You shall not bear the name of Yahweh your God falsely (שָׁוְא)" (Deut 5:11).

This emphasizes the centrality of the divine name to the whole of the Decalogue, while linking it specifically to respect due to persons.

Related to this, the name "Yahweh" appears eight times in the Exodus Decalogue but seven times in the Deuteronomy version, following a pattern of more than sixty key terms repeated exactly seven times. Thus, while Deuteronomy otherwise expands the laws in the Exodus Decalogue, here it makes a decisive reduction. This symbolism likely anticipates the emphasis on the divine name in the Shema (6:4–9) as well as the laws for worship in ch. 12 that occur at "the place where I make my name to dwell." In theological terms, Yahweh has graciously and emphatically attached his name to this people. Consequently, their behavior, for good or bad, will affect God's reputation among the nations.

Deuteronomy adds a Hebrew וְ, translated "and" or "neither," to the final four commands in vv. 17–21 (twice in v. 21). This binds the final commands together as a group of social laws that collectively protect the neighbor's marriage, house, and possessions.

The prohibition against coveting in Exodus first specifies the house, followed by the wife and possessions. In Deuteronomy, the neighbor's wife is listed first with the Hebrew verb חמד ("to covet"). This is independent of a second prohibition with the Hithpael form of אוה ("to desire") for the neighbor's household and property (see below). Deuteronomy also inserts a second וְ between these two prohibitions, thus eliminating the possibility that the wife would be viewed as property within the house. As McConville (2002:131) notes, "The selection of two different verbs is probably not to be explained by different degrees of intensity, but by the intention to mark out the adulterous desire as different in kind."

We can see from this broad overview that Deuteronomy doubles down, in some ways, on the humanitarian and ecological vision of the law as well as the inseparable link between obedience to the commands and honoring Yahweh's name (Block 2012:13–17).

A second feature to keep in mind is the way Deuteronomy connects the Decalogue with the laws in chs. 6–26 by way of its strategic placement of חֻקִּים ("statutes") and מִשְׁפָּטִים ("ordinances"). The two terms are repeated seven times from chs. 4–26 and scholars differ as to whether they are intended to set apart chs. 4–26, 6–26, or 12–26. One could show that all of these are feasible, and all of them support the idea that the laws in the Decalogue have a close relationship with the statutes and ordinances in chs. 12–26. As far as we can tell, this relationship between the "Ten Words" and the laws in Deut 12–26 was probably first noticed by Philo of Alexandria in the first century but then picked up by major figures like Thomas Aquinas, John Calvin, and Martin Luther. Virtually all modern Deuteronomy scholars comment on this relationship as well. While the third command is the most difficult to apply, scholars suggest a relationship within the broader limits of this outline (see McConville 2002:122–23; Walton 2012:93–117):

Decalogue		Applicable chapters in 12–26
1	Worship	chs. 6–11 or 12–13
2	Idolatry	chs. 12–13
3	Divine name	chs. 13–14
4	Sabbath	chs. 15–16

5	Parents / authority	chs. 16–18
6	Murder	chs. 19–21
7	Adultery	chs. 22–23
8	Theft / property	chs. 23–25
9	False witness	chs. 24–25
10	Coveting	chs. 25 or 24–26

Given the overwhelming similarities between the Decalogues of Exodus and Deuteronomy, we can reasonably conclude that the moral order of the world remains fixed. But the slight changes in the Deuteronomy Decalogue and the careful expansions of those laws in chs. 12–26 demonstrate the need to interpret and apply the law in new ways in each individual day and each new generation.

Moreover, we must recognize the central role of God's name in the Decalogue. The first three commands focus on Yahweh: worshiping him alone, not reducing his presence to a local place, not equating him with elements of creation, and not dishonoring his name. Above we highlighted the parallel in Deuteronomy between the third and ninth commands. The divine name, we also noted, appears seven times in these laws. That's over a third of the Decalogue concerned with his "name."

In the ancient world, names were like resumes, or symbols for deeper identities. Just think about the significance of divine naming in the Bible: Abram and Sarai to Abraham and Sarah; Jacob to Israel; and Simon to Cephas (Peter).

As we can imagine, the specificity of the name "Yahweh" is at the heart of the commands. The name resists any clear or simple translation: "I will be who I will be" or "I am who I am." The elusiveness of the name underscores the transcendence of God's nature; he is before and apart from this creation. It is a name *he gives himself* and ties to his works of creation (Gen 2) and redemption of Israel from Egypt (Exod 3–6). This helps us appreciate how the first three commands anticipate the great commandment in Deut 6, which we might translate: "You shall love Yahweh your God with all your heart, with all your life force, and with your muchness" (or very, very much; see Levenson 2016:67–75). This transcendent, self-named God of the covenant is the source of every good thing. It is good and right for him to demand everything from us in return.

Meanwhile, the third command is usually believed to prohibit false oaths in God's name. This common view has some problems. For starters, the verb נשׂא ("to bear, lift up"), which appears twice in 5:11, never describes the making of an oath in the rest of Deuteronomy (Imes 2018:87–100, 140–81). Patrick Miller (2010) further points out that there are in fact other "clear and well-known Hebrew formulations" for false oaths, such as Lev 19:12: "You shall not swear falsely" (וְלֹא־תִשָּׁבְעוּ לְשֶׁקֶר . . .). That phrasing does not appear in the Decalogue, which for Miller "suggests that the formulation in the commandment may have a broader meaning and that the acts in view are not reducible to swearing oaths" (p. 70). Added to this, the laws in chs. 12–26 never mention swearing an oath to God or other gods.

Miller further notices that the prayer in Prov 30:7–9 depicts stealing as an act that profanes the name of Yahweh. This adds weight to the idea that the third commandment concerns more than speech (Miller 2010:97; cf. Imes 2018:83–84). In fact, the verb נשׂא typically means "lift up/carry," and only refers to speech when there are other contextual clues, of which there are none in the twenty appearances of the verb in Deuteronomy.

Carmen Joy Imes (2018) argues that נשׂא functions closer to its root meaning to "lift up" or "carry." Drawing on metaphor theory, she argues that the verb leads one to imagine a journey in which the people "bear" God's name *on their way*, so to speak, and in the place Yahweh chooses, there he "places" (שׂים) his name (e.g., Deut 12:5) (Imes 2018: 87–100). The name functions like a banner or garment that goes with the people.

Here we may point to the provision for the priests to *place God's name on Israel* at the start of the desert journeys in Num 6:24–27. Exodus, using the same verb that is in the third command (נשׂא), describes Aaron "bearing the names of the children of Israel on the breastpiece of judgment" that he dons before entering the sanctuary (28:29). נשׂא is also used for the priests who "carry" the ark of the covenant that symbolizes God's presence and moral guidance (e.g., Deut 31:9). Wearing, bearing, and journeying arise as the dominant images in these contexts, which suggests that the third commandment fits with something that is borne, signifying God's ownership of his covenant people and their obligation to uphold his reputation by the whole way they conduct their lives.

As we will mention again below, the Decalogue has many parallels with the Lord's Prayer, in particular its opening petition "Hallowed be thy name" (Matt 6:9), which echoes the third command. To bear the name and to hallow the name both mean to set it apart in loyalty, giving it the due weight of its glory among the nations. Violating the command, therefore, is not done merely by swearing false oaths but by doing anything that detracts from God's reputation.

Deuteronomy's version of the Decalogue uses the same word שָׁוְא ("falsely") in both the third and ninth command. One valid implication is that the way we treat God's image bearers always reflects our honor of God's reputation. To bear the name is to orient all of life to God's glory.

One final and highly contested question is whether the Decalogue is a "universal" law. Patrick Miller (2004b:17–36) lays out the six most common objections to its claim as universal law:

(1) no concern for justice and mercy for the stranger, orphan, and widow

(2) no emphasis on holiness and purity

(3) does not align with the moral vision in the New Testament

(4) encourages legalism rather than love

(5) a law within homogenous communities and not between diverse
communities

(6) benefits elite classes only, rather than the larger group of poor and
marginalized

Miller counters each of these objections. Here are a few points to summarize
the responses to these objections.

First, there is a strong connection between the Decalogue and the individual
laws in chs. 12–26, to which mercy and justice for the marginalized classes is central (see 10:17–19; 14:22–29; 15:1–18; 24:19–22). Marginalized classes and animals
are also in focus in the Sabbath command, and all ten laws are repeated in the
New Testament. This answers objections 1, 3, and 6.

Second, the Sabbath law also puts the law in the context of purity as does
the emphasis on Israel as a "nation of priests" in Exod 19:6 in the runup to the
Decalogue in Exod 20 (objection 2).

And third, love is at the very heart of Deuteronomy's law (6:5–6; 10:12–19),
answering objection 4.

In a sophisticated way, then, biblical law avoids both the moral relativism and
shallow language of contemporary "love" as well as the legalism of law that lacks
prudence in application and compassion. In its broader literary and canonical
context, the Decalogue stands up very well as a form of universal law.

*　*　*　*　*

A technical note about the Hebrew text of the Decalogue: The Masoretes preserved two distinct (though partially overlapping) reading traditions for the
Decalogue that sometimes differ from each other with respect to cantillation,
versification, and (occasionally) vocalization. The WLC (the Hebrew text that is
the basis for the text found in this volume) follows BHS in presenting these two
systems—the so-called upper and lower cantillation—simultaneously, superim-
posing them over each other. For clarity's sake, we present below only one system
for each verse. In order to have the text below follow the versification of BHS/
WLC, the upper cantillation has been presented for Deut 5:6, 17–20, and the lower
cantillation for 5:7–16; the upper and lower cantillation are the same for 5:21.

6a   אָנֹכִי יְהוָה אֱלֹהֶיךָ אֲשֶׁר הוֹצֵאתִיךָ מֵאֶרֶץ מִצְרָיִם

'ānōḵî YHWH 'ĕlōhêḵā 'ăšer hôṣē'tîḵā mē'ereṣ miṣrayim

"I am Yahweh your God, who brought you out of the land of Egypt,

6b   מִבֵּית עֲבָדִים:

mibbêt 'ăvādîm.

from the house of slaves.

7   לֹא יִהְיֶה לְךָ אֱלֹהִים אֲחֵרִים עַל־פָּנָי:

lō' yihye ləḵā 'ĕlōhîm 'ăhērîm 'al-pānāy.

You shall have no other gods before my face.

8a   לֹא־תַעֲשֶׂה לְךָ פֶסֶל

lō'-ta'ăśe ləḵā fesel

You shall not make for yourself a carved image

8b   כָּל־תְּמוּנָה אֲשֶׁר בַּשָּׁמַיִם מִמַּעַל

kol-təmûnâ 'ăšer baššāmayim mimma'al

of any form that is in the heavens above

8c   וַאֲשֶׁר בָּאָרֶץ מִתָּחַת

wa'ăšer bā'āreṣ mittāḥat

or that is in the earth below

8d   וַאֲשֶׁר בַּמַּיִם| מִתַּחַת לָאָרֶץ:

wa'ăšer bammayim mittaḥat lā'āreṣ.

or that is in the waters below the earth.

9a   לֹא־תִשְׁתַּחֲוֶה לָהֶם וְלֹא תָעָבְדֵם

lō'-tištaḥăwe lāhem wəlō' tā'ovdēm

You shall not bow down to them or serve them.

9b   כִּי אָנֹכִי יְהוָה אֱלֹהֶיךָ אֵל קַנָּא

kî ʾānōḵî YHWH ʾĕlōhêḵā ʾēl qannāʾ

For I, Yahweh your God, am a jealous God,

9c   פֹּקֵד עֲוֹן אָבֹת עַל־בָּנִים וְעַל־שִׁלֵּשִׁים וְעַל־רִבֵּעִים לְשֹׂנְאָי׃

pōqēd ʿăwôn ʾāvōt ʿal-bānîm wəʿal-šillēšîm wəʿal-ribbēʿîm ləśōnəʾāy.

**visiting the guilt of ancestors upon children
to the third and the fourth generations of those who hate me,**

10   וְעֹשֶׂה חֶסֶד לַאֲלָפִים לְאֹהֲבַי וּלְשֹׁמְרֵי מִצְוֹתָי׃

wəʿōśe ḥesed laʾălāfîm ləʾōhăvay ûləšōmrê miṣwōtāy.

**but showing loving faithfulness to thousands,
to those who love me and keep my commands.**

11a   לֹא תִשָּׂא אֶת־שֵׁם־יְהוָה אֱלֹהֶיךָ לַשָּׁוְא

lōʾ tiśśāʾ ʾet-šēm-YHWH ʾĕlōhêḵā laššāwʾ

You shall not bear the name of Yahweh your God falsely.

11b   כִּי לֹא יְנַקֶּה יְהוָה אֵת אֲשֶׁר־יִשָּׂא אֶת־שְׁמוֹ לַשָּׁוְא׃

kî lōʾ yənaqqe YHWH ʾēt ʾăšer-yiśśāʾ ʾet-šəmô laššāwʾ.

**For Yahweh will not hold guiltless
anyone who bears his name falsely.**

12a   שָׁמוֹר אֶת־יוֹם הַשַּׁבָּת לְקַדְּשׁוֹ

šāmôr ʾet-yôm hašabbāt ləqaddəšô

Observe the Sabbath day to keep it holy,

12b   כַּאֲשֶׁר צִוְּךָ יְהוָה אֱלֹהֶיךָ׃

kaʾăšer ṣiwwəḵā YHWH ʾĕlōhêḵā.

as Yahweh your God has commanded you.

13   שֵׁשֶׁת יָמִים תַּעֲבֹד וְעָשִׂיתָ כָּל־מְלַאכְתֶּךָ׃

šēšet yāmîm taʿăvōd wəʿāśîtā kol-məlaʾḵteḵā.

Six days you shall labor and do all of your work.

14a וְיוֹם֙ הַשְּׁבִיעִ֔י שַׁבָּ֖ת לַיהוָ֣ה אֱלֹהֶ֑יךָ

wəyôm haššəvîʿî šabbāt laYHWH *ʾĕlōhêkā*

But the seventh day is a Sabbath to Yahweh your God.

14b לֹ֣א תַעֲשֶׂ֣ה כָל־מְלָאכָ֡ה

lōʾ taʿăśe kol-məlākâ

You shall not do any work—

14c אַתָּ֣ה וּבִנְךָֽ־וּבִתֶּ֣ךָ וְעַבְדְּךָֽ־וַאֲמָתֶ֡ךָ

ʾattâ ûvinkā-ûvittekā wəʿavdəkā-waʾămātekā

you, or your son, or your daughter, or your male or female slave,

14d וְשׁוֹרְךָ֩ וַחֲמֹֽרְךָ֨ וְכָל־בְּהֶמְתֶּ֜ךָ

wəšôrəkā waḥămōrəkā wəkol-bəhemtekā

or your ox, or your donkey, or any livestock,

14e וְגֵרְךָ֙ אֲשֶׁ֣ר בִּשְׁעָרֶ֔יךָ

wəgērəkā ʾăšer bišʿārêkā

or the sojourner who is in your towns—

14f לְמַ֗עַן יָנ֛וּחַ עַבְדְּךָ֥ וַאֲמָתְךָ֖ כָּמֽוֹךָ׃

ləmaʿan yānûaḥ ʿavdəkā waʾămātəkā kāmôkā.

so that your male and female slave may rest as well as you.

15a וְזָכַרְתָּ֞ כִּי־עֶ֣בֶד הָיִ֣יתָ בְּאֶ֣רֶץ מִצְרַ֗יִם

wəzākartā kî ʿeved hāyîtā bəʾereṣ miṣrayim

And you shall remember that you were a slave in the land of Egypt,

15b וַיֹּצִ֨אֲךָ֜ יְהוָ֤ה אֱלֹהֶ֙יךָ֙ מִשָּׁ֔ם

wayyōṣîʾăkā YHWH *ʾĕlōhêkā miššām*

and Yahweh your God brought you out from there

15c בְּיָ֤ד חֲזָקָה֙ וּבִזְרֹ֣עַ נְטוּיָ֔ה

bəyād ḥăzāqâ ûvizrōaʿ nəṭûyâ

with a strong hand and an outstretched arm.

15d עַל־כֵּ֞ן צִוְּךָ֣ יְהוָ֣ה אֱלֹהֶ֔יךָ לַעֲשֹׂ֖ות אֶת־יֹ֥ום הַשַּׁבָּֽת׃

'al-kēn ṣiwwəkā YHWH 'ĕlōhêkā la'ăśôt 'et-yôm hašabbāt.

**Therefore Yahweh your God commanded you
to keep the Sabbath day.**

16a כַּבֵּ֤ד אֶת־אָבִ֙יךָ֙ וְאֶת־אִמֶּ֔ךָ

kabbēd 'et-'āvîkā wə'et-'immekā

Honor your father and your mother,

16b כַּאֲשֶׁ֥ר צִוְּךָ֖ יְהוָ֣ה אֱלֹהֶ֑יךָ

ka'ăšer ṣiwwəkā YHWH 'ĕlōhêkā

as Yahweh your God commanded you,

16c לְמַ֣עַן ׀ יַאֲרִיכֻ֣ן יָמֶ֗יךָ

ləma'an ya'ărîkun yāmêkā

that your days may be prolonged

16d וּלְמַ֙עַן֙ יִ֣יטַב לָ֔ךְ עַ֚ל הָֽאֲדָמָ֔ה אֲשֶׁר־יְהוָ֥ה אֱלֹהֶ֖יךָ נֹתֵ֥ן לָֽךְ׃

ûləma'an yîṭav lāk 'al hā'ădāmâ 'ăšer-YHWH 'ĕlōhêkā nōtēn lāk.

**and that it may go well for you on the land
that Yahweh your God is giving you.**

17 לֹ֖א תִּרְצָֽח׃

lō' tirṣāḥ.

You shall not murder.

18 וְלֹ֖א תִּנְאָֽף׃

wəlō' tin'āf.

And you shall not commit adultery.

19 וְלֹ֖א תִּגְנֹֽב׃

wəlō' tignōv.

And you shall not steal.

20

וְלֹא־תַעֲנֶה בְרֵעֲךָ עֵד שָׁוְא:

wəlō'-ta'ăne vərē'ăkā 'ēd šāw'.

And you shall not answer falsely against your neighbor.

21a

וְלֹא תַחְמֹד אֵשֶׁת רֵעֶךָ

wəlō' tahmōd 'ēšet rē'ekā

And you shall not covet your neighbor's wife.

21b

וְלֹא תִתְאַוֶּה בֵּית רֵעֶךָ שָׂדֵהוּ וְעַבְדּוֹ וַאֲמָתוֹ

wəlō' tit'awwe bêt rē'ekā śādēhû wə'avdô wa'ămātô

**And you shall not desire your neighbor's house,
his field, his male servant or his female servant,**

21c

שׁוֹרוֹ וַחֲמֹרוֹ וְכֹל אֲשֶׁר לְרֵעֶךָ:

šôrô wahămōrô wəkōl 'ăšer lərē'ekā.

his ox, his donkey, or anything belonging to your neighbor."

6a

אָנֹכִי יְהוָה אֱלֹהֶיךָ אֲשֶׁר הוֹצֵאתִיךָ מֵאֶרֶץ מִצְרָיִם

"I am Yahweh your God, who brought you out of the land of Egypt,

אָנֹכִי	I	---	personal
אָנֹכִי	*'ā·nō·kî*	PRON	
יְהוָה	Yahweh	ABS	noun
יהוה	*YHWH*		
אֱלֹהֶיךָ	your God	CST	noun
אֱלֹהִים	*'ĕ·lō·hê·kā*	W/ 2MS SX	
אֲשֶׁר	that/which/who	---	relative
אֲשֶׁר	*'ă·šer*	PRON	
הוֹצֵאתִיךָ	(I) brought/led you out	HIPH PF 1CS	verb
יצא	*hô·ṣē·tî·kā*	W/ 2MS SX	
מֵאֶרֶץ	from (the) land of	CST	noun
אֶרֶץ	*mē·'e·reṣ*	W/ PREP מִן	

| מִצְרָיִם
מִצְרַיִם | Egypt
*miṣ·**ra**·yim* | ABS | noun |

In the Jewish ordering of the "Ten Words," 6a–b is the first "word." Not all the words are commands. In fact, Jewish rabbis and Christians have counted as many as thirteen commands within the "Ten Words." In Protestant and Eastern Orthodox renderings, 6a is the "motive clause" for the first command, that is, the reason, usually a theological one, for keeping the command. The first five commands all have motive clauses.

Other ancient Near Eastern laws only occasionally had motive clauses for their laws. Among the books of the Pentateuch (Gen–Deut), Deuteronomy has by far the most motive clauses (perhaps 50 percent of the laws), which helps us appreciate the strength of its sermonic, impassioned style (Strawn 2003:215–40).

6b	מִבֵּית עֲבָדִים:

from the house of slaves.

| מִבֵּית
בֵּית | from (the) house of
*mib·**bêt*** | CST
W/ PREP מִן | noun |
| עֲבָדִים:
עֶבֶד | slaves/servants
*ʾă·vā·**dîm*** | ABS | noun |

Sometimes translated "house of slavery," Israel's rescue from Egypt is a constant reminder of their obligation to honor Yahweh, their sovereign owner and ruler. The reminder of their experience also leads them to treat slaves, foreigners, and the oppressed classes with a dignity not afforded to Israel's ancestors in Egypt.

7	לֹא יִהְיֶה לְךָ אֱלֹהִים אֲחֵרִים עַל־פָּנָי:

You shall have no other gods before my face.

| לֹא
לֹא | no/not
lō' | --- | particle |
| יִהְיֶה
היה | will be/become
*yih·**ye*** | QAL IMPF 3MS | verb |

לְךָ֖ לְ *lə·ḵā*	to/for you	--- W/ 2MS SX	prep
אֱלֹהִ֣ים אֱלֹהִים *ʾĕ·lō·hîm*	gods	ABS	noun
אֲחֵרִ֖ים אַחֵר *ʾă·ḥē·rîm*	other	MP ATTR	adj
עַל־ עַל *ʿal-*	on/upon/before	---	prep
פָּנָֽי׃ פָּנֶה *pā·nāy*	my face/appearance	CST W/ 1CS SX	noun

The negative particle לֹא used throughout these commands is non-perfective and more forceful than the jussive particle אַל.

The metaphor עַל־פָּנָי, is sometimes paraphrased "before me." As a figure of speech, it need not mean face-to-face, but might suggest a sense that God is always near and aware of our actions.

<table>
<tr><td>8a</td><td colspan="2" align="center">לֹא־תַעֲשֶׂה לְךָ פֶּסֶל</td></tr>
<tr><td></td><td colspan="2" align="center">You shall not make for yourself a carved image</td></tr>
</table>

לֹא־ לֹא *lōʾ*	no/not	---	particle
תַעֲשֶׂה עשׂה *ta·ʿă·śe*	you make	QAL IMPF 2MS	verb
לְךָ לְ *lə·ḵā*	for yourself	--- W/ 2MS SX	prep
פֶּסֶל פֶּסֶל *fe·sel*	idol/image/likeness	ABS	noun

The verb עשׂה places a noticeable emphasis on the effort to hone or craft something, that is, to put one's hands to work to instantiate an idea.

כָּל־תְּמוּנָ֗ה אֲשֶׁ֤ר בַּשָּׁמַ֙יִם֙ מִמַּ֔עַל

of any form that is in the heavens above

כָּל־ כֹּל‪-‬	all/every/any *kol-*	CST	noun
תְּמוּנָ֗ה *tə·mû·nâ*	likeness/form/manifestation	ABS	noun
אֲשֶׁ֤ר *ʾă·šer*	that/which	--- PRON	relative
בַּשָּׁמַ֙יִם֙ שָׁמַיִם *baš·šā·ma·yim*	in the heavens/skies	ABS W/ PREP בְּ + DEF. ART.	noun
מִמַּ֔עַל מַעַל *mim·ma·ʿal*	from above/upwards/ on top of	--- W/ PREP מִן	prep

וַאֲשֶׁ֥ר בָּאָ֖רֶץ מִתָּ֑חַת

or that is in the earth below

וַאֲשֶׁ֥ר אֲשֶׁר *wa·ʾă·šer*	and/or that/which	--- W/ CONJ וְ	relative pron
בָּאָ֖רֶץ אֶרֶץ *bā·ʾā·reṣ*	in the earth/ground	ABS W/ PREP בְּ + DEF. ART.	noun
מִתָּ֑חַת תַּחַת *mit·tā·ḥat*	(from) below/beneath/under	--- W/ PREP מִן	prep

וַאֲשֶׁ֥ר בַּמַּ֖יִם מִתַּ֥חַת לָאָֽרֶץ:

or that is in the waters below the earth.

וַאֲשֶׁ֥ר אֲשֶׁר *wa·ʾă·šer*	and/or that/which	--- W/ CONJ וְ	relative pron
בַּמַּ֖יִם מַיִם *bam·ma·yim*	in the waters	ABS W/ PREP בְּ + DEF. ART.	noun
מִתַּ֥חַת תַּחַת *mit·ta·ḥat*	(from) below/beneath/under	--- W/ PREP מִן	prep

| לָאָֽרֶץ: | to/for the earth | ABS | noun |
| אֶרֶץ | lā·'ā·reṣ | W/ PREP לְ + DEF. ART. | |

Notice the common ancient three-part cosmology of heavens, earth, and sea (8b–d).

<table>
<tr><td>9a</td><td colspan="2" align="center">לֹא־תִשְׁתַּחֲוֶה לָהֶם וְלֹא תָעָבְדֵם</td><td></td></tr>
<tr><td colspan="4" align="center">You shall not bow down to them or serve them.</td></tr>
</table>

לֹא־	no/not	---	particle
אֹל	lō'-		
תִשְׁתַּחֲוֶה	you worship/bow down	HITHPALEL IMPF 2MS	verb
שׁחה	tiš·ta·ḥă·**we**		
לָהֶם	to them	---	prep
לְ	lā·**hem**	W/ 3MP SX	
וְלֹא	and no/not	---	particle
אֹל	wə·**lō'**	W/ CONJ וְ	
תָעָבְדֵם	you serve them	QAL IMPF 2MS	verb
עבד	tā·'ov·**dēm**	W/ 3MP SX	

"Serve" (תָעָבְדֵם) plays upon house of "slaves" (עֲבָדִים) in 6b, the verb "you shall labor" (תַּעֲבֹד) in 13a, עבד ("serve") in 15:12, and "slave" (עֶבֶד) in 15:15 and 17. The laws creatively intertwine worship (תִשְׁתַּחֲוֶה) with forms of work (עבד) in such a way that the work we require of others reflects the genuineness of our worship of Yahweh.

<table>
<tr><td>9b</td><td colspan="2" align="center">כִּי אָנֹכִי יְהוָה אֱלֹהֶיךָ אֵל קַנָּא</td><td></td></tr>
<tr><td colspan="4" align="center">For I, Yahweh your God, am a jealous God,</td></tr>
</table>

כִּי	for/that/when/because	---	conj
כִּי	kî		
אָנֹכִי	I	---	personal pron
אָנֹכִי	'ā·nō·ḵî		
יְהוָה	Yahweh	ABS	noun
יהוה	YHWH		

אֱלֹהֶ֫יךָ	your God	CST	noun
אֱלֹהִים	ʾĕ·lō·**hê**·ḵā	W/ 2MS SX	
אֵל	god/God	ABS	noun
אֵל	**ʾēl**		
קַנָּא	jealous/zealous	MS ATTR	adj
קַנָּא	qan·**nāʾ**		

9c

visiting the guilt of ancestors upon children
to the third and the fourth generations of those who hate me,

פֹּקֵד	visiting/attending/seeking out	QAL PTCP MS	verb
פקד	**pō**·qēd		
עֲוֹן	guilt/sin/iniquity of	CST	noun
עָוֹן	ʿă·**wôn**		
אָבֹת	ancestors	ABS	noun
אָב	ʾā·**vôt**		
עַל־	upon/to	---	prep
עַל	ʿal-		
בָּנִים	sons	ABS	noun
בֵּן	bā·**nîm**		
וְעַל־	upon/to	---	prep
עַל	wə·ʿal-	W/ CONJ וְ	
שִׁלֵּשִׁים	(the) third	MP SUBST	adj
שָׁלֵשׁ	šil·lē·**šîm**		
וְעַל־	and upon/to	---	prep
עַל	wə·ʿal-	W/ CONJ וְ	
רִבֵּעִים	(the) fourth	MP SUBST	adj
רִבֵּעַ	rib·bē·**ʿîm**		
לְשֹׂנְאָי׃	to/of (ones) hating me	QAL PTCP MP	verb
שָׂנֵא	lə·śō·nə·**ʾāy**	W/ PREP לְ + 1CS SX	

The text of vv. 9c–10 also appears at the second giving of the Tablets
in Exod 34:6–7. פקד has a wide range of possible meanings, including
"seek out," "attend," and "care for." The meaning here is undeniably one
of retribution.

וְעֹשֶׂה חֶסֶד לַאֲלָפִים לְאֹהֲבַי וּלְשֹׁמְרֵי מִצְוֹתָי׃

but showing loving faithfulness to thousands,
to those who love me and keep my commands.

וְעֹשֶׂה עשׂה	and/but doing/making *wə·ʿō·śe*	QAL PTCP MS W/ CONJ וְ	verb
חֶסֶד חֶסֶד	lovingkindness/loyalty/ graciousness *ḥe·sed*	ABS	noun
לַאֲלָפִים אֶלֶף	to thousands *la·ʾă·lā·fîm*	ABS W/ PREP לְ	cardinal
לְאֹהֲבַי אהב	to (ones) loving me *lə·ʾō·hă·vay*	QAL PTCP MP W/ PREP לְ + 1CS SX	verb
וּלְשֹׁמְרֵי שׁמר	and (ones) keeping *û·lə·šōm·rê*	QAL (CST) PTCP MP W/ CONJ וְ + PREP לְ	verb
מִצְוֹתָי׃ מִצְוָה	my commandments *miṣ·wō·tāy*	CST W/ 1CS SX	noun

לֹא תִשָּׂא אֶת־שֵׁם־יְהוָה אֱלֹהֶיךָ לַשָּׁוְא

You shall not bear the name of Yahweh your God falsely.

לֹא לֹא	no/not *lō'*	---	particle
תִשָּׂא נשׂא	you lift up/take up *tiś·śā'*	QAL IMPF 2MS	verb
אֶת־ אֵת	(direct object marker) *'et-*	---	particle
שֵׁם־ שֵׁם	(the) name of *šēm-*	CST	noun
יְהוָה יהוה	Yahweh *YHWH*	ABS	noun
אֱלֹהֶיךָ אֱלֹהִים	your God *ʾĕ·lō·hɛ̂·ḵā*	CST W/ 2MS SX	noun
לַשָּׁוְא שָׁוְא	to vanity/emptiness/ worthlessness *laš·šāw'*	ABS W/ PREP לְ + DEF. ART.	noun

שָׁוְא has a broad lexical domain and could be translated "empty" or "vain." In Deuteronomy the word only appears in the Decalogue (5:11a, 11b, 20). This placement serves to tie the third to the ninth command (see Miller 2018:67–68). It is also important to repeat that the divine name יְהוָה appears a symbolic seven times in Deuteronomy's Decalogue, but eight in the list in Exodus.

11b	כִּי לֹא יְנַקֶּה יְהוָה אֵת אֲשֶׁר־יִשָּׂא אֶת־שְׁמוֹ לַשָּׁוְא׃

For Yahweh will not hold guiltless
anyone who bears his name falsely.

כִּי	for/because	---	conj
כִּי	*kî*		
לֹא	no/not	---	particle
לֹא	*lō'*		
יְנַקֶּה	(he) will leave unpunished/ acquitted	PIEL IMPF 3MS	verb
נקה	*yə·naq·qe*		
יְהוָה	Yahweh	ABS	noun
יהוה	*YHWH*		
אֵת	(direct object marker)	---	particle
אֵת	*'ēt*		
אֲשֶׁר־	that/which/who	---	relative pron
אֲשֶׁר	*'ă·šer-*		
יִשָּׂא	(he) lifts up/takes up	QAL IMPF 3MS	verb
נשׂא	*yiś·śā'*		
אֶת־	(direct object marker)	---	particle
אֵת	*'et-*		
שְׁמוֹ	his name	CST W/ 3MS SX	noun
שֵׁם	*šə·mô*		
לַשָּׁוְא׃	to vanity/emptiness/ worthlessness	ABS	noun
שָׁוְא	*laš·šāw'*	W/ PREP לְ + DEF. ART.	

This is the only command in which God threatens consequences for disobedience.

שָׁמוֹר אֶת־יוֹם הַשַּׁבָּת לְקַדְּשׁוֹ

Observe the Sabbath day to keep it holy,

שָׁמוֹר שמר	observe/keep *šā·môr*	QAL INF ABS	verb
אֶת־ אֵת	*(direct object marker)* *'et-*	---	particle
יוֹם יום	(the) day *yôm*	CST	noun
הַשַּׁבָּת שַׁבָּת	the Sabbath *ha·šab·bāt*	ABS W/ DEF. ART.	noun
לְקַדְּשׁוֹ קדש	to hallow/sanctify/set it apart *lə·qad·də·šô*	PIEL INF CST W/ PREP לְ + 3MS SX	verb

This is the first major revision to the Decalogue in Exodus, which used "remember" (זכר) at the start rather than "observe" (שמר), as here. Deuteronomy thus strengthens the command with language of wholehearted observance characteristic of Moses' sermons. "Remember" returns at the end of the command in 15a.

כַּאֲשֶׁר צִוְּךָ יְהוָה אֱלֹהֶיךָ:

as Yahweh your God has commanded you.

כַּאֲשֶׁר אֲשֶׁר	as/according to *ka·'ă·šer*	--- W/ PREP כְּ	relative pron
צִוְּךָ צוה	(he) commanded you *ṣiw·wə·kā*	PIEL PF 3MS W/ 2MS SX	verb
יְהוָה יהוה	Yahweh *YHWH*	ABS	noun
אֱלֹהֶיךָ: אֱלֹהִים	your God *'ĕ·lō·hê·kā*	CST W/ 2MS SX	noun

שֵׁשֶׁת יָמִים תַּעֲבֹד וְעָשִׂיתָ כָּל־מְלַאכְתֶּךָ׃

Six days you shall labor and do all of your work.

שֵׁשֶׁת שֵׁשׁ	six *šē·šet*	CST	cardinal number
יָמִים יוֹם	days *yā·mîm*	ABS	noun
תַּעֲבֹד עבד	you serve/labor/work *ta·ʿă·vōd*	QAL IMPF 2MS	verb
וְעָשִׂיתָ עשׂה	and you do/make *wə·ʿā·śî·tā*	QAL WEQATAL 2MS	verb
כָּל־ כֹּל	all/everything/anything *kol-*	CST	noun
מְלַאכְתֶּךָ׃ מְלָאכָה	your work *mə·laʾk·te·ḵā*	CST W/ 2MS SX	noun

Protestant Reformers viewed labor as a moral obligation (see a similar admonition in 2 Thess 3:10–12). That said, rest is more clearly the focus in this command for several reasons. First, the command relieves Israel of the relentless labor they experienced in Egypt: the right to leisure is protected from the encroaching reach of economics. Second, Israel's rest is not simply what Israel enjoys but what they are required to provide for the rest of creation: humans, animals, and land. Finally, in a world where daily work was viewed as essential to survival, rest posed a psychological risk that the command answers with faith and trust that God will provide.

וְיוֹם הַשְּׁבִיעִי שַׁבָּת לַיהוָה אֱלֹהֶיךָ

But the seventh day is a Sabbath to Yahweh your God.

וְיוֹם יוֹם	and/but day *wə·yôm*	ABS W/ CONJ וְ	noun
הַשְּׁבִיעִי שְׁבִיעִי	the seventh *haš·šə·vî·î*	--- W/ DEF. ART.	ordinal number
שַׁבָּת שַׁבָּת	Sabbath *šab·bāt*	ABS	noun
לַיהוָה יהוה	to Yahweh *la·YHWH*	ABS W/ PREP לְ	noun

| אֱלֹהֶיךָ
אֱלֹהִים | your God
ĕ·lō·hê·kā | CST
W/ 2MS SX | noun |

Although Deuteronomy changes the motivation for the command from the six-day pattern in creation, we should not conclude that that motivation is lost. Deuteronomy does not so much replace Exodus as add to it.

14b לֹא תַעֲשֶׂה כָל־מְלָאכָה

You shall not do any work—

לֹא לֹא	no/not *lō'*	---	particle
תַעֲשֶׂה עשׂה	you work *ta·'ă·śe*	QAL IMPF 2MS	verb
כָל־ כֹּל	all/everything/anything *kol-*	CST	noun
מְלָאכָה מְלָאכָה	work *mə·lā'·kâ*	ABS	noun

14c אַתָּה וּבִנְךָ־וּבִתֶּךָ וְעַבְדְּךָ וַאֲמָתֶךָ

you, or your son, or your daughter, or your male or female slave,

אַתָּה אַתָּה	you *'at·tâ*	---	personal pron
וּבִנְךָ־ בֵּן	and/or your son *û·vin·kā-*	CST W/ CONJ וְ + 2MS SX	noun
וּבִתֶּךָ בַּת	and/or your daughter *û·vit·te·kā*	CST W/ CONJ וְ + 2MS SX	noun
וְעַבְדְּךָ עֶבֶד	and/or your male servant/slave *wa·'av·də·kā-*	CST W/ CONJ וְ + 2MS SX	noun
וַאֲמָתֶךָ אָמָה	and/or your female servant/slave *wa·'ă·mā·te·kā*	CST W/ CONJ וְ + 2MS SX	noun

וְשׁוֹרְךָ֤ וַחֲמֹֽרְךָ֙ וְכָל־בְּהֶמְתֶּ֔ךָ

or your ox, or your donkey, or any of your livestock,

וְשׁוֹרְךָ֤	and/or your ox	CST	noun
שׁוֹר	wə·šô·rə·ḵā	W/ CONJ וְ + 2MS SX	
וַחֲמֹֽרְךָ֙	and/or your donkey	CST	noun
חֲמוֹר	wa·ḥă·mō·rə·ḵā	W/ CONJ וְ + 2MS SX	
וְכָל־	and/or all/every/any of	CST	noun
כֹּל	wə·ḵol-	W/ CONJ וְ	
בְּהֶמְתֶּ֔ךָ	your beast/livestock	CST	noun
בְּהֵמָה	bə·hem·te·ḵā	W/ 2MS SX	

שׁוֹרְךָ ("your ox"), חֲמֹרְךָ ("your donkey"), and כָל־בְּהֶמְתֶּךָ ("any of your livestock") are additions to the Exodus law. *Everything* must rest.

וְגֵרְךָ֖ אֲשֶׁ֣ר בִּשְׁעָרֶ֑יךָ

or your sojourner who is in your towns—

וְגֵרְךָ֖	and/or your sojourner/alien/stranger	CST	noun
גֵּר	wə·gē·rə·ḵā	W/ CONJ וְ + 2MS SX	
אֲשֶׁ֣ר	that/which/who	---	relative
אֲשֶׁר	ʾă·šer		pron
בִּשְׁעָרֶ֑יךָ	in your gates/city entrance	CST	noun
שַׁעַר	biš·ʿā·rɛ̂·ḵā	W/ PREP בְּ + 2MS SX	

בִּשְׁעָרֶיךָ translates literally as "at your gates." The gates were a common place of public traffic and social activity, so it is not clear whether this term signifies something like "in your towns" or those who gathered at the town gates to seek work and help.

לְמַ֣עַן יָנ֗וּחַ עַבְדְּךָ֛ וַאֲמָתְךָ֖ כָּמֽוֹךָ׃

so that your male and female slave may rest as well as you.

לְמַ֣עַן	so that/in order that	---	prep
לְמַעַן	lə·**ma**·ʿan		

יָנוּחַ נוח	(he) rests *yā·nû·aḥ*	QAL IMPF 3MS	verb
עַבְדְּךָ עֶבֶד	your servant/slave *'av·də·kā*	CST W/ 2MS SX	noun
וַאֲמָתְךָ אָמָה	and your female servant/ female slave *wa·'ă·mā·tə·kā*	CST W/ CONJ וְ + 2MS SX	noun
כָּמוֹךָ׃ כְּמוֹ	as well as you/like you *kā·mô·kā*	--- W/ 2MS SX	prep

Rest in the land becomes both a present reality and an eschatological hope in Israel and in the church. See Ps 95 and Heb 3–4.

15a   וְזָכַרְתָּ כִּי עֶבֶד הָיִיתָ בְּאֶרֶץ מִצְרַיִם

And you shall remember that you were a slave in the land of Egypt,

וְזָכַרְתָּ זכר	and you remember *wə·zā·kar·tā*	QAL WEQATAL 2MS	verb
כִּי כִּי	that/for **kî**	---	conj
עֶבֶד עֶבֶד	slave/servant *'e·ved*	ABS	noun
הָיִיתָ היה	you were *hā·yî·tā*	QAL PF 2MS	verb
בְּאֶרֶץ אֶרֶץ	in (the) land of *bə·'e·reṣ*	CST W/ PREP בְּ	noun
מִצְרַיִם מִצְרַיִם	Egypt *miṣ·ra·yim*	ABS	noun

The forms here are singular, even though it clearly refers to Israelites in the plural.

וַיֹּצִֽאֲךָ֧ יְהוָ֛ה אֱלֹהֶ֖יךָ מִשָּֽׁם

and Yahweh your God brought you out from there

וַיֹּצִֽאֲךָ֧ יצא	and (he) brought you out *way·yō·ṣī·'ă·kā*	HIPH WAYY 3MS W/ 2MS SX	verb
יְהוָ֛ה יהוה	Yahweh *YHWH*	ABS	noun
אֱלֹהֶ֖יךָ אֱלֹהִים	your God *'ĕ·lō·hɛ̂·kā*	CST W/ 2MS SX	noun
מִשָּֽׁם שָׁם	from there *miš·šām*	--- W/ PREP מִן	adv

בְּיָ֤ד חֲזָקָ֖ה וּבִזְרֹ֥עַ נְטוּיָֽה

with a strong hand and an outstretched arm.

בְּיָ֤ד יָד	by/with hand *bə·yād*	ABS W/ PREP בְּ	noun
חֲזָקָ֖ה חָזָק	strong *ḥă·zā·qâ*	FS ATTR	adj
וּבִזְרֹ֥עַ זְרוֹעַ	and arm/forearm *û·viz·rō·a'*	ABS W/ CONJ וְ + PREP בְּ	noun
נְטוּיָֽה נטה	outstretched/spread/ lengthened *nə·ṭû·yâ*	QP PTCP FS	verb

עַל־כֵּ֗ן צִוְּךָ֙ יְהוָ֣ה אֱלֹהֶ֔יךָ לַעֲשׂ֖וֹת אֶת־י֥וֹם הַשַּׁבָּֽת׃

Therefore Yahweh your God commanded you
to keep the Sabbath day.

עַל־כֵּ֗ן עַל־כֵּן	thus/for that reason/therefore *'al-kēn*	---	adv
צִוְּךָ֙ צוה	(he) commanded you *ṣiw·wə·kā*	PIEL PF 3MS W/ 2MS SX	verb
יְהוָ֣ה יהוה	Yahweh *YHWH*	ABS	noun

אֱלֹהֶיךָ אֱלֹהִים	your God *ĕ·lō·hê·ḵā*	CST W/ 2MS SX	noun
לַעֲשׂוֹת עשׂה	to do/make *la·ʿă·śôt*	QAL INF CST W/ PREP לְ	verb
אֶת־ אֵת	*(direct object marker)* *ʾet-*	---	particle
יוֹם יוֹם	(the) day of *yôm*	CST	noun
הַשַּׁבָּת: שַׁבָּת	the Sabbath *ha·šab·bāt*	ABS W/ DEF. ART.	noun

<table>
<tr><td>16a</td><td align="center">כַּבֵּד אֶת־אָבִיךָ וְאֶת־אִמֶּךָ</td></tr>
</table>

Honor your father and your mother,

כַּבֵּד כבד	honor/weigh down *kab·bēd*	PIEL IMPV MS	verb
אֶת־ אֵת	*(direct object marker)* *ʾet-*	---	particle
אָבִיךָ אָב	your father *ʾā·vî·ḵā*	CST W/ 2MS SX	noun
וְאֶת־ אֵת	and (+ *direct object marker*) *wə·ʾet-*	--- W/ CONJ וְ	particle
אִמֶּךָ אֵם	your mother *ʾim·me·ḵā*	CST W/ 2MS SX	noun

כַּבֵּד, literally "give weight" or "glory," is to be done to both mother and father. See more in "From Text to Sermon" below.

<table>
<tr><td>16b</td><td align="center">כַּאֲשֶׁר צִוְּךָ יְהוָה אֱלֹהֶיךָ</td></tr>
</table>

as Yahweh your God commanded you,

כַּאֲשֶׁר אֲשֶׁר	as/for/according to *ka·ʾă·šer*	--- W/ PREP כְּ	relative pron
צִוְּךָ צוה	(he) commanded you *ṣiw·wə·ḵā*	PIEL PF 3MS W/ 2MS SX	verb

יְהוָה	Yahweh	ABS	noun
יהוה	*YHWH*		
אֱלֹהֶיךָ	your God	CST	noun
אֱלֹהִים	*ĕ·lō·hê·ḵā*	W/ 2MS SX	

Human authority derives from, and is rooted in, divine authority.

<table>
<tr><td>16c</td><td colspan="3" align="center">לְמַעַן‬ יַאֲרִיכֻן יָמֶיךָ</td></tr>
</table>

that your days may be prolonged

לְמַעַן‬	so that/in order that/ on account of	---	prep
לְמַעַן	*lə·ma·ʿan*		
יַאֲרִיכֻן	(they) will be long/ become long	HIPH IMPF 3MP	verb
ארך	*ya·ʾă·rî·ḵun*	W/ PARAGOGIC ן	
יָמֶיךָ	your days	CST	noun
יום	*yā·mê·ḵā*	W/ 2MS SX	

<table>
<tr><td>16d</td><td colspan="3" align="center">וּלְמַעַן יִיטַב לָךְ עַל הָאֲדָמָה אֲשֶׁר־יְהוָה אֱלֹהֶיךָ נֹתֵן לָךְ:</td></tr>
</table>

and that it may go well for you on the land that Yahweh your God is giving you.

וּלְמַעַן	and so that/in order that/ on account of	---	prep
לְמַעַן	*û·lə·ma·ʿan*	W/ CONJ ו	
יִיטַב	it will be good/well	QAL IMPF 3MS	verb
יטב	*yî·ṭav*		
לָךְ	to/for you	---	prep
ל	*lāḵ*	W/ 2MS SX	
עַל	on/upon/before	---	prep
עַל	*ʿal*		
הָאֲדָמָה	the land	ABS	noun
אֲדָמָה	*hā·ʾă·dā·mâ*	W/ DEF. ART.	
אֲשֶׁר־	that/which	---	relative pron
אֲשֶׁר	*ʾă·šer-*		

יְהוָה יהוה *YHWH*	Yahweh	ABS	noun
אֱלֹהֶיךָ אלהים *ĕ·lō·hê·ḵā*	your God	CST W/ 2MS SX	noun
נֹתֵן נתן *nō·tēn*	giving	QAL PTCP MS	verb
לָךְ: ל *lāḵ*	to you	--- W/ 2MS SX	prep

Long life in the land (אֲדָמָה) mirrors the promise and hope in the Sabbath command. The final clause is repeated in the laws for civic leaders: judges (16:20), kings (17:14), and prophets (18:9). See more in "From Text to Sermon" below.

17	לֹא תִּרְצָח:		
	You shall not murder.		
לֹא לא *lō'*	no/not	---	particle
תִּרְצָח: רצח *tir·ṣāḥ*	you murder/kill/strike down	QAL IMPF 2MS	verb

The Hebrew term רצח is broader than the English word "murder" but more specific than הרג ("kill") or מות (in the Hiphil, "put to death"). The verb is only used for a human killing a human and is not applied to contexts where killing is commanded or authorized and where other figures of speech are common: e.g., דָּמוֹ יִשָּׁפֵךְ, "his blood shall be shed/poured out" (Gen 9:6), and חרם, "put them to the ban" (Deut 7:2).

18	וְלֹא תִּנְאָף:		
	And you shall not commit adultery.		
וְלֹא לא *wə·lō'*	and no/not	--- W/ CONJ ו	particle
תִּנְאָף: נאף *tin·'āf*	you commit adultery	QAL IMPF 2MS	verb

Notice that the וְ ("and") here and in each subsequent line ties the last five commands together. The Hebrew verb נאף ("to commit adultery") occurs four times in the Pentateuch; most of the other twenty-seven occurrences are found in the prophetic literature, where the verb serves as a metaphor for covenant unfaithfulness.

19	וְלֹא תִּגְנֹב:

And you shall not steal.

| וְלֹא
לֹא | and no/not
wə·lō' | ---
W/ CONJ וְ | particle |
| תִּגְנֹב:
גנב | you steal
tig·nōv | QAL IMPF 2MS | verb |

20	וְלֹא־תַעֲנֶה בְרֵעֲךָ עֵד שָׁוְא:

And you shall not answer falsely against your neighbor.

וְלֹא־ לֹא	and no/not wə·lō'-	--- W/ CONJ וְ	particle
תַעֲנֶה ענה	you answer/respond/testify ta·'ă·ne	QAL IMPF 2MS	verb
בְרֵעֲךָ רֵעַ	to/against your friend/ neighbor və·rē·'ă·ḵā	CST W/ PREP בְּ + 2MS SX	noun
עֵד עֵד	witness of 'ēd	CST	noun
שָׁוְא: שָׁוְא	vanity/emptiness/ worthlessness šāw'	ABS	noun

ענה could be translated "testify" here. Compare the related laws in 19:15–21, esp. v. 18.

וְלֹא תַחְמֹד אֵשֶׁת רֵעֶךָ

And you shall not covet your neighbor's wife.

וְלֹא לֹא	and no/not *wə·lōʾ*	--- W/ CONJ וְ	particle
תַחְמֹד חמד	you desire/take pleasure/ treasure *taḥ·mōd*	QAL IMPF 2MS	verb
אֵשֶׁת אִשָּׁה	(the) wife of *ʾē·šet*	CST	noun
רֵעֶךָ רֵעַ	your friend/neighbor *rē·ʿe·ḵā*	CST W/ 2MS SX	noun

In the Exodus Decalogue, the "wife" comes after the "house" in the list of objects not to be coveted.

The verb חמד seems to indicate something more than "desire." Nelson paraphrases this as "scheme to acquire" (Nelson 2004:76). See comparative contexts in Deut 7:25 and Exod 34:24.

וְלֹא תִתְאַוֶּה בֵּית רֵעֶךָ שָׂדֵהוּ וְעַבְדּוֹ וַאֲמָתוֹ

And you shall not desire your neighbor's house, his field, his male servant or his female servant,

וְלֹא לֹא	and no/not *wə·lōʾ*	--- W/ CONJ וְ	particle
תִתְאַוֶּה אוה	you desire/crave *tit·ʾaw·we*	HITH IMPF 2MS	verb
בֵּית בֵּית	(the) house of *bêt*	CST	noun
רֵעֶךָ רֵעַ	your friend/neighbor *rē·ʿe·ḵā*	CST W/ 2MS SX	conj
שָׂדֵהוּ שָׂדֶה	his field/acreage *śā·dē·hû*	CST W/ 3MS SX	noun
וְעַבְדּוֹ עֶבֶד	and/or his male servant/slave *wa·ʿav·dô*	CST W/ CONJ וְ + 3MS SX	noun

| וַאֲמָתוֹ | and/or his female servant/ slave | CST | noun |
| אָמָה | wa·ʾă·mā·**tô** | W/ CONJ וְ + 3MS SX | |

We commented in the introduction that Exod 20:17 uses the verb חמד ("covet") two times. Deuteronomy adds a second command with אוה, "desire" (Hithpael). It then adds a וְ to create at least a partial break between the two commands in this verse: "And do not covet your neighbor's wife. *And* do not desire your neighbor's house, his field, his male servant or his female servant." One conclusion, among others, is that one's wife (marriage) stands on a different moral plane than property.

One might wrongly deduce from this that servants, who appear in the second half of the command, are reduced to the level of property. For one, servants are not bound in the covenant for life as a husband and wife are, so they do not belong in the moral category protected by marriage. Second, as we will see in 15:12–18, servants have legal protections of their own that set them apart from property.

שׁוֹרוֹ וַחֲמֹרוֹ וְכֹל אֲשֶׁר לְרֵעֶךָ:

21c

his ox, his donkey, or anything belonging to your neighbor."

שׁוֹרוֹ	his ox/bull	CST	noun
שׁוֹר	šô·**rô**	W/ 3MS SX	
וַחֲמֹרוֹ	and/or his donkey	CST	noun
חֲמוֹר	wa·ḥă·mō·**rô**	W/ CONJ וְ + 3MS SX	
וְכֹל	and/or all/anything	ABS	noun
כֹּל	wə·**kōl**	W/ CONJ וְ	
אֲשֶׁר	which/that	---	relative pron
אֲשֶׁר	ʾă·**šer**		
לְרֵעֶךָ:	to your friend/neighbor	CST	noun
רֵעַ	lə·rē·**ʾe**·kā	W/ PREP לְ + 2MS SX	

Preachers may want to preach through all Ten Words, possibly by grouping them into several categories such as God, Sabbath, family, possessions, life, and desire. We lack space to tackle all the commands here, but several studies can be helpful. See especially the book by Meilander (2020) and the edited volume by Braaten and Seitz (2005).

All of the commands are mentioned or alluded to in the New Testament, and Craig Evans (2012) offers a short, accessible resource for preaching the Decalogue through the New Testament. In what follows, I suggest ways to address the commands through the lenses of the name of God and wisdom and law.

 *Faith in the Name.* The prophet Joel declares: "Whoever calls on the name of the LORD will be saved" (Joel 2:32). The psalmist also "called on the name of Yahweh" and was saved (116:4). The New Testament authors pick up this Old Testament theme of salvation by the divine name and apply it to salvation in the name of Jesus (Rom 10:13; Acts 2:21; Phil 2:10). It is a name elevated above all other names (Eph 1:21; Phil 2:9; Heb 1:4).

The fact that God's name appears seven times throughout the Decalogue suggests strongly that the name signifies the fullness of everything God represents: his word, his authority, and his promises. When I use my wife's name, for example, I do not just designate a thing, but I point to a rich and complex person: her story, her gifts, her loves. To use her name is to honor all that she is. So too with the divine name.

But to have *faith* in the name signifies something even greater than just saying a name. After all, we are never commanded to believe in a human name. We might say that faith in God's name marks our awakening to believe and trust in God and everything he represents. In this sense, God's name is not just a word spoken haphazardly or a superstitious talisman, as if we can just say "Jesus" and be saved or work miracles. Rather, believing in the name of God is an act of obedient surrender of our whole life to God.

There is another important connection between the third command and the New Testament. Jesus, whose name means "Yahweh saves," is the one who has come to fulfill the promises of Yahweh in the law and the prophets. When Jesus comes to us, he reveals the full expression of all that God is. His name is no longer only Yahweh, but God the Father, Son, and Holy Spirit (cf. Matt 28:19). A congregation can be challenged to connect our belief in the name of Jesus with our entry into a relationship with the deep and mysterious God of the Trinity.

Baptized in the Name. As we just stated, those who have faith in Jesus gain access to God's full revelation in this world—Father, Son, and Spirit. This leads us to the importance of the sacrament of Christian baptism.

The New Testament describes baptism in various ways, such as "into Christ Jesus" (Rom 6:3) or "into Christ" (Gal 3:27). We also notice that Matthew, at the end of his gospel, describes Jesus commanding new disciples to be baptized "in the *name* of the Father, and of the Son, and of the Holy Spirit" (28:19). Baptism in the name of the Triune God signifies both the revelation we have of God in Jesus and the *fellowship* he gives us with God the Trinity. As we begin this new relationship through Jesus, we are to be taught to obey all his instructions (Matt 28:20). Put succinctly, baptism in the name restores our union with the Trinity and sets us on a path of growing as disciples.

We see an almost identical pattern of faith and discipleship in the Decalogue. The first three commandments place Yahweh as the object of Israel's faith. Rather than baptism, circumcision was the sign of their commitment to and relationship with God. Israel's exclusive allegiance to Yahweh also led naturally to obedience to God's prescribed order for their moral lives: work and rest, honoring parents, and living graciously with their neighbors, their spouses, and their property. Faith and discipleship in the Old Testament have been taken up in a new form in the New Testament. People can believe and be baptized and yet fail to notice the obligation to follow through in growth as disciples.

This brings us back to important parallels between the Lord's Prayer and the Decalogue. In Matthew's Gospel, the Lord's Prayer sits precisely in the middle of the Sermon on the Mount, a text historically associated with the Decalogue and Moses' teaching on Mount Horeb (Morrow 2017:58). Significantly, the Lord's Prayer begins with *three* petitions to God: your name be hallowed, your kingdom come, and your will be done, paralleling the three opening commands about God in the Decalogue (Black 2018:35–36). The Lord's Prayer then turns to contentment with our possessions every day (bread), peaceful dealings with our neighbors (forgiving others), and help with obedience in the future (lead us not). In other words, in both the Decalogue and the Lord's Prayer we find a model that connects our faith in God with life in the present, ordering our lives in conformity with God's moral order as we care for our neighbors and the resources we have been given in the creation.

This link between the Lord's Prayer and the commandments has a long and important history in the life of the church. Following Luther's lead, Protestant Reformers insisted on translating the Lord's Prayer and the Decalogue from Latin into the vernacular of the people (e.g., English, German, French), placed these passages together in the communion liturgies, and included them both alongside the creeds as the foundations of faith in the Protestant catechisms (Black 2018:300–301; Cumming 1969:54, 105–7). As Luther once put it:

> For these three [Decalogue, Lord's Prayer, and creeds] contain fully and completely everything that is in the Scriptures, everything that should ever be preached, and everything that a Christian needs to know, all put so briefly and so plainly that no one can make complaint or excuse, saying that what he needs for his salvation is too long or too hard to remember. (Oden 2005:41)

Regarding the Decalogue specifically, Luther says, "This much is certain: those who know the Ten Commandments perfectly know the entire Scriptures and in all affairs and circumstances are able to counsel, help, comfort, judge, and make decisions in both spiritual and temporal matters" (Miller 2018:1). Luther's claim leads naturally to another point or another sermon.

Interpreting the Ten Commandments with Wisdom

Wanting to retain the historical context of the Decalogue, scholars sometimes argue that this is not natural law, or universally applicable across all times and cultures. It is indeed important to remember the historical context of these laws, and our dropping of the opening, "I am the LORD your God who brought you out of the land of Egypt . . ." in modern versions is one particularly regrettable loss. These laws were given to a particular people whose lives were spent wandering in deserts or trying to survive with subsistence farming.

Yet, as outlined in the excursus, there are good reasons to think of these laws as a universal foundation for what law *is* and how it *functions* in society, especially as we find them in Deuteronomy. A sermon might show how law in every society needs to interpret and apply these laws in new times and places, resisting the drift to either antinomianism or legalism. The law, in other words, is a source of wisdom in a changing world (4:5–8).

It is unlikely that Christians in the pews think about this often, but any healthy society is defined and sustained by its law and how it exercises authority and executes justice. Cultures without law simply do not survive. Understanding Israel's laws can make us better citizens in our own day, and it will reveal a built-in pedagogical function that teaches us how to conduct our moral lives in new times and places.

This leads us to make note of two distinctives of Deuteronomy's laws. The first has to do with its additions to the Exodus Decalogue. These reinforce the moral foundations first given at Mount Sinai while adapting them for a more settled life in the land of Israel. Deuteronomy thus looks back with continuity to the past and forward to new challenges in the future (Strawn 2003:224–25). Law must have objective foundations and pliability to adapt to a new moment.

Second, we see a similar pattern of interpreting and applying law within the "decalogic" structure of Deuteronomy, as we noted in the introduction to 5:6–21 above. Each of the Ten Words can be linked to an expanded body of specific laws in chs. 6–26. For example:

Decalogue	**Applicable chapters in 12–26**
Worship	chs. 6–11 or 12–13
Idolatry	chs. 12–13
Divine name	chs. 13–14
Sabbath	chs. 15–16
etc.	

The details are complex, which make any consensus on the exact arrangement unlikely. Yet, as Braulik suggests, one need not show that the laws in chs. 12–26 follow precisely the order of the Decalogue to conclude that they are clear *applications* of the Decalogue to specific occasions at a different time and place than the laws in Exodus (2003:334).

In this way we can make a good case for calling it universal law. It establishes monotheism (love and loyalty to one God) as the primary element necessary for justice and community; it provides laws for work and rest, family, possessions, speech, oaths, and courts; and finally, it targets the desires of the heart that are the rudder of the moral life. Every law in chs. 6–26 can be tied to these basic ethical principles.

Wisdom describes this moral practice of working from the broader moral norms to particular applications. "Do not steal" may be applied to good practices of charity for the poor, giving to the church, and not hoarding possessions. Not committing adultery may be appropriately applied to not looking on someone with lust in our hearts (Matt 5:28).

Wisdom takes us to the heart of a moral idea to consider how it fits with a new context in the here and the now.

In tying the law to wisdom, a preacher may cite from the rhetoric in the book of Proverbs, which has a strong overlap with Deuteronomy: "Get wisdom, get insight" (Prov 4:5) and "Does not Wisdom call? Does not understanding raise her voice?" (8:1). The moral journeys in Proverbs and Deuteronomy alike depend on the discipline of learning wisdom, which includes close study of the moral rules in law and moral sayings in Proverbs as we live our lives conscientiously before God day to day.

This makes it obvious why Moses, at the beginning of Deuteronomy, tells the people to select "wise, discerning, and knowledgeable" people to be heads over the tribes and to judge the legal cases and social disputes that arise (Deut 1:9–18; cf. 1 Tim 3:1–13). Similar guidance is given for appointing "judges" for their "towns" in 16:18–20. Deuteronomy recognizes that a just community requires skilled leaders who know how to interpret and apply broad moral principles and rules to particular cases. Here are just a few examples of how such application is exemplified in the book.

(A) *Wisdom, law, and worship.* The first three commands of the Decalogue offer broad guidelines for remaining faithful to Yahweh. But how do we obey those laws practically? Deuteronomy answers that in both social and ritual dimensions. In the social context, loyalty to God requires our wholehearted love (6:4–9) and catechesis/discipleship of future generations (6:20–24; see Prov 8:17). The teaching was to be grounded upon memories of Israel's past: God's election (Deut 7; Eph 1:3–10), God's gifts of land and home (Deut 8; Jas 1:17), Israel's past rebellion and failures (Deut 9; Eph 2:1–10), and his loving renewal of covenant in each new generation (Deut 10–11; 2 Cor 5:17–21; Heb 9–10).

The second way the commands are applied is through ritual community gatherings for giving thanks and making offerings to God, which serve as a reminder to avoid our inclination to idolatry (Deut 12; 1 Cor 10:1–34; Heb 10:19–25). As we will see in later chapters, this recurrent call to gather also leads God's people to attend to economic inequalities (Acts 2:42–47; 4:32–37; 2 Cor 8:1–15). As such, an important point to grasp is the way proper worship of God moves outward from the individual and family to the worshiping community and then back from community to the family and individual: I am responsible for you and you for me.

(B) *Authority.* With our experiences of abuses, it is natural for a culture to resent authority or authority figures. And yet can we really live without authority in our world? Who makes the decisions when members of a group disagree? Who decides who gets to belong to the group? Who is to be held responsible for failure?

The fifth command offers a way to address these kinds of questions. But the law can easily be misunderstood, especially in an age postured so strongly against authority structures, so we need to unpack it a little. We mentioned already that both father *and* mother are named in the law. Here Christopher Wright rightly warns against "the temptation to see it as a relic of a harshly vindictive patriarchal society" (1996:77). Most scholars, in fact, recognize that the immediate application of the law was for adult children and not a license for authoritarian parenting. This is because the basic economic and social unit of the "father's house" involved two or three generations living together and sharing responsibilities. Wright suggests the law's most obvious applications were for supporting the family's obligations in military service, participation in the agricultural rhythms of life, and teaching and instructing the next generation, all of which were tied to the household. The law naturally applies to younger children as well, but its main force *relies on parental authority to serve broader social well-being.*

Directly related to this, the motive clause for the law promises that Israel's days "will be long" and they will prosper "in the land" (5:16). The authority in the house is directed towards orderly life in communities and in a nation. Turning that around, the nation flourishes when the home is orderly, when children serve diligently, and when elderly parents are not neglected. Ezek 22:6–8 ties honor for parents to care for the "sojourner" and "widow." "Honor" of authority is closely tied to compassionate care of the vulnerable.

When we view the law through this broader social lens, we see its natural application to the legal authorities appointed in the laws in Deut 16:18–18:22. As Patrick Miller has observed, Deuteronomy introduces the passages for the offices of leaders—judges, officers, priests, kings, and prophets—with the phrase "in the land Yahweh your God is giving you." This same phrase appears in the Decalogue promise in 5:16 (2018:210). Like the parents, then, the authority granted to these offices is directed to the flourishing of the people before Yahweh.

Biblical authority is, therefore, anything but a license for power, control, and abuse. In fact, the law places extreme limits on the king: it outlaws the pursuit of wealth and military prowess, forbids the common royal practice of polygamy, balances his rule with the authority of the priests (17:14–20), and disperses his rule through officers, judges, and prophets (16:18–20; 18:9–14).

The writer of Hebrews admonishes his readers, "Obey your leaders and submit to them, for they are keeping watch over your souls, as those who will have to give an account. Let them do this with joy and not with groaning, for that would be of no advantage to you" (13:17). Leading and following are God-given roles that we assume for the well-being of society. Some of us have a role to play in leading and all of us have a role to play in following. Scripture teaches us to pursue these callings in humility and with the flourishing of community life as our goal.

(C) *A humanitarian vision for liberty and rest.* We can briefly point to future sections in this volume for the application of the Sabbath law to provisions for rest, financial forgiveness, and economic recovery in 14:22–16:17. As we will see, the one-in-seven-day pattern of refreshment is expanded to seasonal, yearly, and other long-term practices that gather the people for worship and restore economic and social equalities.

LOVE WRITTEN ON OUR HEARTS

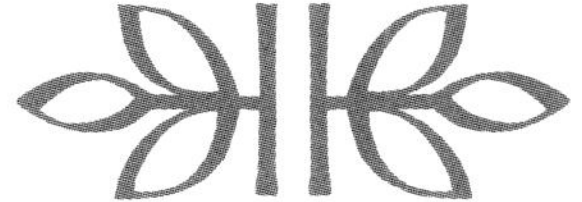

It's a good time to find our place on the map of Deuteronomy. In the companion introduction, we looked at the various ways to think about the structure in Deuteronomy: a law code, a covenant, and series of sermons. Here is a simplified outline.

chs. 1–3	Opening history
chs. 4–5	First sermon and Decalogue
chs. 6–11	Instructional and motivational interlude
chs. 12–26	Main body of laws
chs. 27–34	Covenant renewal and closing

Chapters 4 and 5 anticipate the body of laws that fall under the title הַחֻקִּים וְהַמִּשְׁפָּטִים ("the statutes and the ordinances") in chs. 6–26. While the main body of these individual laws does not begin until ch. 12, ch. 6 repeats this phrase הַחֻקִּים וְהַמִּשְׁפָּטִים as it begins a new section. In this case it serves as a pause to further prepare and motivate readers for the specific laws that will follow. These pauses remind Israel that torah is less a list of rules than a detailed marriage bond of love that holds this covenant together. The statutes and ordinances that will begin in ch. 12 are Israel's means to uphold their part of the bond.

Our short passage is only nine verses, but the material is chock full of difficult linguistic and conceptual challenges. For example: How do we translate the end of 6:4b? "Yahweh alone?" "Yahweh is one?" Maybe something else? How do translate the three nouns in 6:5: בְּכָל־לְבָבְךָ וּבְכָל־נַפְשְׁךָ וּבְכָל־מְאֹדֶךָ? What exactly are הַדְּבָרִים ("the words") that are to be on hearts and bound and written on doors and gates in 6:6, 8–9? Is it all of the Torah? The Decalogue? The whole book of Deuteronomy? And are the commands to "bind" and "write" in 6:8–9 to be taken literally or symbolically?

We'll take up all of this in the text and in the "From Text to Sermon" section below.

LARGER LITERARY CONTEXT › 6:1–25

The apostolic Christian faith is grounded in the opening line of the Nicene Creed: "We believe in *one* God." Just how important is this word "one"? Working with Deuteronomy, and ch. 6 in particular, requires us to spend a little time unpacking any possible claim it has to "monotheism." For, as we see here, the claim is highly contested:

> Deuteronomy does not, at any point, present a doctrine of God that may be described as "monotheism." (MacDonald 2003:209)

> Deuteronomy is uncompromisingly, ruthlessly monotheistic. (Wright 1996:10)

How could scholars disagree so strongly on this point? I think it can be explained by expanding the context a little.

Nathan MacDonald represents many scholars who want us to appreciate the ancient context in which Deuteronomy was written. For example, the risk envisioned by the first commandment was not so much that Israel would worship other gods *instead of Yahweh*, but of worshiping them *alongside Yahweh*. In their world, the more gods the better your odds. And the more likely to get answers to your prayers and returns on your sacrifices. In Deut 4–7 especially, we see that Yahweh will not share the stage with other gods principally because this God made a covenant with them in redeeming them from Egypt. It is what Jon Levenson calls a love of "theopolitical . . . allegiance" (2016:13). Yahweh deserves their undivided loyalty. As to the question, "Do the gods the nations worship even exist?" this group of scholars will say that Deuteronomy never answers explicitly. More to the point, it's not a question that mattered in this context. And, upon a close reading, we can see that the Old Testament sometimes acknowledges other gods, while at other times denying their existence (Pss 115:4–7; 135:15–18; Isa 45:5, 18; Dan 5:23; cf. Rev 9:20).

This takes us back to Christopher Wright, who thinks Deuteronomy is emphatically monotheistic. From his perspective, even if passages like 4:35, 39; 6:4; and 32:39 were *not* meant as statements of monotheism, we can reasonably say that the logic of the whole of Deuteronomy leads us to no other conclusion. For one, Deuteronomy has a distinct missional focus. The nations will say of Israel: Your law is wiser and more righteous (4:6, 8); your God is nearer (4:7); you are holy in our eyes (26:19); our gods are lifeless and meaningless by comparison (4:26); and your God is the origin of all things. All of this ultimately renders other religious myths and beliefs irrelevant (4:35–39). The God of this universe will reduce to nothing the gods of other nations, and he does so in order to attract all people to himself. And that message is often subtle in Deuteronomy and most of the Old Testament.

Most of us have joined the worship of this one God of Israel from other nations. And our creed rightly calls us to confess that, "We believe in *one* God." Among many others, here are three important implications of monotheism.

(1) *Idolatry*. In the ancient world, worshiping many gods was common, and Israel fell into it often. And yet, as McConville suggests, idolatry today is "more likely to take the form of a dichotomy between God and the empirical world when it comes to ethical decision-making, than to carve images from wood or stone." He explains: "[God's] displacement from science, art and public life, with the associated claim to the autonomy of human reason, may be the modern form of having 'other gods in his presence,' or indeed of 'taking his name in vain'" (2002:134–5).

We may not worship a Baal, Asherah, or Dagon, but we do have jobs, homes, hobbies, political ideologies, food preferences, exercise regimens, and many other ways of life that suck us in to worship them like gods. They bid us to find pleasure, satisfaction, and hope in anything other than in God.

(2) *Confidence in the moral order of the world*. To navigate our lives in this world, we need order: a moral map or guide to help us interpret situations, determine right from wrong, and act appropriately. Just imagine a box of puzzle pieces that turn out not to be fit for a final solution. Just random pieces. The same is true for moral decisions. Without an order to the pieces, our decisions become meaningless. But who sets the standard, or order, for right and wrong?

Because God is the one and only Creator of all that exists, we can say with confidence that his commands contain *truth* about this world. We don't simply obey God because he commands us; these "words that I am commanding you today" (6:6) are God's wisdom for our lives. They are clues to the order and design of our world. And so we obey him because his laws are good and wise and the light that leads to life and flourishing (Pss 68; 119:98, 105).

This does not mean that the law requires no interpretation. What counts as idolatry and what does not? Does a polite compliment constitute lying? Is this action in particular an act a theft? Rather than giving us the answer for every case, the laws guide us with wisdom to find the order in the moral map. The law also aids us in building prudence and courage to act rightly in every new day.

It is telling, in this light, that we are not told to keep the law in some abstract way but to love God by keeping his law. More than just a moral map, the law is a personal revelation of the one and only God whose motivations are merciful, guiding us to live well so that we may follow our course to draw near to him in love.

(3) *Finally, our hope in eternal promises.* If there are many gods, the future remains uncertain, subject to competing wills and powers. But the one and only true God has no one who can contest his purposes. God has "promised" (Deut 6:3) to give the Israelites a land, the land he "swore to your fathers" (v. 10). This is the God who determines the course of history, and so he alone can be trusted. Isaiah unites these themes in his prophecy about Israel's failures:

> I am God and there is no other;
> I am God and there is no one like me,
> declaring from the beginning, the end,
> and from ancient times what will be done. . . .
> Surely I have spoken, surely I will bring it to pass.
> I have ordained it,
> surely I will do it. (46:9b, 11b)

Paul makes a similar claim in writing to the church at Corinth. Dismissing the "so-called gods," he directs their trust to the "one God, the Father, from whom are all things and for whom we exist, and one Lord, Jesus Christ, through whom are all things and through whom we exist" (1 Cor 8:5–6 ESV). Christ is the one in whom and through whom all God's promises will come about. Further, because Jesus and the Father are one, we know that all his promises in Christ will be fulfilled.

1a וְזֹאת הַמִּצְוָה הַחֻקִּים֙ וְהַמִּשְׁפָּטִ֔ים

wəzōʾt hammiṣwâ haḥuqqîm wəhammišpāṭîm

And this is the commandment—the statutes and the ordinances—

1b אֲשֶׁר צִוָּה יְהוָה אֱלֹהֵיכֶם

ʾăšer ṣiwwâ YHWH ʾĕlōhêkem

that Yahweh your God commanded

1c לְלַמֵּד אֶתְכֶם לַעֲשׂוֹת

ləlammēd ʾetkem laʿăśôt

to teach you to do

1d בָּאָרֶץ אֲשֶׁר אַתֶּם עֹבְרִים שָׁמָּה לְרִשְׁתָּהּ׃

bāʾāreṣ ʾăšer ʾattem ʿōvərîm šammâ lərištāh.

in the land that you are crossing over to possess,

2a לְמַעַן תִּירָא אֶת־יְהוָה אֱלֹהֶיךָ

ləmaʿan tîrāʾ ʾet-YHWH ʾĕlōhêkā

that you may fear Yahweh your God,

2b לִשְׁמֹר אֶת־כָּל־חֻקֹּתָיו וּמִצְוֺתָיו֙ אֲשֶׁר אָנֹכִי מְצַוְּךָ֔ אַתָּה

lišmōr ʾet-kol-ḥuqqōtāyw ûmiṣwôtāyw ʾăšer ʾānōkî məṣawwekā ʾattâ

by keeping all the statutes and commands
that I am commanding you—

2c וּבִנְךָ וּבֶן־בִּנְךָ֔ כֹּל יְמֵי חַיֶּיךָ

ûvinkā ûven-binkā kōl yəmê ḥayyêkā

you and your children and your children's children,
all the days of your life—

2d וּלְמַעַן יַאֲרִכֻן יָמֶיךָ׃

ûləmaʿan yaʾărikun yāmêkā.

and that your days may be prolonged.

3a
וְשָׁמַעְתָּ יִשְׂרָאֵל וְשָׁמַרְתָּ לַעֲשׂוֹת

wəšāma'tā yiśrā'ēl wəšāmartā la'ăśôt

Hear, O Israel, and guard yourself to do them,

3b
אֲשֶׁר יִיטַב לְךָ וַאֲשֶׁר תִּרְבּוּן מְאֹד

'ăšer yîṭav ləkā wa'ăšer tirbûn mə'ōd

that it may go well with you, and that you may multiply greatly,

3c
כַּאֲשֶׁר דִּבֶּר יְהוָה אֱלֹהֵי אֲבֹתֶיךָ לָךְ

ka'ăšer dibber YHWH 'ĕlōhê 'ăvōtêkā lāk

just as Yahweh, the God of your ancestors, promised you

3d
אֶרֶץ זָבַת חָלָב וּדְבָשׁ:

'ereṣ zāvat ḥālāv ûdəvāš.

a land flowing with milk and honey.

4a
שְׁמַע יִשְׂרָאֵל

šəma' yiśrā'ēl

Hear, O Israel,

4b
יְהוָה אֱלֹהֵינוּ יְהוָה| אֶחָד:

YHWH 'ĕlōhênû YHWH 'eḥād.

Yahweh our God, Yahweh alone.

5a
וְאָהַבְתָּ אֵת יְהוָה אֱלֹהֶיךָ

wə'āhavtā 'ēt YHWH 'ĕlōhêkā

And you shall love Yahweh your God

5b
בְּכָל־לְבָבְךָ וּבְכָל־נַפְשְׁךָ וּבְכָל־מְאֹדֶךָ:

bəkol-ləvāvkā ûvəkol-nafšəkā ûvəkol-mə'ōdekā.

with all your heart, and all your life force, and very, very much.

6
וְהָיוּ הַדְּבָרִים הָאֵלֶּה אֲשֶׁר אָנֹכִי מְצַוְּךָ הַיּוֹם עַל־לְבָבֶךָ:

wəhāyû haddəvārîm hā'elle 'ăšer 'ānōkî məṣawwəkā hayyôm 'al-ləvāvekā.

**And these words that I am commanding you today
shall be on your heart.**

7a

וְשִׁנַּנְתָּ֣ם לְבָנֶ֔יךָ

wəšinnantām ləvānêkā

And you shall teach them to your children

7b

וְדִבַּרְתָּ֖ בָּ֑ם בְּשִׁבְתְּךָ֤ בְּבֵיתֶ֙ךָ֙

wədibbartā bām bəšivtəkā bəvêtekā

וּבְלֶכְתְּךָ֣ בַדֶּ֔רֶךְ וּֽבְשָׁכְבְּךָ֖ וּבְקוּמֶֽךָ׃

ûvəlektəkā badderek ûvəšokbəkā ûvəqûmekā.

**and talk about them when you sit in your house
and when you walk by the way and when you lie down
and when you rise.**

8a

וּקְשַׁרְתָּ֥ם לְא֖וֹת עַל־יָדֶ֑ךָ

ûqəšartām lə'ôt 'al-yādekā

And you shall bind them as a sign on your hand.

8b

וְהָי֥וּ לְטֹטָפֹ֖ת בֵּ֥ין עֵינֶֽיךָ׃

wəhāyû ləṭōṭāfōt bên 'ênêkā.

And they shall be as frontlets between your eyes

9

וּכְתַבְתָּ֛ם עַל־מְזוּזֹ֥ת בֵּיתֶ֖ךָ וּבִשְׁעָרֶֽיךָ׃

ûkətavtām 'al-məzûzōt bêtekā ûviš'ārêkā.

**And you shall write them on the doorposts of your house
and on your gates."**

1a

וְזֹ֣את הַמִּצְוָ֗ה הַֽחֻקִּים֙ וְהַמִּשְׁפָּטִ֔ים

And this is the commandment—the statutes and the ordinances—

וְזֹאת	and this	---		demonstr
זֹאת	*wə·zō't*	W/ CONJ וְ		pron
הַמִּצְוָה	the commandment	ABS		noun
מִצְוָה	*ham·miṣ·wá*	W/ DEF. ART.		

| הַחֻקִּים֙
חֹק | the statutes/regulations
ha·ḥuq·qîm | ABS
W/ DEF. ART. | noun |
| וְהַמִּשְׁפָּטִ֔ים
מִשְׁפָּט | and the judgments/ordinances
wə·ham·miš·pā·ṭîm | ABS
W/ CONJ וְ + DEF. ART. | noun |

<table>
<tr><td>1b</td><td colspan="3" align="center">אֲשֶׁר צִוָּה יְהוָה אֱלֹהֵיכֶם</td></tr>
<tr><td></td><td colspan="3" align="center">that Yahweh your God commanded</td></tr>
</table>

אֲשֶׁר אֲשֶׁר	that/which *'ă·šer*	---	relative pron
צִוָּה צוה	(he) commanded *ṣiw·wâ*	PIEL PF 3MS	verb
יְהוָה יהוה	Yahweh *YHWH*	ABS	noun
אֱלֹהֵיכֶם אֱלֹהִים	your God *'ĕ·lō·hê·kem*	CST W/ 2MP SX	noun

Many translations read "commanded *me*." The "me" is absent in Hebrew but should probably be assumed.

<table>
<tr><td>1c</td><td colspan="3" align="center">לְלַמֵּד אֶתְכֶם לַעֲשׂוֹת</td></tr>
<tr><td></td><td colspan="3" align="center">to teach you to do</td></tr>
</table>

לְלַמֵּד למד	to teach/instruct *lə·lam·mēd*	PIEL INF CST W/ PREP לְ	verb
אֶתְכֶם אֵת	(*direct object marker* +) you *'et·kem*	--- W/ 2MP SX	particle
לַעֲשׂוֹת עשׂה	to do *la·'ă·śôt*	QAL INF CST W/ PREP לְ	verb

1d   בָּאָרֶץ אֲשֶׁר אַתֶּם עֹבְרִים שָׁמָּה לְרִשְׁתָּהּ׃

in the land that you are crossing over to possess,

בָּאָרֶץ אֶרֶץ	in the land *bā·ʾā·reṣ*	ABS W/ PREP בְּ + DEF. ART.	noun
אֲשֶׁר אֲשֶׁר	that/which *ʾă·šer*	---	relative pron
אַתֶּם אַתֶּם	you *ʾat·**tem***	---	personal pron
עֹבְרִים עבר	crossing/passing/passing over *ʿō·və·**rîm***	QAL PTCP MP	verb
שָׁמָּה שָׁם	to there *šām·mâ*	--- W/ LOCATIVE ה	adv
לְרִשְׁתָּהּ׃ ירשׁ	to possess/inherit it *lə·riš·**tāh***	QAL INF CST W/ PREP לְ + 3FS SX	verb

2a   לְמַעַן תִּירָא אֶת־יְהוָה אֱלֹהֶיךָ

that you may fear Yahweh your God,

לְמַעַן לְמַעַן	in order that/so that *lə·**ma**·ʿan*	---	prep
תִּירָא ירא	you fear *tî·**rāʾ***	QAL IMPF 2MS	verb
אֶת־ אֵת	(direct object marker) *ʾet-*	---	particle
יְהוָה יהוה	Yahweh *YHWH*	ABS	noun
אֱלֹהֶיךָ אֱלֹהִים	your God *ʾĕ·lō·**hê**·ḵā*	CST W/ 2MS SX	noun

<table>
<tr><td>2b</td><td colspan="2" align="center">לִשְׁמֹר אֶת־כָּל־חֻקֹּתָיו וּמִצְוֺתָיו אֲשֶׁר אָנֹכִי מְצַוְּךָ</td></tr>
</table>

by keeping all the statutes and commands
that I am commanding you—

לִשְׁמֹר שׁמר	to keep/guard/observe *liš·mōr*	QAL INF CST W/ PREP לְ	verb
אֶת־ אֵת	(direct object marker) *'et-*	---	particle
כָּל־ כֹּל	all/every/each *kol-*	CST	noun
חֻקֹּתָיו חֻקָּה	his statutes/regulations *ḥuq·qō·tāyw*	CST W/ 3MS SX	noun
וּמִצְוֺתָיו מִצְוָה	and his commandments *û·miṣ·wô·tāyw*	CST W/ CONJ וְ + 3MS SX	noun
אֲשֶׁר אֲשֶׁר	that/which *'ă·šer*	---	relative pron
אָנֹכִי אָנֹכִי	I *'ā·nō·kî*	---	personal pron
מְצַוְּךָ צוה	(am) commanding you *mə·ṣaw·we·kā*	PIEL PTCP MS W/ 2MS SX	verb

<table>
<tr><td>2c</td><td colspan="2" align="center">אַתָּה וּבִנְךָ וּבֶן־בִּנְךָ כֹּל יְמֵי חַיֶּיךָ</td></tr>
</table>

you and your children and your children's children,
all the days of your life—

אַתָּה אַתָּה	you *'at·tâ*	---	personal pron
וּבִנְךָ בֵּן	and your child *û·vin·kā*	CST W/ CONJ וְ + 2MS SX	noun
וּבֶן־ בֵּן	and the child of *û·ven-*	CST W/ CONJ וְ	noun
בִּנְךָ בֵּן	your child *bin·kā*	CST W/ 2MS SX	noun
כֹּל כֹּל	all/every/each *kōl*	CST	noun

<table>
<tr><td>יְמֵי
יוֹם</td><td>(the) days of
yə·mê</td><td>CST</td><td>noun</td></tr>
<tr><td>חַיֶּיךָ
חַיִּים</td><td>your life
ḥay·yê·ḵā</td><td>CST
W/ 2MS SX</td><td>noun</td></tr>
</table>

2d — וּלְמַעַן יַאֲרִכֻן יָמֶיךָ׃

and that your days may be prolonged.

<table>
<tr><td>וּלְמַעַן
לְמַעַן</td><td>and in order that/so that
û·lə·ma·ʿan</td><td>---
W/ CONJ וְ</td><td>prep</td></tr>
<tr><td>יַאֲרִכֻן
ארך</td><td>(they) will be long/
become long
ya·ʾă·rī·ḵun</td><td>HIPH IMPF 3MP

W/ PARAGOGIC ן</td><td>verb</td></tr>
<tr><td>יָמֶיךָ׃
יוֹם</td><td>your days
yā·mê·ḵā</td><td>CST
W/ 2MS SX</td><td>noun</td></tr>
</table>

3a — וְשָׁמַעְתָּ יִשְׂרָאֵל וְשָׁמַרְתָּ לַעֲשׂוֹת

Hear, O Israel, and guard yourself to do them,

<table>
<tr><td>וְשָׁמַעְתָּ
שמע</td><td>and you hear/listen/obey
wə·šā·ma·ʿtā</td><td>QAL WEQATAL 2MS</td><td>verb</td></tr>
<tr><td>יִשְׂרָאֵל
יִשְׂרָאֵל</td><td>Israel
yiś·rā·ʾēl</td><td>ABS</td><td>noun</td></tr>
<tr><td>וְשָׁמַרְתָּ
שמר</td><td>and you keep/guard/observe
wə·šā·mar·tā</td><td>QAL WEQATAL 2MS</td><td>verb</td></tr>
<tr><td>לַעֲשׂוֹת
עשׂה</td><td>to do
la·ʿă·śôt</td><td>QAL INF CST
W/ PREP לְ</td><td>verb</td></tr>
</table>

3b — אֲשֶׁר יִיטַב לְךָ וַאֲשֶׁר תִּרְבּוּן מְאֹד

that it may go well with you, and that you may multiply greatly,

<table>
<tr><td>אֲשֶׁר
אֲשֶׁר</td><td>that/which
ʾă·šer</td><td>---</td><td>relative
pron</td></tr>
</table>

יִיטַב יטב *yî·ṭav*	is good/pleasing/agreeable	QAL IMPF 3MS	verb
לְךָ ל *lə·ḵā*	to/for you	--- W/ 2MS SX	prep
וַאֲשֶׁר אֲשֶׁר *wa·'ă·šer*	and that/which	--- W/ CONJ וְ	relative pron
תִּרְבּוּן רבה *tir·bûn*	you multiply/increase/be numerous	QAL IMPF 2MP W/ PARAGOGIC ן	verb
מְאֹד מְאֹד *mə·'ōd*	very/greatly	---	adv

3c

כַּאֲשֶׁר דִּבֶּר יְהוָה אֱלֹהֵי אֲבֹתֶיךָ לָךְ

just as Yahweh, the God of your ancestors, promised you

כַּאֲשֶׁר אֲשֶׁר *ka·'ă·šer*	as/when/according as	--- W/ PREP כְּ	relative pron
דִּבֶּר דבר *dib·ber*	(he) spoke	PIEL PF 3MS	verb
יְהוָה יהוה *YHWH*	Yahweh	ABS	noun
אֱלֹהֵי אֱלֹהִים *'ĕ·lō·hê*	the God of	CST	noun
אֲבֹתֶיךָ אָב *'ă·vō·tê·ḵā*	your ancestors	CST W/ 2MS SX	noun
לָךְ ל *lāḵ*	to/for you	--- W/ 2MS SX	prep

3d

אֶרֶץ זָבַת חָלָב וּדְבָשׁ׃

a land flowing with milk and honey.

אֶרֶץ אֶרֶץ *'e·reṣ*	land	ABS	noun

זָבַ֛ת	flowing/dripping with	QAL (CST) PTCP FS	verb
זוּב	zā·**vat**		
חָלָ֖ב	milk	ABS	noun
חָלָב	ḥā·**lāv**		
וּדְבָ֑שׁ:	and honey	ABS	noun
דְּבַשׁ	û·də·**vāš**	W/ CONJ וְ	

<table>
<tr><td colspan="2" style="text-align:center">4a</td><td style="text-align:center">שְׁמַ֖ע יִשְׂרָאֵ֑ל</td></tr>
</table>

4a	שְׁמַ֖ע יִשְׂרָאֵ֑ל

שְׁמַ֖ע יִשְׂרָאֵ֑ל

Hear, O Israel,

שְׁמַ֖ע	listen/hear/obey	QAL IMPV MS	verb
שמע	šə·**ma**ʿ		
יִשְׂרָאֵ֑ל	Israel	ABS	noun
יִשְׂרָאֵל	yiś·rā·**ʾēl**		

Based upon the first word in this verse, שְׁמַע, ancient Jews instituted a practice called the "Shema" or "Recitation of Shema," which calls for Jews to recite Deut 6:4–9 and 11:18–20 three times each day alongside Num 15:37–41, which commands placing tassels on the corners of Israelite garments. Jewish children are to be taught the Shema and Deut 33:4 as soon as they can speak. Jeffrey Tigay comments, "the Shema serves as the quintessential expression of the most fundamental belief and commitment of Judaism" (Tigay 1996:440–41). One can imagine that for Jesus to call himself the "I am" (John 8:58) and to claim that he and the Father "are one" (John 10:30) suggests that the one true God of Jewish monotheism has shown up in the flesh.

4b	יְהֹוָ֥ה אֱלֹהֵ֖ינוּ יְהֹוָ֥ה ׀ אֶחָֽד:

Yahweh our God, Yahweh alone.

יְהֹוָ֥ה	Yahweh	ABS	noun
יהוה	YHWH		
אֱלֹהֵ֖ינוּ	our God	CST	noun
אֱלֹהִים	ʾĕ·lō·**hê**·nû	W/ 1CP SX	
יְהֹוָ֥ה ׀	Yahweh	ABS	noun
יהוה	YHWH		

אֶחָד:	one/alone/only	ABS	cardinal number
אֶחָד	'e·ḥād		

There are no verbs in this clause, which makes it particularly challenging to translate. Three other major possibilities include:

Yahweh is our God, Yahweh is one

Yahweh is our God, Yahweh alone

Yahweh, our God, is one Yahweh

We should bear two things in mind when considering these options (for an extended study, see MacDonald 2003:59–75). First, יְהוָה אֱלֹהֵינוּ is common in Deuteronomy but always translated appositionally as a name, "Yahweh our God," never with an implied verb, "Yahweh *is* our God" (see 1:6, 19, 20, etc.) (Holmstedt and Jones 2017:21–51). Notice also that when Deuteronomy wants to equate Yahweh and God, it inserts "he" (e.g., 4:35b: יְהוָה הוּא הָאֱלֹהִים).

Second, אֶחָד usually signifies the cardinal number "one." This might mean that God is "unique," or that he is "incomparable," or that he has a "unitary nature" (Nelson 2004:89–90). While these are all possible, they tend to be abstract notions, whereas the overwhelming emphasis of Deuteronomy is Yahweh's exclusive claim to loyalty among other deities:

4:35   Yahweh, he is God, and there is none besides him

4:39   Yahweh, he is God in the heavens above and on the earth beneath, there is no other.

5:7   You shall have no other gods before my face

32:39   I, I am God and there is no other besides me

Recognizing that we cannot be definitive, אֶחָד, translated as "alone," signifies exclusivity and singularity. And this also leads most naturally to why he is owed undivided devotion and love (6:5).

5a וְאָהַבְתָּ אֵת יְהוָה אֱלֹהֶיךָ

And you shall love Yahweh your God

וְאָהַבְתָּ	and you love	QAL WEQATAL 2MS	verb
אהב	wə·'ā·hav·tā		
אֵת	(direct object marker)	---	particle
אֵת	'ēt		

יְהוָה	Yahweh	ABS	noun
יהוה	*YHWH*		
אֱלֹהֶיךָ	your God	CST	noun
אֱלֹהִים	*ĕ·lō·hê·kā*	W/ 2MS SX	

אהב ("to love") is a common requirement in ancient suzerain-vassal treaties. It should be taken as something far beyond Western romantic notions
to express something closer to loyalty and obedience.

<table>
<tr><td>5b</td><td colspan="3" align="center">בְּכָל־לְבָבְךָ וּבְכָל־נַפְשְׁךָ וּבְכָל־מְאֹדֶךָ׃</td></tr>
</table>

with all your heart, and all your life force, and very, very much.

בְּכָל־	with all/the whole of	CST	noun
כֹּל	*bə·kol-*	W/ PREP בְּ	
לְבָבְךָ	your heart	CST	noun
לֵבָב	*lə·vāv·kā*	W/ 2MS SX	
וּבְכָל־	and with all/the whole of	CST	noun
כֹּל	*û·və·kol-*	W/ CONJ וְ + PREP בְּ	
נַפְשְׁךָ	your life/soul/life force	CST	noun
נֶפֶשׁ	*naf·šə·kā*	W/ 2MS SX	
וּבְכָל־	and with all/the whole of	CST	noun
כֹּל	*û·və·kol-*	W/ CONJ וְ + PREP בְּ	
מְאֹדֶךָ׃	your abundance/strength	ABS	noun
מְאֹד	*mə·’ō·de·kā*	W/ 2MS SX	

The three nouns in 5b are notoriously difficult to translate. A sampling
of options includes:

"heart . . . being . . . strength" (McConville 2002:137)

"heart . . . being . . . capability" (Nelson 2004:86)

"heart . . . soul . . . might" JPS (Tigay 1996:77)

"heart . . . life force . . . and very, very much" (Levenson
    2016:69–72)

Each noun requires further comment. In the Old Testament, לֵב ("heart")
is the seat of reason and emotion, whereas in modern culture the heart
is primarily about affection. Deuteronomy's law is not asking for warm

feelings about God but ordering one's intellectual and emotional life to pleasing him.

The Hebrew נֶפֶשׁ is a material thing and can die, so it should not be translated as a ghostly separate part of us as is often imagined in Christian culture of the "soul" (Levenson 2016:69–71). "Life force" is one possible way of improving on most English translations.

And, finally, מְאֹד may be impossible to render accurately in this context. Elsewhere translated "much" or "very" it could be something like "capability" or, as a noun that modifies the first two nouns, i.e., "exceedingly" (Tigay 1996:77). Altogether the phrase could be: "with all your heart and all your life force and very, very much." Taken with 6:5a, the law directs the whole of embodied life in this world to fear and obey God.

The LXX and Synoptic Gospels all record encounters in which Jesus or his interlocutor cite this as the greatest commandment (Matt 22:34–40; Mark 12:28–34; Luke 10:25–28). We find the text cited in a variety of ways (Davies and Allison 1997:235–48)

Text	Speaker	1	2	3	4
Hebrew (MT)	Moses	לֵב	נֶפֶשׁ	מְאֹד	
LXX	Moses	διανοια "understanding"	ψυχε "soul"	δυναμις "might"	
LXX A F	Moses	καρδια "heart"	ψυχε "soul"	δυναμις "might"	
Matt 22:37	Jesus	καρδια "heart"	ψυχε "soul"	διανοια "mind"	
Mark 12:30	Jesus	καρδια "heart"	ψυχε "soul"	διανοια "mind"	ισχυς "strength"
Mark 12:33	Scribe	καρδια "heart"	ουνεσις "understanding"	ισχυς "strength"	
Luke 10:27	Lawyer	καρδια "heart"	ψυχε "soul"	ισχυς "strength"	διανοια "mind"

Of course the preacher who tries to import this data into a sermon will quickly lose the audience. That said, this central passage in Scripture tells us what God most desires from us, so we must come away with something to say about the options. I have two suggestions. First, the LXX seems to take לֵב as the mind or intellect, reinforcing the Jewish understanding we noted above: the heart combines emotions, intellect, and dispositions. This may explain why Jesus and the gospel writers add "mind" to the list.

Second, the versions vary at several points, and even Jesus' two answers differ (Matt 22:37; Mark 12:30). Added to this, the scribe in Mark 12:33 quotes the command back slightly differently than he heard it from Jesus. This seems to be evidence, as Joel Green has said of the terms in Luke, that "although no clear lines can be drawn between these four aspects of the human, each is capable of nuance." Green concludes, "the primary purpose of this fourfold inventory is intended to stress the totality of one's love for God" (1997:428). We take up the meaning of "love" in "From Text to Sermon" below.

<table>
<tr><td>6</td><td colspan="3" dir="rtl">וְהָיוּ הַדְּבָרִים הָאֵלֶּה אֲשֶׁר אָנֹכִי מְצַוְּךָ הַיּוֹם עַל־לְבָבֶךָ׃</td></tr>
</table>

And these words that I am commanding you today
shall be on your heart.

וְהָיוּ היה	and (they) will be *wə·hā·yû*	QAL WEQATAL 3CP	verb
הַדְּבָרִים דָּבָר	(the) words *had·də·vā·rîm*	ABS W/ DEF. ART.	noun
הָאֵלֶּה אֵלֶּה	(the) these *hā·ʾēl·le*	--- W/ DEF. ART.	demonstr pron
אֲשֶׁר אֲשֶׁר	that/which *ʾă·šer*	---	relative pron
אָנֹכִי אָנֹכִי	I *ʾā·nō·ḵî*	---	persona pron
מְצַוְּךָ צוה	(am) commanding you *mə·ṣaw·wə·ḵā*	PIEL PTCP MS W/ 2MS SX	verb
הַיּוֹם יוֹם	today/this day *hay·yôm*	ABS W/ DEF. ART.	noun
עַל־ עַל	on/upon *ʿal-*	---	prep
לְבָבֶךָ׃ לֵבָב	your heart *lə·vā·ve·ḵā*	CST W/ 2MS SX	noun

Recalling that לֵב ("heart") refers to the center of all thought, actions, and affections.

<table>
<tr><td>7a</td><td align="center">וְשִׁנַּנְתָּם לְבָנֶיךָ</td></tr>
</table>

And you shall teach them to your children

וְשִׁנַּנְתָּם שׁנן	and you teach/repeat *wə·šin·nan·tām*	PIEL WEQATAL 2MS W/ 3MP SX	verb
לְבָנֶיךָ בֵּן	to your children *lə·vā·nê·kā*	CST W/ PREP לְ + 2MS SX	noun

<table>
<tr><td>7b</td><td align="center">וְדִבַּרְתָּ בָּם בְּשִׁבְתְּךָ בְּבֵיתֶךָ
וּבְלֶכְתְּךָ בַדֶּרֶךְ וּבְשָׁכְבְּךָ וּבְקוּמֶךָ:</td></tr>
</table>

and talk about them when you sit in your house and when you walk by the way and when you lie down and when you rise.

וְדִבַּרְתָּ דבר	and you speak/talk *wə·dib·bar·tā*	PIEL WEQATAL 2MS	verb
בָּם בְּ	by/with/to them *bām*	--- W/ 3MP SX	prep
בְּשִׁבְתְּךָ ישׁב	when you sit/dwell *bə·šiv·tə·kā*	QAL INF CST W/ PREP בְּ + 2MS SX	verb
בְּבֵיתֶךָ בַּיִת	in your house *bə·vê·te·kā*	CST W/ PREP בְּ + 2MS SX	noun
וּבְלֶכְתְּךָ הלך	and when you walk *û·və·lek·te·kā*	QAL INF CST W/ CONJ וְ + PREP בְּ + 2MS SX	verb
בַדֶּרֶךְ דֶּרֶךְ	in/by the way *bad·de·rek*	ABS W/ PREP בְּ + DEF. ART.	noun
וּבְשָׁכְבְּךָ שׁכב	and when you lie down/sleep *û·və·šok·bə·kā*	QAL INF CST W/ CONJ וְ + PREP בְּ + 2MS SX	verb
וּבְקוּמֶךָ: קום	and when you wake/rise *û·və·qû·me·kā*	QAL INF CST W/ CONJ וְ + PREP בְּ + 2MS SX	verb

The translation "by the way" follows the memorable and more poetic rendering in the KJV family of translations (ESV, RSV, etc.). Many other translations and scholars opt for "on the road" or "on a journey." Whatever we choose, this language resonates closely with Deut 11:19, Ps 1, and Prov 6:22. Commenting on the overlap between Proverbs and Deuteronomy,

Bernd Schipper says, "As in Deut 6:7 and 11:19, 'guiding,' 'watching over,' and 'speaking' have to do with life as a whole" (2019:240).

<table>
<tr><td>8a</td><td colspan="3" align="center">וּקְשַׁרְתָּ֥ם לְא֖וֹת עַל־יָדֶ֑ךָ</td></tr>
<tr><td></td><td colspan="3" align="center">And you shall bind them as a sign on your hand.</td></tr>
</table>

וּקְשַׁרְתָּ֥ם	and you will bind/tie/ hang them	QAL WEQATAL 2MS	verb
קָשַׁר	*û·qə·šar·tām*	W/ 3MP SX	
לְא֖וֹת	to/for sign	ABS	noun
אוֹת	*lə·ʾôt*	W/ PREP לְ	
עַל־	on/upon	---	prep
עַל	*ʿal-*		
יָדֶ֑ךָ	your hand	CST	noun
יָד	*yā·de·ḵā*	W/ 2MS SX	

This is the first of three commands to place "these words" (v. 6) on one's body, home, and gates. While it is possible to speak of the whole of Deuteronomy in the home (v. 7), it is not possible to put that much text in any of the places in vv. 8–9.

<table>
<tr><td>8b</td><td colspan="3" align="center">וְהָי֥וּ לְטֹטָפֹ֖ת בֵּ֥ין עֵינֶֽיךָ׃</td></tr>
<tr><td></td><td colspan="3" align="center">And they shall be as frontlets between your eyes</td></tr>
</table>

וְהָי֥וּ	and they will be	QAL WEQATAL 3CP	verb
הָיָה	*wə·hā·yû*		
לְטֹטָפֹ֖ת	for trim/headdress/bracelet	ABS	noun
טוֹטָפוֹת	*lə·ṭō·ṭā·fōt*	W/ PREP לְ	
בֵּ֥ין	between	---	prep
בֵּין	*bên*		
עֵינֶֽיךָ׃	your eyes	CST	noun
עַיִן	*ʿê·nê·ḵā*	W/ 2MS SX	

The meaning of טֹטָפֹת is uncertain; the word could refer to "headbands" or "pendants." Many translations render בֵּין עֵינֶיךָ as "on your forehead." Clearly something rather small is in view. The same is true for the "hand" in 8a as well as the places the law was to be written in v. 9. This raises two questions that we will address in v. 9.

<table>
<tr><td rowspan="2">9</td><td colspan="3">וּכְתַבְתָּם עַל־מְזוּזֹת בֵּיתֶךָ וּבִשְׁעָרֶיךָ:</td></tr>
<tr><td colspan="3">And you shall write them on the doorposts of your house
and on your gates."</td></tr>
</table>

וּכְתַבְתָּם כתב	and you write them *û·kə·ṯav·tām*	QAL WEQATAL 2MS W/ 3MP SX	verb
עַל־ עַל	on/upon *'al-*	---	prep
מְזוּזֹת מְזוּזָה	(the) doorpost/gatepost of *mə·zû·zōt*	CST	noun
בֵּיתֶךָ בַּיִת	your house *bê·te·ḵā*	CST W/ 2MS SX	noun
וּבִשְׁעָרֶיךָ: שַׁעַר	and on your gates *û·viš·'ā·rê·ḵā*	CST W/ CONJ וְ + PREP בְּ + 2MS SX	noun

בֵּיתֶךָ, "in your house," is singular in the MT (cf. 11:20), but plural ("houses") in the LXX as well as in the Hebrew tephillin (phylactery) manuscripts found at Qumran known as 4QPhyl C and 4QPhyl O. The meaning of the verse is the same. Writing on the "door posts" (מְזוּזֹת) and "gates" (שְׁעָרֶיךָ) brings us back to our two questions. First, what was to be written? There are five possible answers: only 6:4–5, only the Decalogue, only the law code in chs. 12–26, both the Decalogue and the law code, or all of Deuteronomy.

A second and related question is this: Is the command intended to be literal or metaphorical? One can imagine that if the command were literal, it would be impossible to fit the book of Deuteronomy on a hand or something attached to the forehead.

That said, we do have evidence as early as the sixth or seventh century BCE of small inscriptions of Num 6:24–26 as well as phylacteries that were found in the Qumran community from the second century BCE (Weinfeld 1991:341–43). We have also uncovered amulets from other cultures of the time that were blank or had writing that was symbolic of a larger text or covenant. One could, in this way, write the four letters of the divine name to represent the Shema, the Decalogue, or all of

Deuteronomy. Literal writing and symbolic meaning need not be held as mutually exclusive options.

Further, we have good reason to believe that the ultimate meaning or significance was symbolic, especially given the emphasis on לְבָבְךָ "your heart" in v. 5. Compare similar texts such as Proverbs where wisdom is to be "bound" on the heart (Prov 3:3; 7:3) and in Jeremiah where will write on the people's hearts (Jer 31:33). The writing and binding images signify internalization.

Perhaps the major key to interpreting this passage is Moses' command to write. As Sonnet has demonstrated clearly, the theme of writing holds the book of Deuteronomy together (1997:50–58).

| God writes (4:13; 5:22) | the people write (6:9; 11:20) |
| the king writes (17:18) | the people write (27:3, 8) |

It helps to recognize that ancient kings were considered representatives of the gods. In this way the king in Deut 17 is the "model Israelite," the "Torah's arch-reader" (Sonnet 1997:71). The people write in imitation of God and the king, not simply for writing's sake but to become like God.

When the king writes in 17:18 we hear the first mention of a "book." "This book" is mentioned again six times in the final chapters (28:58, 61; 29:19, 20, 26; 30:10). But just what is "this book?" We only learn the answer when Moses writes the book at the end (31:9, 19, 22, 24), circumscribing the sacred words into the form that will live on among the individuals, the nations, and its leaders.

 *A Command to Love?* A sermon might ask whether it seems appropriate to *command* love. Isn't love supposed to arise from the heart and personal initiative? If so, this would make a command seem manipulative, even self-serving.

If that's not problem enough, the earliest Christian readers also raised a possible contradiction in the great love commands for God and neighbor. If I am meant to love God with everything I am and have, then wouldn't I be withholding something from God when I love my neighbor and myself (Lev 19:18)?

A sermon can start by correcting the misconception that biblical love is merely an emotion or attachment. In his book *Love: A History*, philosopher Simon May (2011:11–12) tracks four major historical transformations of the concept of love.

	Timeframe	Major Figures	Transformation
1	1000 BCE – 400 CE	Plato, Moses, Jesus, Paul	love is a "value" and supreme virtue
2	400 CE – 1500 CE	Augustine, Aquinas, Luther	divinely given "power" to love
3	1000 CE – 1800 CE	Spinoza, the troubadours	love as an "object" that can be loved as God had been earlier
4	1700 CE – present	Rousseau	the "*lover*, who becomes authentic through love"

Among other things, what is clear from this history is that our focus on self-love and authenticity today stand in sharp contrast to ancient ideas of ethical love. May comments rather sadly, "as this transformation develops, the lover becomes the focus of love to such an extent that there are moments when the loved one almost drops out of the picture, reduced to a substitutable stage prop in the drama of the lover's life. Love comes to fall in love with itself" (p. 12).

As for the *command* to love, in the context of ancient suzerain-vassal treaties, it was not uncommon for the suzerain, the more powerful party in a covenant, to demand love as an allegiance from the lesser party. Love was a virtue demanded of the lesser party by law. And yet the legal relationship that requires such loyalty is also built upon common affection and the protection of the suzerain. So too, Israel's command to love is rooted in God's prior love and redemption (7:7–8):

It was not because you were more numerous that Yahweh "set his love" [חשק] on you and chose you, for you were the smallest of the nations. But it is because of Yahweh's "love" [אַהֲבָה] for you and his keeping his promise that he swore to Abraham.

Levenson provides a clue to understanding this mystery by pointing out that Israel's election was a "gift," not a "reward," and so it should have inspired gratitude rather than the pride that resulted (Levenson 2016:40–47). The command to love thus arises from an infinite gift of God's own self to Israel. This leads us to two further thoughts.

First, we must recognize that, if we resist the modern tendency to reduce love to mere emotion, we can see how love retains a "moral content" of obedience. Love and law go together (see 1 John 5:3). The command to love our neighbor (and ourselves) in Lev 19:18 is grounded in God's moral ordering of the world, not in a hope that we all just get along. Godly love has a direction and shape based upon the goodness of God.

Our second question asked: If I am supposed to love God with "all" my heart, do I not then rob God when I turn to love my neighbor? Augustine seeks to resolve the problem by saying that the one who loves "relates his love of himself and his neighbor entirely to the love of God, which allows not the slightest trickle to flow away from it and thereby diminish it" (Augustine 1996:XXII.21).

Perhaps we can appreciate how this plays out when we actually get around to loving people around us. Some people want to smother us with their love. Others want to be smothered by ours. Or someone may so want to love and be loved that they never rebuke or correct a friend, or ever want to be corrected. But if my love for a person truly seeks God's love for them, it will require me, at times, to be corrected and to correct. It will require me not just to feel good and be liked by others but to find my satisfaction in God's love. I will also have to resist resenting the one who helps me along to a better way. In the end, obedient love has its life in a community that works together to orient one another to God, who alone fulfills our desires.

To love in this way enables us to love with God's love rather than our own. When we love with our own love, we draw on finite and unavoidably selfish resources. When we draw on God's love for us and in us, we have an inexhaustible resource, just as a candle flame can give light a thousand times and not go out—"light from light," as the early church imagined for us in the Nicene Creed. Human love can only give so much before it is left with no more to give or is extinguished by bitterness, selfishness, fatigue, or loss of hope. But divine love is infinite. If we start loving by receiving God's love as a gift with infinite resources, we make our abode in a source of love that then flows out into the world independent of our limited resources and failing resolve.

🌱 *Habits of Holy Living.* We already observed the close parallels between Deut 6:7; 11:19, Ps 1, and Prov 6:22. These passages address times we walk, lie down, and rise, and exhort us to keep these teachings on our hands, heart, and home. Wisdom, prayer, and law all find their roots in habits of daily life and the traditions passed down in families and communities.

Furthermore, each of the phrases in 6:6–9 opens a dimension of our daily habits. Verse 7 addresses *time*: morning, midday, and night. We humans are forgetful creatures by nature. We get lost in our days and drift. Daily rhythms return us to God's teachings. In this way the law attends to our human weakness; it brings us back to where we find our hope and identity.

The "hand," "forehead," "doorposts," and "gates," meanwhile, imagine the law ordering and enlightening dimensions of our *vocation*: individual, family, and public life (Wright 1996:100). How, the law prompts us to ask three times each day, can I see this law and my love for God shaping my way? And does the law permeate every area of my life?

Finally, we come to the command to "write" on the home and gates. This reminds us of the patterns of *imitation* mentioned above: God writes and the people write; the king writes and people write again. It may be impossible to know whether this writing practice was meant to be literal. Even if physical writing took place, the central point is clearly symbolic. The practices of our lives arise from watching our God and redeemer and imitating his work as we make our way in the world. "Take up your cross and follow me."

In all this, it can be important to say more to a congregation about religious "rituals," especially in those churches where liturgy and ceremony are met with suspicion. Thomas Merton describes an important difference between what he calls a "convention" and a "tradition" that is characteristic of all worshiping communities. A "convention," he says, "is passive and dead . . . a mere repetition of familiar routines [that] follows the line of least resistance." This is often the great concern of low-church Christians who long for spontaneous worship.

But for Merton, tradition is "alive and active," "creative," and "original." "Tradition, which is always old, is at the same time ever new because it is always reviving—born again in each new generation, to be lived and applied in a new and particular way" (Merton 1955:150–51).

This should upend the contrast many make between tradition and spontaneity. For in Deuteronomy, the internalized and active tradition was aimed precisely at renewing one's faith. We should also recognize that everything we do is shaped by tradition in one way or another. Even spontaneous worship falls into patterns that are passed down to the next week, the next month, and to the next generation. And so what's important to recognize is not whether something is more traditional or more spontaneous but what end the action serves. Deuteronomy 6 reminds us that whether ornate or simple, our practices can always become empty and must be born again in love and gratitude—to *tradition* and not *convention*.

In the New Testament, Paul takes up the family model of tradition and passes it on to the family of the church (e.g., 2 Tim 2:2). The echoes here to the Old Testament practices in Psalms, Proverbs, and Deuteronomy ring out: "Let the word of Christ dwell in you richly, teaching and admonishing one another in all wisdom, singing psalms and hymns and spiritual songs with thankfulness in your hearts to God" (Col 3:16 ESV).

MEMORY FOR GRATITUDE

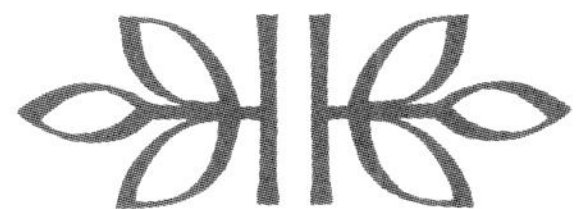

In his book on Jewish memory, Yosef Yerushalmi says: "If Herodotus was the father of history, the fathers of meaning in history are the Jews" (1992:8). This "history" is not simply a chronology of the past or a storied way to hold those events together as we imagine history but a telling of the past *into* the present that gives it purpose. These events between Israel and Yahweh have a good end intended by God. Israel's retelling of this story resets them within God's gracious designs for his whole world (e.g., Gen 1:31; 12:1–3).

Deuteronomy 8 has rightly been called the *"locus classicus"* (paradigmatic passage) of memory and forgetting (Yerushalmi 1992:108). To renew the meaning of their story in each generation, Jews throughout history have maintained rituals that put each individual in Egypt at the Passover and at the mountain before the fire. As it says in the Jewish Passover Haggadah, "In every generation let each man look on himself as if he came forth out of Egypt" (Glatzer 1981:59). In this way of remembering, the past and the present merge in such a way that we become one with those before us, experiencing God's mighty words and works with them and living that common life out in the present called today. All this sheds fresh light on Jesus' command at the Last Supper to "do this in remembrance of me."

LARGER LITERARY CONTEXT ▶ 8:1–9:29

1a

כָּל־הַמִּצְוָה אֲשֶׁר אָנֹכִי מְצַוְּךָ הַיּוֹם

kol-hammiṣwâ ʾăšer ʾānōkî məṣawwəkā hayyôm

"The whole commandment that I am commanding you today—

1b

תִּשְׁמְרוּן לַעֲשׂוֹת

tišmərûn laʿăśôt

be careful to do it,

1c

לְמַעַן תִּחְיוּן וּרְבִיתֶם

ləmaʿan tiḥyûn ûvərîtem

so that you may live and increase

1d

וּבָאתֶם וִירִשְׁתֶּם אֶת־הָאָרֶץ אֲשֶׁר־נִשְׁבַּע יְהוָה לַאֲבֹתֵיכֶם׃

ûvāʾtem wîrištem ʾet-hāʾāreṣ ʾăšer-nišbaʿ YHWH laʾăvōtêkem.

and go in and possess the land that Yahweh swore to your ancestors.

2a

וְזָכַרְתָּ אֶת־כָּל־הַדֶּרֶךְ אֲשֶׁר הֹלִיכֲךָ יְהוָה אֱלֹהֶיךָ

zākartā ʾet-kol-hadderek ʾăšer hōlîkăkā YHWH ʾĕlōhêkā

And remember the whole way that Yahweh your God led you

2b

זֶה אַרְבָּעִים שָׁנָה בַּמִּדְבָּר

ze ʾarbāʿîm šānâ bammidbār

these forty years in the wilderness,

2c

לְמַעַן עַנֹּתְךָ לְנַסֹּתְךָ לָדַעַת אֶת־אֲשֶׁר בִּלְבָבְךָ

ləmaʿan ʿannōtkā lənassōtkā lādaʿat ʾet-ʾăšer bilvāvəkā

to humble you and to test you, to know what was in your hearts,

2d

הֲתִשְׁמֹר מִצְוֹתָיו אִם־לֹא׃

hătišmōr miṣwōtāyw ʾim-lōʾ.

whether you would keep his commands or not.

3a וַיְעַנְּךָ֙ וַיַּרְעִבֶ֔ךָ וַיַּאֲכִלְךָ֤ אֶת־הַמָּן֙
way'annəkā wayyar'ivekā wayya'ăkilkā 'et-hammān

אֲשֶׁ֤ר לֹא־יָדַ֙עְתָּ֙ וְלֹ֣א יָדְע֣וּן אֲבֹתֶ֔יךָ
'ăšer lō-yāda'tā yādə'ûn wəlō' 'ăvōtêkā

**He humbled you and made you hungry and fed you with the manna
that neither you nor your ancestors knew,**

3b לְמַ֣עַן הוֹדִֽעֲךָ֗ כִּ֠י לֹ֣א עַל־הַלֶּ֤חֶם לְבַדּוֹ֙ יִחְיֶ֣ה הָֽאָדָ֔ם
ləma'an hōdî'ăkā kî lō' 'al-halleḥem ləvaddô yiḥye hā'ādām

so that you might know that a man does not live by bread alone

3c כִּ֛י עַל־כָּל־מוֹצָ֥א פִֽי־יְהוָ֖ה יִחְיֶ֥ה הָאָדָֽם׃
kî 'al-kol-môṣā' fî-YHWH yiḥye hā'ādām.

but that a man lives by all that comes from the mouth of God.

4 שִׂמְלָ֨תְךָ֜ לֹ֤א בָֽלְתָה֙ מֵֽעָלֶ֔יךָ וְרַגְלְךָ֖ לֹ֣א בָצֵ֑קָה זֶ֖ה אַרְבָּעִ֥ים שָׁנָֽה׃
śimlātəkā lō' vālətā mē'ālêkā wəragləkā lō' vāṣēqâ ze 'arbā'îm šānâ.

**Your clothing did not wear out on you,
and your foot did not swell these forty years,**

5a וְיָדַעְתָּ֖ עִם־לְבָבֶ֑ךָ כִּ֗י כַּאֲשֶׁ֨ר יְיַסֵּ֥ר אִישׁ֙ אֶת־בְּנ֔וֹ
wəyāda'tā 'im-ləvāvekā kî ka'ăšer yəyassēr 'îš 'et-bənô

that you might know in your heart that as a man disciplines his son,

5b יְהוָ֥ה אֱלֹהֶ֖יךָ מְיַסְּרֶֽךָּ׃
YHWH 'ĕlōhêkā məyassərekā.

so Yahweh your God disciplines you.

6a וְשָׁ֣מַרְתָּ֔ אֶת־מִצְוֺ֖ת יְהוָ֣ה אֱלֹהֶ֑יךָ
wəšāmartā 'et-miṣwōt YHWH 'ĕlōhêkā

And you shall observe the commandments of Yahweh your God

6b לָלֶ֥כֶת בִּדְרָכָ֖יו וּלְיִרְאָ֥ה אֹתֽוֹ׃
lāleket bidvārākāyw ûləyirā' ōtô.

by walking in his ways and fearing him,

7a | כִּי יְהוָה אֱלֹהֶיךָ מְבִיאֲךָ אֶל־אֶרֶץ טוֹבָה

kî YHWH ʾĕlōhêkā məvîʾăkā ʾel-ʾereṣ ṭôvâ

when Yahweh your God brings you into a good land—

7b | אֶרֶץ נַחֲלֵי מָיִם עֲיָנֹת וּתְהֹמֹת

ʾereṣ naḥălê māyim ʿăyānōt ûtəhōmōt

a land with streams of water, springs, and deeps

7c | יֹצְאִים בַּבִּקְעָה וּבָהָר׃

yōṣəʾîm babbiqəʿâ ûvāhār.

flowing out in valley and hill,

8a | אֶרֶץ חִטָּה וּשְׂעֹרָה וְגֶפֶן וּתְאֵנָה וְרִמּוֹן

ʾereṣ ḥiṭṭâ ûśəʾōrâ wəgefen ûtəʾēnâ wərimmôn

a land of wheat and barley, of vines and fig trees and pomegranate trees,

8b | אֶרֶץ־זֵית שֶׁמֶן וּדְבָשׁ׃

ʾereṣ zêt šemen ûdəvāš.

a land of olives bearing oil and honey,

9a | אֶרֶץ אֲשֶׁר לֹא בְמִסְכֵּנֻת תֹּאכַל־בָּהּ לֶחֶם לֹא־תֶחְסַר כֹּל בָּהּ

ʾereṣ ʾăšer lōʾ vəmiskēnut tōʾkal-bāh leḥem lōʾ-teḥsar kōl bāh

**a land in which you will eat bread without scarcity
and in which you will lack nothing,**

9b | אֶרֶץ אֲשֶׁר אֲבָנֶיהָ בַרְזֶל וּמֵהֲרָרֶיהָ תַּחְצֹב נְחֹשֶׁת׃

ʾereṣ ʾăšer ʾăvānêhā varzel ûmēhărārêhā taḥṣōv nəḥōšet.

**a land whose stones are iron and from whose mountains
you will mine copper.**

10a | וְאָכַלְתָּ וְשָׂבָעְתָּ

wəʾākaltā wəśāvāʿtā

When you eat and are satisfied,

10b   וּבֵרַכְתָּ֙ אֶת־יְהוָ֣ה אֱלֹהֶ֔יךָ עַל־הָאָ֥רֶץ הַטֹּבָ֖ה אֲשֶׁ֥ר נָֽתַן־לָֽךְ:

ûvērak̲tā ʾet-YHWH ʾĕlōhêk̲ā ʾal-hāʾāreṣ haṭṭôvâ ʾăšer nātan-lāk̲.

then you shall bless Yahweh your God
on the good land he has given you.

11a   הִשָּׁ֣מֶר לְךָ֗ פֶּן־תִּשְׁכַּ֖ח אֶת־יְהוָ֣ה אֱלֹהֶ֑יךָ

hiššāmer lək̲ā pen-tiškaḥ ʾet-YHWH ʾĕlōhêk̲ā

Be careful, lest you forget Yahweh your God

11b   לְבִלְתִּ֣י שְׁמֹ֤ר מִצְוֺתָיו֙ וּמִשְׁפָּטָ֔יו

ləviltî šəmōr miṣwōtāyw ûmišpāṭāyw

וְחֻקֹּתָ֔יו אֲשֶׁ֛ר אָנֹכִ֥י מְצַוְּךָ֖ הַיּֽוֹם:

wəḥuqqōtāyw ʾăšer ʾānōk̲î məṣawwək̲ā hayyôm.

by not observing his commands and his judgments
and his statutes that I am commanding you today,

12a   פֶּן־תֹּאכַ֖ל וְשָׂבָ֑עְתָּ

pen-tōʾkal wəśāvāʿtā

lest you eat and are full

12b   וּבָתִּ֥ים טוֹבִ֖ים תִּבְנֶ֥ה וְיָשָֽׁבְתָּ:

ûvāttîm ṭôvîm tivne wəyāšāvtā.

and dwell in good houses that you have built,

13a   וּבְקָֽרְךָ֤ וְצֹֽאנְךָ֙ יִרְבְּיֻ֔ן

ûvəqārək̲ā wəṣōʾnək̲ā yirbəyun

and your cattle and your sheep multiply,

13b   וְכֶ֥סֶף וְזָהָ֖ב יִרְבֶּה־לָּ֑ךְ

wək̲esef wəzāhāv yirbe-lāk̲

and your silver and gold multiply,

13c   וְכֹ֥ל אֲשֶׁר־לְךָ֖ יִרְבֶּֽה:

wək̲ōl ʾăšer-lək̲ā yirbe.

and everything you have multiplies,

14a | וָרָ֣ם לְבָבֶ֑ךָ וְשָׁכַחְתָּ֙ אֶת־יְהוָ֣ה אֱלֹהֶ֔יךָ
wərām ləvāvekā wəšākahtā ʾet-YHWH ʾĕlōhêkā

and then your heart is exalted and you forget Yahweh your God,

14b | הַמּוֹצִיאֲךָ֛ מֵאֶ֥רֶץ מִצְרַ֖יִם מִבֵּ֥ית עֲבָדִֽים׃
hammôṣîʾăkā mēʾereṣ miṣrayim mibbêt ʿăvādîm.

who brought you out of the land of Egypt, out of the house of slaves,

15a | הַמּוֹלִֽיכֲךָ֙ בַּמִּדְבָּ֣ר ׀ הַגָּדֹ֤ל וְהַנּוֹרָ֔א
hammôlîkăkā bammidbār haggādōl wəhannôrāʾ

who led you in the great and awesome wilderness—

15b | נָחָ֣שׁ ׀ שָׂרָ֗ף וְעַקְרָ֖ב וְצִמָּא֛וֹן אֲשֶׁ֥ר אֵֽין־מָ֑יִם
nāḥāš śārāf wəʿaqrāv wəṣimmāʾôn ʾăšer ʾēn-māyim

fiery snakes, and scorpions, and dry ground with no water—

15c | הַמּוֹצִ֤יא לְךָ֙ מַ֔יִם מִצּ֖וּר הַחַלָּמִֽישׁ׃
hammôṣîʾ ləkā mayim miṣṣûr haḥallāmîš.

the one who brought out water for you from the flinty rock,

16a | הַמַּאֲכִֽלְךָ֨ מָ֤ן בַּמִּדְבָּר֙ אֲשֶׁ֣ר לֹא־יָדְע֣וּן אֲבֹתֶ֔יךָ
hammaʾăkilkā mān bammidbār ʾăšer lōʾ-yādəʿûn ʾăvōtêkā

who fed you manna that your ancestors did not know,

16b | לְמַ֣עַן עַנֹּֽתְךָ֗ וּלְמַ֙עַן֙ נַסֹּתֶ֔ךָ
ləmaʿan ʿannōtkā ûləmaʿan nassōtekā

to humble you and test you,

16c | לְהֵיטִֽבְךָ֖ בְּאַחֲרִיתֶֽךָ׃
ləhêṭivkā bəʾaḥărîtekā.

to prosper you in the end,

17a | וְאָמַרְתָּ֖ בִּלְבָבֶ֑ךָ
wəʾāmartā bilvāvəkā

and you say in your heart,

17b

כֹּחִ֣י וְעֹ֣צֶם יָדִ֔י עָ֥שָׂה לִ֖י אֶת־הַחַ֥יִל הַזֶּֽה׃

kōḥî wəʿōṣem yādî ʿāśâ lî ʾet-haḥayil hazze.

**'My power and the strength of my hand
have acquired this wealth for me.'**

18a

וְזָֽכַרְתָּ֙ אֶת־יְהֹוָ֣ה אֱלֹהֶ֔יךָ

wəzākartā ʾet-YHWH ʾĕlōhêkā

But remember Yahweh your God,

18b

כִּ֣י ה֗וּא הַנֹּתֵ֥ן לְךָ֛ כֹּ֖חַ לַעֲשׂ֣וֹת חָ֑יִל

kî hûʾ hannōtēn ləkā kōaḥ laʿăśôt ḥāyil

for it is he who gives you strength to acquire wealth,

18c

לְמַ֨עַן הָקִ֧ים אֶת־בְּרִית֛וֹ אֲשֶׁר־נִשְׁבַּ֥ע לַאֲבֹתֶ֖יךָ כַּיּ֥וֹם הַזֶּֽה׃

ləmaʿan hāqîm ʾet-bərîtô ʾăšer-nišbaʿ laʾăvōtêkā kayyôm hazze.

**so that he might establish his covenant,
which he swore to your ancestors, as is the case today."**

1a	כָּל־הַמִּצְוָה אֲשֶׁר אָנֹכִי מְצַוְּךָ הַיּוֹם

"The whole commandment that I am commanding you today—

כָּל־ כֹּל	all/every/each *kol-*	CST	noun
הַמִּצְוָה מִצְוָה	the commandment *ham·miṣ·wâ*	ABS W/ DEF. ART.	noun
אֲשֶׁר אֲשֶׁר	that/which *ʾă·šer*	---	relative pron
אָנֹכִי אָנֹכִי	I *ʾā·nō·kî*	---	personal pron
מְצַוְּךָ צוה	commanding you *mə·ṣaw·wə·kā*	PIEL PTCP MS W/ 2MS SX	verb

| הַיּוֹם | today/this day | ABS | noun |
| יוֹם | *hay·yôm* | W/ DEF. ART. | |

We have been paying careful attention to the variety of legal terms and the way they overlap in Deuteronomy. The phrase כָּל־הַמִּצְוָה ("the whole commandment") reminds us of "these words" (1:1), "this torah" (1:5), as well as the "statutes and rules" and "covenant" (5:1–2).

1b | תִּשְׁמְרוּן לַעֲשׂוֹת

be careful to do it,

תִּשְׁמְרוּן	you shall guard/observe/keep	QAL IMPF 2MP	verb
שׁמר	*tiš·mə·rûn*	W/ PARAGOGIC נ	
לַעֲשׂוֹת	to do	QAL INF CST	verb
עשׂה	*la·ʿă·śôt*	W/ PREP לְ	

This refrain (e.g., 4:1; 5:23; 6:1–3) in Deuteronomy is part of the repetitive rhythm that awakens us again and again to pay attention and live according to what we have heard.

1c | לְמַעַן תִּחְיוּן וּרְבִיתֶם

so that you may live and increase

לְמַעַן	so that/in order that	---	prep
לְמַעַן	*lə·ma·ʿan*		
תִּחְיוּן	you will live	QAL IMPF 2MP	verb
חיה	*tiḥ·yûn*	W/ PARAGOGIC נ	
וּרְבִיתֶם	and you will increase/multiply	QAL WEQATAL 2MP	verb
רבה	*û·və·rî·tem*		

The combination of תִּחְיוּן ("you may live") and רְבִיתֶם ("you may increase") is repeated in 30:16, offering a hope-filled vision of life ahead in the land of Israel.

<table>
<tr><td>1d</td><td align="right" dir="rtl">וּבָאתֶם וִירִשְׁתֶּם אֶת־הָאָרֶץ אֲשֶׁר־נִשְׁבַּע יְהוָה לַאֲבֹתֵיכֶם:</td></tr>
</table>

and go in and possess the land that Yahweh swore to your ancestors.

וּבָאתֶם בּוֹא	and you will go/come *û·vā'·tem*	QAL WEQATAL 2MP	verb
וִירִשְׁתֶּם ירשׁ	and you will inherit/dispossess *wî·riš·tem*	QAL WEQATAL 2MP	verb
אֶת־ אֵת	*(direct object marker)* *'et-*	---	particle
הָאָרֶץ אֶרֶץ	the land *hā·'ā·reṣ*	ABS W/ DEF. ART.	noun
אֲשֶׁר־ אֲשֶׁר	that/which *'ă·šer-*	---	relative pron
נִשְׁבַּע שׁבע	(he) swore *niš·ba'*	NIPH PF 3MS	verb
יְהוָה יהוה	Yahweh *YHWH*	ABS	noun
לַאֲבֹתֵיכֶם: אָב	to your ancestors *la·'ă·vō·tê·kem*	CST W/ PREP לְ + 2MP SX	noun

God's promise (נִשְׁבַּע, "he swore") of land and life takes a central role in motivating Israel to remember.

<table>
<tr><td>2a</td><td align="right" dir="rtl">וְזָכַרְתָּ אֶת־כָּל־הַדֶּרֶךְ אֲשֶׁר הֹלִיכֲךָ יְהוָה אֱלֹהֶיךָ</td></tr>
</table>

And remember the whole way that Yahweh your God led you

וְזָכַרְתָּ זכר	and you remember *zā·kar·tā*	QAL WEQATAL 2MS	verb
אֶת־ אֵת	*(direct object marker)* *'et-*	---	particle
כָּל־ כֹּל	all/every/each *kol-*	CST	noun
הַדֶּרֶךְ דֶּרֶךְ	the way/path *had·de·rek*	ABS W/ DEF. ART.	noun
אֲשֶׁר אֲשֶׁר	that/which *'ă·šer*	---	relative pron

הֹלִיכֲךָ הלך *hō·lî·ḵă·ḵā*	(he) made you walk/go	HIPH PF 3MS W/ 2MS SX	verb
יְהוָה יהוה *YHWH*	Yahweh	ABS	noun
אֱלֹהֶיךָ אלהים *ʾĕ·lō·hê·ḵā*	your God	CST W/ 2MS SX	noun

The command to remember (זכר) is at the heart of Deuteronomy's message (see 5:15; 7:18; 8:18; 9:7, 27; 15:15; 16:3, 12; 24:9, 18, 22; 25:17; 32:7). It is paired in this chapter with a warning to not "forget" (8:11, 14, 19).

2b	זֶה אַרְבָּעִים שָׁנָה בַּמִּדְבָּר

these forty years in the wilderness,

זֶה זֶה *ze*	this/these	---	demonstr pron
אַרְבָּעִים אַרְבָּעִים *ʾar·bā·ʾîm*	forty	ABS	cardinal number
שָׁנָה שָׁנָה *šā·nâ*	year(s)	ABS	noun
בַּמִּדְבָּר מִדְבָּר *bam·mid·bār*	in the wilderness/desert	ABS W/ PREP בְּ + DEF. ART.	noun

The forty years (1:3; 2:7; 29:5; Num 33:38; Amos 2:10) draw upon the forty days of rain with Noah (Gen 7:11). The number forty comes to symbolize a time of punishment and renewal. In his forty days in the wilderness, Jesus picks up Israel's life and failings and brings them, by obedience and a good memory, into the renewal of the kingdom of God.

The LXX omits "these forty years." Yet, vv. 2–4 hang together as a specific memory with "forty years" sitting in parallel on both ends (vv. 2, 4) as well as in the historical report in 2:7 (cf. 29:5 and Amos 2:10). It seems likely the LXX lost something.

לְמַ֨עַן עַנֹּֽתְךָ֜ לְנַסֹּֽתְךָ֗ לָדַ֙עַת֙ אֶת־אֲשֶׁ֣ר בִּלְבָבְךָ֔

to humble you and to test you, to know what was in your hearts,

לְמַ֨עַן לְמַעַן	so that/in order that lə·**ma**·ʿan	---	prep
עַנֹּֽתְךָ֜ ענה	(it/he) will humble/afflict you ʿan·nōt·**ḵā**	PIEL INF CST W/ 2MS SX	verb
לְנַסֹּֽתְךָ֗ נסה	to test you lə·nas·sōt·**ḵā**	PIEL INF CST W/ PREP לְ + 2MS SX	verb
לָדַעַת ידע	to know lā·**da**·ʿat	QAL INF CST W/ PREP לְ	verb
אֶת־ אֵת	(direct object marker) ʾet-	---	particle
אֲשֶׁר אֲשֶׁר	that/which ʾă·**šer**	---	relative pron
בִּלְבָבְךָ לֵבָב	in your heart bil·vā·və·**ḵā**	CST W/ PREP בְּ + 2MS SX	noun

הֲתִשְׁמֹ֥ר מִצְוֺתָ֖יו אִם־לֹֽא׃

whether you would keep his commands or not.

הֲתִשְׁמֹר שׁמר	if/will you keep hă·tiš·**mōr**	QAL IMPF 2MS W/ INTERROGATIVE הֲ	verb
מִצְוֺתָיו מִצְוָה	his commandments miṣ·wō·**tāyw**	CST W/ 3MS SX	noun
אִם־ אִם	if ʾim-	---	conj
לֹא׃ לֹא	no/not lō'	---	particle

וַיְעַנְּךָ וַיַּרְעִבֶּךָ וַיַּאֲכִלְךָ אֶת הַמָּן
אֲשֶׁר לֹא־יָדַעְתָּ וְלֹא יָדְעוּן אֲבֹתֶיךָ

He humbled you and made you hungry and fed you with the manna
that neither you nor your ancestors knew,

וַיְעַנְּךָ	and he humbled/ oppressed you	PIEL WAYY 3MS	verb
ענה	*way·'an·nə·kā*	W/ 2MS SX	
וַיַּרְעִבֶּךָ	and (he) made you hunger/ suffer famine	HIPH WAYY 3MS	verb
רעב	*way·yar·'i·ve·kā*	W/ 2MS SX	
וַיַּאֲכִלְךָ	and (he) made you eat/fed you	HIPH WAYY 3MS	verb
אכל	*way·ya·'ă·kil·kā*	W/ 2MS SX	
אֶת	*(direct object marker)*	---	particle
אֶת	*'et-*		
הַמָּן	the manna	ABS	noun
מָן	*ham·mān*	W/ DEF. ART.	
אֲשֶׁר	that/which	---	relative pron
אֲשֶׁר	*'ă·šer*		
לֹא־	no/not	---	particle
לֹא	*lō'-*		
יָדַעְתָּ	you know	QAL PF 2MS	verb
ידע	*yā·da'·tā*		
וְלֹא	and no/not	---	particle
לֹא	*yā·də·'ûn*	W/ CONJ וְ	
יָדְעוּן	(they) knew	QAL PF 3CP	verb
ידע	*wə·lō'*	W/ PARAGOGIC ן	
אֲבֹתֶיךָ	your ancestors	CST	noun
אָב	*'ă·vō·tê·kā*	W/ 2MS SX	

לְמַעַן הוֹדִעֲךָ כִּי לֹא עַל־הַלֶּחֶם לְבַדּוֹ יִחְיֶה הָאָדָם

so that you might know that a man does not live by bread alone

לְמַעַן	so that/in order that	---	prep
לְמַעַן	*lə·ma·'an*		

הוֹדִעֲךָ ידע	he makes you know *hō·lî·ḵă·ḵā*	HIPH PF 3MS W/ 2MS SX	verb
כִּי כִּי	that/which *kî*	- - -	conj
לֹא לֹא	no/not *lō'*	- - -	particle
עַל־ עַל	on/upon *'al-*	- - -	prep
הַלֶּחֶם לֶחֶם	(the) bread/food *hal·**le**·ḥem*	ABS W/ DEF. ART.	noun
לְבַדּוֹ לְבַד	alone *lə·vad·**dô***	- - - W/ 3MS SX	adv
יִחְיֶה חיה	(he/it) lives *yiḥ·**ye***	QAL IMPF 3MS	verb
הָאָדָם אָדָם	the man/humanity *hā·'ā·**dām***	ABS W/ DEF. ART.	noun

One may prefer to translate אָדָם as a more gender neutral "one," "human," or "human being," but I retain the masculine here so as not to lose the echo here of the first אָדָם in the garden of Eden. See v. 3c below.

3c   כִּי עַל־כָּל־מוֹצָא פִי־יְהוָה יִחְיֶה הָאָדָם:

but that a man lives by all that comes from the mouth of God.

כִּי כִּי	that/which/but *kî*	- - -	conj
עַל־ עַל	on/upon *'al-*	- - -	prep
כָּל־ כֹּל	all/every *kol-*	CST	noun
מוֹצָא מוֹצָא	that which goes out *mô·ṣā'*	ABS	noun
פִי־ פֶּה	(the) mouth of *fî-*	CST	noun
יְהוָה יהוה	Yahweh *YHWH*	ABS	noun

יִחְיֶה	(he) lives	QAL IMPF 3MS	verb
חיה	*yiḥ·ye*		
הָאָדָם:	the man/humanity	ABS	noun
אָדָם	*hā·'ā·dām*	W/ DEF. ART.	

McConville (2002:170) points out that the "whatever comes out of Yahweh's mouth" that satisfies הָאָדָם (v. 3a) recalls God's provision for אָדָם in the garden of Eden as signified by the land as a place of obedient reward and the wilderness as the place of forgetfulness and disorder (cf. Brueggemann 2001:104). The language of "humanity" within creation is strong and clear such that this lesson has a universal meaning: God's self-revelation is our most basic and essential need.

4 שִׂמְלָתְךָ לֹא בָלְתָה מֵעָלֶיךָ וְרַגְלְךָ לֹא בָצֵקָה זֶה אַרְבָּעִים שָׁנָה:

Your clothing did not wear out on you,
and your foot did not swell these forty years,

שִׂמְלָתְךָ	your garment/clothing	CST	noun
שִׂמְלָה	*śim·lā·tə·kā*	W/ 2MS SX	
לֹא	no/not	---	particle
לֹא	*lō'*		
בָלְתָה	wear out/be consumed	QAL PF 3FS	verb
בלה	*vā·lə·tā*		
מֵעָלֶיךָ	from on/upon you	---	prep
עַל	*mē·'ā·lê·kā*	W/ PREP מִן + 2MS SX	
וְרַגְלְךָ	and your foot	CST	noun
רֶגֶל	*wə·rag·lə·kā*	W/ CONJ וְ + 2MS SX	
לֹא	no/not	---	particle
לֹא	*lō'*		
בָצֵקָה	swell	QAL PF 3FS	verb
בצק	*vā·ṣē·qâ*		
זֶה	this/these	---	demonstr pron
זֶה	*ze*		
אַרְבָּעִים	forty	ABS	cardinal number
אַרְבָּעִים	*'ar·bā·'îm*		
שָׁנָה:	year(s)	ABS	noun
שָׁנָה	*šā·nâ*		

Everyone knows the tremendous toll that a very long journey takes on the body and human resources. God protected Israel for a whole generation of forty years (v. 4c; cf. 2:7; 29:5).

5a	וְיָדַעְתָּ עִם־לְבָבֶךָ כִּי כַּאֲשֶׁר יְיַסֵּר אִישׁ אֶת־בְּנוֹ
	that you might know in your heart that, as a man disciplines his son,

וְיָדַעְתָּ	and you know	QAL WEQATAL 2MS	verb
יָדַע	wə·yā·**da**ʿ·tā		
עִם־	with	---	prep
עִם	ʿim-		
לְבָבֶךָ	your heart	CST	noun
לֵבָב	lə·vā·**ve**·ḵā	W/ PREP לְ + 2MS SX	
כִּי	that/which	---	conj
כִּי	**kî**		
כַּאֲשֶׁר	as/according as	---	relative
אֲשֶׁר	ka·ʾă·šer	W/ PREP כְּ	pron
יְיַסֵּר	(he) disciplines/rebukes	PIEL IMPF 3MS	verb
יסר	yə·yas·**sēr**		
אִישׁ	man/person	ABS	noun
אִישׁ	ʾîš		
אֶת־	(direct object marker)	---	particle
אֵת	ʾet-		
בְּנוֹ	his child	CST	noun
בֵּן	bə·**nô**	W/ 3MS SX	

5b	יְהוָה אֱלֹהֶיךָ מְיַסְּרֶךָּ׃
	so Yahweh your God disciplines you.

יְהוָה	Yahweh	ABS	noun
יהוה	YHWH		
אֱלֹהֶיךָ	your God	CST	noun
אֱלֹהִים	ʾĕ·lō·**hê**·ḵā	W/ 2MS SX	

| מְיַסְּרֶֽךָ׃ | (one) disciplining/ rebuking you | PIEL PTCP MS | verb |
| יסר | mə·yas·sə·**re**·ḵā | W/ 2MS SX | |

Verse 5 resembles Prov 3:11–12 (and Heb 12:5–6), reinforcing the wisdom themes of teaching and learning in Deut 6:6–9. We humans are very much like children who naturally drift and forget our many gifts. The discipline of remembering and recentering is a work of love that we do with God's help.

6a וְשָׁמַרְתָּ֙ אֶת־מִצְוֹ֣ת יְהוָ֣ה אֱלֹהֶ֔יךָ

And you shall observe the commandments of Yahweh your God

וְשָׁמַרְתָּ֙	and you keep/guard/observe	QAL WEQATAL 2MS	verb
שמר	wə·šā·mar·**tā**		
אֶת־	(direct object marker)	---	particle
אֵת	ʾet-		
מִצְוֹ֣ת	(the) commandments of	CST	noun
מִצְוָה	miṣ·**wōt**		
יְהוָ֣ה	Yahweh	ABS	noun
יהוה	YHWH		
אֱלֹהֶ֔יךָ	your God	CST	noun
אֱלֹהִים	ʾĕ·lō·**hê**·ḵā	W/ 2MS SX	

6b לָלֶ֥כֶת בִּדְרָכָ֖יו וּלְיִרְאָ֥ה אֹתֽוֹ׃

by walking in his ways and fearing him,

לָלֶ֥כֶת	to walk/go	QAL INF CST	noun
הלך	lā·**le**·ket	W/ PREP לְ	
בִּדְרָכָ֖יו	in his ways	CST	noun
דֶּרֶךְ	bid·vā·rā·**ḵāyw**	W/ PREP בְּ + 3MS SX	
וּלְיִרְאָ֥ה	and to fear	QAL INF CST	verb
ירא	û·lə·yir·**ʾā**	W/ CONJ וְ + PREP לְ	
אֹתֽוֹ׃	him	---	particle
אֵת	ʾō·**tô**	W/ 3MS SX	

כִּי יְהוָה אֱלֹהֶיךָ מְבִיאֲךָ אֶל־אֶרֶץ טוֹבָה

when Yahweh your God brings you into a good land—

כִּי כִּי	for/because *kî*	---	conj
יְהוָה יהוה	Yahweh *YHWH*	ABS	noun
אֱלֹהֶיךָ אֱלֹהִים	your God *ʾĕ·lō·hê·ḵā*	CST W/ 2MS SX	noun
מְבִיאֲךָ בוא	(one) bringing you *mə·vî·ʾă·ḵā*	HIPH PTCP MS W/ 2MS SX	verb
אֶל־ אֶל	to *ʾel-*	---	prep
אֶרֶץ אֶרֶץ	land/earth *ʾe·reṣ*	ABS	noun
טוֹבָה טוֹב	good/pleasant *ṭô·vâ*	FS ATTR	adj

McConville translates אֶרֶץ טוֹבָה as "delightful land," which, in the light of what Israel receives by sheer grace, is certainly an understatement (2002:165).

אֶרֶץ נַחֲלֵי מָיִם עֲיָנֹת וּתְהֹמֹת

a land with streams of water, springs, and deeps

אֶרֶץ אֶרֶץ	land of *ʾe·reṣ*	CST	noun
נַחֲלֵי נַחַל	streams/brooks of *na·ḥă·lê*	CST	noun
מָיִם מַיִם	water/waters *mā·yim*	ABS	noun
עֲיָנֹת עַיִן	springs *ʿă·yā·nōt*	ABS	noun
וּתְהֹמֹת תְּהוֹם	and deeps *û·tə·hō·mōt*	ABS W/ CONJ וְ	noun

יֹצְאִים בַּבִּקְעָה וּבָהָר:

flowing out in valley and hill,

יֹצְאִים	coming/flowing out	QAL PTCP MP	verb
יצא	*yō·ṣə·ʾîm*		
בַּבִּקְעָה	of the plain/valley	ABS	noun
בִּקְעָה	*bab·bi·qə·ʿâ*	W/ PREP בְּ + DEF. ART.	
וּבָהָר:	and the mountain	ABS	noun
הַר	*û·vā·hār*	W/ CONJ וְ + PREP בְּ + DEF. ART.	

אֶרֶץ חִטָּה וּשְׂעֹרָה וְגֶפֶן וּתְאֵנָה וְרִמּוֹן

a land of wheat and barley, of vines and fig trees and pomegranate trees,

אֶרֶץ	and land of	CST	noun
אֶרֶץ	*ʾe·reṣ*		
חִטָּה	wheat	ABS	noun
חִטָּה	*ḥiṭ·ṭâ*		
וּשְׂעֹרָה	and grain/barley	ABS	noun
שְׂעֹרָה	*û·śə·ʿō·râ*	W/ CONJ וְ	
וְגֶפֶן	and vines	ABS	noun
גֶּפֶן	*wə·ge·fen*	W/ CONJ וְ	
וּתְאֵנָה	and figs	ABS	noun
תְּאֵנָה	*û·tə·ʾē·nâ*	W/ CONJ וְ	
וְרִמּוֹן	and pomegranates	ABS	noun
רִמּוֹן	*wə·rim·môn*	W/ CONJ וְ	

אֶרֶץ־זֵית שֶׁמֶן וּדְבָשׁ:

a land of olives bearing oil and honey,

אֶרֶץ־	land of	CST	noun
אֶרֶץ	*ʾe·reṣ*		
זֵית	olive	CST	noun
זַיִת	*zêt*		

שֶׁמֶן	oil	ABS	noun
שֶׁמֶן *še·men*			
וּדְבָשׁ:	and honey	ABS	noun
דְּבַשׁ *û·də·**vāš***		W/ CONJ וְ	

<table>
<tr><th colspan="4">9a   אֶרֶץ אֲשֶׁר לֹא בְמִסְכֵּנֻת תֹּאכַל־בָּהּ לֶחֶם לֹא־תֶחְסַר כֹּל בָּהּ</th></tr>
</table>

a land in which you will eat bread without scarcity
and in which you will lack nothing,

אֶרֶץ	land	ABS	noun
אֶרֶץ *'e·reṣ*			
אֲשֶׁר	that/which	---	relative pron
אֲשֶׁר *'ă·šer*			
לֹא	no/not	---	particle
לֹא *lō'*			
בְמִסְכֵּנֻת	scarcity/poverty	ABS	noun
מִסְכֵּנֻת *və·mis·kē·**nut***		W/ PREP בְּ	
תֹּאכַל־	you eat	QAL IMPF 2MS	verb
אכל *tō'·kal-*			
בָּהּ	in it	---	prep
בְּ *bāh*		W/ 3FS SX	
לֶחֶם	bread/food	ABS	noun
לֶחֶם *le·ḥem*			
לֹא־	no/not	---	particle
לֹא *lō'-*			
תֶחְסַר	you lack	QAL IMPF 2MS	verb
חסר *teḥ·**sar***			
כֹּל	anything	ABS	noun
כֹּל *kōl*			
בָּהּ	in it	---	prep
בְּ *bāh*		W/ 3FS SX	

אֶרֶץ אֲשֶׁר אֲבָנֶיהָ בַרְזֶל וּמֵהֲרָרֶיהָ תַּחְצֹב נְחֹשֶׁת:

9b

a land whose stones are iron and from whose mountains
you will mine copper.

אֶרֶץ *'e·reṣ*	land	ABS	noun
אֲשֶׁר *'ă·šer*	that/which	---	relative pron
אֲבָנֶיהָ *'ă·vā·nê·hā*	stones	CST W/ 3FS SX	noun
בַרְזֶל *var·zel*	iron	ABS	noun
וּמֵהֲרָרֶיהָ *û·mē·hă·rā·rê·hā*	and from (its/her) hill country/mountains	CST W/ CONJ וְ + PREP מִן + 3FS SX	noun
תַּחְצֹב *taḥ·ṣōv*	you dig/hew	QAL IMPF 2MS	verb
נְחֹשֶׁת: *nə·ḥō·šet*	copper	ABS	noun

10a

וְאָכַלְתָּ וְשָׂבָעְתָּ

When you eat and are satisfied,

וְאָכַלְתָּ *wə·'ā·ḵal·tā*	and you eat	QAL WEQATAL 2MS	verb
וְשָׂבָעְתָּ *wə·śā·vā'·tā*	and you are filled/satisfied	QAL WEQATAL 2MS	verb

10b

וּבֵרַכְתָּ אֶת־יְהוָה אֱלֹהֶיךָ עַל־הָאָרֶץ הַטֹּבָה אֲשֶׁר נָתַן־לָךְ:

then you shall bless Yahweh your God
on the good land he has given you.

וּבֵרַכְתָּ *û·vē·raḵ·tā*	and you bless	PIEL WEQATAL 2MS	verb

אֶת־ אֵת	*(direct object marker)* 'et-	---	particle
יְהוָה יהוה	Yahweh *YHWH*	ABS	noun
אֱלֹהֶיךָ אֱלֹהִים	your God *'ĕ·lō·hê·ḵā*	CST W/ 2MS SX	noun
עַל־ עַל	upon/on account of/for *'al-*	---	prep
הָאָרֶץ אֶרֶץ	the land *hā·'ā·reṣ*	ABS W/ DEF. ART.	noun
הַטֹּבָה טוֹב	(the) good *haṭ·ṭô·vâ*	FS ATTR W/ DEF. ART.	adj
אֲשֶׁר אֲשֶׁר	that/which *'ă·šer*	---	relative pron
נָתַן־ נתן	he gave *nā·tan-*	QAL PF 3MS	verb
לָךְ׃ ל	to you *lāḵ*	--- W/ 2MS SX	prep

11a   הִשָּׁמֶר לְךָ פֶּן־תִּשְׁכַּח אֶת־יְהוָה אֱלֹהֶיךָ

Be careful, lest you forget Yahweh your God

הִשָּׁמֶר שמר	take heed *hiš·šā·mer*	NIPH IMPV MS	verb
לְךָ ל	for/to yourself *lə·ḵā*	--- W/ 2MS SX	prep
פֶּן־ פֶּן	lest *pen-*	---	conj
תִּשְׁכַּח שכח	you forget *tiš·kaḥ*	QAL IMPF 2MS	verb
אֶת־ אֵת	*(direct object marker)* 'et-	---	particle
יְהוָה יהוה	Yahweh *YHWH*	ABS	noun

| אֱלֹהֶיךָ | your God | CST | noun |
| אֱלֹהִים | ʾĕ·lō·hê·ḵā | W/ 2MS SX | |

שכח ("to forget") occurs again in v. 14 and is doubled as an emphatic expression in v. 19 (שָׁכֹחַ תִּשְׁכַּח, "surely forget").

<table>
<tr><td>11b</td><td colspan="3" align="center">לְבִלְתִּי שְׁמֹר מִצְוֹתָיו וּמִשְׁפָּטָיו
וְחֻקֹּתָיו אֲשֶׁר אָנֹכִי מְצַוְּךָ הַיּוֹם:</td></tr>
<tr><td></td><td colspan="3" align="center">by not observing his commands and his judgments
and his statutes that I am commanding you today,</td></tr>
</table>

לְבִלְתִּי	not/except	---	conj
לְבִלְתִּי	lə·ḇil·tî		
שְׁמֹר	to keep/observe	QAL INF CST	verb
שׁמר	šə·mōr		
מִצְוֹתָיו	his commandments	CST	noun
מִצְוָה	miṣ·wō·tāyw	W/ 3MS SX	
וּמִשְׁפָּטָיו	and his judgments/ordinances	CST	noun
מִשְׁפָּט	û·miš·pā·ṭāyw	W/ CONJ וְ + 3MS SX	
וְחֻקֹּתָיו	and his statutes/regulations	CST	noun
חֻקָּה	wə·ḥuq·qō·tāyw	W/ CONJ וְ + 3MS SX	
אֲשֶׁר	that/which	---	relative pron
אֲשֶׁר	ʾă·šer		
אָנֹכִי	I	---	personal pron
אָנֹכִי	ʾā·nō·ḵî		
מְצַוְּךָ	command you	PIEL PTCP MS	verb
צוה	mə·ṣaw·wə·ḵā	W/ 2MS SX	
הַיּוֹם:	today	ABS	noun
יוֹם	hay·yôm	W/ DEF. ART.	

<table>
<tr><td>12a</td><td colspan="3" align="center">פֶּן־תֹּאכַל וְשָׂבָעְתָּ</td></tr>
<tr><td></td><td colspan="3" align="center">lest you eat and are full</td></tr>
</table>

| פֶּן־ | lest | --- | conj |
| פֶּן | pen- | | |

<table>
<tr><td>תֹּאכַל
אכל
tō'·ḵal</td><td>you eat</td><td>QAL IMPF 2MS</td><td>verb</td></tr>
<tr><td>וְשָׂבָעְתָּ
שׂבע
wə·śā·vā'·tā</td><td>and are sated/satisfied</td><td>QAL WEQATAL 2MS</td><td>verb</td></tr>
</table>

<table>
<tr><td>12b</td><td colspan="3" align="center">וּבָתִּים טוֹבִים תִּבְנֶה וְיָשָׁבְתָּ׃</td></tr>
<tr><td></td><td colspan="3">and dwell in good houses that you have built,</td></tr>
</table>

וּבָתִּים בַּיִת *û·vāt·tîm*	and houses	ABS W/ CONJ וּ	noun
טוֹבִים טוֹב *ṭô·vîm*	good/pleasant	MP ATTR	adj
תִּבְנֶה בנה *tiv·ne*	you build	QAL IMPF 2MS	verb
וְיָשָׁבְתָּ׃ ישׁב *wə·yā·šāv·tā*	and you dwell/sit/live	QAL WEQATAL 2MS	verb

<table>
<tr><td>13a</td><td colspan="3" align="center">וּבְקָרְךָ וְצֹאנְךָ יִרְבְּיֻן</td></tr>
<tr><td></td><td colspan="3">and your cattle and your sheep multiply,</td></tr>
</table>

וּבְקָרְךָ בָּקָר *û·və·qā·rə·ḵā*	and your cattle	CST W/ CONJ וּ + 2MS SX	noun
וְצֹאנְךָ צֹאן *wə·ṣō'·nə·ḵā*	and your sheep	CST W/ CONJ וְ + 2MS SX	noun
יִרְבְּיֻן רבה *yir·bə·yun*	multiply	QAL IMPF 3MP W/ PARAGOGIC ן	verb

<table>
<tr><td>13b</td><td colspan="3" align="center">וְכֶסֶף וְזָהָב יִרְבֶּה־לָּךְ</td></tr>
<tr><td></td><td colspan="3">and your silver and gold multiply,</td></tr>
</table>

וְכֶסֶף כֶּסֶף *wə·ḵe·sef*	and silver	ABS W/ CONJ וְ	noun

וְזָהָב	and gold	ABS	noun
זָהָב	wə·zā·**hāv**	W/ CONJ וְ	
יִרְבֶּה־	multiply	QAL IMPF 3MS	verb
רבה	yir·**be**-		
לָךְ	to you/your	---	prep
לְ	**lāk**	W/ 2MS SX	

13c וְכֹל אֲשֶׁר־לְךָ יִרְבֶּה׃

and everything you have multiplies,

וְכֹל	and all/everything	ABS	noun
כֹּל	wə·**kōl**	W/ CONJ וְ	
אֲשֶׁר־	that/which	---	relative pron
אֲשֶׁר	ʾă·**šer**-		
לְךָ	to you/your	---	prep
לְ	lə·**kā**	W/ 2MS SX	
יִרְבֶּה׃	multiplies	QAL IMPF 3MS	verb
רבה	yir·**be**		

14a וְרָם לְבָבֶךָ וְשָׁכַחְתָּ אֶת־יְהוָה אֱלֹהֶיךָ

and then your heart is exalted and you forget Yahweh your God,

וְרָם	and (it) raises/exalts	QAL WEQATAL 3MS	verb
רום	wə·**rām**		
לְבָבֶךָ	your heart	CST	noun
לְבָב	lə·vā·**ve**·kā	W/ 2MS SX	
וְשָׁכַחְתָּ	and you forget	QAL WEQATAL 2MS	verb
שכח	wə·šā·**kaḥ**·tā		
אֶת־	(direct object marker)	---	particle
אֵת	ʾet-		
יְהוָה	Yahweh	ABS	noun
יהוה	YHWH		
אֱלֹהֶיךָ	your God	CST	noun
אֱלֹהִים	ʾĕ·lō·**hê**·kā	W/ 2MS SX	

Prosperity—note the heavy repetition of multiplication—tends to encourage pride and self-sufficiency (vv. 7–13). Every good gift in this world is from the grace of God above (Jas 1:17).

14b הַמּוֹצִיאֲךָ מֵאֶרֶץ מִצְרַיִם מִבֵּית עֲבָדִים:

who brought you out of the land of Egypt, out of the house of slaves,

הַמּוֹצִיאֲךָ יצא	the one who brought you out *ham·mô·ṣî·'ă·ḵā*	HIPH PTCP MS W/ DEF. ART. + 2MS SX	verb
מֵאֶרֶץ אֶרֶץ	from (the) land of *mē·'e·reṣ*	CST W/ PREP מִן	noun
מִצְרַיִם מִצְרַיִם	Egypt *miṣ·ra·yim*	ABS	noun
מִבֵּית בַּיִת	from (the) house of *mib·bêt*	CST W/ PREP מִן	noun
עֲבָדִים: עֶבֶד	slaves/servants *'ă·vā·dîm*	ABS	noun

Moses builds his sermons around two divine gifts: the redemption from Egypt into freedom to serve Yahweh, and the giving of a good and plentiful land.

15a הַמּוֹלִיכֲךָ בַּמִּדְבָּר | הַגָּדֹל וְהַנּוֹרָא

who led you in the great and awesome wilderness—

הַמּוֹלִיכֲךָ הלך	the one who led you *ham·mô·lî·ḵă·ḵā*	HIPH PTCP MS W/ DEF. ART. + 2MS SX	verb
בַּמִּדְבָּר | מִדְבָּר	in/through the dessert *bam·mid·bār*	ABS W/ PREP בְּ + DEF. ART.	noun
הַגָּדֹל גָּדוֹל	(the) great *hag·gā·dōl*	MS ATTR W/ DEF. ART.	adj
וְהַנּוֹרָא ירא	and (the) fearful/terrifying *wə·han·nô·rā'*	NIPH PTCP MS W/ CONJ וְ + DEF. ART.	verb

נָחָשׁ ׀ שָׂרָף וְעַקְרָב וְצִמָּאוֹן אֲשֶׁר אֵין־מָיִם

fiery snakes, and scorpions, and dry ground with no water—

נָחָשׁ ׀	snake	ABS	noun
נָחָשׁ	*nā·ḥāš*		
שָׂרָף	burning/venomous	ABS	noun
שָׂרָף	*śā·rāf*		
וְעַקְרָב	and scorpion	ABS W/ CONJ וְ	noun
עַקְרָב	*wə·ʿaq·rāv*		
וְצִמָּאוֹן	and parched/dry land	ABS W/ CONJ וְ	noun
צִמָּאוֹן	*wə·ṣim·mā·ʾôn*		
אֲשֶׁר	that/which	---	relative pron
אֲשֶׁר	*ʾă·šer*		
אֵין־	no	---	particle
אֵין	*ʾên-*		
מָיִם	water/waters/seas	ABS	noun
מָיִם	*mā·yim*		

הַמּוֹצִיא לְךָ מַיִם מִצּוּר הַחַלָּמִישׁ׃

the one who brought out water for you from the flinty rock,

הַמּוֹצִיא	the one who brought out	HIPH PTCP MS W/ DEF. ART.	verb
יצא	*ham·mô·ṣîʾ*		
לְךָ	for you	--- W/ 2MS SX	prep
לְ	*lə·kā*		
מַיִם	water/waters	ABS	noun
מַיִם	*ma·yim*		
מִצּוּר	from rock	CST W/ PREP מִן	noun
צוּר	*miṣ·ṣûr*		
הַחַלָּמִישׁ׃	the flinty	ABS W/ DEF. ART	noun
חַלָּמִישׁ	*ha·ḥal·lā·mîš*		

הַמַּאֲכִלְךָ מָן בַּמִּדְבָּר אֲשֶׁר לֹא־יָדְעוּן אֲבֹתֶיךָ

who fed you manna that your ancestors did not know,

הַמַּאֲכִלְךָ אכל	the one who fed you *ham·ma·ʾă·ḵil·ḵā*	HIPH PTCP MS W/ DEF. ART. + 2MS SX	verb
מָן מָן	manna *mān*	ABS	noun
בַּמִּדְבָּר מִדְבָּר	in the wilderness/desert *bam·mid·bār*	ABS W/ PREP בְּ + DEF. ART.	noun
אֲשֶׁר אֲשֶׁר	that/which *ʾă·šer*	---	relative pron
לֹא־ לֹא	no/not *lō·*	---	particle
יָדְעוּן ידע	(they) knew *yā·də·ʿûn*	QAL PF 3CP W/ PARAGOGIC נ	verb
אֲבֹתֶיךָ אָב	your ancestors *ʾă·vō·tê·ḵā*	CST W/ 2MS SX	noun

לְמַעַן עַנֹּתְךָ וּלְמַעַן נַסֹּתֶךָ

to humble you and test you,

לְמַעַן לְמַעַן	so that/in order that *lə·ma·ʿan*	---	prep
עַנֹּתְךָ ענה	to humble you *ʿan·nōt·ḵā*	PIEL INF CST W/ 2MS SX	verb
וּלְמַעַן לְמַעַן	and so that/in order that *û·lə·ma·ʿan*	--- W/ CONJ וְ	prep
נַסֹּתֶךָ נסה	to test you *nas·sō·te·ḵā*	PIEL INF CST W/ 2MS SX	verb

לְהֵיטִבְךָ בְּאַחֲרִיתֶךָ:

to prosper you in the end,

לְהֵיטִבְךָ יטב	to do good for you/to you lə·hê·ṭiv·ḵā	HIPH INF CST W/ PREP לְ + 2MS SX	verb
בְּאַחֲרִיתֶךָ: אַחֲרִית	in the end/after these things ba·'a·ḥă·rî·te·ḵā	CST W/ PREP בְּ + 2MS SX	noun

וְאָמַרְתָּ בִּלְבָבֶךָ

and you say in your heart,

וְאָמַרְתָּ אמר	and you will say wə·'ā·mar·tā	QAL WEQATAL 2MS	verb
בִּלְבָבֶךָ לֵבָב	in your heart bil·vā·və·ḵā	ABS W/ PREP בְּ + 2MS SX	noun

This is a moment that ethicists call "conscience," or moral reflection on one's actions and motives. Despite what may seem to be a simple phrase, "in your heart" points to a complex moral concept and the immensely challenging task of testing the motives that lie behind our actions.

כֹּחִי וְעֹצֶם יָדִי עָשָׂה לִי אֶת־הַחַיִל הַזֶּה:

'My power and the strength of my hand
have acquired this wealth for me.'

כֹּחִי כֹּחַ	my power/strength kō·ḥî	ABS W/ 1CS SX	noun
וְעֹצֶם עֹצֶם	and (the) strength of wə·'ō·ṣem	CST W/ CONJ וְ	noun
יָדִי יָד	my hand yā·dî	ABS W/ 1CS SX	noun
עָשָׂה עשה	(it) made 'ā·śâ	QAL PF 3MS	verb
לִי לְ	for me lî	--- W/ 1CS SX	prep

אֶת־	(direct object marker)	---	particle
אֵת	*'et-*		
הַחַיִל	(the) wealth	ABS	noun
חַיִל	*ha·ḥa·yil*	W/ DEF. ART.	
הַזֶּה	(the) this	---	demonst
זֶה	*haz·ze*	W/ DEF. ART.	pron

18a   וְזָכַרְתָּ אֶת־יְהוָה אֱלֹהֶיךָ

But remember Yahweh your God,

וְזָכַרְתָּ	and you will remember	QAL WEQATAL 2MS	verb
זכר	*wə·zā·ḵar·tā*		
אֶת־	(direct object marker)	---	particle
אֵת	*'et-*		
יְהוָה	Yahweh	ABS	proper noun
יהוה	*YHWH*		
אֱלֹהֶיךָ	your God	ABS	noun
אֱלֹהִים	*'ĕ·lō·hê·ḵā*	W/ 2MS SX	

Remembering God's grace to us (see v. 18b) is the antidote to pride.

18b   כִּי הוּא הַנֹּתֵן לְךָ כֹּחַ לַעֲשׂוֹת חָיִל

for it is he who gives you strength to acquire wealth,

כִּי	for/because	---	conj
כִּי	*kî*		
הוּא	he	---	personal pron
הוּא	*hû'*		
הַנֹּתֵן	the one who gives	QAL PTCP MS	verb
נתן	*han·nō·tēn*	W/ DEF. ART.	
לְךָ	to you	---	prep
לְ	*lə·ḵā*	W/ 2MS SX	
כֹּחַ	power/strength	ABS	noun
כֹּחַ	*kō·aḥ*		

לַעֲשׂוֹת	to make	QAL INF CST	verb
עשׂה	la·ʿă·śôt	W/ PREP לְ	
חַיִל	wealth	ABS	noun
חַיִל	ḥā·yil		

18c לְמַ֫עַן הָקִים אֶת־בְּרִיתוֹ אֲשֶׁר־נִשְׁבַּע לַאֲבֹתֶיךָ כַּיּוֹם הַזֶּה:

so that he might establish his covenant,
which he swore to your ancestors, as is the case today."

לְמַ֫עַן	so that/in order that	---	conj
לְמַעַן	lə·ma·ʿan		
הָקִים	he will/may establish	HIPH INF CST	verb
קום	hā·qîm		
אֶת־	(direct object marker)	---	particle
אֶת	ʾet-		
בְּרִיתוֹ	his covenant	ABS	noun
בְּרִית	bə·rî·tô	W/ 3MS SX	
אֲשֶׁר־	that/which	---	relative pron
אֲשֶׁר	ʾă·šer-		
נִשְׁבַּע	he swore	NIPH PF 3MS	verb
שׁבע	niš·baʿ		
לַאֲבֹתֶיךָ	to your ancestors	ABS	noun
אָב	la·ʾă·vō·tê·ḵā	W/ PREP לְ + 2MS SX	
כַּיּוֹם	as/like (the) day	ABS	noun
יוֹם	kay·yôm	W/ DEF. ART. + PREP כְּ	
הַזֶּה	(the) this	---	demonstr pron
זֶה	haz·ze	W/ DEF. ART.	

Gifts, Gratitude, and Memory

 *Gift.* In the "From Text to Sermon" section on 1:1–8, we reflected on the relationship between God's unfolding gift and hope—our faith in a promise laid up for us in the future. In this chapter, God's generosity is turned around to a memory of gifts given *in the past.*

In his book *The Gift*, Kenneth Schmitz examines the difference between a present and a gift (1982:45–48). We all give presents as a matter of friendly exchange. There is nothing wrong with presents of course, but social convention has made us not only expect them but also seek to reciprocate with something of similar value. In this way, a present stands apart from a gift, which is not an exchange but giving characterized by "contingency," "vulnerability," and "surprise" (p. 44). Rather than giving a present in return, the only appropriate response to a gift is reception and gratitude. In this way, we can see that presents bless us in mostly expected ways, while gifts surprise us and turn us to admiration for the giver.

This helps us pull together the flow of the argument that started in Deut 6–7. God has set his love upon Israel, not in exchange, and not on the basis of merit, but contingently and surprisingly (7:7–8). He gives because of his sheer goodness, as Augustine recognized so well. Moses labors to characterize redemption from Egypt (8:14), protection in the wilderness (8:2–4), and provision of the land ahead (8:7–10) as being the result of God's promise and his contingent (uncompelled) giving. It is simply impossible for us to reciprocate anything to God that matches these gifts.

Theologically, this teaching about gifts points to the broader context of three great divine gifts. In the first great gift, the eternal Father eternally begets a Son. We may easily pass by the way "begetting" manifests giving. But to have a Son is to have been generous in giving from all eternity. Likewise, through the Son, the Father breathes forth the Spirit. From before time, then, these three persons of the Trinity are marked by inner goodness and generosity; the three persons are constantly engaged in the giving and receiving of their mutual love.

Second, God's giving flows out "in the beginning" (Gen 1:1) when he creates the world and crafts a place in which to further share his internal giving and receiving. This is an answer to what may be the deepest of all philosophical questions: "Why is there anything at all?" Psalm 104 offers a long meditation on God's work of creation and the fruitfulness and flourishing that come from his hand. God's creatures proclaim in response, "all wait for you to feed them in their time" (v. 27). God made the creation to await the reception of his good gifts. Why is there anything at all? At the very least, the world exists because of God's infinite love and generosity.

Third, God sent forth his Son as a redeeming gift to a fallen world. Echoing the words of Genesis, Jesus is the "firstborn of all creation" (Col 1:15), the λόγος (word, explanation, divine mind, order) who was "in the beginning" (John 1:1). In Jesus, it is right to see the gift of a new creation (2 Cor 5:17–21; Rom 8:19–23). Looking upon Christ, we are reminded of the renewed gift of ourselves, our world, and of himself in love and union.

 *Gratitude.* We know a gift can be refused, just as it can be received with gratitude. Paul commends us to give thanks "always" (Eph 5:20), "in all things" (1 Thess 5:18), and to "be thankful" (Col 3:15). After all, the creation, our lives, our callings, our families, our daily blessings, and our salvation are all from God. "What do you have that you did not receive?" (1 Cor 4:7).

As Israel enters the land, Moses' words remind them that their suffering in the wilderness was meant to teach them a lesson: the miraculous provision of water, manna, and clothing that did not wear out all came from a good and great Giver of gifts.

Having learned to live in dependency, they will enter the land and soon begin to grow, reproduce, plant, eat, and build. Without extreme care and discipline, they will soon imagine these things as the result of their own work (Deut 8:11–16)—to see themselves as merited, rather than recipients of blessing. We can look ahead from Deuteronomy to places like Ps 50 where Israel, in the midst of trouble, multiplies its burnt offerings in hope of God's help. Twice God tells them that what he desires in the end is not sacrifice but "thanksgiving" (vv. 14, 23; cf. Ps 95). What he most wants from us is to remember our Giver.

Memory. The primary form gratitude takes in Deut 8 is remembrance. In his book *The Shallows*, Nicholas Carr aptly warns us, "Outsource memory and culture withers" (2010:197). Carr is addressing the way increasing addiction to technology and distraction inhibits the life and storytelling of a community. This leads to the death of long-term cultural memory and the identity of a people. The danger was just as real for Israel. Distracted by the present, they would forget God's work in the past, leading them straight to apostasy in the future.

As we can see in Deut 8, we are not interested in memory for memory's sake but in memory's power to renew gratitude and our focus on the Giver. In the first century, the Roman philosopher Seneca penned his book *De beneficiis*, which was likely the most influential book on gratitude among Christian theologians until the nineteenth century (when we started to forget gratitude). Seneca pointed out that many things get in the way of gratitude such as greed and envy, but nothing compares to the tragedy of forgetfulness (in Leithart 2014:44–55). "The man is ungrateful who denies that he has received a benefit; who pretends that he has not received it; who does not return it. The most ungrateful man of all is he who forgets it" (*De beneficiis* 3.2). Thus Ps 106 recites God's many works while reminding Israel that they "did not remember" (v. 7). This led God to do more mighty works, yet again they "forgot" (v. 13), and "forgot" (v. 21). In the end, Yahweh was the one to "remember" his covenant and deliver them (v. 45). God's perfect memory renews his mercy towards those who forget.

It should be obvious, then, that "memory makes a person grateful" (Leithart 2014:51). One can illustrate this well with the story of Mordecai in the book of Esther. On the night that king Ahasuerus lay awake, sleepless, he asked for a "book of memories" (סֵפֶר הַזִּכְרֹנוֹת) to be brought to him (Esther 6:1). As the book is read, he hears the story of Mordecai uncovering a plot to assassinate him. Ahasuerus' memory of the event sparks the king's gratitude, which leads the king to honor Mordecai, which eventually results in the protection of the Jews. From memory to gratitude to mercy.

So how can we go about remembering in our communities? In his book on Jewish memory, Yosef Yerushalmi reminds us that forgetting can occur "abruptly or by a process of erosion" (1982:109). The tradition we find in the Old Testament retains memory through the two "channels" of "ritual and recital" (p. 11)—lives that ritualize gathering and storytelling. The rituals provide the times and physical habits for the community to gather where they rehearse the significance of the ritual in word, prayer, and song.

Passover and other major feasts may be the most obvious rituals in our minds. These feasts also closely resemble the Christian sacraments of baptism and the Lord's Supper, which makes sense as almost all of the earliest Christians were Jewish. This may also shed some light on the history of adopting holy days and seasons such Advent, Christmas, Epiphany, Ash Wednesday, and Lent. Liturgical scholar Massey Shepherd (1952:104) comments:

Every season and every holy day of the Christian year is for us an advent, a coming in the present time of God's mighty acts of old in His Christ and in His saints. When we "make memorial" of them we relive them as though we ourselves were the very historic participants in the drama, the very ones who were summoned to make a choice and take a stand for God and for his Christ.

Shepherd thus highlights the *responsibility* inherent in community memory. We all are participants in this process. Here is how Yerushalmi (1982:109) puts it:

When we say a people "remembers," we are really saying that a past has been actively transmitted to the present generation and that this past has been accepted as meaningful. Conversely, a people forgets when the generation that now possesses the past does not convey it to the next, or when the latter rejects what it receives and does not pass it onward.

When Jesus commands the church to "do this in remembrance of me," we take up our commitment to do, remember, and give thanks to the Giver of all, and to pass this habit on to the next generation in the basic ritual of breaking bread and blessing wine.

LOVE, FEAR, SERVE YAHWEH

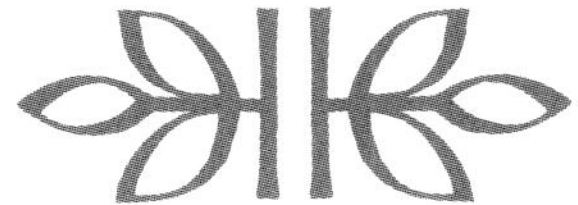

Many scholars view Deut 10–11 as a long closure to the sermon that began in 6:1. Its long list of imperatives prepares the audience to hear and keep the laws in chs. 12–26. Richard Nelson (2004:133) summarizes it this way:

> Recurring admonitions accumulate with persistent force. . . . The reader is repeatedly urged to "love" (10:2; 11:1, 13, 22), "fear" and "serve" (10:12, 20), "walk" (10:12; 11:22), "cling" (10:20; 11:22), and "keep" the law (10:13; 11:1, 8, 22; cf. 11:16).

This leaves the reader anxious to finally begin reading the laws, warned that future life in the land will depend on giving everything they have to the way of the Lord.

LARGER LITERARY CONTEXT ▸ 10:1–11:32

12a
וְעַתָּה֙ יִשְׂרָאֵ֔ל מָ֚ה יְהוָ֣ה אֱלֹהֶ֔יךָ שֹׁאֵ֖ל מֵעִמָּ֑ךְ

wəʿattâ yiśrāʾēl māh YHWH ʾĕlōhêḵā šōʾēl mēʿimmāḵ

And now, O Israel, what does Yahweh your God demand of you?—

12b
כִּ֣י אִם־לְיִרְאָ֞ה אֶת־יְהוָ֤ה אֱלֹהֶ֙יךָ֙

kî ʾim-ləyirʾâ ʾet-YHWH ʾĕlōhêḵā

but only to fear Yahweh your God,

12c
לָלֶ֙כֶת֙ בְּכָל־דְּרָכָ֔יו

lāleḵet bəḵol-dərāḵāyw

to walk in all his ways,

12d
וּלְאַהֲבָ֣ה אֹת֔וֹ

ûləʾahăvâ ʾōtô

and to love him,

12e
וְלַעֲבֹד֙ אֶת־יְהוָ֣ה אֱלֹהֶ֔יךָ

wəlaʿăvōd ʾet-YHWH ʾĕlōhêḵā

to serve Yahweh your God

12f
בְּכָל־לְבָבְךָ֖ וּבְכָל־נַפְשֶֽׁךָ׃

bəḵol-ləvāvḵā ûvəḵol-nafšeḵā.

with all your heart and with all your life force,

13
לִשְׁמֹ֞ר אֶת־מִצְוֺ֣ת יְהוָ֗ה

lišmōr ʾet-miṣwōt YHWH

וְאֶת־חֻקֹּתָ֛יו אֲשֶׁ֥ר אָנֹכִ֖י מְצַוְּךָ֣ הַיּ֑וֹם לְט֖וֹב לָֽךְ׃

wəʾet-ḥuqqōtāyw ʾăšer ʾānōḵî məṣawwəḵā hayyôm ləṭôv lāḵ.

to keep the commands of Yahweh [your God]
and the ordinances that I am commanding you today for your good.

14a   הֵן לַיהוָה אֱלֹהֶיךָ הַשָּׁמַיִם וּשְׁמֵי הַשָּׁמָיִם

hēn la*YHWH ʾĕlōhêkā haššāmayim ûšəmê haššāmāyim*

See, to Yahweh your God belong heaven and the highest heavens,

14b   הָאָרֶץ וְכָל־אֲשֶׁר־בָּהּ׃

hāʾāreṣ vəkol-ʾăšer-bāh.

the earth and all that is in it.

15a   רַק בַּאֲבֹתֶיךָ חָשַׁק יְהוָה לְאַהֲבָה אוֹתָם

raq baʾăvōtêkā ḥāšaq YHWH ləʾahăvâ ʾôtām

Yet it was only your ancestors that Yahweh desired to love,

15b   וַיִּבְחַר בְּזַרְעָם אַחֲרֵיהֶם

wayyivḥar bəzarʿām ʾaḥărêhem

and he chose their descendants after them—

15c   בָּכֶם מִכָּל־הָעַמִּים כַּיּוֹם הַזֶּה׃

bākem mikkol-hāʿammîm kayyôm hazze.

you—from among all peoples, as it is to this day.

16a   וּמַלְתֶּם אֵת עָרְלַת לְבַבְכֶם

ûmaltem ʾēt ʿorlat ləvāvkem

Circumcise the foreskin of your heart,

16b   וְעָרְפְּכֶם לֹא תַקְשׁוּ עוֹד׃

wəʿorpəkem lōʾ taqšû ʿôd.

and stiffen your neck no longer.

17a   כִּי יְהוָה אֱלֹהֵיכֶם הוּא אֱלֹהֵי הָאֱלֹהִים וַאֲדֹנֵי הָאֲדֹנִים

kî YHWH ʾĕlōhêkem hûʾ ʾĕlōhê hāʾĕlōhîm waʾădōnê hāʾădōnîm

For Yahweh your God—he is God of gods and Lord of lords,

17b   הָאֵל הַגָּדֹל הַגִּבֹּר וְהַנּוֹרָא

hāʾēl haggādōl haggibbōr wəhannôrāʾ

the great, the mighty, and the awesome God,

17c   אֲשֶׁר֙ לֹא־יִשָּׂ֣א פָנִ֔ים וְלֹ֥א יִקַּ֖ח שֹֽׁחַד׃

ʾăšer lōʾ-yiśśāʾ fānîm wəlōʾ yiqqaḥ šōḥad.

who does not show favor or take a bribe,

18a   עֹשֶׂ֛ה מִשְׁפַּ֥ט יָת֖וֹם וְאַלְמָנָ֑ה

ʿōśe mišpaṭ yātôm wəʾalmānâ

doing justice to the orphan and widow

18b   וְאֹהֵ֣ב גֵּ֔ר לָ֥תֶת ל֖וֹ לֶ֥חֶם וְשִׂמְלָֽה׃

wəʾōhēv gēr lātet lô leḥem wəśimlâ.

and loving the sojourner, giving them clothing.

19   וַאֲהַבְתֶּ֖ם אֶת־הַגֵּ֑ר כִּֽי־גֵרִ֥ים הֱיִיתֶ֖ם בְּאֶ֥רֶץ מִצְרָֽיִם׃

waʾăhavtem ʾet-haggēr kî-gērîm hĕyîtem bəʾereṣ miṣrāyim.

So you shall love the sojourner, for you were sojourners
in the land of Egypt.

20a   אֶת־יְהוָ֧ה אֱלֹהֶ֛יךָ תִּירָ֖א

ʾet-YHWH ʾĕlōhêkā tîrāʾ

Yahweh your God you shall fear;

20b   אֹת֣וֹ תַעֲבֹ֑ד וּב֣וֹ תִדְבָּ֔ק וּבִשְׁמ֖וֹ תִּשָּׁבֵֽעַ׃

ʾōtô taʿăvōd ûvô tidbāq ûvišmô tiššāvēaʿ.

him you shall serve, and to him you shall cling,
and in his name you shall swear.

21   ה֥וּא תְהִלָּתְךָ֖ וְה֣וּא אֱלֹהֶ֑יךָ אֲשֶׁר־עָשָׂ֣ה אִתְּךָ֗

hûʾ təhillātəkā wəhûʾ ʾĕlōhêkā ʾăšer-ʿāśâ ʾittəkā

אֶת־הַגְּדֹלֹ֤ת וְאֶת־הַנּֽוֹרָאֹת֙ הָאֵ֔לֶּה אֲשֶׁ֥ר רָא֖וּ עֵינֶֽיךָ׃

ʾet-haggədōlōt wəʾet-hannôrāʾōt hāʾelle ʾăšer rāʾû ʿênêkā.

He is your praise, and he is your God, who did for you
these great and awesome things your eyes have seen.

22a   בְּשִׁבְעִ֣ים נֶ֔פֶשׁ יָרְד֥וּ אֲבֹתֶ֖יךָ מִצְרָ֑יְמָה

bəšivʿîm nefeš yārədû ʾăvōtêkā miṣrāyəmāh

As seventy people your ancestors went down to Egypt,

וְעַתָּה שָׂמְךָ֙ יְהוָ֣ה אֱלֹהֶ֔יךָ כְּכוֹכְבֵ֥י הַשָּׁמַ֖יִם לָרֹֽב׃

wəʿattâ śāməkā YHWH ʾĕlōhêkā kəkôkəvê haššāmayim lārōv.

but now Yahweh your God has made you as numerous as the stars of heaven.

12a	וְעַתָּה יִשְׂרָאֵל מָה יְהוָה אֱלֹהֶיךָ שֹׁאֵל מֵעִמָּךְ

And now, O Israel, what does Yahweh your God demand of you?—

וְעַתָּה	And now	---	adv
עַתָּה	*wə·ʿat·tâ*	W/ CONJ וְ	
יִשְׂרָאֵל	Israel	ABS	noun
יִשְׂרָאֵל	*yiś·rā·ʾēl*		
מָה	what	---	interr
מָה	*māh*		pron
יְהוָה	Yahweh	ABS	noun
יהוה	*YHWH*		
אֱלֹהֶיךָ	your God	CST	noun
אֱלֹהִים	*ʾĕ·lō·hê·kā*	W/ 2MS SX	
שֹׁאֵל	ask/asking	QAL PTCP MS	verb
שאל	*šō·ʾēl*		
מֵעִמָּךְ	from you/from with you	---	prep
עִם	*mē·ʿim·māk*	W/ PREP מִן + 2MS SX	

וְעַתָּה ("and now") marks a transition from ch. 9 and the long history of Israel's rebellion, Moses' intercession, and God's mercy. Israel's proper response, as stated in ch. 8, is to receive God's gifts and share them within the community.

כִּי אִם־לְיִרְאָה אֶת־יְהוָה אֱלֹהֶיךָ

but only to fear Yahweh your God,

כִּי אִם־	except/but	---	conj
כִּי אִם־	*kî ʾim-*		
לְיִרְאָה	to fear	QAL INF CST W/ PREP לְ	verb
ירא	*lə·yir·ʾâ*		
אֶת־	*(direct object marker)*	---	particle
אֶת	*ʾet-*		
יְהוָה	Yahweh	ABS	noun
יהוה	*YHWH*		
אֱלֹהֶיךָ	your God	CST W/ 2MS SX	noun
אֱלֹהִים	*ĕ·lō·hê·kā*		

Verse 12 makes these three requirements—reverence, obedience, and fear—nearly synonymous.

לָלֶכֶת בְּכָל־דְּרָכָיו

to walk in all his ways,

לָלֶכֶת	to walk/go	QAL INF CST W/ PREP לְ	verb
הלך	*lā·le·ket*		
בְּכָל־	in all of	CST W/ PREP בְּ	noun
כֹּל	*bə·kol-*		
דְּרָכָיו	his ways	CST W/ 3MS SX	noun
דֶּרֶךְ	*də·rā·kāyw*		

וּלְאַהֲבָה אֹתוֹ

and to love him,

וּלְאַהֲבָה	and to love	QAL INF CST W/ CONJ וְ + PREP לְ	verb
אהב	*û·lə·ʾa·hă·vâ*		
אֹתוֹ	him	---	particle
אֵת	*ʾō·tô*	W/ 3MS SX	

See 6:5 and 11:1. Love in this context points to both affection and loyal obedience, as clearly indicated by עבד ("serve") below.

<table>
<tr><td>12e</td><td colspan="3" align="center">וּֽלְעָבֹד֙ אֶת־יְהוָ֣ה אֱלֹהֶ֔יךָ</td></tr>
<tr><td></td><td colspan="3" align="center">to serve Yahweh your God</td></tr>
</table>

וּֽלְעָבֹד֙ עבד	and to serve *wə·la·ʿă· vōd*	QAL INF CST W/ CONJ וּ + PREP לְ	verb
אֶת־ אֵת	*(direct object marker)* *ʾet-*	---	particle
יְהוָ֣ה יהוה	Yahweh *YHWH*	ABS	noun
אֱלֹהֶ֔יךָ אֱלֹהִים	your God *ʾĕ·lō·hê·kā*	CST W/ 2MS SX	noun

<table>
<tr><td>12f</td><td colspan="3" align="center">בְּכָל־לְבָבְךָ֖ וּבְכָל־נַפְשֶֽׁךָ׃</td></tr>
<tr><td></td><td colspan="3" align="center">with all your heart and with all your life force,</td></tr>
</table>

בְּכָל־ כֹּל	with all *bə·kol-*	CST W/ PREP בְּ	noun
לְבָבְךָ֖ לֵבָב	your heart *lə·vāv·kā*	CST W/ 2MS SX	noun
וּבְכָל־ כֹּל	and with all *û·və·kol-*	CST W/ CONJ וּ + PREP בְּ	noun
נַפְשֶֽׁךָ׃ נֶפֶשׁ	your soul/life/life force *naf·še·kā*	CST W/ 2MS SX	noun

Chapters 10–11 begin to close the sermon that began in 6:1, reemphasizing the total commitment required of Yahweh's people.

לִשְׁמֹר אֶת־מִצְוֺת יְהוָה
וְאֶת־חֻקֹּתָיו אֲשֶׁר אָנֹכִי מְצַוְּךָ הַיּוֹם לְטוֹב לָךְ:

to keep the commands of Yahweh [your God]
and the ordinances that I am commanding you today for your good.

לִשְׁמֹר שׁמר	to keep/guard *liš·mōr*	QAL INF CST W/ PREP לְ	verb
אֶת־ אֵת	(direct object marker) *ʾet-*	---	particle
מִצְוֺת מִצְוָה	(the) commandments of *miṣ·wōt*	CST	noun
יְהוָה יהוה	Yahweh *YHWH*	ABS	noun
וְאֶת־ אֵת	and (+ *direct object marker*) *wə·ʾet-*	--- W/ CONJ וְ	particle
חֻקֹּתָיו חֻקָּה	his statutes/regulations *ḥuq·qō·tāyw*	CST W/ 3MS SX	noun
אֲשֶׁר אֲשֶׁר	that/which *ʾă·šer*	---	relative pron
אָנֹכִי אָנֹכִי	I *ʾā·nō·kî*	---	personal pron
מְצַוְּךָ צוה	command/(am) commanding you *mə·ṣaw·wə·kā*	PIEL PTCP MS W/ 2MS SX	verb
הַיּוֹם יוֹם	today *hay·yôm*	ABS W/ DEF. ART.	noun
לְטוֹב טוֹב	for good/that it may go well *lə·ṭôv*	ABS W/ PREP לְ	noun
לָךְ: לְ	with/for you *lāk*	--- W/ 2MS SX	prep

Several ancient versions add אֱלֹהֶיךָ ("your God") after יְהוָה ("Yahweh") to keep the verse in parallel with the typical formula (4:2; 6:17; 8:6; 11:27–28, etc.; Nelson 2002:131).

See also variations of the phrase "for your good" in 6:24 and 8:14. It bears remembering that while the law was a burden because of human sin (Rom 7:13), its purpose was always to make Israel flourish and live long in the land.

See, to Yahweh your God belong heaven and the highest heavens,

הֵן	see/behold	---	particle
הֵן	*hēn*		
לַיהוָה	to Yahweh	ABS W/ PREP לְ	noun
יהוה	*la·YHWH*		
אֱלֹהֶיךָ	your God	CST W/ 2MS SX	noun
אֱלֹהִים	*ʾĕ·lō·hê·ḵā*		
הַשָּׁמַיִם	(are) the heavens	ABS W/ DEF. ART.	noun
שָׁמַיִם	*haš·šā·ma·yim*		
וּשְׁמֵי	and (the) heaven(s) of	CST W/ CONJ וְ	noun
שָׁמַיִם	*û·šə·mê*		
הַשָּׁמָיִם	the heavens	ABS W/ DEF. ART.	noun
שָׁמַיִם	*haš·šā·mā·yim*		

The Hebrew "heaven of heavens" is a superlative. See v. 17a.

the earth and all that is in it.

הָאָרֶץ	the earth	ABS W/ DEF. ART.	noun
אֶרֶץ	*hā·ʾā·reṣ*		
וְכָל־	and all	ABS W/ CONJ וְ	noun
כֹּל	*və·ḵol-*		
אֲשֶׁר־	that/which	---	relative pron
אֲשֶׁר	*ʾă·šer-*		
בָּה׃	(is) in it	--- W/ 3FS SX	prep
בְּ	*bāh*		

God's possession of all good gifts (see "From Text to Sermon" for Deut 8 above; cf. Ps 24) grounds our understanding of human life and benefits. Everything is given to us.

Yet it was only your ancestors that Yahweh desired to love,

רַק	only	---	adv
רַק	*raq*		
בַּאֲבֹתֶיךָ	in/on your fathers	CST	noun
אָב	*ba·ʾă·vō·tɛ̂·ḵā*	W/ PREP בְּ + 2MS SX	
חָשַׁק	(he) attached/set	QAL PF 3MS	verb
חשק	*ḥā·šaq*		
יְהוָה	Yahweh	ABS	noun
יהוה	*YHWH*		
לְאַהֲבָה	to love	QAL INF CST	verb
אהב	*lə·ʾa·hă·vâ*	W/ PREP לְ	
אוֹתָם	them	---	particle
אֵת	*ʾô·tām*	W/ 3MP SX	

Also used of Yahweh in 7:7, חשק is difficult to render. Some choose "set his heart on," or "desire." We should compare the passionate, even scandalous connotation of חשק in 21:11. Suffice it to say, this is not just banal kindness and admiration, but inflamed love (Levenson 2016:40–42, 172–78).

and he chose their descendants after them—

וַיִּבְחַר	and he chose	QAL WAYY 3MS	verb
בחר	*way·yiv·ḥar*		
בְּזַרְעָם	(in) their seed/offspring	CST	noun
זֶרַע	*bə·zar·ʾām*	W/ PREP בְּ + 3MP SX	
אַחֲרֵיהֶם	after them	---	prep
אַחֲרֵי	*ʾa·ḥă·rê·hem*	W/ 3MP SX	

בחר ("to choose") recalls God's free and passionate choice of Israel in 7:6–8.

בָּכֶם מִכָּל־הָעַמִּים כַּיּוֹם הַזֶּה׃

| 15c | you—from among all peoples, as it is to this day. |

בָּכֶם	(in) you	---	prep
בְּ	*bā·kem*	W/ 2MP SX	
מִכָּל־	from all	CST	noun
כֹּל	*mik·kol-*	W/ PREP מִן	
הָעַמִּים	the peoples/nations	ABS	noun
עַם	*hā·'am·mîm*	W/ DEF. ART.	
כַּיּוֹם	as (the) day	ABS	noun
יוֹם	*kay·yôm*	W/ PREP כְּ + DEF. ART.	
הַזֶּה׃	(the) this	---	demonsrt
זֶה	*haz·ze*	W/ DEF. ART.	pron

וּמַלְתֶּם אֵת עָרְלַת לְבַבְכֶם

| 16a | Circumcise the foreskin of your heart, |

וּמַלְתֶּם	and circumcise	QAL WEQATAL 2MS	verb
מוּל	*û·mal·tem*		
אֵת	*(direct object marker)*	---	particle
אֵת	*'ēt*		
עָרְלַת	(the) foreskin of	CST	noun
עָרְלָה	*'or·lat*		
לְבַבְכֶם	your heart	CST	noun
לֵבָב	*lə·vāv·kem*	W/ 2MP SX	

The risk of future disobedience looms darkly over the whole book. Moses returns to the necessity for God to circumcise the heart in 30:6 (cf. Jer 4:4). Before his death, Stephen appears to draw on this saying in his accusation of the Jewish people (Acts 7:51).

וְעָרְפְּכֶם לֹא תַקְשׁוּ עוֹד׃

| 16b | and stiffen your neck no longer. |

וְעָרְפְּכֶם	and your neck	CST	noun
עֹרֶף	*wə·'or·pə·kem*	W/ CONJ וְ + 2MP SX	

לֹא	no/not	---	particle
לֹא	*lōʾ*		
תַקְשׁוּ	you (all) stiffen	HIPH IMPF 2MP	verb
קשה	*taq·šû*		
עֽוֹד׃	anymore	---	adv
עוֹד	*ʿôd*		

The stiff neck is the second bodily metaphor (see the hard heart in v. 16a), emphasizing the drastic commitment Israel will have to make to remembering, repenting, and returning to God. It is, as we will see in 30:6, too great a demand.

> **17a** כִּי יְהוָה אֱלֹהֵיכֶם הוּא אֱלֹהֵי הָאֱלֹהִים וַאֲדֹנֵי הָאֲדֹנִים
>
> For Yahweh your God—he is God of gods and Lord of lords,

כִּי	For/so that/because	---	conj
כִּי	*kî*		
יְהוָה	Yahweh	ABS	noun
יהוה	*YHWH*		
אֱלֹהֵיכֶם	your God	CST	noun
אֱלֹהִים	*ʾĕ·lō·hê·ḵem*	W/ 2MP SX	
הוּא	he	---	personal
הוּא	*hûʾ*		pron
אֱלֹהֵי	(is) God	CST	noun
אֱלֹהִים	*ʾĕ·lō·hê*		
הָאֱלֹהִים	of (the) gods	ABS	noun
אֱלֹהִים	*hā·ʾĕ·lō·hîm*	W/ DEF. ART.	
וַאֲדֹנֵי	and Lord	CST	noun
אָדוֹן	*wa·ʾă·dō·nê*	W/ CONJ וְ	
הָאֲדֹנִים	of (the) lords	ABS	noun
אָדוֹן	*hā·ʾă·dō·nîm*	W/ DEF. ART.	

These superlatives echo the superlative in v. 14.

הָאֵל הַגָּדֹל הַגִּבֹּר וְהַנּוֹרָא

the great, the mighty, and the awesome God,

הָאֵל אֵל	(the) God *hā·ʾēl*	ABS W/ DEF. ART.	noun
הַגָּדֹל גָּדוֹל	the great *hag·gā·dōl*	MS ATTR W/ DEF. ART.	adj
הַגִּבֹּר גִּבּוֹר	the mighty *hag·gib·bōr*	MS ATTR W/ DEF. ART.	adj
וְהַנּוֹרָא ירא	the awesome/terrifying *wə·han·nô·rāʾ*	NIPH PTCP MS W/ CONJ וְ + DEF. ART.	verb

אֲשֶׁר לֹא־יִשָּׂא פָנִים וְלֹא יִקַּח שֹׁחַד׃

who does not show favor or take a bribe,

אֲשֶׁר אֲשֶׁר	who/that/which *ʾă·šer*	---	relative pron
לֹא־ לֹא	no/not *lōʾ-*	---	particle
יִשָּׂא נשא	(he) lifts up (prefers) *yiś·śāʾ*	QAL IMPF 3MS	verb
פָנִים פָּנֶה	faces *fā·nîm*	ABS	noun
וְלֹא לֹא	and no/not *wə·lōʾ*	W/ CONJ וְ	particle
יִקַּח לקח	(he) takes *yiq·qaḥ*	QAL IMPF 3MS	verb
שֹׁחַד׃ שֹׁחַד	bribe *šō·ḥad*	ABS	noun

To "lift up the face" is obviously a figure of speech (cf. 2 Chr 19:7; Job 34:19). Also, God's just character, וְלֹא יִקַּח שֹׁחַד ("he does not take a bribe") is meant to be imitated by the leaders and individual Israelites (16:19; 27:25).

עֹשֶׂה מִשְׁפַּט יָתוֹם וְאַלְמָנָה

doing justice to the orphan and widow

עֹשֶׂה עֹשֶׂה	(one) doing/making *ʿō·śe*	QAL PTCP MS	verb
מִשְׁפַּט מִשְׁפָּט	justice of/for *miš·paṭ*	CST	noun
יָתוֹם יָתוֹם	(the) orphan *yā·tôm*	ABS	noun
וְאַלְמָנָה אַלְמָנָה	and (the) widow *wə·ʾal·mā·nâ*	ABS W/ CONJ וְ	noun

עֹשֶׂה מִשְׁפַּט can also be translated as "one who does justice." As in v. 17c, God's actions are manifested in the requirements of the laws (16:14; 24:17)

וְאֹהֵב גֵּר לָתֶת לוֹ לֶחֶם וְשִׂמְלָה:

and loving the sojourner, giving them clothing.

וְאֹהֵב אהב	and (one) loving *wə·ʾō·hēv*	QAL PTCP MS W/ CONJ וְ	verb
גֵּר גֵּר	(the) foreigner/sojourner *gēr*	ABS	noun
לָתֶת נתן	to give *lā·tet*	QAL INF CST W/ PREP לְ	verb
לוֹ לְ	to him *lô*	--- W/ 3MS SX	prep
לֶחֶם לֶחֶם	food/bread *le·ḥem*	ABS	noun
וְשִׂמְלָה: שִׂמְלָה	and clothing *wə·śim·lâ*	ABS W/ CONJ וְ	noun

It could not be clearer here that love is action that cares for the needs of others.

In the Old Testament, גֵּר ("sojourner") appears most often in the law and should be taken as a legal term for something like a "displaced foreigner" or "landless immigrant." We saw their protections in the Sabbath law (5:14) and will return to Israel's obligation to them in 14:29; 16:11, 14 and 24:14–20 (for an extended study, see Glanville 2018).

19 וַאֲהַבְתֶּם אֶת־הַגֵּר כִּי־גֵרִים הֱיִיתֶם בְּאֶרֶץ מִצְרָיִם:

So you shall love the sojourner, for you were sojourners
in the land of Egypt.

וַאֲהַבְתֶּם אהב *wa·ʾă·hav·tem*	and you (all) shall love	QAL WEQATAL 2MP	verb
אֶת־ אֵת *ʾet-*	(direct object marker)	---	particle
הַגֵּר גֵּר *hag·gēr*	the foreigner/sojourner	ABS W/ DEF. ART.	noun
כִּי־ כִּי *kî-*	for	---	conj
גֵרִים גֵּר *gē·rîm*	foreigners/sojourners	ABS	noun
הֱיִיתֶם היה *hĕ·yî·tem*	you were	QAL PF 2MP	verb
בְּאֶרֶץ אֶרֶץ *bə·ʾe·reṣ*	in (the) land of	CST W/ PREP בְּ	noun
מִצְרָיִם: מִצְרָיִם *miṣ·rā·yim*	Egypt	ABS	noun

Yet again, Israel's actions are reflections of Yahweh's actions. He is holy; they are to be holy. He loves; they are to love.

20a אֶת־יְהוָה אֱלֹהֶיךָ תִּירָא

Yahweh your God you shall fear;

אֶת־ אֵת *ʾet-*	(direct object marker)	---	particle
יְהוָה יהוה *YHWH*	Yahweh	ABS	noun
אֱלֹהֶיךָ אֱלֹהִים *ʾĕ·lō·hê·ḵā*	your God	CST W/ 2MS SX	noun

<table>
<tr><td>תִּירָא
יָרא</td><td>you will fear
tî·rā'</td><td>QAL IMPF 2MS</td><td>verb</td></tr>
</table>

אֹתוֹ תַעֲבֹד וּבוֹ תִדְבָּק וּבִשְׁמוֹ תִּשָּׁבֵעַ׃

him you shall serve, and to him you shall cling,
and in his name you shall swear.

אֹתוֹ אֵת	him 'ō·tô	--- W/ 3MS SX	particle
תַעֲבֹד עבד	you will serve ta·'ă·vōd	QAL IMPF 2MS	verb
וּבוֹ בְּ	and to/with him û·vô	--- W/ CONJ וְ + 3MS SX	prep
תִדְבָּק דבק	you will cling tid·bāq	QAL IMPF 2MS	verb
וּבִשְׁמוֹ שֵׁם	and in his name û·viš·mô	CST W/ CONJ וְ + PREP בְּ + 3MS SX	noun
תִּשָּׁבֵעַ׃ שבע	you will swear tiš·šā·vē·a'	NIPH IMPF 2MS	verb

הוּא תְהִלָּתְךָ וְהוּא אֱלֹהֶיךָ אֲשֶׁר־עָשָׂה אִתְּךָ אֶת־הַגְּדֹלֹת וְאֶת־הַנּוֹרָאֹת הָאֵלֶּה אֲשֶׁר רָאוּ עֵינֶיךָ׃

He is your praise, and he is your God, who did for you
these great and awesome things your eyes have seen.

הוּא הוּא	he hû'	---	personal pron
תְהִלָּתְךָ תְּהִלָּה	(is) your praise tə·hil·lā·tə·kā	CST W/ 2MS SX	noun
וְהוּא הוּא	and he wə·hû'	--- W/ CONJ וְ	personal pron
אֱלֹהֶיךָ אֱלֹהִים	(is) your God 'ĕ·lō·hê·kā	CST W/ 2MS SX	noun
אֲשֶׁר־ אֲשֶׁר	who 'ă·šer-	---	relative pron

עָשָׂה עשׂה	(he) did/made *'ā·śâ*	QAL PF 3MS ---	verb
אִתְּךָ אֵת	you *'it·tə·ḵā*	--- W/ 2MS SX	prep
אֶת־ אֵת	(direct object marker) *'et-*	---	particle
הַגְּדֹלֹת גָּדוֹל	the great things *hag·gə·dō·lōt*	FP SUBST W/ DEF. ART.	adj
וְאֶת־ אֵת	and (+ *direct object marker*) *wə·'et-*	--- W/ CONJ וְ	particle
הַנּוֹרָאֹת ירא	(the) awesome/terrifying things *han·nô·rā·'ōt*	NIPH PTCP FP W/ DEF. ART.	verb
הָאֵלֶּה אֵלֶּה	(the) these *hā·'êl·le*	--- W/ DEF. ART.	demonstr pron
אֲשֶׁר אֲשֶׁר	that/which *'ă·šer*	---	relative pron
רָאוּ ראה	(they) saw *rā·'û*	QAL PF 3CP	verb
עֵינֶיךָ׃ עַיִן	your eyes *'ê·nê·ḵā*	CST W/ 2MS SX	noun

Some translations begin, "he is your glory."

The phrase רָאוּ עֵינֶיךָ ("your eyes have seen") appears in this way especially in chs. 4 and 29 to emphasize the objective historical basis for Israel's indebtedness to Yahweh. In the narrative of Deuteronomy, however, most of the people who saw these great wonders would now have died. The phrase thus serves to confirm the reliability of the report that has been passed down through generations. Paul uses the appearance of the risen Jesus to the same effect (1 Cor 15:1–11).

22a	בְּשִׁבְעִים נֶפֶשׁ יָרְדוּ אֲבֹתֶיךָ מִצְרָיְמָה

As seventy people your ancestors went down to Egypt,

בְּשִׁבְעִים שִׁבְעִים	in/by seventy *bə·šiv·'îm*	ABS W/ PREP בְּ	cardinal number

נֶפֶשׁ / נֶפֶשׁ *ne·feš*	life/soul/person	ABS	noun
יָרְדוּ / ירד *yā·rə·dû*	(they) went down	QAL PF 3CP	verb
אֲבֹתֶיךָ / אָב *ʾă·vō·tê·ḵā*	your fathers	CST W/ 2MS SX	noun
מִצְרָיְמָה / מִצְרַיִם *miṣ·rāy·māh*	to Egypt	ABS W/ LOCATIVE ה	noun

22b וְעַתָּה שָׂמְךָ יְהוָה אֱלֹהֶיךָ כְּכוֹכְבֵי הַשָּׁמַיִם לָרֹב:

but now Yahweh your God has made you as numerous as the stars of heaven.

וְעַתָּה / עַתָּה *wə·'at·tâ*	and now	--- W/ CONJ וְ	adv
שָׂמְךָ / שִׂים *śā·mə·ḵā*	(he) has set/arranged/ established you	QAL PF 3MS W/ 2MS SX	verb
יְהוָה / יהוה *YHWH*	Yahweh	ABS	noun
אֱלֹהֶיךָ / אֱלֹהִים *ʾĕ·lō·hê·ḵā*	your God	CST W/ 2MS SX	noun
כְּכוֹכְבֵי / כּוֹכָב *kə·ḵô·ḵə·vê*	as (the) stars of	CST W/ PREP כְּ	noun
הַשָּׁמַיִם / שָׁמַיִם *haš·šā·ma·yim*	the heavens	ABS W/ DEF. ART.	noun
לָרֹב: / רֹב *lā·rōv*	as/for a multitude	ABS W/ PREP לְ	noun

As a final confirmation of God's past faithfulness, Israel's present size is a fulfillment of the promise to Abraham who had no child and whose wife was old and barren (Gen 15:5). For those who believe in him, this God can be trusted to do what seems impossible.

 *Divine Love.* This section of Deuteronomy rests on the book's two central themes: God's gratuitous love of Israel in choosing them and setting his passion on them (7:6–7; 10:15), and Israel's response of love for God (6:4; 10:12). Deuteronomy communicates these themes in a way that echoes the framework of an ancient suzerainty covenant. This was not a treaty between two equal parties but one in which a higher power bound himself and his love to one lower in standing.

The unequal love exhibited here raises an interesting problem, or at least it has for theologians for thousands of years.

Jon Levenson presents the problem as a question: how can a perfect God experience a human passion like love? (2016:172–79). In other words, if God is perfect, eternal, and unchanging—as Christian and Jewish traditions have held—how can such a God get caught up in worldly emotions like love? Doesn't that mean that God changes? That he has passions? That he is not perfect?

Theologians in the patristic and medieval eras argued that not all passions are a response to need. Love and joy arise not out of God's imperfection but out of his character as a person: they are his own personal perfections. This provided Christians a way to understand how divine eternal love could enter a finite world—through *relationship* with us.

These issues are obviously complex. But I belabor the point so that we don't overlook just how perfect this love is and how extraordinary it is that we share in it in this finite and sinful world. As Levenson recognizes, Deuteronomy leaves us unavoidably and undeniably with "God's mysterious and (to many) scandalous love for Israel." Perfect and eternal love has fallen upon our world in extravagant excess. Such a love "demands love in return, one manifested most obviously and explicitly in Israel's undivided and heartfelt service of the LORD alone" (Levenson 2016:178).

In the New Testament, the love shared with God in Israel's covenant takes its form in the Son. John makes this clear when he connects the gift of the Son to the love of God (John 3:16). You might have seen this issue rising in the background already. It is not simply that the Son has come into the world but that he has come as fully God and fully man. Thus, we find him able to say both that the Father loved him before the foundation of the world (17:24) and that he has loved his disciples just as he was loved by the Father (15:9). Now we are at the very heart of the mystery of the Christian gospel: perfect love has become incarnate and taken up life within us.

More importantly, as we see in Deut 10, God's love becomes the basis for how we live in the world, just as it was for Jesus' disciples (John 13:34–35; 15:12).

🌱 *Love the Stranger.* According to Deut 10:18–19, one central way to reflect God's love is to care for the "sojourner." This landless person (גֵּר) is sometimes translated "stranger," which accents their propensity to be vulnerable, lost, overlooked, and underprioritized in social life. God reserves special love for such people, and he commands us to do the same, for we were lost and displaced before we knew him (cf. Luke 15:1–32).

Two scenes in the New Testament further reveal the depth of Jesus' commission to love the stranger. The first, in the book of Acts, narrates Jesus' words to Paul at his conversion:

> "Saul, Saul, why do you persecute me?"
> "Who are you, Lord?"
> "I am Jesus, whom you are persecuting." (9:4–5)

Saul's threats and persecution were aimed at Jesus' followers (9:1), but Jesus presents himself as suffering with and alongside these followers. On the one hand, this gives us extraordinary assurance that God is with us in our suffering. On the other hand, that he suffers with his followers means that when we love others in times of need, we love God who is with them and within them.

The empathy of love also plays out in the story of the "Good Samaritan" who attends to a man beaten and left for dead on the side of the road (Luke 10:29–37). Considering Deut 10:18–19, we might ask if it's not more appropriate to call this story "The Compassionate Stranger," since it is the differences among the three classes in the story—the anonymous man in need, the priest and Levite, and the Samaritan—that press the bounds of Jewish social obligation. Who is my neighbor? Anyone in need. Elsewhere, in the Sermon on the Mount, Jesus makes the point emphatic: "For if you love those who love you, what reward do you have? Do not even the tax collectors do the same?" (Matt 5:46).

🌱 *The Love of Neighbors.* Verses 18–19 take us to Yahweh's particular concern for the orphan, widow, and sojourner (landless immigrant). The imperative Moses gives Israel, then, follows a particular logic: God loves the sojourner, he loved you as sojourners in Egypt, therefore you should love the sojourner. Our interest here is in the way God took his people out of slavery, oppression, and homelessness and gave them freedom, love, and a home. The love that Israel should seek, therefore, should take this same shape in acts of deliverance, compassion, and restoration.

Putting this another way, the love of God we see in Deuteronomy brings people and nations into a place of flourishing where they fulfill what he most desires for them. God takes great pleasure in finding people in need and giving them a place where they truly become themselves. The laws we will visit in chs. 14–16 and 24 all provide more particular ways to furnish people with the freedom and property they need to live their lives: relieving poverty, forming community bonds that welcome the stranger, and protecting the vulnerable.

One good way to preach Deut 10, then, could be to explore the *shape* of love, which is not simply an abstract affection but action that seeks to manifest God and his ordained will. This love will by necessity have two sides.

 ***Love and Hope.*** On the one hand, love is eschatologically driven. I am often asked to include 1 Cor 13 when I officiate at wedding services. While it works well at weddings, the chapter is really a future-looking exhortation that applies universally to Christian love among individuals and communities.

An oft-overlooked saying appears in v. 12: "For now we see in a mirror, dimly, but then we will see face to face. Now I know only in part; then I will know fully, even as I have been fully known" (NRSV). Only then does Paul go on to speak of faith, hope, and *love*. Which is to say that love, tied to hope, looks forward to when we will be "fully known" (v. 12). The love of neighbor has an eschatological trajectory: with it, we seek to bring another into the new creations we are destined to become in Christ—a future perfect self "hidden with Christ in God" (Col 3:3).

Gerard Manley Hopkins observed in his poem "As Kingfishers Catch Fire" (1918:54) that the "just man" (i.e., the Christian)

> Acts in God's eye what in God's eye he is—
> Christ—for Christ plays in ten thousand places

Hopkins lyrically orients us to the future vision of our neighbor in their eschatological perfection, where we see the face of Christ. We love our neighbor into that future vision where Christ has so taken up his place in us that we reflect his glory perfectly.

 ***Love and Discipline.*** Second, discipline is a form of love (Deut 8:5; Prov 3:12; Heb 12:5). Many will be aware of fads in parenting that are "permissive" or "child-centered." Sensitivity about abuse must not be dismissed. Yet very often child-rearing philosophies arise as people pull back from

the hard work of parenting, allowing the child to dictate the terms of the family and home. Children left untaught and undisciplined in this way only end up as burdens to society, believing the world is obliged to bend and mold itself around their wishes. *Loving* children means fitting them for the world, teaching them virtues of patience, discipline, and kindness as well as sharing, listening, abstaining, helping, and loving.

Like children, we too need corrective love. The French philosopher Simone Weil once controversially described punishment as "a vital need of the human soul" (1952:22). If we are honest, we know that we all err in life and need the loving correction to return to the right path. As the proverb has it:

> Faithful are the wounds from the beloved,
> but excessive the kisses of the enemy. (Prov 27:6)

It bears remembering here that the love expressed in Deut 10 is a love that has restored Israel from the rebellion described in 9:1–10:11. And this leads us to]repentance.

☙ *Deep Penitence.*

> *"Circumcise the foreskin of your heart,
> and stiffen your neck no longer." (Deut 10:16)*

Love as discipline complements the penitence required to love God. The command of Moses in v. 16 looks back to the golden calf rebellion and God's desire at that time to destroy the nation of Israel (see 9:13–14). What follows in ch. 9 is highly significant: Moses lays prostrate in prayer for forty days on behalf of the sin of his people. Then God forgives them (9:17–21). Recalling the phrase "stiff neck" in the context of the present in ch. 10, Moses is preparing the people for life without him. They will need to learn the same penitent response to their future sin and rebellion, and to remember how susceptible they will be to turning away from God.

Notice how the metaphors of the hard heart and stiff neck emphasize a stubborn resistance to spiritual pliability and contrition. To be faithful to the Lord requires breaking through the skin and relaxing our spiritual posture to allow God and his word to work over us and in us. (The same metaphors reappear in the call to be generous to the needy in 15:1–18.)

It should be clear by now that Deut 10 (and chs. 6–11) is about the inner spirit behind the law. The theological concept of the "spirit of the law" (see 2 Cor 3:3–6) also seems to suggest something deeper than the law, involving a whole catalogue of virtues like remembrance, penitence, humility, love, and gratitude. The law can and does point to these, but it cannot translate them simply by reading or hearing the words. Something more is needed: a violent circumcision of our inner being.

Moses exemplifies this for us in his submissive prayer in 9:17–21. Thomas Merton (1955:41) helps us connect prayer to the reflection that leads us back to righteous living:

> The whole function of the life of prayer is, then, to enlighten and strengthen our conscience so that it not only knows and perceives the outward, written precepts of the moral and divine laws, but above all lives God's law in concrete reality by perfect and continual union with his will.

Merton goes on to say that the enlightened and disciplined conscience is necessary to "solve the problems of life" (p. 42). It should become clear to us that the hundreds of laws that lie ahead of us in Deut 12–26 can, if we are diligent, take up residence in our prayer in such a way that our conscience is strengthened and equipped to confront these problems with wisdom.

ALL WILL FEAST BEFORE THE LORD

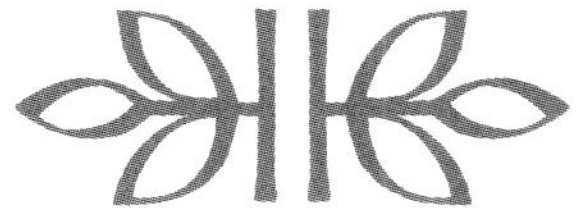

This section of law focuses on feasting practices "at the place (God) chooses to place his name [בַּמָּקוֹם אֲשֶׁר־יִבְחַר לְשַׁכֵּן שְׁמוֹ שָׁם]" (v. 23). Often called the "centralization formula," this phrase first appears in 12:5 and is then repeated in 12:11; 14:23; 16:2, 6, 11; and 26:2 (cf. Jer. 7:12; Ezra 6:12; Neh 1:9). It also appears in a parallel form לְשׂוּם שְׁמוֹ שָׁם, which we translate "to set his name" (Deut 12:5, 21; 14:24; 1 Kgs 9:3; 11:36; 14:21; 2 Kgs 21:4, 7).

Sandra Richter has argued that both phrases, לְשַׁכֵּן שֵׁם שָׁם and לְשׂוּם שֵׁם שָׁם, are based on an Akkadian idiom that means to "place the name" (2007:342–66). It appears that these phrases describe the building of a monument recognizing God's works and the gift of the land, just as we find in the ceremony on Mount Ebal in Deut 27. At the same time, monuments to other gods were to be destroyed (12:1–3), which complements the command not to make idols or worship them (5:8–10). This combination of destroying and making memorials signified unqualified loyalty to Yahweh.

Scholars variously try to associate the "place" with Shechem, Shiloh, Bethel, Gilgal, Gerizim, Ebal, or Jerusalem. So why doesn't Deuteronomy just name the place it has in mind and eliminate the ambiguity? Probably because Deuteronomy is meant to be heard and lived out in every new "today," and each new "place" where it is read and heard. So while Ebal was likely the first site of a ceremony for placing the name as Israel looked out over the promised land, future generations would be able to apply it in their time and place. Thus, God and his law had perpetual force among Israelites.

Chapter 14 makes clear that loyalty to Yahweh has a distinct shape in community life. Such loyalty (v. 23) should give way to tithing to supply feasts that gather the whole community in rejoicing. As we will see below, while tithes in the ancient world were common, we have no evidence of prior laws that gave the tithe back to the people for feasting.

LARGER LITERARY CONTEXT ▸ 12:1–14:29; 16:1–17; 26:1–15

22a

עַשֵּׂר תְּעַשֵּׂר אֵת כָּל־תְּבוּאַת זַרְעֶךָ

'aśśēr tə'aśśēr 'ēt kol-təvû'at zar'ekā

You shall surely tithe all the produce of your seed

22b

הַיֹּצֵא הַשָּׂדֶה שָׁנָה שָׁנָה:

hayyōṣē' haśśāde šānâ šānâ.

that is brought from the field year by year.

23a

וְאָכַלְתָּ לִפְנֵי| יְהוָה אֱלֹהֶיךָ

wə'ākaltā lifnê YHWH 'ĕlōhêkā

And you shall eat it before Yahweh your God

23b

בַּמָּקוֹם אֲשֶׁר־יִבְחַר לְשַׁכֵּן שְׁמוֹ שָׁם

bammāqôm 'ăšer-yivḥar ləšakkēn šəmô šām

in the place where he chooses to place his name—

23c

מַעְשַׂר דְּגָנְךָ תִּירֹשְׁךָ וְיִצְהָרֶךָ וּבְכֹרֹת בְּקָרְךָ וְצֹאנֶךָ

ma'śar dəgānəkā tîrōškā wəyiṣhārekā ûvəkōrōt bəqārəkā wəṣō'nekā

a tithe from your grain, your wine, and your oil,
and the firstborn of your herd and your flock—

23d

לְמַעַן תִּלְמַד לְיִרְאָה אֶת־יְהוָה אֱלֹהֶיךָ כָּל־הַיָּמִים:

ləma'an tilmad ləyir'â 'et-YHWH 'ĕlōhêkā kol-hayyāmîm.

that you may learn to fear Yahweh your God always.

24a

וְכִי־יִרְבֶּה מִמְּךָ הַדֶּרֶךְ

wəkî-yirbe mimməkā hadderek

And if the way is too great for you,

24b

כִּי לֹא תוּכַל שְׂאֵתוֹ

kî lō' tûkal śə'ētô

so that you are not able to carry it,

24c כִּי־יִרְחַק מִמְּךָ הַמָּקוֹם אֲשֶׁר יִבְחַר֩

kî-yirḥaq mimməkā hammāqôm ʾăšer yivḥar

יְהוָה אֱלֹהֶיךָ לָשׂוּם שְׁמוֹ שָׁם

YHWH ʾĕlōhêkā lāśûm šəmô šām

so that the place Yahweh your God chooses
to set his name is too far for you—

24d כִּי יְבָרֶכְךָ יְהוָה אֱלֹהֶיךָ׃

kî yəvārekəkā YHWH ʾĕlōhêkā.

because Yahweh your God will bless you—

25a וְנָתַתָּה בַּכָּסֶף וְצַרְתָּ הַכֶּסֶף בְּיָדְךָ

wənātattâ bakkāsef wəṣartā hakkesef bəyādəkā

then you may sell it for money and bind the money in your hand

25b וְהָלַכְתָּ אֶל־הַמָּקוֹם אֲשֶׁר יִבְחַר יְהוָה אֱלֹהֶיךָ בּוֹ׃

wəhālaktā ʾel-hammāqôm ʾăšer yivḥar YHWH ʾĕlōhêkā bô.

and go to the place where Yahweh your God chooses.

26a וְנָתַתָּה הַכֶּסֶף בְּכֹל אֲשֶׁר־תְּאַוֶּה נַפְשְׁךָ

wənātattâ hakkesef bəkol ʾăšer-təʾawwe nafšəkā

And you may spend the money on anything you desire,

26b בַּבָּקָר וּבַצֹּאן וּבַיַּיִן וּבַשֵּׁכָר

babbāqār ûvaṣōʾn ûvayyayin ûvaššēkār

on cattle or flocks or wine or strong drink

26c וּבְכֹל אֲשֶׁר תִּשְׁאָלְךָ נַפְשֶׁךָ

ûvəkōl ʾăšer tišʾāləkā nafšekā

or on anything you wish.

26d וְאָכַלְתָּ שָּׁם לִפְנֵי יְהוָה אֱלֹהֶיךָ

wəʾākaltā šām lifnê YHWH ʾĕlōhêkā

And you shall eat there before Yahweh your God,

26e

וְשָׂמַחְתָּ אַתָּה וּבֵיתֶךָ:

wəśāmaḥtā 'attâ ûvêtekā.

and you shall rejoice, you and your household.

27a

וְהַלֵּוִי אֲשֶׁר־בִּשְׁעָרֶיךָ לֹא תַעַזְבֶנּוּ

wəhallēwî 'ăšer bišʿārêkā lō' taʿazvennû

And you shall not abandon the Levite who is in your towns,

27b

כִּי אֵין לוֹ חֵלֶק וְנַחֲלָה עִמָּךְ:

kî 'ên lô ḥēleq wənaḥălâ ʿimmāk.

for he has no portion or inheritance with you.

עַשֵּׂר תְּעַשֵּׂר אֵת כָּל־תְּבוּאַת זַרְעֶךָ		
You shall surely tithe all the produce of your seed		

עַשֵּׂר עשׂר	to give/pay a tenth *'aś·śēr*	PIEL INF ABS	verb
תְּעַשֵּׂר עשׂר	you give/pay a tenth *tə·'aś·śēr*	PIEL IMPF 2MS	verb
אֵת אֵת	(direct object marker) *'ēt*	---	particle
כָּל־ כֹּל	all *kol-*	CST	noun
תְּבוּאַת תְּבוּאָה	(the) produce/yield/harvest of *tə·vû·'at*	CST	noun
זַרְעֶךָ זֶרַע	your seed *zar·'e·kā*	CST W/ 2MS SX	noun

The emphasis created by using an infinitive absolute and finite verb from the same root (here עַשֵּׂר תְּעַשֵּׂר, "you shall surely tithe") is common in Deuteronomy.

<table>
<tr><td>22b</td><td align="center">הַיֹּצֵא הַשָּׂדֶה שָׁנָה שָׁנָה:</td></tr>
</table>

that is brought from the field year by year.

הַיֹּצֵא יצא	the bringing out/brought out *hay·yō·ṣē'*	QAL PTCP MS W/ DEF. ART.	verb
הַשָּׂדֶה שָׂדֶה	the field *haś·śā·**de***	ABS W/ DEF. ART.	noun
שָׁנָה שָׁנָה	year *šā·**nâ***	ABS	noun
שָׁנָה: שָׁנָה	(by) year *šā·**nâ***	ABS	noun

<table>
<tr><td>23a</td><td align="center">וְאָכַלְתָּ לִפְנֵי| יְהוָה אֱלֹהֶיךָ</td></tr>
</table>

And you shall eat it before Yahweh your God

וְאָכַלְתָּ אכל	and you will eat *wə·'ā·ḵal·**tā***	QAL WEQATAL 2MS	verb
לִפְנֵי| לִפְנֵי	before *lif·**nê***	- - -	prep
יְהוָה יהוה	Yahweh *YHWH*	ABS	noun
אֱלֹהֶיךָ אֱלֹהִים	your God *'ĕ·lō·**hê***·ḵā	CST W/ 2MS SX	noun

The presence of God in Israel's daily life is easy to overlook, but it was central to God's vision for this unique nation whose God is "so near" (4:7).

<table>
<tr><td>23b</td><td align="center">בַּמָּקוֹם אֲשֶׁר־יִבְחַר לְשַׁכֵּן שְׁמוֹ שָׁם</td></tr>
</table>

in the place where he chooses to place his name—

בַּמָּקוֹם מָקוֹם	in the place *bam·mā·**qôm***	ABS W/ PREP בְּ + DEF. ART.	noun
אֲשֶׁר־ אֲשֶׁר	that/which *'ă·šer-*	- - -	relative pron

Hebrew	Meaning	Parsing	Part of Speech
יִבְחַר֑ בחר *yiv·ḥar*	he will choose	QAL IMPF 3MS	verb
לְשַׁכֵּ֥ן שכן *lə·šak·kēn*	to establish/cause to dwell	PIEL INF CST W/ PREP לְ	verb
שְׁמ֖וֹ שֵׁם *šə·mô*	his name	CST W/ 3MS SX	noun
שָׁ֑ם שָׁם *šām*	there	---	adv

See the introduction to this section for discussion of the phrase לְשַׁכֵּן שְׁמוֹ שָׁם ("to place his name") and its close parallel in v. 24c, לָשׂוּם שְׁמוֹ שָׁם ("to set his name").

23c   מַעְשַׂר דְּגָנְךָ֩ תִּירֹשְׁךָ֨ וְיִצְהָרֶ֜ךָ וּבְכֹרֹת בְּקָרְךָ֣ וְצֹאנֶ֗ךָ

a tithe from your grain, your wine, and your oil,
and the firstborn of your herd and your flock—

Hebrew	Meaning	Parsing	Part of Speech
מַעְשַׂר מַעֲשֵׂר *maʿ·śar*	tithe/tenth of	CST	noun
דְּגָנְךָ֩ דָּגָן *də·gā·nə·ḵā*	your grain	CST W/ 2MS SX	noun
תִּירֹשְׁךָ֨ תִּירוֹשׁ *tî·rōš·ḵā*	your wine	CST W/ 2MS SX	noun
וְיִצְהָרֶ֜ךָ יִצְהָר *wə·yiṣ·hā·re·ḵā*	and your olive oil	CST W/ CONJ וְ + 2MS SX	noun
וּבְכֹרֹת בְּכוֹר *û·və·ḵō·rōt*	and (the) firstborn of	CST W/ CONJ וְ	noun
בְּקָרְךָ֣ בָּקָר *bə·qā·rə·ḵā*	your herd	CST W/ 2MS SX	noun
וְצֹאנֶ֗ךָ צֹאן *wə·ṣō·ne·ḵā*	and your flock/sheep	CST W/ CONJ וְ + 2MS SX	noun

לְמַ֣עַן תִּלְמַ֗ד לְיִרְאָ֛ה אֶת־יְהוָ֥ה אֱלֹהֶ֖יךָ כָּל־הַיָּמִֽים׃

that you may learn to fear Yahweh your God always.

לְמַ֣עַן	so that/in order that	---	prep
לְמַעַן	lə·**ma**·ʿan		
תִּלְמַ֗ד	you will learn	QAL IMPF 2MS	verb
למד	til·**mad**		
לְיִרְאָ֛ה	to fear	QAL INF CST	verb
ירא	lə·yir·**ʾâ**	W/ PREP לְ	
אֶת־	(direct object marker)	---	particle
אֶת	ʾet-		
יְהוָ֥ה	Yahweh	ABS	noun
יהוה	YHWH		
אֱלֹהֶ֖יךָ	your God	CST	noun
אֱלֹהִים	ʾĕ·lō·**hɛ̂**·ḵā	W/ 2MS SX	
כָּל־	all	CST	noun
כֹּל	kol-		
הַיָּמִֽים׃	the days	ABS	noun
יוֹם	hay·yā·**mîm**	W/ DEF. ART.	

Deuteronomy repeats this aim תִּלְמַד לְיִרְאָה ("you may learn to fear") using history to tie the people together in time: for the people at Horeb, repeated today for children tomorrow (4:10), for the people every year in the land (14:23), for the king daily (17:19), and future generations forever (31:13).

וְכִֽי־יִרְבֶּ֤ה מִמְּךָ֙ הַדֶּ֔רֶךְ

And if the way is too great for you,

וְכִֽי־	but/and if	---	conj
כִּי	wə·**ḵî**-	W/ CONJ וְ	
יִרְבֶּ֤ה	(it) is (too) great	QAL IMPF 3MS	verb
רבה	yir·**be**		
מִמְּךָ֙	for you	---	prep
מִן	mim·mə·**ḵā**	W/ 2MS SX	
הַדֶּ֔רֶךְ	the way	ABS	noun
דֶּרֶךְ	had·**de**·reḵ	W/ DEF. ART.	

כִּי לֹא תוּכַל שְׂאֵתוֹ

so that you are not able to carry it,

כִּי kî	so that	---	conj
לֹא lōʾ	no/not	---	particle
תוּכַל ykl tû·kal	you are able	QAL IMPF 2MS	verb
שְׂאֵתוֹ nśʾ śə·ʾē·tô	to lift/carry it	QAL INF CST W/ 3MS SX	verb

Notice the subtle indication that, if Israel obeys Yahweh, he will bless them with so much land that gathering will become too difficult (Altmann 2011:233).

כִּי־יִרְחַק מִמְּךָ הַמָּקוֹם אֲשֶׁר יִבְחַר יְהוָה אֱלֹהֶיךָ לָשׂוּם שְׁמוֹ שָׁם

so that the place Yahweh your God chooses
to set his name is too far for you—

כִּי־ kî-	so that	---	conj
יִרְחַק rḥq yir·ḥaq	(it) is too far	QAL IMPF 3MS	verb
מִמְּךָ mn mim·mə·kā	from/for you	W/ 2MS SX	prep
הַמָּקוֹם māqôm ham·mā·qôm	the place	ABS W/ DEF. ART.	noun
אֲשֶׁר ʾăšer ʾă·šer	that/which	---	relative pron
יִבְחַר bḥr yiv·ḥar	(he) will choose	QAL IMPF 3MS	verb
יְהוָה YHWH	Yahweh	ABS	noun
אֱלֹהֶיךָ ʾĕlōhîm ʾĕ·lō·hê·kā	your God	CST W/ 2MS SX	noun

לָשׂוּם שִׂים	to set/place *lā·śûm*	QAL INF CST W/ PREP לְ	verb
שְׁמוֹ שֵׁם	his name *šə·mô*	CST W/ 3MS SX	noun
שָׁם שָׁם	there *šām*	---	adv

<table>
<tr><td>24d</td><td colspan="2" align="center">כִּי יְבָרֶכְךָ יְהוָה אֱלֹהֶיךָ׃</td></tr>
<tr><td></td><td colspan="2" align="center">because Yahweh your God will bless you—</td></tr>
</table>

כִּי כִּי	for/so that *kî*	---	conj
יְבָרֶכְךָ ברך	he will bless you *yə·vā·re·kə·kā*	PIEL IMPF 3MS W/ 2MS SX	verb
יְהוָה יהוה	Yahweh *YHWH*	ABS	noun
אֱלֹהֶיךָ׃ אֱלֹהִים	your God *ĕ·lō·hê·kā*	CST W/ 2MS SX	noun

<table>
<tr><td>25a</td><td colspan="2" align="center">וְנָתַתָּה בַּכֶּסֶף וְצַרְתָּ הַכֶּסֶף בְּיָדְךָ</td></tr>
<tr><td></td><td colspan="2" align="center">then you may sell it for money and bind the money in your hand</td></tr>
</table>

וְנָתַתָּה נתן	and you will give/exchange (it) *wə·nā·tat·tâ*	QAL WEQATAL 2MS	verb
בַּכֶּסֶף כֶּסֶף	into silver/money *bak·kā·sef*	ABS W/ PREP בְּ + DEF. ART.	noun
וְצַרְתָּ צור	and you will bind up *wə·ṣar·tā*	QAL WEQATAL 2MS	verb
הַכֶּסֶף כֶּסֶף	the silver/money *hak·ke·sef*	ABS W/ DEF. ART.	noun
בְּיָדְךָ יָד	in your hand *bə·yā·də·kā*	CST W/ PREP בְּ + 2MS SX	noun

וְהָלַכְתָּ אֶל־הַמָּקוֹם אֲשֶׁר יִבְחַר יְהוָה אֱלֹהֶיךָ בּוֹ׃

and go to the place where Yahweh your God chooses.

וְהָלַכְתָּ הלך	and you shall go *wə·hā·lāḵ·tā*	QAL WEQATAL 2MS	verb
אֶל־ אֶל	to *'el-*	---	prep
הַמָּקוֹם מָקוֹם	the place *ham·mā·qôm*	ABS W/ DEF. ART.	noun
אֲשֶׁר אֲשֶׁר	that/which *'ă·šer*	---	relative pron
יִבְחַר בחר	(he) will choose *yiv·ḥar*	QAL IMPF 3MS	verb
יְהוָה יהוה	Yahweh *YHWH*	ABS	noun
אֱלֹהֶיךָ אֱלֹהִים	your God *'ĕ·lō·hê·ḵā*	CST W/ 2MS SX	noun
בּוֹ׃ בְּ	for him/it *bô*	--- W/ 3MS SX	prep

וְנָתַתָּה הַכֶּסֶף בְּכֹל אֲשֶׁר־תְּאַוֶּה נַפְשְׁךָ

And you may spend the money on anything you desire,

וְנָתַתָּה נתן	and you shall give/exchange *wə·nā·tat·tâ*	QAL WEQATAL 2MS	verb
הַכֶּסֶף כֶּסֶף	the silver/money *hak·ke·sef*	ABS W/ DEF. ART.	noun
בְּכֹל כֹּל	for all/anything *bə·ḵol*	ABS W/ PREP בְּ	noun
אֲשֶׁר־ אֲשֶׁר	that/which *'ă·šer-*	---	relative pron
תְּאַוֶּה אוה	(it) desires *tə·'aw·we*	PIEL IMPF 3FS	verb
נַפְשְׁךָ נֶפֶשׁ	your life/soul *naf·šə·ḵā*	CST W/ 2MS SX	noun

בַּבָּקָר וּבַצֹּאן וּבַיַּיִן וּבַשֵּׁכָר

on cattle or flocks or wine or strong drink

בַּבָּקָר בָּקָר	for oxen/cattle *bab·bā·qār*	ABS W/ PREP בְּ + DEF. ART.	noun
וּבַצֹּאן צֹאן	and/or for sheep/goats *û·va·ṣōʾn*	ABS W/ CONJ וְ + PREP בְּ + DEF. ART.	noun
וּבַיַּיִן יַיִן	and/or for wine *û·vay·ya·yin*	ABS W/ CONJ וְ + PREP בְּ + DEF. ART.	noun
וּבַשֵּׁכָר שֵׁכָר	and/or for strong drink *û·vaš·šē·kār*	ABS W/ CONJ וְ + PREP בְּ + DEF. ART.	noun

וּבְכֹל אֲשֶׁר תִּשְׁאָלְךָ נַפְשֶׁךָ

or on anything you wish.

וּבְכֹל כֹּל	or for anything *û·və·kōl*	ABS W/ CONJ וְ + PREP בְּ	noun
אֲשֶׁר אֲשֶׁר	that/which *ʾă·šer*	---	relative pron
תִּשְׁאָלְךָ שָׁאל	(it) desires *tiš·ʾā·lə·kā*	QAL IMPF 3FS W/ 2MS SX	verb
נַפְשֶׁךָ נֶפֶשׁ	your soul/life *naf·še·kā*	CST W/ 2MS SX	noun

וְאָכַלְתָּ שָׁם לִפְנֵי יְהוָה אֱלֹהֶיךָ

And you shall eat there before Yahweh your God,

וְאָכַלְתָּ אכל	and you will eat *wə·ʾā·kal·tā*	QAL WEQATAL 2MS	verb
שָׁם שָׁם	there *šām*	---	adv
לִפְנֵי לִפְנֵי	before/in the presence of *lif·nê*	---	prep

| יְהוָה | Yahweh | ABS | noun |
| יהוה | *YHWH* | | |

| אֱלֹהֶיךָ | your God | CST | noun |
| אֱלֹהִים | *ʾĕ·lō·hê·kā* | W/ 2MS SX | |

26e   וְשָׂמַחְתָּ אַתָּה וּבֵיתֶךָ׃

and you shall rejoice, you and your household.

| וְשָׂמַחְתָּ | and you will rejoice | QAL WEQATAL 2MS | verb |
| שׂמח | *wə·śā·maḥ·tā* | | |

| אַתָּה | you | --- | personal pron |
| אַתָּה | *ʾat·tâ* | | |

| וּבֵיתֶךָ׃ | and your household | CST | noun |
| בַּיִת | *û·vê·te·kā* | W/ CONJ וְ + 2MS SX | |

27a   וְהַלֵּוִי אֲשֶׁר־בִּשְׁעָרֶיךָ לֹא תַעַזְבֶנּוּ

And you shall not abandon the Levite who is in your towns,

| וְהַלֵּוִי | and the Levite | MS SUBST | adj |
| לֵוִי | *wə·hal·lē·wî* | W/ CONJ וְ + DEF. ART. | |

| אֲשֶׁר־ | who/that/which | --- | relative pron |
| אֲשֶׁר | *ʾă·šer* | | |

| בִּשְׁעָרֶיךָ | (is) in your gates | CST | noun |
| שַׁעַר | *biš·ʿā·rê·kā* | W/ PREP בְּ + 2MS SX | |

| לֹא | no/not | --- | particle |
| לֹא | *lōʾ* | | |

| תַעַזְבֶנּוּ | you will leave/abandon/ neglect | QAL IMPF 2MS | verb |
| עזב | *ta·ʿaz·ven·nû* | W/ 3MS SX | |

כִּי אֵין לְוֹ חֵלֶק וְנַחֲלָה עִמָּךְ׃

for he has no portion or inheritance with you.

כִּי	for/that	---	con
כִּי	*kî*		
אֵין	there is not	---	particle
אֵין	*'ên*		
לְוֹ	to him	---	prep
לְ	*lô*	W/ 3MS SX	
חֵלֶק	portion/lot	ABS	noun
חֵלֶק	*ḥē·leq*		
וְנַחֲלָה	or inheritance	ABS	noun
נַחֲלָה	*wə·na·ḥă·lâ*	W/ CONJ וְ	
עִמָּךְ׃	with you	---	prep
עִם	*'im·māḵ*	W/ 2MS SX	

28a

מִקְצֵה | שָׁלֹשׁ שָׁנִים תּוֹצִיא

miqṣē šālōš šānîm tôṣî'

אֶת־כָּל־מַעְשַׂר תְּבוּאָתְךָ בַּשָּׁנָה הַהִוא

'et-kol-ma'śar təvû'ātəkā baššānâ hahî'

At the end of the third year, you shall bring out
a full tithe of your produce for that year

28b

וְהִנַּחְתָּ בִּשְׁעָרֶיךָ:

wəhinnaḥtā biš'ārêkā.

and store it in your towns.

29a

וּבָא הַלֵּוִי כִּי אֵין־לוֹ חֵלֶק וְנַחֲלָה עִמָּךְ

ûvā' hallēwî kî 'ēn-lô ḥēleq wənaḥălâ 'immāk

And the Levite, because he has no inheritance with you, shall come—

29b

וְהַגֵּר וְהַיָּתוֹם וְהָאַלְמָנָה אֲשֶׁר בִּשְׁעָרֶיךָ

wəhaggēr wəhayyātôm wəhā'almānâ 'ăšer biš'ārêkā

and the sojourner, and the orphan and the widow
who are in your towns—

29c

וְאָכְלוּ וְשָׂבֵעוּ

wə'ākəlû wəśāvē'û

and they shall eat and be satisfied,

29d

לְמַעַן יְבָרֶכְךָ יְהוָה אֱלֹהֶיךָ בְּכָל־מַעֲשֵׂה יָדְךָ אֲשֶׁר תַּעֲשֶׂה:

ləma'an yəvārekəkā YHWH 'ĕlōhêkā bəkōl-ma'ăśē yādəkā 'ăšer ta'ăśe.

so that Yahweh your God may bless you
in all the work of your hand that you do.

מִקְצֵה| שָׁלֹשׁ שָׁנִים תּוֹצִיא
אֶת־כָּל־מַעְשַׂר תְּבוּאָתְךָ בַּשָּׁנָה הַהִוא

At the end of the third year, you shall bring out
a full tithe of your produce for that year

מִקְצֵה|	from end of	CST	noun
קָצֶה	miq·ṣē	W/ PREP מִן	
שָׁלֹשׁ	three	ABS	cardinal
שָׁלֹשׁ	šā·lōš		number
שָׁנִים	years	ABS	noun
שָׁנָה	šā·nîm		
תּוֹצִיא	you will bring	HIPH IMPF 2MS	verb
יצא	tô·ṣî'		
אֶת־	(direct object marker)	---	particle
אֵת	'et-		
כָּל־	all	CST	noun
כֹּל	kol-		
מַעְשַׂר	the tithe of	CST	noun
מַעֲשֵׂר	ma'·śar		
תְּבוּאָתְךָ	your produce/crop	CST	noun
תְּבוּאָה	tə·vû·'ā·tə·ḵā	W/ 2MS SX	
בַּשָּׁנָה	in (the) year	ABS	noun
שָׁנָה	baš·šā·nâ	W/ PREP בְּ + DEF. ART.	
הַהִוא	(the) that/same	---	demonstr
הִיא	ha·hī'	W/ DEF. ART.	pron

וְהִנַּחְתָּ בִּשְׁעָרֶיךָ:

and store it in your towns.

וְהִנַּחְתָּ	and rest/lay it up	HIPH WEQATAL 2MS	verb
נוח	wə·hin·naḥ·tā		
בִּשְׁעָרֶיךָ:	in your gates/towns	CST	noun
שַׁעַר	biš·'ā·rê·ḵā	W/ PREP בְּ + 2MS SX	

וּבָא הַלֵּוִי כִּי אֵין־לוֹ חֵלֶק וְנַחֲלָה עִמָּךְ

And the Levite, because he has no inheritance with you, shall come—

וּבָא	and (he) will come	QAL WEQATAL 3MS	verb
בוא	*û·vā'*		
הַלֵּוִי	the Levite	MS SUBST W/ DEF. ART.	adj
לֵוִי	*hal·lē·wî*		
כִּי	for/because	---	conj
כִּי	*kî*		
אֵין־	there is no/not	---	particle
אַיִן	*'ên-*		
לוֹ	to him	--- W/ 3MS SX	prep
ל	*lô*		
חֵלֶק	portion/lot	ABS	noun
חֵלֶק	*ḥē·leq*		
וְנַחֲלָה	or inheritance	ABS W/ CONJ וְ	noun
נַחֲלָה	*wə·na·ḥă·lâ*		
עִמָּךְ	with you	--- W/ 2MS SX	prep
עִם	*'im·māḵ*		

וְהַגֵּר וְהַיָּתוֹם וְהָאַלְמָנָה אֲשֶׁר בִּשְׁעָרֶיךָ

and the sojourner, and the orphan and the widow
who are in your towns—

וְהַגֵּר	and the sojourner/foreigner	ABS W/ CONJ וְ + DEF. ART.	noun
גֵּר	*wə·hag·gēr*		
וְהַיָּתוֹם	and the fatherless/orphan	ABS W/ CONJ וְ + DEF. ART.	noun
יָתוֹם	*wə·hay·yā·tôm*		
וְהָאַלְמָנָה	and the widow	ABS W/ CONJ וְ + DEF. ART.	noun
אַלְמָנָה	*wə·hā·'al·mā·nâ*		
אֲשֶׁר	who/that/which	---	relative pron
אֲשֶׁר	*'ă·šer*		
בִּשְׁעָרֶיךָ	(is) in your gates/towns	CST W/ PREP בְּ + 2MS SX	noun
שַׁעַר	*biš·'ā·rê·ḵā*		

and they shall eat and be satisfied,

| וְאָכְלוּ
אכל | and they will eat
wə·ʾā·ḵə·lû | QAL WEQATAL 3CP | verb |
| וְשָׂבֵעוּ
שׂבע | and they will be satisfied/filled
wə·śā·vē·ʿû | QAL WEQATAL 3CP | verb |

This promise is repeated five times: 6:11; 8:10; 11:15; 31:20. It also appears in Ps 78:29, Ruth 2:14, and Neh 9:25.

so that Yahweh your God may bless you
in all the work of your hand that you do.

לְמַעַן לְמַעַן	in order that *lə·ma·ʿan*	- - -	prep
יְבָרֶכְךָ ברך	(he) will bless you *yə·vā·re·ḵə·ḵā*	PIEL IMPF 3MS W/ 2MS SX	verb
יְהוָה יהוה	Yahweh *YHWH*	ABS	noun
אֱלֹהֶיךָ אֱלֹהִים	your God *ʾĕ·lō·hê·ḵā*	CST W/ 2MS SX	noun
בְּכָל־ כֹּל	in all *bə·ḵōl-*	CST W/ PREP בְּ	noun
מַעֲשֵׂה מַעֲשֶׂה	the work of *ma·ʿă·śē*	CST	noun
יָדֶךָ יָד	your hand *yā·də·ḵā*	CST W/ 2MS SX	noun
אֲשֶׁר אֲשֶׁר	that/which *ʾă·šer*	- - -	relative pron
תַּעֲשֶׂה׃ עשׂה	you make/do *ta·ʿă·śe*	QAL IMPF 2MS	verb

The phrase "the work of your hand(s)," מַעֲשֵׂה יָדֶ(י)ךָ, occurs six times in Deuteronomy, more than in any other Old Testament book (2:7; 14:29; 16:15; 24:19; 28:12; 30:9). See "From Text to Sermon" for more.

 *The Tithe and the Food That Teach a Community to Fear Yahweh.*

> *[Eating] is the first and most urgent activity*
> *of all animal and human life. We are*
> *only because we eat. (Kass 1992:2)*

> *Food communicates class, ethnic group, lifestyle*
> *affiliation, and other social positions. Eating is usually*
> *a social matter, and people eat every day. Thus, food*
> *is available for management as a way of showing the*
> *world many things about the eater. It naturally takes*
> *on much of the role of communicating everything.*
> *Indeed, it may be second only to language as a social*
> *communication system. (Anderson 2005:124)*

This is the second of four communal meal passages in Deuteronomy (12:13–27; 14:22–29; 16:1–17; 26:1–15). We will look closely at 16:1–17 in a future section, but it's important for the reader to be well acquainted with the passages in chs. 12 and 26 as they are tied closely to 14:22–29. These meals in Israel's law shape its culture, its memories, its social consciousness, and its hope for the future. Our present passage in 14:22–29 consists of two tithes. The first is an annual tithe brought to God's chosen place for the purposes of worship and feasting (vv. 22–27). The second is a triennial tithe that is eaten in local "towns" (vv. 28–29). I'll break down the passage topically to help draw out some ideas for preaching, beginning with a background on ancient feasts.

 *The Tithe: Old Testament and Ancient Near Eastern Background on the Banquet.* We find nothing comparable to these tithe laws in the rest of the Old Testament. There is no tithe in the Book of the Covenant (Exod 22–24), and the tithe in Num 18:21–32 appears to be a narrower law focused on compensating the Levites for their service. The tithes in Lev 27:30–33, meanwhile, went to the sanctuary while tithes in Amos 4:4–5 are voluntary sacrifices (Nelson 2004:184).

From what we know about comparable tithes in Egypt and Ugarit, the proceeds went to the royal house. It is no coincidence that, in response to Israel's desire for a king, Samuel warns Israel about royal power and abuses of this very practice (1 Sam 8:10–18). In the Neo-Babylonian and Neo-Assyrian periods, meanwhile, the proceeds of a tithe went to the temple. And so among all the tithes in the ancient world, only Deuteronomy retains the food for public consumption. At Altmann puts it: "The Israelites are to eat their taxes" (2011:224–26).

At first glance, the absence of the king in this passage may seem striking. After all, taxes in the ancient world were almost always based on royal decrees. But in the context of Deuteronomy, Israel's king is in the background. Deuteronomy calls him one "from among your brothers" and forbids him from "multiplying silver and gold to himself" (17:14–20). More than that, the king is one with the people at this feast who are meant to "learn to fear Yahweh your God" (14:23; 17:19). Israel will indeed bring their tithe, but to Yahweh their divine king who gives it all back (Glanville 2018:153).

🌿 ***The Food.*** The choice of food for the annual tithe is lavish and is likely based on the foods listed in the introduction to the tithe and the gathering of the people at "the place" in 12:18–28. Eating ten percent of the annual harvest at one feast would seem an absurdly wasteful amount of food today. Yet is it not uncommon for what we know of ancient royal feasts. Altmann (2011:234–35) sums up the scene well:

> The inclusion of portions of the entire yield (meat, grains, grapes, and oil) implies that the foodstuffs take on the character of and should be understood as an exquisite feast, thereby portraying the people of [Deuteronomy's] banquets as Yhwh's chosen guests at a sumptuous banquet, akin to the those portrayed in the Neo-Assyrian palace reliefs.

Deuteronomy thus draws on a common ritual to refresh the memory of their story in the heart of every Israelite. Two main lessons stand out.

(1) *Grace.* The many similarities between this tithe and the food specified in laws for worship in 12:13–21 link the tithe to God's generous blessing in the land. Everything Israel owns will have come from him. All is grace and nothing communicates grace so naturally as a sumptuous, extravagant feast. This is the central theme in Isak Dinesen's short story "Babette's Feast." In the middle of a banquet that cost Babette her whole life's savings, her distinguished guest General Löewenhielm addresses the room:

> But the moment comes when our eyes are opened, and we see and realize that grace is infinite. Grace, my friends, demands nothing

from us but that we shall await it with confidence and acknowledge it in gratitude. Grace, brothers, makes no conditions and singles out none of us in particular; grace takes us all to its bosom and proclaims general amnesty. . . . For mercy and truth have met together, and righteousness and bliss have kissed one another! (Dinesen 2010:38–39)

(2) *Called to a life of gratitude.* The wonderful breadth of food is the result of Israel's grateful obedience to Yahweh. Whereas the Sabbath law emphasized rest for Israel, this promise that God will bless מַעֲשֵׂה יָדְךָ ("the work of your hand," 14:29) reflects future habits of diligent work the other six days of the week. Meat, grain, oil, and wine will not just fall from the sky but result from the union of hard work and divine blessing.

Similarly, the Valiant Woman in Prov 31:10–31 is praised for the "fruit of her hands" (v. 31). Scholars recognize the way her "hand" and "palm" hold the activities of the chapter together (vv. 13, 16, 19, 20, 31) such that her hands come to represent the great breadth of her accomplishments: cooking, agriculture, real estate, textiles, parenting, marriage, care for the poor, and teaching. In this way, "hands" in Deuteronomy and Prov 31 represent God's blessing on our particular vocations in this world.

 ***The Community That Fears Yahweh.*** I have an economist friend who boasts that food is the center of economics. After all, if we cannot eat, other economic goods don't matter. But then there is also all the harvesting, storing, shipping, selling, and cooking of food that we do for billions and billions of people every day, all of them driving their own massive economies. More people in this world work in some area of agribusiness than in any other field. Food economies are truly at the heart of every culture.

By centering its religion on regular feasting, Deuteronomy effortlessly weaves its message into the warp and woof of Israelite life: economics, family, politics, education, and social order. More importantly, these tithing rituals serve to shape Israel into a certain kind of people, namely, those who "learn to fear Yahweh your God" (14:23). As an important aside, it is worth highlighting here that the woman in Prov 31 was also distinguished as one who "fears Yahweh" (31:30). In both passages (Deut and Prov) we can see that the fear of Yahweh is more than simply a theological idea: it is a social way of living that honors God through diligence, communal love, food, generosity, and rejoicing.

Each tithe (vv. 22–27, 28–29) has its own focus. The first is the annual tithe that results in a feast at "the place" Yahweh chooses. The law specifically directs Israel to gather by household, and to not "abandon the Levite" who "has no portion or inheritance with you." The Levites were able to have gardens for food, but they did not have large parcels of land to contribute significantly to a feast. We must also recognize that Deuteronomy's strict restriction of worship to a single "place" would mean that Levites, who served when altars were dispersed throughout the land, would gradually lose their place in local communities as worship came to a central place (12:1–7) (Altmann, 2011:235). The Levites' calling was also to keep Israel focused on its covenant obligations to be holy to Yahweh (14:2). By including this isolated group, the law serves both as a way to broadly welcome guests and a reminder of Israel's call to holiness.

The second tithe was consumed in Israel's towns every three years, focusing on landless residents in Israel: the Levite, sojourner, the orphan, and the widow (v. 29). While scholars often interpret this tithe as collection for the poor, which would certainly be one result, this feast has a larger focus. Notice first that these groups are not poor by definition; widows and Levites could have significant resources. Further, neither the word for "poor" (אֶבְיוֹן) or "needy" (עָנִי) appear in this section as they do in 15:4–11 and 24:12–15. The law thus serves two interrelated roles. It gives those most easily isolated common access to the local stores of accumulated wealth, and it provides a means for gathering, belonging, and rejoicing (Deut 14:26) (McConville 2002:252).

🌱 *Hospitality and Fearing God.* A sermon could paint a mental picture of the annual and triennial feasts. Who is sitting where? And who has the best food? More than anything, meals have the power to unite and to divide people. Weddings, dinner parties, and cafeteria lunch tables all naturally separate those on the inside from those on the outside. In the same way, ancient Near Eastern royal banquets determined who was worthy to feast with the king and who was of a lesser class. Deuteronomy turns these sorting practices on their heads, welcoming everyone equally to the feast Yahweh gives (Glanville 2018:153). Exclusionary and elitist attitudes are thus transformed into practices of hospitality aimed at the one most vulnerable to loneliness and isolation—the stranger. Leon Kass observes:

> Hospitality recognizes simultaneously the neediness and vulnerability and also the humanity of the stranger. Sympathy and fellow feeling are aroused by the sight of another human being away from hearth and home, without the sustenance and nurture they provide. . . . The stranger knows that we know that we both know

what it is to be estranged and necessitous. To feed the stranger
is to make him feel less his absence from his own. (1999:105–6)

We looked earlier at Samuel's warning to Israel that future kings would lay a heavy burden upon them, conscripting the men for military service and putting women to work in service of the king's comforts (1 Sam 8:10–18). In sharp contrast, we find David taking his throne and seeking to show kindness to anyone who might be forgotten. This brings to his mind Jonathan's physically disabled son Mephibosheth. David invites him to eat at his table the rest of his days (2 Sam 9:1–13). A stranger becomes a friend at a feast. Two types of possible kings emerge in the narrative.

To "learn to fear Yahweh," then, means faithfully engaging in practices of eating and remembering that engrain in Israel a dual sense of loyalty to God alongside solidarity, rejoicing, and mutual care among the ones most likely to be forgotten (Nelson 2004:185).

Jesus was publicly criticized for his own determination to gather with outcasts at tables—the sick, the physically disabled, prostitutes, sinners, and tax collectors. Yet we find already in the early church that Christians were prone to lose this vision, calling for frequent reminders:

So then, my brothers and sisters, when you come together to
eat, wait for one another. (1 Cor 11:33 NRSV)

Welcome one another, therefore, just as Christ has welcomed
you, for the glory of God. (Rom 15:7 NRSV)

The vision in Deuteronomy thus lives on in the church. Christ becomes the royal host who invites us; he also becomes the tithe we share, the brother who turns strangers into friends, and the one through whom we give thanks to the Father.

FREEDOM FOR THE OPPRESSED AND THE MORALITY OF KINSHIP

While we only cover the first eleven verses of ch. 15 in this volume, it is important to recognize that there are two sets of interrelated laws for the seventh-year Sabbath: the release of debts (vv. 1–11) and the release of bond slaves (manumission) (vv. 12–18). From the perspective of jurisprudence, the laws follow a design similar to what Stephen Toulmin calls "warrants" that combine data with conclusions based on sound premises (2003:89–107). The following outline of the laws is taken from material in Hamilton (1992:26):

15:1	Heading Law	15:12
15:2–3	Warrant	15:13–14
15:4–6	Call to Obedience	15:15
15:7–11	Consequence in Specific Situation	15:16–18
15:11	Surprise	15:16

In our study of the Decalogue, we have emphasized the close connection between the Ten Words and the groupings of laws in chs. 12–26. For example:

(1)	Deut 12:2–13:19	One Temple, One God
(2)	Deut 14:1–21	Bearing God's Name Falsely
(3)	Deut 14:22–16:17	Sabbath, Land, Food, Time
(4)	Deut 16:18–18:22	Authority in the Home, City, and Nation

While these connections are debated, the link between the Sabbath command and these laws in chs. 14–16 is one that receives almost unanimous recognition. The weekly rest God gives becomes the basis for bringing grace and aid to the gaps in Israel's economic and social life.

LARGER LITERARY CONTEXT ▸ 15:1–18

Sermons on this passage (and perhaps also on the manumission law in vv. 12–18) require some historical background on what we know of ancient economies and debts. In the ancient agrarian world, one was always in a place of vulnerability: low crop yields, human sickness, animal sickness, mold, blight, drought, theft, and the simple failures that come with trying to plant and gather productively. Need and inequality were constant realities.

A worker in financial trouble at the start of the year could take a loan of seed or animals from a lender and offer up material goods like land, animals, or money as a pledge to secure the loan. Subsequent loans would add to the debt and require further pledges. As a result, a borrower could have two growing debts. In a dire situation, the borrower would have to sell a member of the household into debt slavery, as described in 15:12. In the very worst case, the borrower would default on the loan altogether, losing the pledge of land in the process. Here we can see an emerging world of monopolies of land among the elite and increasing wealth gaps between rich and poor.

To attend to this socially unsettling tendency, the Mosaic law provides what Patrick Miller (2004a) describes as a "trajectory" of Sabbath laws that stretch from the weekly day of rest to the seven-year cycle of provisions in Deut 15 and then to a 49-year Sabbath at the Jubilee in Lev 25. Each law provided humanitarian relief where previous Sabbath laws fell short (2004a:10–11).

The two laws in this chapter put a limit on debts and helped the borrower recover from a downward spiral of debt. The first law requires owners to grant a remission in the seventh year. Interpreters are uncertain as to whether the release was simply a deferral for one year or a cancellation, and about whether the release applied only to pledges, or to loans as well as pledges. One may consult the discussion and bibliography in Baker, who believes that it is a permanent cancelation of the loan (2009:278–79).

Baker's view is supported by the presentation of loans in the sixth year (vv. 9–10). Giving a loan in the sixth year would mean the lender could not claim the loan or any pledges for at least two years, if at all. A loan in the first year or two offered at least a chance at recuperation. The obvious temptation was to "look meanly on your brother" and refuse the loan. The law counters this temptation with theological and spiritual motivations. Theologically, it warns that if the poor man cries out to God, it will be counted as sin against the lender, perhaps inviting a curse of his land and crops (see 28:15–68). God is always watching. Spiritually, it reminds them of God's ongoing blessing with an encouragement to be generous and empathetic to the needy person. As we will see below, this will lead to several possible angles for preaching this text.

1

מִקֵּץ שֶׁבַע־שָׁנִים תַּעֲשֶׂה שְׁמִטָּה׃

miqqēṣ ševa'-šānîm ta'ăśe šəmiṭṭâ.

At the end of seven years, you shall make a release.

2a

וְזֶה דְּבַר הַשְּׁמִטָּה שָׁמוֹט

wəze dəvar haššəmiṭṭâ šāmôṭ

And this is the manner of the release:

2b

כָּל־בַּעַל מַשֵּׁה יָדוֹ אֲשֶׁר יַשֶּׁה בְּרֵעֵהוּ

kol-ba'al maššē yādô 'ăšer yašše bərē'ēhû

every creditor who has a loan shall release it to his neighbor;

2c

לֹא־יִגֹּשׂ אֶת־רֵעֵהוּ וְאֶת־אָחִיו

lō'-yiggōś 'et-rē'ēhû wə'et-'āḥîw

he shall not exact it of his neighbor, his brother.

2d

כִּי־קָרָא שְׁמִטָּה לַיהוָה׃

kî-qārā' šəmiṭṭâ laYHWH.

For Yahweh's release has been proclaimed.

3a

אֶת־הַנָּכְרִי תִּגֹּשׂ

'et-hannokrî tiggōś

Of the stranger, he may exact it;

3b

וַאֲשֶׁר יִהְיֶה לְךָ אֶת־אָחִיךָ תַּשְׁמֵט יָדֶךָ׃

wa'ăšer yihye ləkā 'et-'āḥîkā tašmēt yādekā.

**but whatever claim you have against your brother,
you must release it.**

4a

אֶפֶס כִּי לֹא יִהְיֶה־בְּךָ אֶבְיוֹן

'efes kî lō' yihye-bəkā 'evyôn

Only there shall be no poor among you,

4b   כִּי־בָרֵךְ יְבָרֶכְךָ֫ יְהוָ֖ה בָּאָ֑רֶץ

kî-vārēk yəvārekəkā YHWH bāʾāreṣ

אֲשֶׁר֙ יְהוָ֣ה אֱלֹהֶ֔יךָ נֹתֵן־לְךָ֖ נַחֲלָ֣ה לְרִשְׁתָּֽהּ׃

ʾăšer YHWH ʾĕlōhêkā nōtēn-ləkā naḥălâ ləristāh.

because Yahweh will surely bless you in the land
that Yahweh your God is giving you as an inheritance to possess,

5a   רַ֗ק אִם־שָׁמ֤וֹעַ תִּשְׁמַע֙ בְּק֖וֹל יְהוָ֣ה אֱלֹהֶ֔יךָ

raq ʾim-šāmôaʿ tišmaʿ bəqôl YHWH ʾĕlōhêkā

if only you listen intently to the voice of Yahweh your God

5b לִשְׁמֹ֨ר לַעֲשׂ֜וֹת אֶת־כָּל־הַמִּצְוָ֣ה הַזֹּ֗את אֲשֶׁ֧ר אָנֹכִ֛י מְצַוְּךָ֖ הַיּֽוֹם׃

lišmōr laʿăśôt ʾet-kol-hammiṣwâ hazzōʾt ʾăšer ʾānōkî məṣawwəkā hayyôm.

by keeping and doing all this commandment
that I am commanding you today.

6a   כִּֽי־יְהוָ֤ה אֱלֹהֶ֙יךָ֙ בֵּֽרַכְךָ֔ כַּאֲשֶׁ֖ר דִּבֶּר־לָ֑ךְ

kî-YHWH ʾĕlōhêkā bērakəkā kaʾăšer dibber-lāk

For Yahweh your God will bless you, just as he promised you.

6b   וְהַֽעֲבַטְתָּ֞ גּוֹיִ֤ם רַבִּים֙ וְאַתָּ֣ה לֹ֣א תַעֲבֹ֔ט

wəhaʿăvaṭtā gôyim rabbîm wəʾattâ lōʾ taʿăvōṭ

And you will lend to many nations, but you shall not borrow;

6c   וּמָֽשַׁלְתָּ֙ בְּגוֹיִ֣ם רַבִּ֔ים וּבְךָ֖ לֹ֥א יִמְשֹֽׁלוּ׃

ûmāšaltā bəgôyim rabbîm ûvəkā lōʾ yimšōlû.

and you will rule over many nations, but over you they will not rule.

מִקֵּץ שֶׁבַע־שָׁנִים תַּעֲשֶׂה שְׁמִטָּה:

At the end of seven years, you shall make a release.

מִקֵּץ	at (the) end of	CST	noun
קֵץ	*miq·qēṣ*	W/ PREP מִן	
שֶׁבַע־	seven	ABS	cardinal
שֶׁבַע	*še·vaʿ-*		number
שָׁנִים	years	ABS	noun
שָׁנָה	*šā·nîm*		
תַּעֲשֶׂה	you will do/make	QAL IMPF 2MS	verb
עשׂה	*ta·ʿă·śe*		
שְׁמִטָּה:	release	ABS	noun
שְׁמִטָּה	*šə·miṭ·ṭâ*		

Nelson describes v. 1 as a "legislative jussive," which he translates, "you shall perform a debt remission" (2004:187, 189). We will see the legal force of the law arise alongside rhetorical and theological persuasion.

Somewhat relatedly, Hamilton has suggested that, more important than "phrasing, vocabulary, and syntax," the key to Deuteronomy is understanding its "anatomy of evocation and exhortation" (1992:9). That is, how does it appeal uniquely to the human sense of duty and obligation?

וְזֶה דְּבַר הַשְּׁמִטָּה שָׁמוֹט

And this is the manner of the release:

וְזֶה	and this	---	demonstr
זֶה	*wə·ze*	W/ CONJ וְ	pron
דְּבַר	word/manner/thing of	CST	noun
דְּבֶר	*də·var*		
הַשְּׁמִטָּה	the release	ABS	noun
שְׁמִטָּה	*haš·šə·miṭ·ṭâ*	W/ DEF. ART.	
שָׁמוֹט	to release/let go	QAL INF ABS	verb
שמט	*šā·môṭ*		

Hamilton observes that this parenthetical remark sets Israel's remission off from other laws of *šemittah*, or cancellation, in the ancient Near East (1992:17). Deuteronomy's version looks to be an expansion of the fallow year of "release" for the land in Exod 23:10–11.

כָּל־בַּֽעַל מַשֵּׁה יָדוֹ אֲשֶׁר יַשֶּׁה בְּרֵעֵהוּ

Every creditor who has a loan shall release it to his neighbor;

כָּל־ כֹּל	all/everything *kol-*	CST	noun
בַּֽעַל בַּעַל	owner/lord/master of *ba·'al*	ABS	noun
מַשֵּׁה מַשֶּׁה	(the) loan of *maš·šē*	CST	noun
יָדוֹ יָד	his hand *yā·dô*	CST W/ 3MS SX	noun
אֲשֶׁר אֲשֶׁר	that/which *'ă·šer*	---	relative pron
יַשֶּׁה נשה	he loaned *yaš·še*	HIPH IMPF 3MS	verb
בְּרֵעֵהוּ רֵעַ	to his friend/neighbor *bə·rē·'ē·hû*	CST W/ PREP בְּ + 3MS SX	noun

In the framework of jurisprudence, this phrase answers the question, "Who has to give a remission?" Everyone does. It is not clear here whether מַשֶּׁה refers to a loan or a pledge or security put up for an outstanding loan (Wright 1990:169–73).

לֹא־יִגֹּשׂ אֶת־רֵעֵהוּ וְאֶת־אָחִיו

he shall not exact it of his neighbor, his brother.

לֹא־ לֹא	no/not *lō'-*	---	particle
יִגֹּשׂ נגשׂ	he will press/exact *yig·gōš*	QAL IMPF 3MS	verb
אֶת־ אֵת	(direct object marker) *'et-*	---	particle
רֵעֵהוּ רֵעַ	his friend/neighbor *rē·'ē·hû*	CST W/ 3MS SX	noun
וְאֶת־ אֵת	and (+ direct object marker) *wə·'et-*	--- W/ CONJ וְ	particle

אָחִיו	his brother	CST	noun
אָח	'ā·ḥîw	W/ 3MS SX	

This clause answers two questions of jurisprudence: Who is eligible for remission? Answer: All Israelites. And, why? Answer: Because we are all kin.

2d — כִּי־קָרָא שְׁמִטָּה לַיהוָה:

For Yahweh's release has been proclaimed.

כִּי־	for/that/because	---	conj
כִּי	kî-		
קָרָא	it was proclaimed/declared	QAL PF 3MS	verb
קרא	qā·rā'		
שְׁמִטָּה	the release	ABS	noun
שְׁמִטָּה	šə·miṭ·ṭâ		
לַיהוָה:	of Yahweh	ABS	noun
יהוה	la·YHWH	W/ PREP לְ	

The motivation to love your kindred is backed up by the legal grounding of this law: Yahweh has commanded it.

3a — אֶת־הַנׇּכְרִי תִּגֹּשׂ

Of the stranger, he may exact it;

אֶת־	(direct object marker)	---	particle
אֶת	'et-		
הַנׇּכְרִי	the foreigner/stranger	MS SUBST	adj
נׇכְרִי	han·nok̠·rî	W/ DEF. ART.	
תִּגֹּשׂ	you will/may press/exact	QAL IMPF 2MS	verb
נגשׂ	tig·gōš		

This need not be taken as discrimination against strangers or foreigners, as they have several provisions for their vulnerability in Deuteronomy (e.g., 14:28–29). Rather, it specifies that this law is aimed at long-term financial stability between Israelite clans and families who own the land, and not foreign traders who may have financial dealings with Israelites.

וַאֲשֶׁר יִהְיֶה לְךָ אֶת־אָחִיךָ תַּשְׁמֵט יָדֶךָ׃

but whatever claim you have against your brother,
you must release it.

וַאֲשֶׁר אֲשֶׁר *wa·ʾă·šer*	and that/which/whatever	--- W/ CONJ וְ	relative pron
יִהְיֶה היה *yih·ye*	it will be	QAL IMPF 3MS	verb
לְךָ ל *lə·ḵā*	to/for you	--- W/ 2MS SX	prep
אֶת־ אֵת *ʾet-*	(direct object marker)	---	particle
אָחִיךָ אָח *ʾā·ḥî·ḵā*	your brother	CST W/ 2MS SX	noun
תַּשְׁמֵט שמט *taš·mēt*	you will release	HIPH IMPF 2MS	verb
יָדֶךָ׃ יָד *yā·de·ḵā*	your hand	CST W/ 2MS SX	noun

To the question, "What kinds of claims are included in this law?" the answer is everything. When translated literally, the Hebrew phrase תַּשְׁמֵט יָדֶךָ means "you must/will release your hand." This may arise from an Akkadian phrase which means "to loosen the hand" (Weinfeld 1995:162–63).

אֶפֶס כִּי לֹא יִהְיֶה־בְּךָ אֶבְיוֹן

Only there shall be no poor among you,

אֶפֶס אֶפֶס *ʾe·fes*	nothing/no	ABS	noun
כִּי כִּי *kî*	that/which	---	conj
לֹא לֹא *lō'*	no/not	---	particle
יִהְיֶה־ היה *yih·ye-*	there will be	QAL IMPF 3MS	verb
בְּךָ בְּ *bə·ḵā*	of/among you	--- W/ 2MS SX	prep

| אֶבְיוֹן | poor | MS SUBST | adj |
| אֶבְיוֹן | 'ev·yôn | | |

This is the social goal, or the vision of an ideal community. Compare this to v. 11.

4b כִּי־בָרֵךְ יְבָרֶכְךָ֫ יְהוָֹה בָּאָ֫רֶץ
אֲשֶׁר יְהוָה אֱלֹהֶיךָ נֹתֵן־לְךָ֫ נַחֲלָה לְרִשְׁתָּהּ׃

because Yahweh will surely bless you in the land
that Yahweh your God is giving you as an inheritance to possess,

כִּי־	for/that/because	---	conj
כִּי	kî-		
בָרֵךְ	to bless	PIEL INF ABS	verb
ברך	vā·rēk		
יְבָרֶכְךָ	(he) will bless you	PIEL IMPF 3MS W/ 2MS SX	verb
ברך	yə·vā·re·kə·kā		
יְהוָֹה	Yahweh	ABS	noun
יהוה	YHWH		
בָּאָ֫רֶץ	in the land	ABS W/ PREP בְּ + DEF. ART.	noun
אֶרֶץ	bā·'ā·reṣ		
אֲשֶׁר	that/which	---	relative pron
אֲשֶׁר	'ă·šer		
יְהוָה	Yahweh	ABS	noun
יהוה	YHWH		
אֱלֹהֶיךָ	your God	CST W/ 2MS SX	noun
אֱלֹהִים	'ĕ·lō·hê·kā		
נֹתֵן־	(is) giving	QAL PTCP MS	verb
נתן	nō·tēn-		
לְךָ	to you	--- W/ 2MS SX	prep
ל	lə·kā		
נַחֲלָה	(as) an inheritance	ABS	noun
נַחֲלָה	na·ḥă·lâ		
לְרִשְׁתָּהּ׃	to possess it	QAL INF CST W/ PREP לְ + 3FS SX	verb
ירשׁ	lə·riš·tāh		

As Hamilton observes, this is the first of eight times that ch. 15 uses an infinitive absolute plus imperfect verb of the same root, which has an intensifying force (here in v. 4: "Yahweh will surely bless"), far more than any other chapter in Deuteronomy (1992:13). The language is both legal (i.e., "you *must* do this") and rhetorical (i.e., "*please* be gracious"), demonstrating "the care which is being taken to dictate the way in which this text effects its audience" (1992:13).

<table>
<tr><td>5a</td><td colspan="3" align="center">רַק אִם־שָׁמֹועַ תִּשְׁמַע בְּקֹול יְהוָה אֱלֹהֶיךָ</td></tr>
</table>

	if only you listen intently to the voice of Yahweh your God		
רַק	surely/only	---	adv
רק	*raq*		
אִם־	if	---	conj
אם	*'im-*		
שָׁמֹועַ	to listen	QAL INF ABS	verb
שמע	*šā·mô·a'*		
תִּשְׁמַע	you listen	QAL IMPF 2MS	verb
שמע	*tiš·ma'*		
בְּקֹול	to (the) voice of	CST	noun
קול	*bə·qôl*	W/ PREP בְּ	
יְהוָה	Yahweh	ABS	noun
יהוה	*YHWH*		
אֱלֹהֶיךָ	your God	CST	noun
אלהים	*'ĕ·lō·hê·kā*	W/ 2MS SX	

Again, the rhetorical emphasis comes through in רַק אִם ("if only"). The conditional clause probably applies to both v. 4a and v. 4b: if you obey, there will be no poor, because Yahweh will bless you.

<table>
<tr><td>5b</td><td colspan="3" align="center">לִשְׁמֹר לַעֲשֹׂות אֶת־כָּל־הַמִּצְוָה הַזֹּאת אֲשֶׁר אָנֹכִי מְצַוְּךָ הַיֹּום:</td></tr>
</table>

	by keeping and doing all this commandment that I am commanding you today.		
לִשְׁמֹר	to guard/keep	QAL INF CST	verb
שמר	*liš·mōr*	W/ PREP לְ	
לַעֲשֹׂות	to do/make	QAL INF CST	verb
עשה	*la·'ă·śôt*	W/ PREP לְ	

אֶת־ אֵת *’et-*	(direct object marker)	---	particle
כָּל־ כֹּל *kol-*	all/every	CST	noun
הַמִּצְוָה מִצְוָה *ham·miṣ·wâ*	(the) commandment	ABS W/ DEF. ART.	noun
הַזֹּאת זֹאת *haz·zōʼt*	(the) this	--- W/ DEF. ART.	demonstr pron
אֲשֶׁר אֲשֶׁר *ăšer*	that/which	---	relative pron
אָנֹכִי אָנֹכִי *ā·nō·kî*	I	---	personal pron
מְצַוְּךָ צוה *mə·ṣaw·wə·kā*	(am) commanding you	PIEL PTCP MS W/ 2MS SX	verb
הַיּוֹם: יוֹם *hay·yôm*	today	ABS W/ DEF. ART.	noun

Verse 5b links Moses' authority both to Yahweh's authority (v. 2d) and to God's promise to bless Israel for obedience (v. 6a).

6a	כִּי־יְהוָה אֱלֹהֶיךָ בֵּרַכְךָ כַּאֲשֶׁר דִּבֶּר־לָךְ

For Yahweh your God will bless you, just as he promised you.

כִּי־ כִּי *kî-*	for/that/because	---	conj
יְהוָה יהוה *YHWH*	Yahweh	ABS	noun
אֱלֹהֶיךָ אֱלֹהִים *ĕ·lō·hê·kā*	your God	CST W/ 2MS SX	noun
בֵּרַכְךָ ברך *bē·ra·kə·kā*	(he) will bless you	PIEL PF 3MS W/ 2MS SX	verb
כַּאֲשֶׁר אֲשֶׁר *ka·ʼă·šer*	according to/just as	--- W/ PREP כְּ	relative pron
דִּבֶּר־ דבר *dib·ber-*	he spoke/promised	PIEL PF 3MS	verb

לָ֔ךְ לְ *lāk*	to you	--- W/ 2MS SX	prep

6b

וְהַעֲבַטְתָּ֙ גּוֹיִ֣ם רַבִּ֔ים וְאַתָּה֙ לֹ֣א תַעֲבֹ֔ט

And you will lend to many nations, but you shall not borrow;

וְהַעֲבַטְתָּ֙ עבט *wə·ha·ʿă·vaṭ·tā*	you will give/lend	HIPH WEQATAL 2MS	verb
גּוֹיִ֣ם גּוֹי *gô·yim*	(to) nations	ABS	noun
רַבִּ֔ים רַב *rab·bîm*	many/numerous	MP ATTR	adj
וְאַתָּה֙ אַתָּה *wə·ʾat·tâ*	and/but you	--- W/ CONJ וְ	personal pron
לֹ֣א לֹא *lō'*	no/not	---	particle
תַעֲבֹ֔ט עבט *ta·ʿă·vōṭ*	(you) will borrow	QAL IMPF 2MS	verb

The ideal vision of this community pictures a system of such gracious sharing and meeting of needs that they will have no reason to call upon other nations for help during economic distress.

6c

וּמָשַׁלְתָּ֙ בְּגוֹיִ֣ם רַבִּ֔ים וּבְךָ֖ לֹ֣א יִמְשֹֽׁלוּ׃

and you will rule over many nations, but over you they will not rule.

וּמָשַׁלְתָּ֙ משל *û·mā·šal·tā*	and you will rule	QAL WEQATAL 2MS	verb
בְּגוֹיִ֣ם גּוֹי *bə·gô·yim*	over nations	ABS W/ PREP בְּ	noun
רַבִּ֔ים רַב *rab·bîm*	many/numerous	MP ATTR	adj
וּבְךָ֖ בְּ *û·və·kā*	and/but over you	--- W/ CONJ וְ + 2MS SX	prep

לֹא	no/not	---	particle
לֹא	*lōʾ*		
יִמְשֹׁלוּ:	they will rule	QAL IMPF 3MP	verb
מׁשל	*yim·šō·lû*		

This motivation clause anticipates the blessing in 28:13.

7a
כִּי־יִהְיֶה בְךָ֙ אֶבְיוֹן֙ מֵאַחַ֣ד אַחֶ֔יךָ

kî-yihye vəkā 'evyôn mē'aḥad 'aḥêkā

"When there is a poor person among one of your brothers,

7b
בְּאַחַ֣ד שְׁעָרֶ֔יךָ בְּאַרְצְךָ֖ אֲשֶׁר־יְהוָ֥ה אֱלֹהֶ֖יךָ נֹתֵ֣ן לָ֑ךְ

bə'aḥad šə'ārêkā bə'arṣəkā 'ăšer YHWH 'ĕlōhêkā nōtēn lāk

**in one of your towns in the land
that Yahweh your God is giving you,**

7c
לֹ֧א תְאַמֵּ֛ץ אֶת־לְבָבְךָ֖

lō' tə'ammēṣ 'et-ləvāvkā

do not harden your heart,

7d
וְלֹ֤א תִקְפֹּץ֙ אֶת־יָ֣דְךָ֔ מֵאָחִ֖יךָ הָאֶבְיֽוֹן׃

wəlō' tiqpōṣ 'et-yādəkā mē'āḥîkā hā'evyôn.

and do not shut your hand against your poor brother.

8a
כִּי־פָתֹ֧חַ תִּפְתַּ֛ח אֶת־יָדְךָ֖ ל֑וֹ

kî-fātōaḥ tiftaḥ 'et-yādəkā lô

But open your hand to him,

8b
וְהַעֲבֵט֙ תַּעֲבִיטֶ֔נּוּ דֵּ֚י מַחְסֹר֔וֹ אֲשֶׁ֥ר יֶחְסַ֖ר לֽוֹ׃

wəha'ăvēṭ ta'ăvîṭennû dê maḥsōrô 'ăšer yeḥsar lô.

and surely lend to him what is sufficient for what he lacks.

9a
הִשָּׁ֣מֶר לְךָ֗ פֶּן־יִהְיֶ֣ה דָבָר֩ עִם־לְבָבְךָ֨ בְלִיַּ֜עַל

hiššāmer ləkā pen-yihye dāvār 'im-ləvāvkā vəliyya'al

Be careful, lest you have a wicked thought in your heart,

9b
לֵאמֹ֗ר קָרְבָ֣ה שְׁנַת־הַשֶּׁ֩בַע֩ שְׁנַ֨ת הַשְּׁמִטָּ֜ה

lē'mōr qārəvâ šənat-hašševa' šənat haššəmiṭṭâ

saying, 'The seventh year, the year of release, is near,'

9c וְרָעָ֣ה עֵֽינְךָ֗ בְּאָחִ֙יךָ֙ הָֽאֶבְי֔וֹן וְלֹ֥א תִתֵּ֖ן לֽוֹ

wərāʿâ ʿênəkā bəʾāḥîkā hāʾevyôn wəlōʾ tittēn lô

and you look meanly at your brother, the one who is poor,
and you give him nothing,

9d וְקָרָ֤א עָלֶ֙יךָ֙ אֶל־יְהוָ֔ה וְהָיָ֥ה בְךָ֖ חֵֽטְא׃

wəqārāʾ ʿālêkā ʾel-YHWH wəhāyâ vəkā ḥēṭ.

and he cries out against you to Yahweh, and it is sin for you.

10a נָת֤וֹן תִּתֵּן֙ ל֔וֹ וְלֹא־יֵרַ֥ע לְבָבְךָ֖ בְּתִתְּךָ֣ לֽוֹ

nātôn tittēn lô wəlōʾ-yēraʿ ləvāvkā bətittəkā lô

You shall give freely to him, and it shall not seem mean
in your heart when you give to him.

10b כִּ֞י בִּגְלַ֣ל ׀ הַדָּבָ֣ר הַזֶּ֗ה יְבָרֶכְךָ֙ יְהוָ֣ה אֱלֹהֶ֔יךָ

kî biglal haddāvār hazze yəvārekəkā YHWH ʾĕlōhêkā

בְּכָל־מַעֲשֶׂ֔ךָ וּבְכֹ֖ל מִשְׁלַ֥ח יָדֶֽךָ׃

bəkol-maʿăśekā ûvəkōl mišlaḥ yādekā.

For because of this thing Yahweh your God will bless you
in all your works and in all your hand undertakes.

11a כִּ֛י לֹא־יֶחְדַּ֥ל אֶבְי֖וֹן מִקֶּ֣רֶב הָאָ֑רֶץ

kî lōʾ-yeḥdal ʾevyôn miqqerev hāʾāreṣ

For there shall not cease to be poor in the land.

11b עַל־כֵּ֞ן אָנֹכִ֤י מְצַוְּךָ֙ לֵאמֹ֔ר

ʿal-kēn ʾānōkî məṣawwəkā lēʾmōr

Thus I command you, saying,

11c פָּתֹ֧חַ תִּפְתַּ֛ח אֶת־יָדְךָ֖ לְאָחִ֑יךָ

pātōaḥ tiftaḥ ʾet-yādəkā ləʾāḥîkā

'Open your hand generously to your brother,

11d לַעֲנִיֶּ֥ךָ וּלְאֶבְיֹנְךָ֖ בְּאַרְצֶֽךָ׃

laʿăniyyekā ûləʾevyōnəkā bəʾarṣekā.

to your needy, and to your poor in your land.'"

Verses 7–11 turn the emphasis to inward attitudes that contrast closed hands, mean hearts, and evil eyes with open hands and generous hearts.

7a	כִּי־יִהְיֶה בְךָ אֶבְיוֹן מֵאַחַד אַחֶיךָ
	"When there is a poor person among one of your brothers,

כִּי־	for/that/because	---	conj
כִּי	*kî-*		
יִהְיֶה֙	there is	QAL IMPF 3MS	verb
היה	*yih·ye*		
בְךָ֜	with/among you	---	prep
בְּ	*və·ḵā*	W/ 2MS SX	
אֶבְיוֹן	poor	MS SUBST	adj
אֶבְיוֹן	*'ev·yôn*		
מֵאַחַד	from one of	CST	cardinal
אֶחָד	*mē·'a·ḥad*	W/ PREP מִן	number
אַחֶיךָ	your brothers	CST	noun
אָח	*'ā·ḥê·ḵā*	W/ 2MS SX	

Verse 7 has a chiastic shape that begins with "poor . . . among your brothers" (v. 7a) and ends with "from your brother who is poor" (v. 7d).

7b	בְּאַחַד שְׁעָרֶיךָ בְּאַרְצְךָ אֲשֶׁר־יְהוָה אֱלֹהֶיךָ נֹתֵן לָךְ
	in one of your towns in the land that Yahweh your God is giving you,

בְּאַחַד	in one of	CST	cardinal
אֶחָד	*bə·'a·ḥad*	W/ PREP בְּ	number
שְׁעָרֶיךָ	your gates/towns	CST	noun
שַׁעַר	*šə·'ā·rɛ̂·ḵā*	W/ 2MS SX	
בְּאַרְצְךָ	in your land	CST	noun
אֶרֶץ	*bə·'ar·ṣə·ḵā*	W/ PREP בְּ + 2MS SX	
אֲשֶׁר־	that/which	---	relative
אֲשֶׁר	*'ă·šer*		pron

יְהוָה	Yahweh	ABS	noun
יהוה	*YHWH*		
אֱלֹהֶיךָ	your God	CST	noun
אֱלֹהִים	*ʾĕ·lō·hê·ḵā*	W/ 2MS SX	
נֹתֵן	(is) giving	QAL PTCP MS	verb
נתן	*nō·tēn*		
לָךְ	to you	---	prep
ל	*lāḵ*	W/ 2MS SX	

It should not go unnoticed that the whole law is premised on the gift of the land; everything Israel will have to give was given them in the first place.

<table>
<tr><td>7c</td><td colspan="3" align="center">לֹא תְאַמֵּץ אֶת־לְבָבְךָ</td></tr>
</table>

do not harden your heart,

לֹא	no/not	---	particle
לא	*lō'*		
תְאַמֵּץ	you will make strong/harden	PIEL IMPF 2MS	verb
אמץ	*tə·'am·mēṣ*		
אֶת־	(direct object marker)	---	particle
את	*'et-*		
לְבָבְךָ	your heart	CST	noun
לְבָב	*lə·vāv·ḵā*	W/ 2MS SX	

The Piel of אמץ typically means "strengthen," but see Deut 2:30, where there is a similar use of this verb to describe "hardening" of the heart.

<table>
<tr><td>7d</td><td colspan="3" align="center">וְלֹא תִקְפֹּץ אֶת־יָדְךָ מֵאָחִיךָ הָאֶבְיוֹן׃</td></tr>
</table>

and do not shut your hand against your poor brother.

וְלֹא	and no/not	---	particle
לא	*wə·lō'*	W/ CONJ וְ	
תִקְפֹּץ	you draw together/close	QAL IMPF 2MS	verb
קפץ	*tiq·pōṣ*		
אֶת־	(direct object marker)	---	particle
את	*'et-*		

יָדְךָ יָד *yā·ḏə·ḵā*	your hand	CST W/ 2MS SX	noun
מֵאָחִיךָ אָח *mē·'ā·ḥî·ḵā*	from your brother	CST W/ PREP מִן + 2MS SX	noun
הָאֶבְיוֹן: אֶבְיוֹן *hā·'ev·yôn*	(the) poor	MS PRED W/ DEF. ART.	adj

8a   כִּי־פָתֹחַ תִּפְתַּח אֶת־יָדְךָ לוֹ

But open your hand to him,

כִּי־ כִּי *kî-*	for/that/because	---	conj
פָתֹחַ פתח *fā·tō·aḥ*	to open	QAL INF ABS	verb
תִּפְתַּח פתח *tif·taḥ*	you will open	QAL IMPF 2MS	verb
אֶת־ אֵת *'et-*	*(direct object marker)*	---	particle
יָדְךָ יָד *yā·ḏə·ḵā*	your hand	CST W/ 2MS SX	noun
לוֹ לְ *lô*	to him	--- W/ 3MS SX	prep

See Prov 31:20 for the same image with different vocabulary (פָּרַשׂ כַּף).

8b   וְהַעֲבֵט תַּעֲבִיטֶנּוּ דֵּי מַחְסֹרוֹ אֲשֶׁר יֶחְסַר לוֹ:

and surely lend to him what is sufficient for what he lacks.

וְהַעֲבֵט עבט *wə·ha·'ă·vēṭ*	and to lend	HIPH INF ABS W/ CONJ וְ	verb
תַּעֲבִיטֶנּוּ עבט *ta·'ă·vî·ṭen·nû*	you will lend him	HIPH IMPF 2MS W/ 3MS SX	verb
דֵּי דַּי *dê*	sufficient/enough of/for	CST	noun

מַחְסֹרֹו	his need/poverty/lack	CST W/ 3MS SX	noun
מַחְסֹור	*maḥ·sō·**rô***		
אֲשֶׁר	that/which	---	relative pro
אֲשֶׁר	*'ă·**šer***		
יֶחְסַר	he lacks/needs	QAL IMPF 3MS	verb
חסר	*yeḥ·**sar***		
לֹו׃	to him	--- W/ 3MS SX	prep
לְ	***lô***		

Notice paired verbs "open," "open," and "lend," "lend" (v. 8a–b) alongside the doubling of the nominal and verbal forms of חסר, "the need he needs." *Any* kind of need must be met with sufficient gestures of generosity.

9a הִשָּׁמֶר לְךָ פֶּן־יִהְיֶה דָבָר עִם־לְבָבְךָ בְלִיַּעַל

Be careful, lest you have a wicked thought in your heart,

הִשָּׁמֶר	Guard/observe	NIPH IMPV MS	verb
שׁמר	*hiš·šā·**mer***		
לְךָ	for you/yourself	--- W/ 2MS SX	prep
לְ	*lə·**ḵā***		
פֶּן־	lest	---	conj
פֶּן	*pen-*		
יִהְיֶה	(it) will be	QAL IMPF 3MS	verb
היה	*yih·**ye***		
דָבָר	thing/word/thought	ABS	noun
דָּבָר	*dā·**vār***		
עִם־	with/among	---	prep
עִם	*'im-*		
לְבָבְךָ	your heart	CST W/ 2MS SX	noun
לֵבָב	*lə·vāv·**ḵā***		
בְּלִיַּעַל	useless/worthless/wicked	ABS	noun
בְּלִיַּעַל	*bə·liy·**ya·**'al*		

לֵאמֹר קָרְבָה שְׁנַת־הַשֶּׁבַע שְׁנַת הַשְּׁמִטָּה

saying, 'The seventh year, the year of release, is near,'

לֵאמֹר אמר	to say/saying *lē'·mōr*	QAL INF CST W/ PREP לְ	verb
קָרְבָה קרב	(it) draws near *qā·rə·vâ*	QAL PF 3FS	verb
שְׁנַת־ שָׁנָה	(the) year (of) *šə·nat-*	CST	noun
הַשֶּׁבַע שֶׁבַע	the seventh *haš·še·va'*	ABS W/ DEF. ART.	cardinal number
שְׁנַת שָׁנָה	(the) year of *šə·nat*	CST	noun
הַשְּׁמִטָּה שְׁמִטָּה	the release *haš·šə·miṭ·ṭâ*	ABS W/ DEF. ART.	noun

וְרָעָה עֵינְךָ בְּאָחִיךָ הָאֶבְיוֹן וְלֹא תִתֵּן לוֹ

and you look meanly at your brother, the one who is poor,
and you give him nothing,

וְרָעָה רעע	and (it) is grudging *wə·rā·'â*	QAL WEQATAL 3FS	verb
עֵינְךָ עַיִן	your eye *'ê·nə·ḵā*	CST W/ 2MS SX	noun
בְּאָחִיךָ אָח	on/against your brother *bə·'ā·ḥî·ḵā*	CST W/ PREP בְּ + 2MS SX	noun
הָאֶבְיוֹן אֶבְיוֹן	the poor one *hā·'ev·yôn*	MS PRED W/ DEF. ART.	adj
וְלֹא לֹא	and no/not *wə·lō'*	--- W/ CONJ וְ	particle
תִתֵּן נתן	you give/lend *tit·tēn*	QAL IMPF 2MS	verb
לוֹ לְ	to him *lô*	--- W/ 3MS SX	prep

וְקָרָא עָלֶ֫יךָ אֶל־יְהוָ֫ה וְהָיָה בְךָ חֵטְא׃

and he cries out against you to Yahweh, and it is sin for you.

וְקָרָא	and he calls/cries out	QAL WEQATAL 3MS	verb
קרא	wə·qā·rā'		
עָלֶ֫יךָ	over/against you	---	prep
עַל	'ā·lê·ḵā	W/ 2MS SX	
אֶל־	to	---	prep
אֶל	'el-		
יְהוָ֫ה	Yahweh	ABS	noun
יהוה	YHWH		
וְהָיָה	and it be	QAL WEQATAL 3MS	verb
היה	wə·hā·yâ		
בְךָ	to/against you	---	prep
בְּ	və·ḵā	W/ 2MS SX	
חֵטְא׃	sin/guilt	ABS	noun
חֵטְא	ḥēṭ'		

See 24:15 for a passage where the withholding of wages leads to a poor worker crying out to Yahweh. Surely the Israelites could hear in these passages an echo of Israel's cry to God in Egypt that moved him to deliver them (Exod 2:24; 3:9). God's concern for nations applies also to the most marginalized in the community.

נָתוֹן תִּתֵּן לוֹ וְלֹא־יֵרַע לְבָבְךָ בְּתִתְּךָ לוֹ

You shall give freely to him, and it shall not seem mean
in your heart when you give to him.

נָתוֹן	to give	QAL INF ABS	verb
נתן	nā·tôn		
תִּתֵּן	you will give/lend	QAL IMPF 2MS	verb
נתן	tit·tēn		
לוֹ	to him	---	prep
לְ	lô	W/ 3MS SX	
וְלֹא־	and no/not	---	particle
לֹא	wə·lō'-	W/ CONJ וְ	

יֵרַע רעע *yē·ra'*	(it) will be grudging	QAL IMPF 3MS	verb
לְבָבְךָ לֵבָב *lə·vāv·ḵā*	your heart	CST W/ 2MS SX	noun
בְּתִתְּךָ נתן *bə·tit·tə·ḵā*	when you give	QAL INF CST W/ PREP בְּ + 2MS SX	verb
לוֹ לְ *lô*	to him	--- W/ 3MS SX	prep

10b

For because of this thing Yahweh your God will bless you
in all your works and in all your hand undertakes.

כִּי כִּי *kî*	for/that/because	---	conj
בִּגְלַל | בִּגְלַל *big·lal*	on account of	---	prep
הַדָּבָר דָּבָר *had·dā·vār*	(the) thing/matter	ABS W/ DEF. ART.	noun
הַזֶּה זֶה *haz·ze*	(the) this	--- W/ DEF. ART.	demonstr pron
יְבָרֶכְךָ ברך *yə·vā·re·ḵə·ḵā*	(he) will bless you	PIEL IMPF 3MS W/ 2MS SX	verb
יְהוָה יהוה *YHWH*	Yahweh	ABS	noun
אֱלֹהֶיךָ אֱלֹהִים *ĕ·lō·hê·ḵā*	your God	CST W/ 2MS SX	noun
בְּכָל־ כֹּל *bə·ḵol-*	in all/every	CST W/ PREP בְּ	noun
מַעֲשֶׂךָ מַעֲשֶׂה *ma·ă·śe·ḵā*	your work	CST W/ 2MS SX	noun
וּבְכֹל כֹּל *û·və·ḵōl*	and in all/every	CST W/ CONJ וְ + PREP בְּ	noun
מִשְׁלַח מִשְׁלַח *miš·laḥ*	outstretching/undertaking of	CST	noun

| יָדֶ֑ךָ | your hand | CST | noun |
| יָד | *yā·de·kā* | W/ 2MS SX | |

11a   כִּי לֹא־יֶחְדַּל אֶבְיוֹן מִקֶּרֶב הָאָרֶץ

For there shall not cease to be poor in the land.

כִּי	for/that/because	---	con
כִּי	*kî*		
לֹא־	no/not	---	particle
לֹא	*lō'-*		
יֶחְדַּל	(it) will cease	QAL IMPF 3MS	verb
חדל	*yeḥ·dal*		
אֶבְיוֹן	poor	MS SUBST	adj
אֶבְיוֹן	*'ev·yôn*		
מִקֶּרֶב	in the midst of	CST	noun
קֶרֶב	*miq·qe·rev*	W/ PREP מִן	
הָאָרֶץ	the land	ABS	noun
אֶרֶץ	*hā·'ā·reṣ*	W/ DEF. ART.	

As we saw in the introduction, the law ends with a surprise that contrasts the promise in v. 4. See "From Text to Sermon" below. Jesus' three quotations of this passage in the gospels occur in the context of a woman anointing him for his death (Matt 26:11; Mark 14:7; John 12:8; Luke 7:36–38 has a similar scene). John identifies the woman as Mary of Bethany. On the one hand the passage recognizes the immeasurable cost of Jesus' death and of the life he gives to us. On the other hand, the ineradicable reality of poverty reminds the church of its need to be persistent in acts of mercy.

11b   עַל־כֵּן אָנֹכִי מְצַוְּךָ לֵאמֹר

Thus I command you, saying,

עַל־כֵּן	thus/for that reason	---	adv
עַל־כֵּן	*'al-kēn*		
אָנֹכִי	I	---	personal pron
אָנֹכִי	*'ā·nō·kî*		

<table>
<tr><td>מְצַוְּךָ
צוה
mə·ṣaw·wə·ḵā</td><td>(am) commanding you</td><td>PIEL PTCP MS
W/ 2MS SX</td><td>verb</td></tr>
<tr><td>לֵאמֹר
אמר
lē·mōr</td><td>to say/saying</td><td>QAL INF CST
W/ PREP לְ</td><td>verb</td></tr>
</table>

<table>
<tr><td>11c</td><td colspan="3" align="center">פָּתֹחַ תִּפְתַּח אֶת־יָדְךָ לְאָחִיךָ</td></tr>
<tr><td></td><td colspan="3" align="center">'Open your hand generously to your brother,</td></tr>
</table>

פָּתֹחַ פתח *pā·tō·aḥ*	to open	QAL INF ABS	verb
תִּפְתַּח פתח *tif·taḥ*	you open	QAL IMPF 2MS	verb
אֶת־ אֵת *'et-*	(direct object marker)	---	particle
יָדְךָ יָד *yā·də·ḵā*	your hand	CST W/ 2MS SX	noun
לְאָחִיךָ אָח *lə·'ā·ḥî·ḵā*	to your brother	CST W/ PREP לְ + 2MS SX	noun

The many doubled verbs in this chapter are often difficult to translate into English. One might prefer "Surely open your hand." See v. 4b above.

<table>
<tr><td>11d</td><td colspan="3" align="center">לַעֲנִיֶּךָ וּלְאֶבְיֹנְךָ בְּאַרְצֶךָ:</td></tr>
<tr><td></td><td colspan="3" align="center">to your needy, and to your poor in your land.'"</td></tr>
</table>

לַעֲנִיֶּךָ עָנִי *la·'ă·niy·ye·ḵā*	to your afflicted/needy	MS SUBST W/ PREP לְ + 2MS SX	adj
וּלְאֶבְיֹנְךָ אֶבְיֹון *û·lə·'ev·yō·nə·ḵā*	and to your poor	MS SUBST W/ CONJ וְ + PREP לְ + 2MS SX	adj
בְּאַרְצֶךָ: אֶרֶץ *bə·'ar·ṣe·ḵā*	in your land	CST W/ PREP בְּ + 2MS SX	noun

The doubling of objects, "poor" and "needy," makes the law inclusive of any need in the community.

The Vision for a Generous and Compassionate Society. Biblical laws do not solve the world's economic problems, let alone Israel's much smaller economic inequalities in their time. They merely put limits on poverty and wealth, leaving persisting inequalities behind. And yet, while these laws are only stopgap measures in economic terms, they communicate a deeper vision that we can see on three levels.

First, vv. 4–6 set up what Hamilton describes as an "ideal portrait" of an obedient people living under the blessing of God. It is very easy for us to feel insignificant within the massive economies around us. It was not so different in Israel's world. In this law, those individuals with economic means find themselves faced with their ability to push the nation toward one end or another, to blessing or to curse (Hamilton 1992:15–16). Our part always matters.

Second, the law is bound together by bodily metaphors of open hands, tight fists, hard and mean hearts, and evil eyes. We already commented on the way bodily metaphors give depth to the nature of love in 10:1–12. Modern cognitive science reveals that metaphors spark a chain of activity in the network of our body and emotions. Just think of the difference between the command to "be generous" and to "open your hand wide." The second command immediately triggers the sense of our fingers loosening our grip on things we cherish and crave. So too for the way we look at people with our eyes and have compassion on them in our hearts. Generosity is a commitment of the whole person to the well-being of others.

Finally, both laws offer a rhetorical surprise. The first surprise is that there will always be poor in the land (v. 11; cf. Matt 6:11; Mark 14:7; John 12:8), which is to say that no matter where I fall on the economic spectrum, *there will always be people needier than I.* The need for compassion and mercy is ever present. The second surprise comes in the law of manumission in vv. 12–18: "And if [the slave] says to you, 'I will not leave you,' because he loves you and your household and it is good for him to be with you . . ." (v. 16). This encourages the slave owner to ask, "What if I'm so gracious that my bond slave decides to stay with me and my house?" There is a way of going beyond the law that will knit the community together as kin. Taken together, the two surprises evoke the attitudes and desires that make for an ideal economic community.

 *Liturgy and Habits of Grace.* Comparing Deut 15 to similar Mesopotamian laws, Hamilton observes, "the only certain time in which a *mišarum* act [act of "righteousness" or "equity"] could be expected was shortly after the ascension of a new king." The release was often recorded in the annals of the king and not in the law codes, relieving the king and economic well-doers of an obligation to care for the needy (1992:50, 53).

By contrast, the Bible builds a trajectory of relief into its calendar— Deuteronomy's tithes (14:22–29), seventh-year Sabbaths (15:1–18), and the Jubilee year (Lev 25:8–34). These accomplish two important things. First, by not mentioning the king, the laws stand as Yahweh's command for which no human king or magistrate could take credit (15:2; Lev 25:4; cf. Matt 6:2–4). Second, by tying the law to a specific calendar, the poor may always have hope of a day of relief, and the rich(er) have a regular reminder to give thanks to God and extend a hand of generosity.

A Community of Kin. This topic might be a sermon or two on its own, es-pecially as it picks up on themes in 14:28–29. We should begin by recog-nizing that, for all their sophistication, our advanced capitalist economic systems have only accentuated the gaps between rich and poor. Harvard professor Michael Sandel carefully diagnoses this worsening phenom-enon in our time. He shows that in 1970, for example, CEOs made thirty times more than the average worker. By 2014 that rose to three hundred times more (2021:197).

Such a gap in income might seem incidental: there aren't all that many CEOs after all, are there? Sandel shows that the disparity is not merely a financial tale of a few billionaires but a key indicator of decreasing access to social mobility throughout our society. Children whose parents are in the upper 1 percent are more likely get good test scores, get into good col-leges, make more money after graduation, etc. One of many representative examples is that if you come from the upper 1 percent in America, your chances of getting into an Ivy League school "are 77 times greater than if you come from a poor family (bottom 20%)" (2021:167). And so rich kids go to school with other rich kids, marry, and produce more rich kids. And the pool of wealth and opportunity gets smaller and more tightly knit.

Meanwhile those in poor families and neighborhoods have a decreas-ing likelihood of breaking out. Here is how Jonathan Tran describes the plight of urban dwellers today:

> Three times as many urban neighborhoods have poverty rates exceeding 30 percent as was true in 1970, and the number of poor people living in these neighborhoods has doubled. The result of

these trends is that the poor in the nation's metropolitan areas are increasingly segregated into neighborhoods of concentrated poverty. (2022:6)

We return to Sandel, who describes the interpersonal result:

We live and work and shop and play in different places; our children go to different schools. And when the meritocratic sorting machine has done its work, those on top find hard to resist the thought that they deserve their success and that those on the bottom deserve their place as well. (2021:226)

This is surely the death of community and the spirit of the "common good." Meanwhile, the solutions proposed by the political left and the right are either more government or more industry, respectively. They both wrongly assume that a better distribution of material goods is the solution to our problems.

Like our liberal economic policy, Deut 14–16 implements a redistribution of wealth, or more accurately, it ensures that the poorest have access to the overall growth of wealth within the community. More than that, Deuteronomy aims beyond material distribution of goods to the deeper dignity of the human beings in this system—especially those in concentrated areas of poverty.

To do this, Deut 15 uses the Hebrew word אָח ("brother" or "kin") a remarkable seven times (vv. 2, 3, 7 [twice], 9, 11, 12), significantly more than in any other chapter in the book. This provides a further contrast to other ancient Near Eastern laws in the way it institutes a "brotherhood" or "kinship" among the covenant people.

Patrick Miller observes a striking parallel of this frequent use of אָח in Gen 4:1–16 when Cain slays his brother and where we witness the first tragic breakdown of brotherhood and family (1990:136–37). In a similar way, Deuteronomy teaches that true brotherhood (kinship) isn't a matter of birth but a "moral category" we live out in community life. Miller continues, "Those with whom one lives as a brother and sister always have a proper claim upon one's compassion and care" (1990:136).

Thus, as Deuteronomy teaches us to attend to growing material disparities in our midst, it gives us a deeper vision of community and the infinite dignity of the image bearers who live around us. Paralleling Deuteronomy, Mary Hirschfeld calls for correction to our overreliance on financial or material answers to our problems. What we need is a "more organic" view of society in which "the joys of others enhance our own well-being. And by the same token, the sufferings of others diminish our own well-being, making it more natural to look after those in need" (2019:265). Open your hand to your poor brother in the land.

 ***Jesus and the Great Release.*** The discussion on economics above exposes capitalist tendencies to equate material prosperity with happiness, what Jonathan Tran describes as, "flattening everything out to *homo economicus*" (2022:16). By contrast, the orthodox Christian tradition has long valued material goods as only a *means* in life, not our goal. Our ultimate fulfillment is found in our participation in the divine life, community and friendship, and growth in virtue.

This should help us understand why the liberation and release passages in Deut 15 and Lev 25 take on a "spiritual and eschatological sense" in Luke 4:16–21 (Wright 1990:176). That is, the release Christ proclaims is not primarily of financial and economic restoration but of forgiveness from sin and guilt, and rebirth from death to righteousness and life. Just why has Jesus laid aside the economic vision of the Old Testament in this way?

This brings us to the logic behind a move of the New Testament writers that we see already at work in the Prophets. The greatest tragedy of sin is not economic in nature, but the loss of fellowship between creature and Creator. Cut off from God's grace and fellowship, we plunge headlong into a desperate grasp on the things of this world that create the very economic mismanagement we see around us every day. This is why God begins our redemption by breaking our bond to sin and death, lifting us back to himself. It is a move from *homo economicus* back to an economy of gift and of grace (Matt 6:25–34).

Reconciled to God, we encounter a new life welling up within us. God's deposit of living grace from above satisfies our longings, loosening our grip on things in this world and enabling us to restore reciprocal bonds with our neighbors. We come to see that the physical and economic release and mercy we provide to others now works on a different plane than the charity of the economic world around us, since it draws upon and regifts the infinite treasure of God's loving gift of himself.

When we turn back to Deut 15, we read of a debt slave who chooses to stay with the lender, or owner (15:16–18). This should not be taken as a blanket endorsement for debt slavery but rather as an ideal image of reciprocation: a gift of service in return for a gift of freedom. Surely this exchange anticipates the bondage we give to God in response to the free gift of salvation we receive in Christ Jesus (1 Cor 7:22–23; 1 Pet 2:16). God has treated us so lavishly, how could we not dedicate our lives to him?

THREE ANNUAL FEASTS AND THE RENEWAL OF FAITH AND COMMUNITY

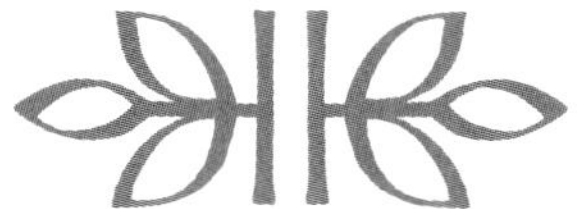

Deuteronomy 16 stipulates requirements for the three annual Feasts of Passover and Unleavened Bread, Weeks, and Booths. Altmann observes important parallels between these feasts and feasts in West Semitic ritual and narrative texts (2011:134–85). All of these cultural rituals emphasize the gathering of all levels of society at a common feast. Yet, in 14:22–27 and 16:9–15, we can mark this difference:

> All should eat and drink until satisfied on a banquet provided by Yhwh through the multiplicity of households instead of the royal house. This particular emphasis conceives of a corporate identity re-articulated and created afresh with a focus on individual households (likely something of the *bêt 'ab*), rather than a politically centralized focus on the human monarch found in the banqueting of the Ugaritic narratival corpus. (2011:185)

Or, one might say, the role of the king is reduced to nothing so that the role of Yahweh binding his people together takes center stage. These three meals all rehearse a common tradition from the past that gives the nation its identity. According to the anthropologist Margaret Visser,

> Feasts, by means of structure and ritual, deliberately use the powerful connotations of food to recall origins and earlier times. They also attempt to be events in themselves unforgettable, in order to furnish recollections of the future. The food served at festivals is, therefore, not only richer and more splendid than we usually eat, but also traditional, inherited from the past and intended to be experienced as ancient custom. (2008:37)

As such, the gatherings go beyond simply feasting: they serve to nurture a common sense of national identity grounded in Yahweh's past work of redemption and future promises of flourishing.

LARGER LITERARY CONTEXT ▸ 14:22–16:17

1a

שָׁמוֹר֙ אֶת־חֹ֣דֶשׁ הָאָבִ֔יב

šāmôr ʾet-ḥōdeš hāʾāvîv

Observe the month of Abib,

1b

וְעָשִׂ֣יתָ פֶּ֔סַח לַיהוָ֖ה אֱלֹהֶ֑יךָ

wəʿāśîtā pesaḥ laYHWH ʾĕlōhêḵā

and keep the Passover to Yahweh your God.

1c

כִּ֞י בְּחֹ֣דֶשׁ הָאָבִ֗יב הוֹצִֽיאֲךָ֞ יְהוָ֧ה אֱלֹהֶ֛יךָ מִמִּצְרַ֖יִם לָֽיְלָה׃

kî bəḥōdeš hāʾāvîv hôṣîʾăḵā YHWH ʾĕlōhêḵā mimmiṣrayim lāylâ.

**For in the month of Abib, Yahweh your God
brought you out of the land of Egypt by night.**

2a

וְזָבַ֥חְתָּ פֶּ֛סַח לַיהוָ֥ה אֱלֹהֶ֖יךָ צֹ֣אן וּבָקָ֑ר

wəzāvaḥtā pesaḥ laYHWH ʾĕlōhêḵā ṣōʾn ûvāqār

**And you shall sacrifice a Passover offering to Yahweh your God,
sheep and livestock,**

2b

בַּמָּקוֹם֙ אֲשֶׁר־יִבְחַ֣ר יְהוָ֔ה לְשַׁכֵּ֥ן שְׁמ֖וֹ שָֽׁם׃

bammāqôm ʾăšer-yivḥar YHWH ləšakkēn šəmô šām.

at the place where Yahweh chooses to place his name.

3a

לֹא־תֹאכַ֤ל עָלָיו֙ חָמֵ֔ץ

lōʾ-tōʾkal ʿālāyw ḥāmēṣ

You shall not eat leavened bread with it.

3b

שִׁבְעַ֥ת יָמִ֛ים תֹּֽאכַל־עָלָ֥יו מַצּ֖וֹת לֶ֣חֶם עֹ֑נִי

šivʿat yāmîm tōʾkal-ʿālāyw maṣṣôt leḥem ʿōnî

Seven days you shall eat unleavened bread, the bread of affliction—

3c

כִּ֣י בְחִפָּז֗וֹן יָצָ֙אתָ֙ מֵאֶ֣רֶץ מִצְרַ֔יִם

kî vəḥippāzôn yāṣāʾtā mēʾereṣ miṣrayim

for in haste you went out of the land of Egypt—

3d   לְמַ֣עַן תִּזְכֹּר֩ אֶת־י֨וֹם צֵאתְךָ֜ מֵאֶ֣רֶץ מִצְרַ֗יִם כֹּ֖ל יְמֵ֥י חַיֶּֽיךָ׃

ləmaʿan tizkōr ʾet-yôm ṣēʾtḵā mēʾereṣ miṣrayim kōl yəmê ḥayyêḵā.

so that you remember the day that you came out
of the land of Egypt all the days of your life.

4a   וְלֹא־יֵרָאֶ֨ה לְךָ֥ שְׂאֹ֛ר בְּכָל־גְּבֻלְךָ֖ שִׁבְעַ֣ת יָמִ֑ים

wəlō-yērāʾe ləḵā śəʾōr bəḵol-gəvulḵā šivʿat yāmîm

No leaven shall be seen within any of your territory for seven days,

4b   וְלֹא־יָלִ֣ין מִן־הַבָּשָׂ֗ר אֲשֶׁ֨ר תִּזְבַּ֥ח בָּעֶ֛רֶב בַּיּ֥וֹם הָרִאשׁ֖וֹן לַבֹּֽקֶר׃

wəlō-yālîn min-habbāśār ʾăšer tizbaḥ bāʿerev bayyôm hāriʾšôn labbōqer.

nor shall the meat that you sacrifice on the evening
of the first day remain until the morning.

5a   לֹ֥א תוּכַ֖ל לִזְבֹּ֣חַ אֶת־הַפָּ֑סַח

lō tûḵal lizbōaḥ ʾet-happāsaḥ

You are not permitted to sacrifice the Passover offering

5b   בְּאַחַ֣ד שְׁעָרֶ֔יךָ אֲשֶׁר־יְהוָ֥ה אֱלֹהֶ֖יךָ נֹתֵ֥ן לָֽךְ׃

bəʾaḥad šəʿārêḵā ʾăšer YHWH ʾĕlōhêḵā nōtēn lāḵ.

in any of your towns that Yahweh your God is giving you,

6a   כִּ֣י אִם־אֶל־הַמָּק֗וֹם

kî ʾim-ʾel-hammāqôm

except in the place

6b   אֲשֶׁר־יִבְחַ֨ר יְהוָ֤ה אֱלֹהֶ֨יךָ֙ לְשַׁכֵּ֣ן שְׁמ֣וֹ שָׁ֔ם

ʾăšer-yivḥar YHWH ʾĕlōhêḵā ləšakkēn šəmô šām

where Yahweh your God chooses to place his name.

6c   תִּזְבַּ֧ח אֶת־הַפֶּ֛סַח בָּעֶ֖רֶב כְּב֣וֹא הַשָּׁ֑מֶשׁ

tizbaḥ ʾet-happesaḥ bāʿārev kəvô haššemeš

Sacrifice the Passover offering in the evening,
when the sun goes down,

6d   מוֹעֵד צֵאתְךָ מִמִּצְרָיִם׃

môʿēd ṣēʾtkā miṣrayim.

at the time you went out from Egypt.

7a   וּבִשַּׁלְתָּ וְאָכַלְתָּ בַּמָּקוֹם אֲשֶׁר יִבְחַר יְהוָה אֱלֹהֶיךָ בּוֹ

ûviššaltā waʾākaltā bammāqôm ʾăšer yivḥar YHWH ʾĕlōhêkā bô

You shall boil it and eat it at the place
that Yahweh your God chooses.

7b   וּפָנִיתָ בַבֹּקֶר וְהָלַכְתָּ לְאֹהָלֶיךָ׃

ûfānîtā vabbōqer wahālaktā laʾōhālêkā.

In the morning, turn and go back to your tents.

8a   שֵׁשֶׁת יָמִים תֹּאכַל מַצּוֹת

šēšet yāmîm tûkal maṣṣôt

Six days you shall eat unleavened bread,

8b   וּבַיּוֹם הַשְּׁבִיעִי עֲצֶרֶת לַיהוָה אֱלֹהֶיךָ

ûvayyôm haššəvîʿî ʿăṣeret laYHWH ʾĕlōhêkā

and on the seventh day there shall be a solemn assembly
to Yahweh your God.

8c   לֹא תַעֲשֶׂה מְלָאכָה׃

lōʾ taʿăśe məlākâ.

Do not do any work.

1a	שָׁמוֹר אֶת־חֹדֶשׁ הָאָבִיב
	Observe the month of Abib,

	שָׁמוֹר	keep/observe	QAL INF ABS	verb
	שמר	*šā·môr*		

אֶת־	(direct object marker)	---	particle
אֵת	ʾet-		
חֹדֶשׁ	(the) month of	CST	noun
חֹדֶשׁ	ḥō·deš		
הָאָבִיב	(the) Abib	ABS	noun
אָבִיב	hā·ʾā·vîv	W/ DEF. ART.	

אָבִיב could be translated "ripe" or "new grain." The feast clearly marks the beginning of agricultural life and fruits.

1b	וְעָשִׂיתָ פֶּסַח לַיהוָה אֱלֹהֶיךָ

and keep the Passover to Yahweh your God.

וְעָשִׂיתָ	and do/make/keep	QAL WEQATAL 2MS	verb
עשׂה	wə·ʿā·śî·tā		
פֶּסַח	(the) Passover	ABS	noun
פֶּסַח	pe·saḥ		
לַיהוָה	to/for Yahweh	ABS	noun
יהוה	la·YHWH	W/ DEF. ART.	
אֱלֹהֶיךָ	your God	CST	noun
אֱלֹהִים	ʾĕ·lō·hê·ḵā	W/ 2MS SX	

Based on context, I have translated פֶּסַח as "the Passover" here, as "Passover offering" in v. 2a, and as "the Passover offering" in vv. 5a and 6c where the Hebrew includes the definite article.

1c	כִּי בְּחֹדֶשׁ הָאָבִיב הוֹצִיאֲךָ יְהוָה אֱלֹהֶיךָ מִמִּצְרַיִם לָיְלָה:

For in the month of Abib, Yahweh your God
brought you out of the land of Egypt by night.

כִּי	for/that/because	---	conj
כִּי	kî		
בְּחֹדֶשׁ	in (the) month of	CST	noun
חֹדֶשׁ	bə·ḥō·deš	W/ PREP בְּ	
הָאָבִיב	(the) Abib	ABS	noun
אָבִיב	hā·ʾā·vîv	W/ DEF. ART.	

הוֹצִיאֲךָ֖ יצא *hô·ṣî·ʾă·kā*	(he) brought you out	HIPH PF 3MS W/ 2MS SX	verb
יְהוָ֥ה יהוה *YHWH*	Yahweh	ABS	noun
אֱלֹהֶ֔יךָ אֱלֹהִים *ʾĕ·lō·hê·kā*	your God	CST W/ 2MS SX	noun
מִמִּצְרַ֖יִם מִצְרַיִם *mim·miṣ·ra·yim*	from Egypt	ABS W/ PREP מִן	noun
לָֽיְלָה׃ לַיְלָה *lāy·lâ*	(at/by) night	ABS	noun

2a

And you shall sacrifice a Passover offering to Yahweh your God,
sheep and livestock,

וְזָבַחְתָּ֥ זבח *wə·zā·vaḥ·tā*	and you will sacrifice/offer	QAL WEQATAL 2MS	verb
פֶּ֖סַח פֶּסַח *pe·saḥ*	Passover (offering)	ABS	noun
לַיהוָ֣ה יהוה *la·YHWH*	to Yahweh	ABS W/ PREP לְ	noun
אֱלֹהֶ֑יךָ אֱלֹהִים *ʾĕ·lō·hê·kā*	your God	CST W/ 2MS SX	noun
צֹ֣אן צֹאן *ṣō'n*	sheep	ABS	noun
וּבָקָ֑ר בָּקָר *û·vā·qār*	and cattle	ABS W/ CONJ וְ	noun

2b

at the place where Yahweh chooses to place his name.

בַּמָּקוֹם֙ מָקוֹם *bam·mā·qôm*	at the place	ABS W/ PREP בְּ + DEF. ART.	noun
אֲשֶׁר־ אֲשֶׁר *ʾă·šer-*	that/which	---	relative pron

יִבְחַר	(he) chooses	QAL IMPF 3MS	verb
בחר	*yiv·ḥar*		
יְהוָֹה	Yahweh	ABS	noun
יהוה	*YHWH*		
לְשַׁכֵּן	to make dwell/place/settle	PIEL INF CST W/ PREP לְ	verb
שׁכן	*lə·šak·kēn*		
שְׁמוֹ	his name	CST W/ 3MS SX	noun
שֵׁם	*šə·mô*		
שָׁם:	there	---	adv
שָׁם	*šām*		

See comments on 14:23.

3a — לֹא־תֹאכַל עָלָיו חָמֵץ

You shall not eat leavened bread with it.

לֹא־	no/not	---	particle
לֹא	*lō'-*		
תֹאכַל	you will eat	QAL IMPF 2MS	verb
אכל	*tō'·kal*		
עָלָיו	to/before/with it	---	prep
עַל	*'ā·lāyw*	W/ 3MS SX	
חָמֵץ	that which is leavened	ABS	noun
חָמֵץ	*ḥā·mēṣ*		

Deuteronomy weaves together the Feasts of Passover and Unleavened Bread (see Exod 13:3–10). The Passover establishes Israel in the memory of their redemption from Egypt while the Feast of Unleavened Bread can only be celebrated in the land God promised to give to them (Wright 1996:198–99).

3b — שִׁבְעַת יָמִים תֹּאכַל־עָלָיו מַצּוֹת לֶחֶם עֹנִי

Seven days you shall eat unleavened bread, the bread of affliction—

| שִׁבְעַת | seven (of) | CST | cardinal number |
| שֶׁבַע | *šiv·'at* | | |

יָמִים יוֹם	days *yā·mîm*	ABS	noun
תֹּאכַל־ אכל	you will eat *tō·ḵal-*	QAL IMPF 2MS	verb
עָלָיו עַל	to/before/with it *'ā·lāyw*	--- W/ 3MS SX	prep
מַצּוֹת מַצָּה	bread/unleavened bread *maṣ·ṣôt*	ABS	noun
לֶחֶם לֶחֶם	(the) bread of *le·ḥem*	CST	noun
עֳנִי עֳנִי	affliction *'ō·nî*	ABS	noun

3c — כִּי בְחִפָּזוֹן יָצָאתָ מֵאֶרֶץ מִצְרָיִם

for in haste you went out of the land of Egypt—

כִּי כִּי	for/that/because *kî*	---	conj
בְחִפָּזוֹן חִפָּזוֹן	in haste *və·ḥip·pā·zôn*	ABS W/ PREP בְּ	noun
יָצָאתָ יצא	you went out *yā·ṣā'·tā*	QAL PF 2MS	verb
מֵאֶרֶץ אֶרֶץ	from (the) land of *mē·'e·reṣ*	CST W/ PREP מִן	noun
מִצְרָיִם מִצְרָיִם	Egypt *miṣ·ra·yim*	ABS	noun

3d — לְמַעַן תִּזְכֹּר אֶת־יוֹם צֵאתְךָ מֵאֶרֶץ מִצְרַיִם כֹּל יְמֵי חַיֶּיךָ:

so that you remember the day that you came out
of the land of Egypt all the days of your life.

| לְמַעַן
לְמַעַן | so that/in order that
lə·ma·'an | --- | prep |

תִּזְכֹּר זכר	you might remember *tiz·kōr*	QAL IMPF 2MS	verb
אֶת־ אֵת	(direct object marker) *ʾet-*	---	particle
יוֹם יוֹם	(the) day ***yôm***	ABS	noun
צֵאתְךָ יצא	you came out *ṣēʾt·kā*	QAL INF CST W/ 2MS SX	verb
מֵאֶרֶץ אֶרֶץ	from (the) land of *mē·ʾe·reṣ*	CST W/ PREP מִן	noun
מִצְרַיִם מִצְרַיִם	Egypt *miṣ·**ra**·yim*	ABS	noun
כֹּל כֹּל	all ***kōl***	CST	noun
יְמֵי יוֹם	(the) days of *yə·**mê***	CST	noun
חַיֶּיךָ: חַיִּים	your life *ḥāy·**yê**·kā*	CST W/ 2MS SX	noun

<table>
<tr><td>4a</td><td style="text-align:right">וְלֹא־יֵרָאֶה לְךָ שְׂאֹר בְּכָל־גְּבֻלְךָ שִׁבְעַת יָמִים</td></tr>
</table>

No leaven shall be seen within any of your territory for seven days,

וְלֹא־ לֹא	and no/not *wə·lō̄ʾ-*	--- W/ CONJ וְ	particle
יֵרָאֶה ראה	(it) will be seen *yē·rā·ʾe*	NIPH IMPF 3MS	verb
לְךָ לְ	to/among you *lə·kā*	--- W/ 2MS SX	prep
שְׂאֹר שְׂאֹר	leaven/yeast *śə·ʾōr*	ABS	noun
בְּכָל־ כֹּל	in all *bə·kol-*	CST W/ PREP בְּ	noun
גְּבֻלְךָ גְּבוּל	your boundary/territory *gə·vul·kā*	CST W/ 2MS SX	noun

שִׁבְעַ֖ת	seven (of)	CST	cardinal number
שֶׁ֫בַע *šiv·ʿat*			
יָמִ֑ים	days	ABS	noun
יוֹם *yā·mîm*			

בְּכָל־גְּבֻלְךָ could be translated as "in all your borders."

4b וְלֹא־יָלִין מִן־הַבָּשָׂר אֲשֶׁר תִּזְבַּח בָּעֶ֫רֶב בַּיּוֹם הָרִאשׁוֹן לַבֹּ֫קֶר׃

nor shall the meat that you sacrifice on the evening
of the first day remain until the morning.

וְלֹא־	and no/not	---	particle
לֹא *wə·lō̄ʾ-*		W/ CONJ וְ	
יָלִין	(it) stays/remains overnight	QAL IMPF 3MS	verb
לין *yā·lîn*			
מִן־	from/with	---	prep
מִן *min-*			
הַבָּשָׂר	the flesh/meat	ABS	noun
בָּשָׂר *hab·bā·śār*		W/ DEF. ART.	
אֲשֶׁר	that/which	---	relative pron
אֲשֶׁר *ʾă·šer*			
תִּזְבַּח	you will sacrifice	QAL IMPF 2MS	verb
זבח *tiz·baḥ*			
בָּעֶ֫רֶב	in (the) evening	ABS	noun
עֶ֫רֶב *bā·ʿe·rev*		W/ PREP בְּ + DEF. ART.	
בַּיּוֹם	on the day	ABS	noun
יוֹם *bay·yôm*		W/ PREP בְּ + DEF. ART.	
הָרִאשׁוֹן	(the) first	---	ordinal number
רִאשׁוֹן *hā·ri·šôn*		W/ DEF. ART.	
לַבֹּ֫קֶר׃	to the morning	ABS	noun
בֹּ֫קֶר *lab·bō·qer*		W/ PREP לְ + DEF. ART.	

לֹא תוּכַל לִזְבֹּחַ אֶת־הַפֶּסַח

You are not permitted to sacrifice the Passover offering

לֹא לֹא *lō'*	no/not	---	particle
תוּכַל יכל *tû·ḵal*	you will be able	QAL IMPF 2MS	verb
לִזְבֹּחַ זבח *liz·bō·aḥ*	to sacrifice	QAL INF CST W/ PREP לְ	verb
אֶת־ את *'et-*	(direct object marker)	---	particle
הַפֶּסַח פֶּסַח *hap·pā·saḥ*	the Passover (offering)	ABS W/ DEF. ART.	noun

בְּאַחַד שְׁעָרֶיךָ אֲשֶׁר־יְהוָה אֱלֹהֶיךָ נֹתֵן לָךְ:

in any of your towns that Yahweh your God is giving you,

בְּאַחַד אֶחָד *bə·'a·ḥad*	in one of	CST W/ PREP בְּ	cardinal number
שְׁעָרֶיךָ שַׁעַר *šə·'ā·rɛ·ḵā*	your gates/towns	CST W/ 2MS SX	noun
אֲשֶׁר־ אֲשֶׁר *'ă·šer*	that/which	---	relative pron
יְהוָה יהוה *YHWH*	Yahweh	ABS	noun
אֱלֹהֶיךָ אֱלֹהִים *'ĕ·lō·hɛ·ḵā*	your God	CST W/ 2MS SX	noun
נֹתֵן נתן *nō·tēn*	is giving	QAL PTCP MS	verb
לָךְ: לְ *lāḵ*	to you	--- W/ 2MS SX	prep

In the "From Text to Sermon" section below, we will comment on the requirement to gather at Passover.

כִּ֣י אִם־אֶל־הַמָּק֔וֹם

except in the place

כִּ֣י אִם־	only/except	- - -	conj
כִּי אִם־	*kî ʾim-*		
אֶל־	to	- - -	prep
אֶל	*ʾel-*		
הַמָּק֔וֹם	the place	ABS W/ DEF. ART.	noun
מָקוֹם	*ham·mā·qôm*		

A singular place emphasizes both a singular God and the unity of the people.

אֲשֶׁר־יִבְחַ֞ר יְהוָ֤ה אֱלֹהֶ֙יךָ֙ לְשַׁכֵּ֣ן שְׁמ֣וֹ שָׁ֔ם

where Yahweh your God chooses to place his name.

אֲשֶׁר־	that/which	- - -	relative pron
אֲשֶׁר	*ʾă·šer-*		
יִבְחַ֞ר	(he) chooses	QAL IMPF 3MS	verb
בחר	*yiv·ḥar*		
יְהוָ֤ה	Yahweh	ABS	noun
יהוה	*YHWH*		
אֱלֹהֶ֙יךָ֙	your God	CST W/ 2MS SX	noun
אֱלֹהִים	*ʾĕ·lō·hê·ḵā*		
לְשַׁכֵּ֣ן	to make dwell/place/settle	PIEL INF CST W/ PREP לְ	verb
שכן	*lə·šak·kēn*		
שְׁמ֣וֹ	his name	CST W/ 3MS SX	noun
שֵׁם	*šə·mô*		
שָׁ֔ם	there	- - -	adv
שָׁם	*šām*		

God's name, as noted many times already, signifies God's covenant with his people and the honor he demands from his people.

תִּזְבַּח אֶת־הַפֶּסַח בָּעֶרֶב כְּבוֹא הַשֶּׁמֶשׁ

Sacrifice the Passover offering in the evening,
when the sun goes down,

תִּזְבַּח זבח	you will sacrifice *tiz·baḥ*	QAL IMPF 2MS	verb
אֶת־ אֵת	(direct object marker) *'et-*	---	particle
הַפֶּסַח פֶּסַח	the Passover (offering) *hap·pe·saḥ*	ABS W/ DEF. ART.	noun
בָּעֶרֶב עֶרֶב	in the evening *bā·ʿā·rev*	ABS W/ PREP בְּ + DEF. ART.	noun
כְּבוֹא בוא	when it comes/goes *kə·vô'*	QAL INF CST W/ PREP כְּ	verb
הַשֶּׁמֶשׁ שֶׁמֶשׁ	the sun *haš·še·meš*	ABS W/ DEF. ART.	noun

מוֹעֵד צֵאתְךָ מִמִּצְרָיִם:

at the time you went out from Egypt.

מוֹעֵד מוֹעֵד	time *mô·ʿēd*	ABS	noun
צֵאתְךָ יצא	you came/went out *ṣē't·kā*	QAL INF CST W/ 2MS SX	verb
מִמִּצְרָיִם: מִצְרַיִם	from Egypt *miṣ·ra·yim*	ABS W/ PREP מִן	noun

וּבִשַּׁלְתָּ וְאָכַלְתָּ בַּמָּקוֹם אֲשֶׁר יִבְחַר יְהוָה אֱלֹהֶיךָ בּוֹ

You shall boil it and eat it at the place
that Yahweh your God chooses.

וּבִשַּׁלְתָּ בשל	and you will cook *û·viš·šal·tā*	PIEL WEQATAL 2MS	verb
וְאָכַלְתָּ אכל	and you will eat *wə·'ā·kal·tā*	QAL WEQATAL 2MS	verb

בַּמָּקוֹם מָקוֹם	in the place *bam·mā·qôm*	ABS W/ PREP בְּ + DEF. ART.	noun
אֲשֶׁר אֲשֶׁר	that/which *ʾă·šer*	---	relative pron
יִבְחַר בחר	(he) will choose *yiv·ḥar*	QAL IMPF 3MS	verb
יְהוָה יהוה	Yahweh *YHWH*	ABS	noun
אֱלֹהֶיךָ אֱלֹהִים	your God *ʾĕ·lō·hê·ḵā*	CST W/ 2MS SX	noun
בּוֹ בְּ	(with) it *bô*	--- W/ 3MS SX	prep

7b   וּפָנִיתָ בַבֹּקֶר וְהָלַכְתָּ לְאֹהָלֶיךָ׃

In the morning, turn and go back to your tents.

וּפָנִיתָ פנה	and you will turn *û·fā·nî·tā*	QAL WEQATAL 2MS	verb
בַּבֹּקֶר בֹּקֶר	in the morning *vab·bō·qer*	ABS W/ PREP בְּ + DEF. ART.	noun
וְהָלַכְתָּ הלך	and you will go *wǝ·hā·laḵ·tā*	QAL WEQATAL 2MS	verb
לְאֹהָלֶיךָ׃ אֹהֶל	to your tents *lǝ·ʾō·hā·lê·ḵā*	CST W/ PREP לְ + 2MS SX	noun

The return to tents allows for the holiness experienced in the "place" to return to each home, sanctifying the whole land.

8a   שֵׁשֶׁת יָמִים תֹּאכַל מַצּוֹת

Six days you shall eat unleavened bread,

| שֵׁשֶׁת
שֵׁשׁ | six (of)
šē·šet | CST | cardinal
number |
| יָמִים
יוֹם | days
yā·mîm | ABS | noun |

תֹּאכַ֖ל	you will eat	QAL IMPF 2MS	verb
אכל	tû·**ḵal**		
מַצּ֑וֹת	unleavened bread	ABS	noun
מַצָּה	maṣ·**ṣôt**		

וּבַיּ֣וֹם הַשְּׁבִיעִ֗י עֲצֶ֙רֶת֙ לַיהוָ֣ה אֱלֹהֶ֔יךָ

and on the seventh day there shall be a solemn assembly
to Yahweh your God.

וּבַיּ֣וֹם	and on the day	ABS	noun
יוֹם	û·vay·**yôm**	W/ CONJ וְ + PREP בְּ + DEF. ART.	
הַשְּׁבִיעִ֗י	(the) seventh	---	ordinal
שְׁבִיעִי	haš·šə·vî·**î**	W/ DEF. ART.	number
עֲצֶ֙רֶת֙	an assembly	ABS	noun
עֲצָרָה	ă·ṣe·ret		
לַיהוָ֣ה	to Yahweh	ABS	noun
יהוה	la·YHWH	W/ PREP לְ	
אֱלֹהֶ֔יךָ	your God	CST	noun
אֱלֹהִים	ĕ·lō·**hê**·ḵā	W/ 2MS SX	

עֲצָרָה, "assembly," has a strong association with priestly, sacred gatherings
(e.g., Lev 23:36; 1 Kgs 10:20; Isa 1:13).

לֹ֥א תַעֲשֶׂ֖ה מְלָאכָֽה׃

Do not do any work.

לֹ֥א	no/not	---	particle
לֹא	lō'		
תַעֲשֶׂ֖ה	you will do/make	QAL IMPF 2MS	verb
עשׂה	ta·ă·śe		
מְלָאכָֽה׃	work/labor	ABS	noun
מְלָאכָה	mə·lā'·ḵâ		

This is a clear echo of the Sabbath command in 5:14.

9a

שִׁבְעָ֥ה שָׁבֻעֹ֖ת תִּסְפָּר־לָ֑ךְ

šiv'â šāvu'ōt tispār-lāk

Count seven weeks for yourself.

9b

מֵהָחֵ֤ל חֶרְמֵשׁ֙ בַּקָּמָ֔ה תָּחֵ֣ל לִסְפֹּ֔ר שִׁבְעָ֖ה שָׁבֻעֽוֹת׃

mēhāḥēl ḥermēš baqqāmâ tāḥēl lispōr šiv'â šāvu'ôt.

**Begin to count seven weeks from when you first put the sickle
to the standing grain.**

10a

וְעָשִׂ֜יתָ חַ֤ג שָׁבֻעוֹת֙ לַיהוָ֣ה אֱלֹהֶ֔יךָ

wə'āśîtā hag šāvu'ôt YHWH 'ĕlōhêkā

Then you shall keep the Feast of Weeks to Yahweh your God.

10b

מִסַּ֛ת נִדְבַ֥ת יָדְךָ֖ אֲשֶׁ֣ר תִּתֵּ֑ן

missat nidvat yādəkā 'ăšer tittēn

You shall give a freewill offering of your hand in proportion

10c

כַּאֲשֶׁ֥ר יְבָרֶכְךָ֖ יְהוָ֥ה אֱלֹהֶֽיךָ׃

ka'ăšer yəvārekəkā YHWH 'ĕlōhêkā.

to all that Yahweh your God has blessed you with.

11a

וְשָׂמַחְתָּ֞ לִפְנֵ֣י ׀ יְהוָ֣ה אֱלֹהֶ֗יךָ

wəśāmaḥtā lifnê YHWH 'ĕlōhêkā

And you shall rejoice before Yahweh your God—

11b

אַתָּ֨ה וּבִנְךָ֤ וּבִתֶּ֙ךָ֙ וְעַבְדְּךָ֣ וַאֲמָתֶ֔ךָ וְהַלֵּוִ֖י אֲשֶׁ֥ר בִּשְׁעָרֶֽיךָ

'attâ ûvinkā ûvittekā wə'avdəkā wə'ămātêkā wəhallēwî 'ăšer bišʿārêkā

**you and your son and your daughter and your male slave
and female slave and the Levite who is in your towns**

11c וְהַגֵּר וְהַיָּתוֹם וְהָאַלְמָנָה אֲשֶׁר בְּקִרְבֶּךָ

wəhaggēr wəhayyātôm wəhā'almānâ 'ăšer bəqirbekā

**and the sojourner and the orphan
and the widow who are among you—**

11d בַּמָּקוֹם אֲשֶׁר יִבְחַר יְהוָה אֱלֹהֶיךָ לְשַׁכֵּן שְׁמוֹ שָׁם:

bammāqôm 'ăšer-yivḥar YHWH 'ĕlōhêkā ləšakkēn šəmô šām.

in the place where Yahweh your God chooses to place his name.

12a וְזָכַרְתָּ כִּי־עֶבֶד הָיִיתָ בְּמִצְרָיִם

wəzākartā kî-'eved hāyîtā bəmiṣrāyim

And you shall remember that you were slaves in Egypt.

12b וְשָׁמַרְתָּ וְעָשִׂיתָ אֶת־הַחֻקִּים הָאֵלֶּה:

wəšāmartā wə'āśîtā 'et-haḥuqqîm hā'ēlle.

And be careful to keep these statutes.

9a	שִׁבְעָה שָׁבֻעֹת תִּסְפָּר־לָךְ		
	Count seven weeks for yourself.		

שִׁבְעָה *šiv·'â* / שֶׁבַע	seven	ABS	cardinal number
שָׁבֻעֹת *šā·vu·'ōt* / שָׁבוּעַ	sevens/weeks	ABS	noun
תִּסְפָּר־ *tis·pār-* / ספר	you will count	QAL IMPF 2MS	verb
לָךְ *lāk* / ל	for yourself	W/ 2MS SX	prep

מֵהָחֵל חֶרְמֵשׁ בַּקָּמָה תָּחֵל לִסְפֹּר שִׁבְעָה שָׁבֻעוֹת:

Begin to count seven weeks from when you first put the sickle to the standing grain.

מֵהָחֵל חלל *mē·hā·ḥēl*	from the beginning of	HIPH INF CST W/ PREP מִן	verb
חֶרְמֵשׁ חֶרְמֵשׁ *ḥer·mēš*	the sickle	ABS	noun
בַּקָּמָה קָמָה *baq·qā·mâ*	in the standing grain	ABS W/ PREP בְּ + DEF. ART.	noun
תָּחֵל חלל *tā·ḥēl*	you will begin	HIPH IMPF 2MS	verb
לִסְפֹּר ספר *lis·pōr*	to count	QAL INF CST W/ PREP לְ	verb
שִׁבְעָה שֶׁבַע *šiv·ʿâ*	seven	ABS	cardinal number
שָׁבֻעוֹת: שָׁבוּעַ *šā·vu·ʿôt*	sevens/weeks	ABS	noun

The Hebrew here is literally, "from the beginning of the sickle in the standing grain."

וְעָשִׂיתָ חַג שָׁבֻעוֹת לַיהוָה אֱלֹהֶיךָ

Then you shall keep the Feast of Weeks to Yahweh your God.

וְעָשִׂיתָ עשה *wə·ʿā·śî·tā*	then you will do/keep	QAL WEQATAL 2MS	verb
חַג חַג *ḥag*	(the) feast of	CST	noun
שָׁבֻעוֹת שָׁבוּעַ *šā·vu·ʿôt*	sevens/weeks	ABS	noun
לַיהוָה יהוה *YHWH*	to Yahweh	ABS W/ PREP לְ	noun
אֱלֹהֶיךָ אֱלֹהִים *ʾĕ·lō·hê·kā*	your God	CST W/ 2MS SX	noun

You shall give a freewill offering of your hand in proportion

מִסַּת מִסַּת	from (the) measure of *mis·sat*	CST	noun
נִדְבַת נְדָבָה	the freewill offering of *nid·vat*	CST	noun
יָדְךָ יָד	your hand *yā·də·ḵā*	CST W/ 2MS SX	noun
אֲשֶׁר אֲשֶׁר	that/which *ʾă·šer*	---	relative pron
תִּתֵּן נתן	you will give *tit·tēn*	QAL IMPF 2MS	verb

מִסָּה is a *hapax legomenon*, sometimes translated "sufficient."

to all that Yahweh your God has blessed you with.

כַּאֲשֶׁר אֲשֶׁר	according to/just as *ka·ʾă·šer*	W/ PREP כְּ	relative pron
יְבָרֶכְךָ ברך	(he) blesses you *yə·vā·re·ḵə·ḵā*	PIEL IMPF 3MS W/ 2MS SX	verb
יְהוָה יהוה	Yahweh *YHWH*	ABS	noun
אֱלֹהֶיךָ׃ אֱלֹהִים	your God *ʾĕ·lō·hê·ḵā*	CST W/ 2MS SX	noun

And you shall rejoice before Yahweh your God—

וְשָׂמַחְתָּ שׂמח	and you will rejoice *wə·śā·maḥ·tā*	QAL WEQATAL 2MS	verb
לִפְנֵי׀ לִפְנֵי	before *lif·nê*	---	prep

יְהוָה	Yahweh	ABS	noun
יהוה	*YHWH*		
אֱלֹהֶיךָ	your God	CST	noun
אֱלֹהִים	*ĕ·lō·hê·kā*	W/ 2MS SX	

11b	אַתָּה וּבִנְךָ וּבִתֶּךָ וְעַבְדְּךָ וַאֲמָתֶךָ וְהַלֵּוִי אֲשֶׁר בִּשְׁעָרֶיךָ

you and your son and your daughter and your male slave
and female slave and the Levite who is in your towns

אַתָּה	you	---	personal pron
אַתָּה	*'at·tâ*		
וּבִנְךָ	and your son	CST	noun
בֵּן	*û·vin·kā*	W/ CONJ וְ + 2MS SX	
וּבִתֶּךָ	and your daughter	CST	noun
בַּת	*û·vit·te·kā*	W/ CONJ וְ + 2MS SX	
וְעַבְדְּךָ	and your male slave	CST	noun
עֶבֶד	*wə·'av·də·kā*	W/ CONJ וְ + 2MS SX	
וַאֲמָתֶךָ	and your female slave	CST	noun
אָמָה	*wə·'ă·mā·tê·kā*	W/ CONJ וְ + 2MS SX	
וְהַלֵּוִי	and the Levite	MS SUBST	adj
לֵוִי	*wə·hal·lē·wî*	W/ CONJ וְ + DEF. ART.	
אֲשֶׁר	who/which	---	relative pron
אֲשֶׁר	*'ă·šer*		
בִּשְׁעָרֶיךָ	is in your gates/towns	CST	noun
שַׁעַר	*biš·'ā·rê·kā*	W/ PREP בְּ + 2MS SX	

By the piling up of וְ after וְ, the passage emphasizes the inclusion of all
social classes (also v. 11c).

11c	וְהַגֵּר וְהַיָּתוֹם וְהָאַלְמָנָה אֲשֶׁר בְּקִרְבֶּךָ

and the sojourner and the orphan
and the widow who are among you—

| וְהַגֵּר | and the sojourner/foreigner | ABS | noun |
| גֵּר | *wə·hag·gēr* | W/ CONJ וְ + DEF. ART. | |

וְהַיָּתוֹם	and the fatherless/orphan	ABS	noun
יָתוֹם	wə·hay·yā·**tôm**	W/ CONJ וְ + DEF. ART.	
וְהָאַלְמָנָה	and the widow	ABS	noun
אַלְמָנָה	wə·hā·'al·mā·**nâ**	W/ CONJ וְ + DEF. ART.	
אֲשֶׁר	who/which	---	relative pron
אֲשֶׁר	'ă·šer		
בְּקִרְבֶּךָ	(is) in your midst	CST	noun
קֶרֶב	bə·qir·**be**·ḵā	W/ PREP בְּ + 2MS SX	

11d

in the place where Yahweh your God chooses to place his name.

בַּמָּקוֹם	in the place	ABS	noun
מָקוֹם	bam·mā·**qôm**	W/ PREP בְּ + DEF. ART.	
אֲשֶׁר	that/which	---	relative pron
אֲשֶׁר	'ă·šer-		
יִבְחַר	(he) will choose	QAL IMPF 3MS	verb
בחר	yiv·**ḥar**		
יְהוָה	Yahweh	ABS	noun
יהוה	YHWH		
אֱלֹהֶיךָ	your God	CST	noun
אֱלֹהִים	'ĕ·lō·**hê**·ḵā	W/ 2MS SX	
לְשַׁכֵּן	to set/place/make dwell	PIEL INF CST	verb
שׁכן	lə·šak·**kēn**	W/ PREP לְ	
שְׁמוֹ	his name	CST	noun
שֵׁם	šə·**mô**	W/ 3MS SX	
שָׁם:	there	---	adv
שָׁם	šām		

Yahweh, rather than the priests or king, is the host of the feast.

12a — וְזָכַרְתָּ כִּי־עֶבֶד הָיִיתָ בְּמִצְרָיִם

And you shall remember that you were slaves in Egypt.

וְזָכַרְתָּ֖ זכר	and you will remember *wə·zā·ḵar·tā*	QAL WEQATAL 2MS	verb
כִּי־ כִּי	that *kî-*	---	conj
עֶבֶד עֶבֶד	slave *'e·ved*	ABS	noun
הָיִיתָ היה	you were *hā·yî·tā*	QAL PF 2MS	verb
בְּמִצְרָיִם מִצְרַיִם	in Egypt *bə·miṣ·rā·yim*	ABS W/ PREP בְּ	noun

וְזָכַרְתָּ ("And you shall remember") clearly ties the feasts to the Sabbath command in the Decalogue (5:15).

12b — וְשָׁמַרְתָּ וְעָשִׂיתָ אֶת־הַחֻקִּים הָאֵלֶּה:

And be careful to keep these statutes.

וְשָׁמַרְתָּ שמר	and you will guard/keep *wə·šā·mar·tā*	QAL WEQATAL 2MS	verb
וְעָשִׂיתָ עשה	to do *wə·'ā·śî·tā*	QAL WEQATAL 2MS	verb
אֶת־ אֵת	(direct object marker) *'et-*	---	particle
הַחֻקִּים חֹק	(the) statutes/regulations *ha·ḥuq·qîm*	ABS W/ DEF. ART.	noun
הָאֵלֶּה: אֵלֶּה	(the) these *hā·'ēl·le*	--- W/ DEF. ART.	demonstr pron

13a חַג הַסֻּכֹּת תַּעֲשֶׂה לְךָ שִׁבְעַת יָמִים

ḥag hassukkōt taʿăśe ləkā šivʿat yāmîm

You shall keep the Feast of Booths for seven days

13b בְּאָסְפְּךָ מִגָּרְנְךָ וּמִיִּקְבֶךָ׃

bəʾāsəpəkā miggārnəkā ûmiyyiqvekā.

after you gather from the threshing floor and winepress.

14a וְשָׂמַחְתָּ בְּחַגֶּךָ אַתָּה וּבִנְךָ וּבִתֶּךָ

wəśāmaḥtā wəḥaggekā ʾattâ ûvinkā ûvittekā

וְעַבְדְּךָ וַאֲמָתֶךָ וְהַלֵּוִי

wəʿavdəkā waʾămātekā wəhallēwî

**Rejoice in your feast, you and your son and your daughter
and your male slave and your female slave and the Levite**

14b וְהַגֵּר וְהַיָּתוֹם וְהָאַלְמָנָה אֲשֶׁר בִּשְׁעָרֶיךָ׃

wəhaggēr wəhayyātôm wəhāʾalmānâ ʾăšer bišʿārêkā.

**and the sojourner and the orphan and the widow
who are in your towns.**

15a שִׁבְעַת יָמִים תָּחֹג לַיהוָה אֱלֹהֶיךָ

šivʿat yāmîm tāḥōg laYHWH ʾĕlōhêkā

Seven days you shall feast to Yahweh your God

15b בַּמָּקוֹם אֲשֶׁר־יִבְחַר יְהוָה

bammāqôm ʾăšer-yivḥar YHWH

in the place that Yahweh chooses.

15c כִּי יְבָרֶכְךָ יְהוָה אֱלֹהֶיךָ בְּכֹל תְּבוּאָתְךָ וּבְכֹל מַעֲשֵׂה יָדֶיךָ

kî yəvārekəkā YHWH ʾĕlōhêkā bəkōl təvûʾātəkā ûvəkōl maʿăśē yādêkā

**For Yahweh your God will bless you in all your produce
and in all the work of your hands.**

15d | וְהָיִיתָ אַךְ שָׂמֵחַ:

wəhāyîtā ʾak śāmēaḥ.

And you shall surely be joyful.

13a | חַג הַסֻּכֹּת תַּעֲשֶׂה לְךָ שִׁבְעַת יָמִים

You shall keep the Feast of Booths for seven days

חַג חַג	(the) feast of *ḥag*	CST	noun
הַסֻּכֹּת סֻכָּה	(the) booths *has·suk·kōt*	ABS W/ DEF. ART.	noun
תַּעֲשֶׂה עשׂה	you will do/keep *ta·ʿă·śe*	QAL IMPF 2MS	verb
לְךָ לְ	you/for you *lə·kā*	--- W/ 2MS SX	prep
שִׁבְעַת שֶׁבַע	seven (of) *šiv·ʿat*	CST	cardinal number
יָמִים יוֹם	days *yā·mîm*	ABS	noun

13b | בְּאָסְפְּךָ מִגָּרְנְךָ וּמִיִּקְבֶךָ:

after you gather from the threshing floor and winepress.

בְּאָסְפְּךָ אסף	when you gather *bə·ʾā·sə·pə·kā*	QAL INF CST W/ PREP בְּ + 2MS SX	verb
מִגָּרְנְךָ גֹּרֶן	from the threshing floor *mig·gā·rə·nə·kā*	CST W/ PREP מִן + 2MS SX	noun
וּמִיִּקְבֶךָ: יֶקֶב	and the winepress *û·miy·yiq·ve·kā*	CST W/ CONJ וְ + PREP מִן + 2MS SX	noun

וְשָׂמַחְתָּ בְּחַגֶּךָ אַתָּה וּבִנְךָ וּבִתֶּךָ
וְעַבְדְּךָ וַאֲמָתֶךָ וְהַלֵּוִי

Rejoice in your feast, you and your son and your daughter
and your male slave and your female slave and the Levite

וְשָׂמַחְתָּ שׂמח	and you will rejoice *wə·śā·mah·tā*	QAL WEQATAL 2MS	verb
בְּחַגֶּךָ חַג	in your feast *wə·hag·ge·kā*	CST W/ PREP בְּ + 2MS SX	noun
אַתָּה אַתָּה	you *'at·tâ*	---	personal pron
וּבִנְךָ בֵּן	and your son *û·vin·kā*	CST W/ CONJ וְ + 2MS SX	noun
וּבִתֶּךָ בַּת	and your daughter *û·vit·te·kā*	CST W/ CONJ וְ + 2MS SX	noun
וְעַבְדְּךָ עֶבֶד	and your male slave *wə·'av·də·kā*	CST W/ CONJ וְ + 2MS SX	noun
וַאֲמָתֶךָ אָמָה	and your female slave *wa·'ă·mā·te·kā*	CST W/ CONJ וְ + 2MS SX	noun
וְהַלֵּוִי לֵוִי	and the Levite *wə·hal·lē·wî*	MS SUBST W/ CONJ וְ + DEF. ART.	adj

It must be remembered that this communal gathering centers around mutual joy (שׂמח).

וְהַגֵּר וְהַיָּתוֹם וְהָאַלְמָנָה אֲשֶׁר בִּשְׁעָרֶיךָ׃

and the sojourner and the orphan and the widow
who are in your towns.

וְהַגֵּר גֵּר	and the sojourner/foreigner *wə·hag·gēr*	ABS W/ CONJ וְ + DEF. ART.	noun
וְהַיָּתוֹם יָתוֹם	and the fatherless/orphan *wə·hay·yā·tôm*	ABS W/ CONJ וְ + DEF. ART.	noun
וְהָאַלְמָנָה אַלְמָנָה	and the widow *wə·hā·'al·mā·nâ*	ABS W/ CONJ וְ + DEF. ART.	noun
אֲשֶׁר אֲשֶׁר	that/which *'ă·šer*	---	relative pron

| בִּשְׁעָרֶיךָ: | (is) in your gates/towns | CST | noun |
| שַׁעַר | biš·ʿā·rê·ḵā | W/ PREP בְּ + 2MS SX | |

15a שִׁבְעַת יָמִים תָּחֹג לַיהוָה אֱלֹהֶיךָ

Seven days you shall feast to Yahweh your God

שִׁבְעַת	seven (of)	CST	cardinal number
שֶׁבַע	šiv·ʿat		
יָמִים	days	ABS	noun
יוֹם	yā·mîm		
תָּחֹג	you will feast	QAL IMPF 2MS	verb
חגג	tā·ḥōg		
לַיהוָה	to Yahweh	ABS	noun
יהוה	la·YHWH	W/ PREP לְ	
אֱלֹהֶיךָ	your God	CST	noun
אֱלֹהִים	ĕ·lō·hê·ḵā	W/ 2MS SX	

Once again, the seventh-year pattern of the Sabbath is in the background of these laws (see vv. 3, 8, 9, 12, 13).

15b בַּמָּקוֹם אֲשֶׁר־יִבְחַר יְהוָה

in the place that Yahweh chooses.

בַּמָּקוֹם	in the place	ABS	noun
מָקוֹם	bam·mā·qôm	W/ PREP בְּ + DEF. ART.	
אֲשֶׁר־	that/which	---	relative pron
אֲשֶׁר	ʾă·šer-		
יִבְחַר	(he) chooses	QAL IMPF 3MS	verb
בחר	yiv·ḥar		
יְהוָה	Yahweh	ABS	noun
יהוה	YHWH		

כִּי יְבָרֶכְךָ֣ יְהוָה אֱלֹהֶיךָ בְּכֹל תְּבוּאָתְךָ֗ וּבְכֹל מַעֲשֵׂה יָדֶיךָ

For Yahweh your God will bless you in all your produce
and in all the work of your hands.

כִּי	for/because	---	conj
כִּי	*kî*		
יְבָרֶכְךָ֣	(he) will bless you	PIEL IMPF 3MS	verb
ברך	*yə·vā·re·ḵə·ḵā*	W/ 2MS SX	
יְהוָה	Yahweh	ABS	noun
יהוה	*YHWH*		
אֱלֹהֶיךָ	your God	CST	noun
אֱלֹהִים	*ʾĕ·lō·hê·ḵā*	W/ 2MS SX	
בְּכֹל	in all	CST	noun
כֹּל	*bə·ḵōl*	W/ PREP בְּ	
תְּבוּאָתְךָ	your produce/yield	CST	noun
תְּבוּאָה	*tə·vû·ʾā·tə·ḵā*	W/ 2MS SX	
וּבְכֹל	and in all	CST	noun
כֹּל	*û·və·ḵōl*	W/ CONJ וְ + PREP בְּ	
מַעֲשֵׂה	(the) work of	CST	noun
מַעֲשֶׂה	*ma·ʿă·śē*		
יָדֶיךָ	your hands	CST	noun
יָד	*yā·dê·ḵā*	W/ 2MS SX	

וְהָיִיתָ אַךְ שָׂמֵחַ׃

And you shall surely be joyful.

וְהָיִיתָ	and you will be	QAL WEQATAL 2MS	verb
היה	*wə·hā·yî·tā*		
אַךְ	surely	---	adv
אַךְ	*ʾaḵ*		
שָׂמֵחַ׃	joyful/rejoicing	MS PRED	adj
שָׂמֵחַ	*śā·mē·aḥ*		

16a
שָׁל֣וֹשׁ פְּעָמִ֣ים ׀ בַּשָּׁנָ֗ה יֵרָאֶ֨ה כָל־זְכוּרְךָ֜
šālôš pəʿāmîm baššānâ yērāʾe kol-zəkûrəkā

אֶת־פְּנֵ֣י ׀ יְהוָ֣ה אֱלֹהֶ֗יךָ בַּמָּק֖וֹם אֲשֶׁ֣ר יִבְחָ֑ר
ʾet-pənê YHWH ʾĕlōhêkā bammāqôm ʾăšer yivḥar

**Three times each year all your males shall appear
before Yahweh your God in the place that he chooses**

16b
בְּחַ֣ג הַמַּצּ֗וֹת וּבְחַ֤ג הַשָּׁבֻעוֹת֙ וּבְחַ֣ג הַסֻּכּ֔וֹת
bəḥag hammaṣṣôt ûvəḥag haššāvuʿôt ûvəḥag hassukkôt

**at the Feast of Unleavened Bread, and at the Feast of Weeks,
and at the Feast of Booths.**

16c
וְלֹ֧א יֵרָאֶ֛ה אֶת־פְּנֵ֥י יְהוָ֖ה רֵיקָֽם׃
wəlōʾ yērāʾe ʾet-pənê YHWH rêqām.

And he shall not appear before Yahweh empty handed:

17
אִ֖ישׁ כְּמַתְּנַ֣ת יָד֑וֹ כְּבִרְכַּ֛ת יְהוָ֥ה אֱלֹהֶ֖יךָ אֲשֶׁ֥ר נָֽתַן־לָֽךְ׃
ʾîš kəmatənat yādô kəvirkat YHWH ʾĕlōhêkā ʾăšer nātan-lāk.

**each man with a gift of his hand, according to the blessing
that Yahweh your God has given you.**

16a
שָׁל֣וֹשׁ פְּעָמִ֣ים ׀ בַּשָּׁנָ֗ה יֵרָאֶ֨ה כָל־זְכוּרְךָ֜
אֶת־פְּנֵ֣י ׀ יְהוָ֣ה אֱלֹהֶ֗יךָ בַּמָּק֖וֹם אֲשֶׁ֣ר יִבְחָ֑ר

Three times each year all your males shall appear
before Yahweh your God in the place that he chooses

שָׁל֣וֹשׁ	three		ABS	cardinal
שָׁלֹשׁ	*šā·lôš*			number

פְּעָמִים | פַּעַם	times/steps/occurrences *pa·ʿă·**mîm***	ABS	noun
בַּשָּׁנָה שָׁנָה	in the year *baš·šā·**nâ***	ABS W/ PREP בְּ + DEF. ART.	noun
יֵרָאֶה ראה	(he/it) will appear *yē·rā·**ʾe***	NIPH IMPF 3MS	verb
כָּל־ כֹּל	all/every *ḵol-*	CST	noun
זְכוּרְךָ זָכוּר	your male *zə·ḵû·rə·**ḵā***	CST W/ 2MS SX	noun
אֶת־ אֵת	*(direct object marker)* *ʾet-*	---	particle
פְּנֵי | פָּנֶה	(the) face of *pə·**nê***	CST	noun
יְהֹוָה יהוה	Yahweh *YHWH*	ABS	noun
אֱלֹהֶיךָ אֱלֹהִים	your God *ʾĕ·lō·**hê**·ḵā*	CST W/ 2MS SX	noun
בַּמָּקוֹם מָקוֹם	in the place *bam·mā·**qôm***	ABS W/ PREP בְּ + DEF. ART.	noun
אֲשֶׁר אֲשֶׁר	that/which *ʾă·**šer***	---	relative pron
יִבְחָר בחר	he will choose *yiv·**ḥar***	QAL IMPF 3MS	verb

בְּחַג הַמַּצּוֹת וּבְחַג הַשָּׁבֻעוֹת וּבְחַג הַסֻּכּוֹת

at the Feast of Unleavened Bread, and at the Feast of Weeks,
and at the Feast of Booths.

בְּחַג חַג	at (the) feast of *bə·**ḥag***	CST W/ PREP בְּ	noun
הַמַּצּוֹת מַצָּה	(the) unleavened bread *ham·maṣ·**ṣôt***	ABS W/ DEF. ART.	noun
וּבְחַג חַג	and at (the) feast of *û·və·**ḥag***	CST W/ CONJ וְ + PREP בְּ	noun

הַשָּׁבֻעוֹת שָׁבוּעַ	(the) sevens/weeks *haš·šā·vu·ʿôt*	ABS W/ DEF. ART.	noun
וּבְחַג חַג	and at (the) feast of *û·va·ḥag*	CST W/ CONJ וְ + PREP בְּ	noun
הַסֻּכּוֹת סֻכָּה	(the) booths *has·suk·kōt*	ABS W/ DEF. ART.	noun

---

16c — וְלֹא יֵרָאֶה אֶת־פְּנֵי יְהוָה רֵיקָם׃

And he shall not appear before Yahweh empty handed:

וְלֹא לֹא	and no/not *wə·lōʾ*	--- W/ CONJ וְ	particle
יֵרָאֶה רָאה	he will appear *yē·rā·ʾe*	NIPH IMPF 3MS	verb
אֶת־ אֵת	(direct object marker) *ʾet-*	---	particle
פְּנֵי פָּנֶה	(the) face of *pə·nê*	CST	noun
יְהוָה יהוה	Yahweh *YHWH*	ABS	noun
רֵיקָם׃ רֵיקָם	empty-handed/without possessions *rê·qām*	---	adv

The verb ראה here and in 16a is in the Niphal: "shall appear." The BHS editorial note suggests pointing these as Qal: יִרְאֶה, "you shall see (the face of Yahweh)" (cf. 2 Sam 3:13; 14:28, 32). The Niphal pointing might have been used to distinguish the act of appearing before YHWH from that of seeing his face, which might have been inferred had the Qal been used.

---

17 — כְּבִרְכַּת יְהוָה אֱלֹהֶיךָ אֲשֶׁר נָתַן־לָךְ׃ אִישׁ כְּמַתְּנַת יָדוֹ

each man with a gift of his hand, according to the blessing that Yahweh your God has given you.

אִישׁ אִישׁ	each/man *ʾîš*	ABS	noun

כְּמַתְּנַת מַתָּנָה	according to the gift *kə·ma·tə·nat*	CST W/ PREP כְּ	noun
יָדֹו יָד	of his hand *yā·dô*	CST W/ 3MS SX	noun
כְּבִרְכַּת בְּרָכָה	according to (the) blessing of *kə·vir·kat*	CST W/ PREP כְּ	noun
יְהוָה יהוה	Yahweh *YHWH*	ABS	noun
אֱלֹהֶיךָ אֱלֹהִים	your God *ʾĕ·lō·hê·ḵā*	CST W/ 2MS SX	noun
אֲשֶׁר אֲשֶׁר	that/which *ʾă·šer*	---	relative pron
נָתַן־ נתן	he has given *nā·tan-*	QAL PF 3MS	verb
לָךְ׃ ל	to you *lāḵ*	--- W/ 2MS SX	prep

Travel, Time, and Holy Land.

> *"Do not come near here; remove your sandals, for the place on which you stand is holy ground." (Exod 3:5)*

Redemption from Egypt did not end with political freedom for Israel but pointed forward to God's deeper desire to gather with his people in sacred places in the future. The promise to "place his name" in 16:2 is an oft-repeated refrain in Deuteronomy that signifies this hallowing of Israel's land as a place of divine intimacy.

It is, therefore, no minor point that all three pilgrimage feasts require the people (as represented by the men) to travel to the chosen *place* for worship and then to return home; the liturgy is not simply about what happens at the "place" but the whole process of moving there and back. Dru Johnson has shown that the rituals laid out in the Bible can be tied to habits that lead back from the sanctuary where sacrifices happened to the homes and fields where the foods and animals are grown and prepared (2016:33–56). The rituals *at* the sanctuary thus seep their way back into every crack and contour of our lives at home. Paying close attention to these movements in time and place opens windows into the meaning of these feasts.

The opening Feast of Passover follows the movement from "towns" to the "place" (vv. 5–6) and back to "tents" (v. 7). This is paralleled by the provision that no leaven should be seen in "any of your territory" (v. 4a). In this way, all the land is included in the interwoven tapestry of rituals. The pilgrimage thus takes God's sacred presence from the one chosen place into every place in the land. Further, with the journey from Egypt as the central memory, the liturgy unites the nation around the gifts of freedom and the land beneath their feet.

Finally, the anonymous "you" behind each of the commands makes the head of the father's household responsible for this rhythm of gathering at Yahweh's feasts and returning home again. And so, while the feasts gather the nation as one, the identity of individual households is never lost. The unity that binds the nation together in Yahweh at "one place" does the same for each family household together with the needy and the marginalized who live in their midst. As we will see below, journey and place create a unique kind of community.

🌱 *Community.* The annual feasts play a powerful role in forming a people as a community—that is, people who *communicate*, in the original sense of the word (Latin, *communicare*), which describes how people *share* their lives, goods, land, and homes (not simply their words).

Notice first that the Feast of Passover emphasizes the individual Israelite, as if to say, "every one of you is included in this people." But then the second two feasts emphasize the unity of all social groups as one. The Israelite must recognize individual membership in God's covenant and a corresponding obligation to others in the land.

It should be obvious that unity within social classes and ethnicities comes naturally: we are prone to look to those like us, or at our worst, look up to those who have more than us. But the lists in these feasts disrupt this instinct, pointing each Israelite to look down to those below them and outward to those different from them as they share their food. As Walter Houston has put it, "Such is the function of the kind of patronage feasts envisioned in Deut 16: Yhwh offers hospitality in return for homage" (2009:12). Yahweh has given Israel this land and this produce, and he asks for practices of generous hospitality in return.

Gathering across ethnic, geographic, and economic classes is not merely awkward at times but naturally forces buried divisions and conflicts to the surface when we encounter each other face to face. "So you're the people who bought up all the land from my family." "Oh, you're the family that fled famine in your own land and keep gleaning in my fields." As a result, an implicit part of the work and ritual in worship is in reconciling with my neighbor. Jesus makes this point emphatic in the Sermon on the Mount when he teaches us to reconcile with our neighbor before bringing our gift to the altar (Matt 5:23–24). This is not simply peace before worship but peace as worship.

There seems little doubt that Jesus' teachings have their roots in passages like this in the Old Testament. Compare for example God's rejection and acceptance of two kinds of sacrifices in Ps 51:16–19. The sacrifices are only acceptable when the offeror has humbly dealt with sin. Citing the anthropologist Victor Turner, Altmann summarizes this same social power of Deut 16: "[Deuteronomy's] ritual meal texts postulate the meals as 'fundamentally a response to the divisiveness, alienation, and exploitation that are associated with everyday social structure'" (2011:209).

We might say that food has a central role in what Ephraim Radner describes as "self-repair" in societies (2016:212). Radner reminds us of the climactic feast of reconciliation at the Lord's Table. When we call Christ our "Passover," we place his body, life, death, and resurrection at the center of a new gathering and worshiping community. When we eat his body and drink his blood, we restore our unity with God the Trinity and with one another. This community is the very thing for which Jesus prayed: "that they may be one as we are one," and "I in them and you in me that they may become completely one" (John 17:11, 23).

 *Joy.* I often wonder if we haven't watered down Christian joy with our holiday cards and placid scenes of fireplaces and family reunions, as if joy were a warm sentimental setting with just the right mood and lighting—a good feeling among friends. It's certainly good to be joyful in such simple things. But when it comes to the joy in Scripture, Georg Braulik's warning is well placed: "The joy spoken of in Deuteronomy is by no means a harmless, naively positive attitude. On the contrary, [one] cannot imagine anything more critical than this joy" (1994b:40). One can, as we know well, rejoice in the absence of material goods (Hab 3:17–19) and even in our suffering (Matt 5:12; Rom 5:3–5; Col 1:24; Jas 1:2).

Such joy is central to Deuteronomy's message. Note that the verbal form שׂמח ("rejoice" rather than the nonverbal forms "joy" or "joyful") is used more in Deuteronomy than in any other book besides the Psalms (Braulik 1994b:39–40). Moses commands rejoicing three times in the Sabbath laws (14:26; 16:11, 14) along with the adjectival form, "you shall surely be joyful" (16:15).

Joy in all these passages accompanies an interconnected string of activities: the produce of work (12:18), gathering and sharing (16:11, 14–15), and recognition of all the gifts that come from Yahweh (26:11). Joy thus arises in unity, divine provision, and bodily rest and satisfaction. It should not go unnoticed in these contexts that joy is attached to the goodness of the created world in this life as it reminds us of the gifts of God.

The optimism we meet in Deuteronomy is countered by the struggle to find joy in the fallen and ephemeral world of Ecclesiastes. The seven exhortations to "rejoice" in food and daily life come up against the stark reality that joy often eludes us (3:12, 22; 5:18; 8:15; 10:19; 11:8, 9). Qoheleth's struggle to find joy amidst much despair only finds a way forward in his admonition to "remember your creator in the days of your youth" (Eccl 12:1). Remember the goodness of God's world, his providence, and grace. Here is the secret to joy (on joy in Ecclesiastes, see Bartholomew 2009:228–31).

The tension between joy and despair is broken once and for all at the announcement of the incarnation in the words of Mary's Magnificat: "My soul magnifies the Lord, and my spirit rejoices in God my Savior" (Luke 1:46–47). Mary is the first to receive the Creator in her life and in her body. One must pause at this point at which God unites himself with his creation and becomes one with us. A great cosmic link has fastened the world to God and it cannot be broken. We follow Mary into this joy.

Finally, Christian joy surpasses momentary happiness because it is a gift of the Holy Spirit within us (Rom 14:17; 15:13); it is not something we do by ourselves or from our own resources. As David Ford has said, the Christian is "completely in the arms of God and completely in the world" (Ford 1999:260). Having been rescued by God, we "abide" in his love in this life and come to know the fullness of joy (John 15:11).

 ***Deuteronomy and Liturgy Today.*** In 1 Cor 14, Paul addresses what seems to be a range of disruptive activities during worship, admonishing them that, "God is not a God of disorder, but of peace . . . but everything should be done decently and in order" (14:33, 40).

This recalls a major liturgical renewal movement in the latter half of the twentieth century. The Roman Catholic tradition reformed its worship to allow masses in local languages and began to allow lay involvement in worship. Many liturgical denominations saw growth and others returned to more historic liturgies. Movements like this are usually responses to the shortcomings of a previous generation. People had a longing for *meaning* in what they were doing when they gathered and for deeper ways to connect with God. While there is not one "right" way to worship, we should recognize that there are better ways and worse ways, some more decent and in order than others. How might the Sabbath rituals in Deuteronomy help churches think about their worship?

For one, it should make us *think* about worship. The liturgical scholar Louis Weil (2013:5–9) relays a story of years of travel to churches around the country where he asked pastors the reasons for their ceremonial actions and patterns in worship. The most common answer was that these pastors had learned their worship from their mentor, and that mentor from a previous mentor. Weil advises us that we ought to know why we do things and, even more, that we make it clear to the congregation why worship proceeds as it does. This might prompt questions like: Why this song? Why here? How long is the sermon and how does it fit into the shape of this liturgy? What is the meaning of what we have just done together?

Deuteronomy's feasts also work on deeper levels. As we saw above, the Sabbath festivals have an intentional flow that connects every person in the household to the nation gathered in the holy place while turning their eyes to those most in need around them. We might say that the experience of God in worship comes home with us, sanctifying along the way the land in which we live. Worship also engaged the people in a memory of the past and a hope for the future, much as the ancient creeds and reading of Scripture do for us today. We gather and worship to rehearse our story.

At the center of our liturgies, we can find ourselves being restored individually and relationally, affirming the good gift of God's creation, and glorifying God as the center of our life. We might ask if our worship does these kinds of things every week, and if not, how we might deepen, enrich, and renew it.

WISDOM IN THE INDIVIDUAL LAWS

The three sets of laws we covered in chs. 14–16 are all related to the Sabbath command in the Decalogue. Meanwhile, the laws concerning authority in 16:18–18:22 are naturally linked to the fifth command to honor father and mother. The laws we now visit in chs. 22–25 are expansions, or applications, of the laws in the Decalogue pertaining to life, marriage, court testimony, and possessions.

In these laws we notice a consistent emphasis on "your brother" or "kindred" that is not found in other books in the Pentateuch. In this way, Deuteronomy portrays the community in solidarity, bound together by the strongest humanitarian laws we know of in the ancient world (Morrow 2017:246–47).

LARGER LITERARY CONTEXT ▸ 19:1–25:19

22:1a

לֹא־תִרְאֶה אֶת־שׁוֹר אָחִ֫יךָ אוֹ אֶת־שֵׂיוֹ נִדָּחִים

lōʾ-tirʾe ʾet-šôr ʾāḥîḵā ʾô ʾet-śēyô niddāḥîm

You shall not see your brother's ox or his sheep straying

22:1b

וְהִתְעַלַּמְתָּ מֵהֶם

wəhitʿallamtā mēhem

and ignore them.

22:1c

הָשֵׁב תְּשִׁיבֵם לְאָחִ֫יךָ׃

hāšēv təšîvēm ləʾāḥîḵā.

You shall surely return them to your brother.

22:2a

וְאִם־לֹא קָרוֹב אָחִ֫יךָ אֵלֶ֫יךָ וְלֹא יְדַעְתּוֹ

wəʾim-lōʾ qārôv ʾāḥîḵā ʾēlêḵā wəlōʾ yədaʿtô.

And if your brother is not near to you or you do not know him,

22:2a

וַאֲסַפְתּוֹ אֶל־תּוֹךְ בֵּיתֶ֫ךָ

waʾăsaftô ʾel-tôḵ bêteḵā

then you shall gather it within your house.

22:2b

וְהָיָה עִמְּךָ עַד דְּרֹשׁ אָחִ֫יךָ אֹתוֹ וַהֲשֵׁבֹתוֹ לוֹ׃

wəhāyâ ʿimməḵā ʿad dərōš ʾāḥîḵā ʾōtô wahăšēvōtô lô.

**And it shall be with you until your brother comes seeking it;
then you shall return it to him.**

22:3a

וְכֵן תַּעֲשֶׂה לַחֲמֹרוֹ

wəḵēn taʿăśe laḥămōrô

And so you shall do for his donkey,

22:3b

וְכֵן תַּעֲשֶׂה לְשִׂמְלָתוֹ

wəḵēn taʿăśe ləśimlātô

and so you shall do for his garment,

22:3c וְכֵן תַּעֲשֶׂה לְכָל־אֲבֵדַת אָחִיךָ

wək̄ēn taʿăśe lək̄ol-ʾăvēdat ʾāḥîk̄ā

and so you shall do for any lost property of your brother's

22:3d אֲשֶׁר־תֹּאבַד מִמֶּנּוּ וּמְצָאתָהּ

ʾăšer-tōʾvad mimmennû ûməṣāʾtāh

that is lost to him and that you find.

22:3e לֹא תוּכַל לְהִתְעַלֵּם׃

lōʾ tûk̄al ləhitʿallēm.

You shall not be capable of ignoring it.

22:4a לֹא־תִרְאֶה אֶת־חֲמוֹר אָחִיךָ אוֹ שׁוֹרוֹ נֹפְלִים בַּדֶּרֶךְ

lōʾ-tirʾe ʾet-ḥămôr ʾāḥîk̄ā ʾô šôrô nōfəlîm badderek̄

You shall not see your brother's donkey or ox fallen by the way

22:4b וְהִתְעַלַּמְתָּ מֵהֶם

wəhitʿallamtā mēhem

and ignore them.

22:4c הָקֵם תָּקִים עִמּוֹ׃

hāqēm tāqîm ʿimmô.

You shall surely help him lift it.

22:1a	לֹא־תִרְאֶה אֶת־שׁוֹר אָחִיךָ אוֹ אֶת־שֵׂיוֹ נִדָּחִים
	You shall not see your brother's ox or his sheep straying

לֹא־	no/not	---	particle
לֹא	*lō-*		
תִרְאֶה	you will see	QAL IMPF 2MS	verb
ראה	*tir·ʾe*		

אֶת־	*(direct object marker)*	---	particle
אֵת	*'et-*		
שׁוֹר	ox of	CST	noun
שׁוֹר	*šôr*		
אָחִיךָ	your brother	CST W/ 2MS SX	noun
אָח	*'ā·ḥî·ḵā*		
אוֹ	or	---	conj
אוֹ	*'ô*		
אֶת־	*(direct object marker)*	---	particle
אֵת	*'et-*		
שֵׂיוֹ	his sheep/goat	CST W/ 3MS SX	noun
שֶׂה	*śē·yô*		
נִדָּחִים	scattered/led astray	NIPH PTCP MP	verb
נדח	*nid·dā·ḥîm*		

Note the frequent use of אָחִיךָ ("your brother") in these laws.

22:1b	וְהִתְעַלַּמְתָּ מֵהֶם
	and ignore them.

וְהִתְעַלַּמְתָּ	and you ignore	HITH WEQATAL 2MS	verb
עלם	*wə·hit·'al·lam·tā*		
מֵהֶם	(from) them	---	personal
הֵם	*mē·hem*	W/ PREP מִן	pron

The Hithpael of עלם occurs only here and in v. 4b in Deuteronomy. One might translate this "hide from them," nicely anticipating those who passed by the man on the side of the road in Luke 10:25–37.

22:1c	הָשֵׁב תְּשִׁיבֵם לְאָחִיךָ:
	You shall surely return them to your brother.

הָשֵׁב	to return	HIPH INF ABS	verb
שׁוב	*hā·šēv*		
תְּשִׁיבֵם	you shall return them	HIPH IMPF 2MS W/ 3MP SX	verb
שׁוב	*tə·šî·vēm*		

<table>
<tr><td>לְאָחִֽיךָ׃
אָח</td><td>to your brother
lə·ʾā·ḥî·ḵā</td><td>CST
W/ PREP לְ + 2MS SX</td><td>noun</td></tr>
</table>

22:2a   וְאִם־לֹא קָרוֹב אָחִיךָ אֵלֶיךָ וְלֹא יְדַעְתֹּו

And if your brother is not near to you or you do not know him,

<table>
<tr><td>וְאִם־
אִם</td><td>and if
wə·ʾim-</td><td>---
W/ CONJ וְ</td><td>conj</td></tr>
<tr><td>לֹא
לֹא</td><td>not/no
lō·ʾ</td><td>---</td><td>particle</td></tr>
<tr><td>קָרוֹב
קָרוֹב</td><td>near
qā·rôv</td><td>MS PRED</td><td>adj</td></tr>
<tr><td>אָחִיךָ
אָח</td><td>your brother
ʾā·ḥî·ḵā</td><td>CST
W/ 2MS SX</td><td>noun</td></tr>
<tr><td>אֵלֶיךָ
אֶל</td><td>to you
ʾē·lɛ̂·ḵā</td><td>---
W/ 2MS SX</td><td>prep</td></tr>
<tr><td>וְלֹא
לֹא</td><td>and no/not
wə·lō·ʾ</td><td>---
W/ CONJ וְ</td><td>particle</td></tr>
<tr><td>יְדַעְתֹּו
ידע</td><td>you know him
yə·daʿ·tô</td><td>QAL PF 2MS
W/ 3MS SX</td><td>verb</td></tr>
</table>

The "brother/kindred" is expanded to include people we do not know.

22:2a   וַאֲסַפְתֹּו אֶל־תֹּוךְ בֵּיתֶךָ

then you shall gather it within your house.

<table>
<tr><td>וַאֲסַפְתֹּו
אסף</td><td>and you will gather it
wa·ʾă·saf·tô</td><td>QAL WEQATAL 2MS
W/ 3MS SX</td><td>verb</td></tr>
<tr><td>אֶל־
אֶל</td><td>to
ʾel-</td><td>---</td><td>prep</td></tr>
<tr><td>תֹּוךְ
תֹּוךְ</td><td>the middle/midst of
tôḵ</td><td>CST</td><td>noun</td></tr>
<tr><td>בֵּיתֶךָ
בֵּית</td><td>your house
bê·te·ḵā</td><td>CST
W/ 2MS SX</td><td>noun</td></tr>
</table>

Literally, "in the midst of," though the implication seems to be to keep it with your own animals.

<table>
<tr><td>22:2b</td><td colspan="3" align="center">וְהָיָ֣ה עִמְּךָ֗ עַ֣ד דְּרֹ֤שׁ אָחִ֙יךָ֙ אֹת֔וֹ וַהֲשֵׁבֹת֖וֹ לֽוֹ׃</td></tr>
</table>

And it shall be with you until your brother comes seeking it;
then you shall return it to him.

וְהָיָ֣ה היה	and it will be *wə·hā·yâ*	QAL WEQATAL 3MS	verb
עִמְּךָ֗ עִם	with you *'im·mə·kā*	--- W/ 2MS SX	prep
עַ֣ד עַד	until *'ad*	---	prep
דְּרֹ֤שׁ דרש	(he) seeks *də·rōš*	QAL INF CST	verb
אָחִ֙יךָ֙ אָח	your brother *'ā·ḥî·kā*	CST W/ 2MS SX	noun
אֹת֔וֹ אֵת	(direct object marker +) it *'ō·tô*	--- W/ 3MS SX	particle
וַהֲשֵׁבֹת֖וֹ שׁוּב	and you will return it *wa·hă·šē·vō·tô*	HIPH WEQATAL 2MS W/ 3MS SX	verb
לֽוֹ׃ לְ	to him *lô*	--- W/ 3MS SX	prep

<table>
<tr><td>22:3a</td><td align="center">וְכֵ֤ן תַּעֲשֶׂה֙ לַחֲמֹר֔וֹ</td></tr>
</table>

And so you shall do for his donkey,

וְכֵ֤ן כֵּן	and thus/so *wə·kēn*	--- W/ CONJ וְ	adv
תַּעֲשֶׂה֙ עשׂה	you will do *ta·'ă·śe*	QAL IMPF 2MS	verb
לַחֲמֹר֔וֹ חֲמוֹר	for his donkey *la·ḥă·mō·rô*	CST W/ PREP לְ + 3MS SX	noun

וְכֵן תַּעֲשֶׂה לְשִׂמְלָתוֹ

and so you shall do for his garment,

וְכֵן	and so/thus	---	adv
כֵּן	wə·*kēn*	W/ CONJ וְ	
תַּעֲשֶׂה	you will do	QAL IMPF 2MS	verb
עשׂה	ta·'ă·*śe*		
לְשִׂמְלָתוֹ	for his garment	CST	noun
שִׂמְלָה	lə·śim·lā·*tô*	W/ PREP לְ + 3MS SX	

וְכֵן תַּעֲשֶׂה לְכָל־אֲבֵדַת אָחִיךָ

and so you shall do for any lost property of your brother's

וְכֵן	and thus/so	---	adv
כֵּן	wə·*kēn*	W/ CONJ וְ	
תַּעֲשֶׂה	you will do	QAL IMPF 2MS	verb
עשׂה	ta·'ă·*śe*		
לְכָל־	for all	CST	noun
כֹּל	lə·*kol*-	W/ PREP לְ	
אֲבֵדַת	lost property of	CST	noun
אֲבֵדָה	'ă·vē·*dat*		
אָחִיךָ	your brother	CST	noun
אָח	'ā·*ḥî*·kā	W/ 2MS SX	

אֲשֶׁר־תֹּאבַד מִמֶּנּוּ וּמְצָאתָהּ

that is lost to him and that you find.

אֲשֶׁר־	that/which	---	relative pron
אֲשֶׁר	'ă·*šer*-		
תֹּאבַד	is lost/missing	QAL IMPF 3FS	verb
אבד	tō'·*vad*		
מִמֶּנּוּ	from him	---	prep
מִן	mim·*men*·nû	W/ 3MS SX	

| וּמְצָאתָהּ | and (that) you find it | QAL WEQATAL 2MS | verb |
| מצא | û·mə·ṣā'·**tāh** | W/ 3FS SX | |

22:3e לֹא תוּכַל לְהִתְעַלֵּם:

You shall not be capable of ignoring it.

לֹא	no/not	---	particle
לֹא	lō'		
תוּכַל	you will be able	QAL IMPF 2MS	verb
יכל	tû·**kal**		
לְהִתְעַלֵּם:	to ignore them	HITH INF CST	verb
עלם	lə·hit·'al·**lēm**	W/ PREP לְ	

The verb תוּכַל ("you shall [not] be capable") is difficult to render in English. One could say "must not ignore it" or "dare not remain indifferent" (Nelson 2002:252).

22:4a לֹא־תִרְאֶה אֶת־חֲמוֹר אָחִיךָ אוֹ שׁוֹרוֹ נֹפְלִים בַּדֶּרֶךְ

You shall not see your brother's donkey or ox fallen by the way

לֹא־	no/not	---	particle
לֹא	lō'-		
תִרְאֶה	you will see	QAL IMPF 2MS	verb
ראה	tir·'e		
אֶת־	(direct object marker)	---	particle
אֶת	'et-		
חֲמוֹר	donkey of	CST	noun
חֲמוֹר	ḥă·**môr**		
אָחִיךָ	your brother	CST	noun
אָח	'ā·ḥî·**kā**	W/ 2MS SX	
אוֹ	or	---	conj
אוֹ	'ô		
שׁוֹרוֹ	his sheep/goat	CST	noun
שׁוֹר	šô·**rô**	W/ 3MS SX	

נֹפְלִים נפל	fallen/fallen down *nō·fə·lîm*	QAL PTCP MP	verb
בַּדֶּרֶךְ דֶּרֶךְ	on the way/path *bad·de·reḵ*	ABS W/ PREP בְּ + DEF. ART.	noun

Notice the powerful connection to the man beaten and left on the side of road in the parable of the Good Samaritan (Luke 10:29–37).

<table>
<tr><td>22:4b</td><td colspan="3" align="center">וְהִתְעַלַּמְתָּ מֵהֶם</td></tr>
<tr><td></td><td colspan="3" align="center">and ignore them.</td></tr>
</table>

וְהִתְעַלַּמְתָּ עלם	and you hide yourself/ignore *wə·hit·ʿal·lam·tā*	HITH WEQATAL 2MS	verb
מֵהֶם מִן	(from) them *mē·hem*	--- W/ 3MP SX	prep

The only other Hithpael of this root in Deuteronomy is in v. 1 above.

<table>
<tr><td>22:4c</td><td colspan="3" align="center">הָקֵם תָּקִים עִמּוֹ:</td></tr>
<tr><td></td><td colspan="3" align="center">You shall surely help him lift it.</td></tr>
</table>

הָקֵם קום	to lift up *hā·qēm*	HIPH INF ABS	verb
תָּקִים קום	you will lift up *tā·qîm*	HIPH IMPF 2MS	verb
עִמּוֹ: עִם	with him *ʿim·mô*	--- W/ 3MS SX	prep

24:14a

לֹא־תַעֲשֹׁק שָׂכִיר עָנִי וְאֶבְיֹון

lō'-ta'ăšōq śākîr 'ānî wə'evyôn

Do not afflict a wage earner who is poor and needy

24:14b

מֵאַחֶיךָ אֹו מִגֵּרְךָ אֲשֶׁר בְּאַרְצְךָ בִּשְׁעָרֶיךָ׃

mē'aḥêkā 'ô miggērkā 'ăšer bə'arṣəkā biš'ārêkā.

**from among your brothers or from your sojourner
who is in your land, within your towns.**

24:15a

בְּיֹומֹו תִתֵּן שְׂכָרֹו וְלֹא־תָבֹוא עָלָיו הַשֶּׁמֶשׁ

bəyômô tittēn śəkārô wəlō'-tāvô' 'ālāyw haššemeš

Give his wages each day, and do not let the sun go down on him,

24:15b

כִּי עָנִי הוּא וְאֵלָיו הוּא נֹשֵׂא אֶת־נַפְשֹׁו

kî 'ānî hû' wə'ēlāyw hû' nōśē' 'et-nafšô

for he is needy and his life depends on it,

24:15c

וְלֹא־יִקְרָא עָלֶיךָ אֶל־יְהוָה וְהָיָה בְךָ חֵטְא׃

wəlō'-yiqrā' 'ālêkā 'el-YHWH wəhāyâ vəkā ḥēṭ'.

**so that he does not cry out against you to Yahweh
and it be sin for you.**

24:14a	לֹא־תַעֲשֹׁק שָׂכִיר עָנִי וְאֶבְיֹון

Do not afflict a wage earner who is poor and needy

לֹא־	no/not	---	particle
לֹא־	*lō'-*		
תַעֲשֹׁק	you will oppress	QAL IMPF 2MS	verb
עשק	*ta·'ă·šōq*		

שָׂכִיר	the worker/hired worker	MS SUBST	adj
שָׂכִיר *śā·**kîr***			
עָנִי	who is afflicted/poor	MS ATTR	adj
עָנִי *'ā·**nî***			
וְאֶבְיוֹן	and poor/needy	MS ATTR	adj
אֶבְיוֹן *wə·'ev·**yôn***		W/ CONJ וְ	

<table>
<tr><td>24:14b</td><td colspan="3" dir="rtl">מֵאַחֶיךָ אוֹ מִגֵּרְךָ אֲשֶׁר בְּאַרְצְךָ בִּשְׁעָרֶיךָ:</td></tr>
</table>

from among your brothers or from your sojourner
who is in your land, within your towns.

מֵאַחֶיךָ	from among your brothers	CST	noun
אָח *mē·'ā·**ḥê**·kā*		W/ PREP מִן + 2MS SX	
אוֹ	or	---	conj
אוֹ *'ô*			
מִגֵּרְךָ	from among your sojourner/ foreigner	CST	noun
גֵּר *mig·gêr·**kā***		W/ PREP מִן + 2MS SX	
אֲשֶׁר	that/which	---	relative pron
אֲשֶׁר *'ă·**šer***			
בְּאַרְצְךָ	in your land	CST	noun
אֶרֶץ *bə·'ar·ṣə·**kā***		W/ PREP בְּ + 2MS SX	
בִּשְׁעָרֶיךָ:	in your gates/towns	CST	noun
שַׁעַר *biš·'ā·**rê**·kā*		W/ PREP בְּ + 2MS SX	

Notice how the "brother" and "sojourner" are brought together with the same protections.

<table>
<tr><td>24:15a</td><td colspan="3" dir="rtl">בְּיוֹמוֹ תִתֵּן שְׂכָרוֹ וְלֹא־תָבוֹא עָלָיו הַשֶּׁמֶשׁ</td></tr>
</table>

Give his wages each day, and do not let the sun go down on him,

| בְּיוֹמוֹ | on that day | CST | noun |
| יוֹם *bə·yô·**mô*** | | W/ PREP בְּ + 3MS SX | |

תִּתֵּן	you will give	QAL IMPF 2MS	verb
נתן	*tit·tēn*		
שְׂכָרוֹ	his wages	CST	noun
שָׂכָר	*śə·kā·rô*	W/ 3MS SX	
וְלֹא־	and no/not	---	particle
לֹא	*wə·lō-*	W/ CONJ וְ	
תָבוֹא	(it) will go/goes	QAL IMPF 3FS	verb
בוא	*tā·vô*		
עָלָיו	upon him/it	---	prep
עַל	*ʿā·lāyw*	W/ 3MS SX	
הַשֶּׁמֶשׁ	the sun	ABS	noun
שֶׁמֶשׁ	*haš·še·meš*	W/ DEF. ART.	

24:15b כִּי עָנִי הוּא וְאֵלָיו הוּא נֹשֵׂא אֶת־נַפְשׁוֹ

for he is needy and his life depends on it,

כִּי	for/then/because	---	conj
כִּי	*kî*		
עָנִי	poor	MS PRED	adj
עָנִי	*ʿā·nî*		
הוּא	he (is)	---	personal pron
הוּא	*hû'*		
וְאֵלָיו	and on it	---	prep
אֶל	*wə·ʾē·lāyw*	W/ CONJ וְ + 3MS SX	
הוּא	he/it	---	personal pron
הוּא	*hû'*		
נֹשֵׂא	lifts/carries	QAL PTCP MS	verb
נשא	*nō·śē'*		
אֶת־	(direct object marker)	---	particle
אֶת	*ʾet-*		
נַפְשׁוֹ	his soul/life/self	CST	noun
נֶפֶשׁ	*naf·šô*	W/ 3MS SX	

וְאֵלָיו הוּא נֹשֵׂא אֶת־נַפְשׁוֹ is literally "he lifts up his soul to it." More colloquially, this may mean "he longs for it," as in Jer 22:27 and 44:14. See also Pss 25:1 and 143:8.

<table>
<tr><td>24:15c</td><td colspan="3" style="text-align:center">וְלֹא־יִקְרָא עָלֶיךָ אֶל־יְהוָה וְהָיָה בְךָ חֵטְא׃</td></tr>
<tr><td></td><td colspan="3" style="text-align:center">so that he does not cry out against you to Yahweh
and it be sin for you.</td></tr>
</table>

וְלֹא־ לֹא	and no/not *wə·lō'-*	--- W/ CONJ וְ	particle
יִקְרָא קרא	he will cry out *yiq·rā'*	QAL WAYY 3MS	verb
עָלֶיךָ עַל	against you *'ā·lê·ḵā*	--- W/ 2MS SX	prep
אֶל־ אֶל	to *'el-*	---	prep
יְהוָה יהוה	Yahweh *YHWH*	ABS	noun
וְהָיָה היה	and it be/will be *wə·hā·yâ*	QAL WEQATAL 3MS	verb
בְךָ בְּ	to you *və·ḵā*	--- W/ 2MS SX	prep
חֵטְא׃ חֵטְא	sin *ḥēṭ'*	ABS	noun

The same warning occurs in 15:9.

24:17a

לֹא תַטֶּה מִשְׁפַּט גֵּר יָתֹום

lō' taṭṭe mišpaṭ gēr yātôm

Do not pervert the justice due the sojourner or orphan.

24:17b

וְלֹא תַחֲבֹל בֶּגֶד אַלְמָנָה:

wəlō' taḥăvōl beged 'almānâ.

And do not seize a widow's garment.

24:18a

וְזָכַרְתָּ כִּי עֶבֶד הָיִיתָ בְּמִצְרַיִם

wəzākartā kî-'eved hāyîtā bəmiṣrayim

But remember that you were a slave in Egypt,

24:18b

וַיִּפְדְּךָ יְהוָה אֱלֹהֶיךָ מִשָּׁם

wayyifdəkā YHWH 'ĕlōhêkā miššām

and Yahweh your God redeemed you from there.

24:18c

עַל־כֵּן אָנֹכִי מְצַוְּךָ לַעֲשׂוֹת אֶת־הַדָּבָר הַזֶּה:

'al-kēn 'ānōkî məṣawwəkā la'ăśôt 'et-haddāvār hazze.

Therefore I command you to do this thing.

24:17a	לֹא תַטֶּה מִשְׁפַּט גֵּר יָתֹום		
	Do not pervert the justice due the sojourner or orphan.		

לֹא	no/not	---	particle
לֹא	*lō'*		
תַטֶּה	pervert	HIPH IMPF 2MS	verb
נטה	*taṭ·ṭe*		
מִשְׁפַּט	justice of/for	CST	noun
מִשְׁפָּט	*miš·paṭ*		

גֵּר	(the) sojourner/foreigner	ABS	noun
גֵּר	*gēr*		
יָתוֹם	(the) orphan/fatherless	ABS	noun
יָתוֹם	*yā·tôm*		

The "and/or" has to be inserted here.

<table>
<tr><td colspan="4" align="center">24:17b   וְלֹא תַחֲבֹל בֶּגֶד אַלְמָנָה׃</td></tr>
<tr><td colspan="4" align="center">And do not seize a widow's garment.</td></tr>
</table>

וְלֹא	and no/not	--- W/ CONJ וְ	particle
לֹא	*wə·lō'*		
תַחֲבֹל	seize/take as pledge	QAL IMPF 2MS	verb
חבל	*ta·ḥă·vōl*		
בֶּגֶד	garment/clothing of	CST	noun
בֶּגֶד	*be·ged*		
אַלְמָנָה׃	(the) widow	ABS	noun
אַלְמָנָה	*'al·mā·nâ*		

<table>
<tr><td colspan="4" align="center">24:18a   וְזָכַרְתָּ כִּי עֶבֶד הָיִיתָ בְּמִצְרָיִם</td></tr>
<tr><td colspan="4" align="center">But remember that you were a slave in Egypt,</td></tr>
</table>

וְזָכַרְתָּ	and/but you remember	QAL WEQATAL 2MS	verb
זכר	*wə·zā·kar·tā*		
כִּי	that	---	conj
כִּי	*kî-*		
עֶבֶד	slave	ABS	noun
עֶבֶד	*'e·ved*		
הָיִיתָ	you were	QAL PF 2MS	verb
היה	*hā·yî·tā*		
בְּמִצְרָיִם	in Egypt	ABS W/ PREP בְּ	noun
מִצְרָיִם	*bə·miṣ·ra·yim*		

וַיִּפְדְּךָ יְהוָה אֱלֹהֶיךָ מִשָּׁם

and Yahweh your God redeemed you from there.

וַיִּפְדְּךָ	and (he) redeemed you	QAL WAYY 3MS	verb
פדה	*way·yif·də·kā*	W/ 2MS SX	
יְהוָה	Yahweh	ABS	noun
יהוה	*YHWH*		
אֱלֹהֶיךָ	your God	CST	noun
אֱלֹהִים	*ʾĕ·lō·hê·kā*	W/ 2MS SX	
מִשָּׁם	from there	---	adv
שָׁם	*miš·šām*	W/ PREP מִן	

עַל־כֵּן אָנֹכִי מְצַוְּךָ לַעֲשׂוֹת אֶת־הַדָּבָר הַזֶּה:

Therefore I command you to do this thing.

עַל־כֵּן	thus/therefore		adv
עַל־כֵּן	*ʿal-kēn*		
אָנֹכִי	I	---	personal pron
אָנֹכִי	*ʾā·nō·kî*		
מְצַוְּךָ	command/am commanding you	PIEL PTCP MS	verb
צוה	*mə·ṣaw·wə·kā*	W/ 2MS SX	
לַעֲשׂוֹת	to do	QAL INF CST	verb
עשה	*la·ʿă·śôt*	W/ PREP לְ	
אֶת־	(direct object marker)	---	particle
אֵת	*ʾet-*		
הַדָּבָר	(the) thing	ABS	noun
דָּבָר	*had·dā·vār*	W/ DEF. ART.	
הַזֶּה:	this	---	demonstr
זֶה	*haz·ze*	W/ DEF. ART.	

24:19a כִּי תִקְצֹר קְצִירְךָ בְשָׂדֶךָ וְשָׁכַחְתָּ עֹמֶר בַּשָּׂדֶה

kî tiqṣōr qəṣîrḵā vəśādeḵā wəšāḵaḥtā ʿōmer baśśāde

**When you reap your harvest in your field
and forget a sheaf in the field,**

24:19b לֹא תָשׁוּב לְקַחְתּוֹ

lōʾ tāšûv ləqaḥtô

do not return to get it.

24:19c לַגֵּר לַיָּתוֹם וְלָאַלְמָנָה יִהְיֶה

laggēr layyātôm wəlāʾalmānâ yihye

It will be for the sojourner, the orphan, and the widow,

24:19d לְמַעַן יְבָרֶכְךָ יְהוָה אֱלֹהֶיךָ

ləmaʿan yəvārekəḵā YHWH ʾĕlōhêḵā

so that Yahweh your God may bless you

24:19e בְּכֹל מַעֲשֵׂה יָדֶיךָ׃

bəḵōl maʿăśē yādêḵā.

in all the work of your hands.

24:20a כִּי תַחְבֹּט זֵיתְךָ

kî taḥbōṭ zêtəḵā

When you beat your olive trees,

24:20b לֹא תְפַאֵר אַחֲרֶיךָ

lōʾ təfaʾēr ʾaḥărêḵā

you shall not search through the branches again.

24:20c לַגֵּר לַיָּתוֹם וְלָאַלְמָנָה יִהְיֶה׃

laggēr layyātôm wəlāʾalmānâ yihye.

It will be for the sojourner, the orphan, and the widow.

24:21a

כִּי תִבְצֹר כַּרְמְךָ
kî tivṣōr karməḵā

When you gather grapes from your vineyard,

24:21b

לֹא תְעוֹלֵל אַחֲרֶיךָ
lō' təʿôlēl 'aḥărêḵā

you shall not go over them again.

24:21c

לַגֵּר לַיָּתוֹם וְלָאַלְמָנָה יִהְיֶה:
laggēr layyātôm wəlā'almānâ yihye.

It will be for the sojourner, the orphan, and the widow.

24:22a

וְזָכַרְתָּ כִּי־עֶבֶד הָיִיתָ בְּאֶרֶץ מִצְרָיִם
wəzāḵartā kî-ʿeved hāyîtā bə'ereṣ bəmiṣrāyim

And you shall remember that you were a slave in the land of Egypt.

24:22b

עַל־כֵּן אָנֹכִי מְצַוְּךָ לַעֲשׂוֹת אֶת־הַדָּבָר הַזֶּה:
'al-kēn 'ānōḵî məṣawwəḵā laʿăśôt 'et-haddāvār hazze.

Therefore I command you to do this thing.

24:19a	כִּי תִקְצֹר קְצִירְךָ בְשָׂדֶךָ וְשָׁכַחְתָּ עֹמֶר בַּשָּׂדֶה

When you reap your harvest in your field
and forget a sheaf in the field,

	כִּי	for/then/because	---	conj
	כִּי	*kî*		
תִקְצֹר		you reap	QAL IMPF 2MS	verb
קצר		*tiq·ṣōr*		
קְצִירְךָ		your reaping	CST	noun
קָצִיר		*qə·ṣîr·ḵā*	W/ 2MS SX	
בְשָׂדֶךָ		in your field	CST	noun
שָׂדֶה		*və·śā·de·ḵā*	W/ PREP בְּ + 2MS SX	

וְשָׁכַחְתָּ	and you forget	QAL WEQATAL 2MS	verb
שכח	wə·šā·kaḥ·**tā**		
עֹמֶר	sheaf/omer	ABS	noun
עֹמֶר	**'ō**·mer		
בַּשָּׂדֶה	in the field	ABS	noun
שָׂדֶה	baś·śā·**de**	W/ PREP בְּ + DEF. ART.	

לֹא תָשׁוּב לְקַחְתּוֹ

do not return to get it.

לֹא	no/not	---	particle
לֹא	**lō'**		
תָשׁוּב	you return	QAL IMPF 2MS	verb
שׁוּב	tā·**šûv**		
לְקַחְתּוֹ	to get/collect it	QAL INF CST	verb
לקח	lə·qaḥ·**tô**	W/ PREP לְ + 3MS SX	

לַגֵּר לַיָּתוֹם וְלָאַלְמָנָה יִהְיֶה

It will be for the sojourner, the orphan, and the widow,

לַגֵּר	for the sojourner/foreigner	ABS	noun
גֵּר	lag·**gēr**	W/ PREP לְ + DEF. ART.	
לַיָּתוֹם	for the orphan/fatherless	ABS	noun
יָתוֹם	lay·yā·**tôm**	W/ PREP לְ + DEF. ART.	
וְלָאַלְמָנָה	and for the widow	ABS	noun
אַלְמָנָה	wə·lā·'al·mā·**nâ**	W/ CONJ וְ + PREP לְ + DEF. ART.	
יִהְיֶה	it will be	QAL IMPF 3MS	verb
היה	yih·**ye**		

לְמַעַן יְבָרֶכְךָ יְהוָה אֱלֹהֶיךָ

so that Yahweh your God may bless you

לְמַעַן לְמַעַן	so that/in order that lə·**ma**·ʿan	---	prep
יְבָרֶכְךָ ברך	(he) will bless you yə·vā·re·kə·**kā**	PIEL IMPF 3MS W/ 2MS SX	verb
יְהוָה יהוה	Yahweh YHWH	ABS	noun
אֱלֹהֶיךָ אֱלֹהִים	your God ʾĕ·lō·**hê**·kā	CST W/ 2MS SX	noun

בְּכֹל מַעֲשֵׂה יָדֶיךָ׃

in all the work of your hands.

בְּכֹל כֹּל	in every bə·**kōl**	CST W/ PREP בְּ	noun
מַעֲשֵׂה מַעֲשֶׂה	work of ma·ʿă·**śē**	CST	noun
יָדֶיךָ׃ יָד	your hands yā·**dê**·kā	CST W/ 2MS SX	noun

כִּי תַחְבֹּט זֵיתְךָ

When you beat your olive trees,

כִּי כִּי	for/when **kî**	---	conj
תַחְבֹּט חבט	you will beat taḥ·**bōṭ**	QAL IMPF 2MS	verb
זֵיתְךָ זַיִת	your olive/olive tree zê·tə·**kā**	CST W/ 2MS SX	noun

<table>
<tr><td>24:20b</td><td colspan="4" align="center">לֹא תְפָאֵר אַחֲרֶיךָ</td></tr>
</table>

you shall not search through the branches again.

לֹא	no/not	---	particle
לֹא	*lō'*		
תְפָאֵר	you will go over branches	PIEL IMPF 2MS	verb
פאר	*tə·fā·'ēr*		
אַחֲרֶיךָ	after you	---	prep
אַחֲרֵי	*'a·hă·rê·ḵā*	W/ 2MS SX	

<table>
<tr><td>24:20c</td><td colspan="4" align="center">לַגֵּר לַיָּתוֹם וְלָאַלְמָנָה יִהְיֶה:</td></tr>
</table>

It will be for the sojourner, the orphan, and the widow.

לַגֵּר	for the sojourner/foreigner	ABS W/ PREP לְ + DEF. ART.	noun
גֵּר	*lag·gēr*		
לַיָּתוֹם	for the orphan/fatherless	ABS W/ PREP לְ + DEF. ART.	noun
יָתוֹם	*lay·yā·tôm*		
וְלָאַלְמָנָה	and for the widow	ABS W/ CONJ וְ + PREP לְ + DEF. ART.	noun
אַלְמָנָה	*wə·lā·'al·mā·nâ*		
יִהְיֶה:	it will be	QAL IMPF 3MS	verb
היה	*yih·ye*		

<table>
<tr><td>24:21a</td><td colspan="4" align="center">כִּי תִבְצֹר כַּרְמְךָ</td></tr>
</table>

When you gather grapes from your vineyard,

כִּי	when	---	conj
כִּי	*kî*		
תִבְצֹר	you gather (grapes)	QAL IMPF 2MS	verb
בצר	*tiv·ṣōr*		
כַּרְמְךָ	(from) your vineyard	CST W/ 2MS SX	noun
כֶּרֶם	*kar·mə·ḵā*		

לֹא תְעוֹלֵל אַחֲרֶיךָ

you shall not go over them again.

לֹא	no/not	---	particle
לֹא	*lōʾ*		
תְעוֹלֵל	glean/gather	POEL IMPF 2MS	verb
עלל	*tə·ʿô·lēl*		
אַחֲרֶיךָ	after you	---	prep
אַחֲרֵי	*ʾa·ḥă·rê·kā*	W/ 2MS SX	

לַגֵּר לַיָּתוֹם וְלָאַלְמָנָה יִהְיֶה:

It will be for the sojourner, the orphan, and the widow.

לַגֵּר	for the sojourner/foreigner	ABS	noun
גֵּר	*lag·gēr*	W/ PREP לְ + DEF. ART.	
לַיָּתוֹם	for the orphan/fatherless	ABS	noun
יָתוֹם	*lay·yā·tôm*	W/ PREP לְ + DEF. ART.	
וְלָאַלְמָנָה	and for the widow	ABS	noun
אַלְמָנָה	*wə·lā·ʾal·mā·nâ*	W/ CONJ וְ + PREP לְ + DEF. ART.	
יִהְיֶה:	it will be	QAL IMPF 3MS	verb
היה	*yih·ye*		

וְזָכַרְתָּ כִּי־עֶבֶד הָיִיתָ בְּאֶרֶץ מִצְרָיִם

And you shall remember that you were a slave in the land of Egypt.

וְזָכַרְתָּ	you will remember	QAL WEQATAL 2MS	verb
זכר	*wə·zā·kar·tā*		
כִּי־	that	---	conj
כִּי	*kî-*		
עֶבֶד	slave	ABS	noun
עֶבֶד	*ʿe·ved*		
הָיִיתָ	you were	QAL PF 2MS	verb
היה	*hā·yi·tā*		

בָּאֶרֶץ	in (the) land of	CST	noun
אֶרֶץ	bə·'e·reṣ	W/ PREP בְּ	
מִצְרַיִם	Egypt	ABS	noun
מִצְרַיִם	bə·miṣ·rā·yim		

24:22b   עַל־כֵּן אָנֹכִי מְצַוְּךָ לַעֲשׂוֹת אֶת־הַדָּבָר הַזֶּה:

Therefore I command you to do this thing.

עַל־כֵּן	thus/therefore	---	adv
עַל־כֵּן	'al-kēn		
אָנֹכִי	I	---	personal pron
אָנֹכִי	'ā·nō·kî		
מְצַוְּךָ	command/am commanding you	PIEL PTCP MS	verb
צוה	mə·ṣaw·wə·kā	W/ 2MS SX	
לַעֲשׂוֹת	to do	QAL INF CST	verb
עשה	la·'ă·śôt	W/ PREP לְ	
אֶת־	(direct object marker)	---	particle
אֵת	'et-		
הַדָּבָר	(the) word/thing	ABS	noun
דָּבָר	had·dā·vār	W/ DEF. ART.	
הַזֶּה:	(the) this	---	demonstr pron
זֶה	haz·ze	W/ DEF. ART.	

25:13a

לֹא־יִהְיֶה לְךָ בְּכִיסְךָ
lōʾ-yihye ləḵā bəkîsḵā

Do not have in your bag

25:13b

אֶבֶן וָאֶבֶן גְּדוֹלָה וּקְטַנָּה:
ʾeven wāʾāven gədôlâ ûqṭannâ.

a stone and a stone, one large and one small.

25:14a

לֹא־יִהְיֶה לְךָ בְּבֵיתְךָ
lōʾ-yihye ləḵā bəvêtəḵā

Do not have in your house

25:14b

אֵיפָה וְאֵיפָה גְּדוֹלָה וּקְטַנָּה:
ʾêfâ wəʾêfâ gədôlâ ûqṭannâ.

a weight and a weight, one large and one small.

25:15a

אֶבֶן שְׁלֵמָה וָצֶדֶק יִהְיֶה־לָּךְ
ʾeven šəlēmâ wāṣedeq yihye-lāḵ

You shall have a whole and just stone;

25:15b

אֵיפָה שְׁלֵמָה וָצֶדֶק יִהְיֶה־לָּךְ
ʾêfâ šəlēmâ wāṣedeq yihye-lāḵ

you shall have a whole and just weight,

25:15c

לְמַעַן יַאֲרִיכוּ יָמֶיךָ עַל הָאֲדָמָה
ləmaʿan yaʾărîḵû yāmêḵā ʿal hāʾădāmâ

so that your days may be prolonged on the land

25:15d

אֲשֶׁר־יְהוָה אֱלֹהֶיךָ נֹתֵן לָךְ:
ʾăšer YHWH ʾĕlōhêḵā nōtēn lāḵ.

that Yahweh your God is giving you.

25:16a

כִּי תוֹעֲבַת יְהוָה אֱלֹהֶיךָ

kî tôʿăvat YHWH ʾĕlōhêkā

For they are an abomination to Yahweh your God—

25:16b

כָּל־עֹשֵׂה אֵלֶּה כֹּל עֹשֵׂה עָוֶל׃

kol-ʿōśē ʾēlle kōl ʿōśē ʿāwel.

all who do these things, everyone who acts unjustly.

25:13a	לֹא־יִהְיֶה לְךָ בְּכִיסְךָ

Do not have in your bag

לֹא־ לֹא	no/not *lō'-*	---	particle
יִהְיֶה היה	it will be *yih·ye*	QAL IMPF 3MS	verb
לְךָ ל	to/for you *lə·kā*	--- W/ 2MS SX	prep
בְּכִיסְךָ כִּיס	in your bag *bə·kîs·kā*	CST W/ PREP בְּ + 2MS SX	noun

25:13b	אֶבֶן וָאֶבֶן גְּדוֹלָה וּקְטַנָּה׃

a stone and a stone, one large and one small.

אֶבֶן אֶבֶן	stone *'e·ven*	ABS	noun
וָאֶבֶן אֶבֶן	and stone *wā·'ā·ven*	ABS W/ CONJ וְ	noun
גְּדוֹלָה גָּדוֹל	large *gə·dô·lâ*	FS SUBST	adj
וּקְטַנָּה׃ קָטָן	and small *ûq·ṭan·nâ*	FS SUBST W/ CONJ וְ	adj

Compare the similar figure of speech אֶבֶן וָאֶבֶן אֵיפָה וְאֵיפָה (literally: "a stone and a stone, an ephah [measure/weight] and an ephah," typically translated as "unequal weights, unequal measures") in Prov 20:10. In both passages, duplicity is captured in Hebrew's terse colloquial poetics, which is lost in the English translation, "unequal weights."

<table>
<tr><td>25:14a</td><td colspan="3" align="center">לֹא־יִהְיֶה לְךָ בְּבֵיתְךָ</td></tr>
<tr><td></td><td colspan="3" align="center">Do not have in your house</td></tr>
</table>

לֹא־	no/not	- - -	particle
לֹא	*lō-*		
יִהְיֶה	it will be	QAL IMPF 3MS	verb
היה	*yih·ye*		
לְךָ	to/for you	- - -	prep
ל	*lə·kā*	W/ 2MS SX	
בְּבֵיתְךָ	in your house	CST	noun
בַּיִת	*bə·vê·tə·kā*	W/ PREP בְּ + 2MS SX	

<table>
<tr><td>25:14b</td><td colspan="3" align="center">אֵיפָה וְאֵיפָה גְדוֹלָה וּקְטַנָּה:</td></tr>
<tr><td></td><td colspan="3" align="center">a weight and a weight, one large and one small.</td></tr>
</table>

אֵיפָה	measure	ABS	noun
אֵיפָה	*ê·fâ*		
וְאֵיפָה	and measure	ABS	noun
אֵיפָה	*wə·'ê·fâ*	W/ CONJ וְ	
גְדוֹלָה	great	FS PRED	adj
גָּדוֹל	*gə·dô·lâ*		
וּקְטַנָּה:	and small	FS PRED	adj
קָטָן	*ûq·ṭan·nâ*	W/ CONJ וְ	

The translation "two weights," while correct, ruins the poetic balance between the first and second half of the lines (cf. v. 13b).

אֶבֶן שְׁלֵמָה וָצֶדֶק יִהְיֶה־לָּךְ

You shall have a whole and just stone;

אֶבֶן	stone	ABS	noun
אֶבֶן	'e·ven		
שְׁלֵמָה	full/whole	FS ATTR	adj
שָׁלֵם	šə·lē·**mâ**		
וָצֶדֶק	and just/fair	ABS W/ CONJ וְ	noun
צֶדֶק	wā·ṣe·deq		
יִהְיֶה־	it will be	QAL IMPF 3MS	verb
היה	yih·ye-		
לָּךְ	to/for you	--- W/ 2MS SX	prep
ל	lāḵ		

אֵיפָה שְׁלֵמָה וָצֶדֶק יִהְיֶה־לָּךְ

you shall have a whole and just weight,

אֵיפָה	measure	ABS	noun
אֵיפָה	'ê·**fâ**		
שְׁלֵמָה	full/whole	FS ATTR	adj
שָׁלֵם	šə·lē·**mâ**		
וָצֶדֶק	and just/fair	ABS W/ CONJ וְ	noun
צֶדֶק	wā·ṣe·deq		
יִהְיֶה־	it will be	QAL IMPF 3MS	verb
היה	yih·ye-		
לָּךְ	to/for you	--- W/ 2MS SX	prep
ל	lāḵ		

לְמַעַן יַאֲרִיכוּ יָמֶיךָ עַל הָאֲדָמָה

so that your days may be prolonged on the land

| לְמַעַן | for/so that | --- | prep |
| לְמַעַן | lə·**ma**·'an | | |

יַאֲרִיכוּ	(they) will be long	HIPH IMPF 3MP	verb
אָרַךְ	*ya·ʾă·rî·ḵû*		
יָמֶיךָ	your days	CST W/ 2MS SX	noun
יוֹם	*yā·mê·ḵā*		
עַל	on/upon	---	prep
עַל	*ʿal*		
הָאֲדָמָה	the land	ABS W/ DEF. ART.	noun
אֲדָמָה	*hā·ʾă·dā·mâ*		

25:15d — אֲשֶׁר־יְהוָה אֱלֹהֶיךָ נֹתֵן לָךְ׃

that Yahweh your God is giving you.

אֲשֶׁר־	that/which	---	relative pron
אֲשֶׁר	*ʾă·šer*		
יְהוָה	Yahweh	ABS	noun
יהוה	*YHWH*		
אֱלֹהֶיךָ	your God	CST W/ 2MS SX	noun
אֱלֹהִים	*ʾĕ·lō·hê·ḵā*		
נֹתֵן	is giving	QAL PTCP MS	verb
נתן	*nō·tēn*		
לָךְ׃	to you	--- W/ 2MS SX	prep
ל	*lāḵ*		

25:16a — כִּי תוֹעֲבַת יְהוָה אֱלֹהֶיךָ

For they are an abomination to Yahweh your God—

כִּי	for/then/because	---	conj
כִּי	*kî*		
תוֹעֲבַת	abomination of/to	CST	noun
תוֹעֵבָה	*tô·ʿă·vat*		
יְהוָה	Yahweh	ABS	noun
יהוה	*YHWH*		
אֱלֹהֶיךָ	your God	CST W/ 2MS SX	noun
אֱלֹהִים	*ʾĕ·lō·hê·ḵā*		

כָּל־עֹשֵׂה אֵלֶּה כֹּל עֹשֵׂה עָוֶל:

all who do these things, everyone who acts unjustly.

כָּל־ כֹּל *kol-*	all/everyone	CST	noun
עֹשֵׂה עשׂה *'ō·śē*	those doers/ those who do	QAL PTCP MS	verb
אֵלֶּה אֵלֶּה *'ēl·le*	these	---	demonstr pron
כֹּל כֹּל *kōl*	all/everyone	CST	noun
עֹשֵׂה עשׂה *'ō·śē*	who does/acts	QAL PTCP MS	verb
עָוֶל: עָוֶל *'ā·wel*	unjustly/dishonestly	ABS	noun

 *Neighbor as Kin.* Blood is thicker than water, reports the ancient proverb. There is a subconscious hierarchy from family to friend and neighbor that becomes more complicated under scrutiny. "Better is a friend who is near than a brother far away" (Prov 27:10b). What matters, it seems, is having someone who can provide sympathy and aid in a time of need, and sometimes a friend does that better than a relative.

Like the proverb above, Deuteronomy's law stretches the natural limits of family and instructs us to gather with and care for those who do not have a family to help them.

In the textual analysis, we showed that the law in 22:1–4 uses אָח ("brother") five times, replacing "enemy" in a similar law in Exod 23:4–5 (compare the discussion of 15:1–11 above). It is naïve to view this change in Deuteronomy as a departure from caring for enemies (see Deut 22:2. Rather, the new emphasis highlights a communal bond at the heart of Deuteronomy's law.

To appreciate this, consider that the covenant code in Exod 20–23 never uses אָח, whereas Deuteronomy's parallel to those laws in chs. 12–26 uses אָח thirty-five times (six times in chs. 22 and 24). The אָח can be everyone from the king who is "from the midst of your brothers" (17:15) to the person who seeks a loan (23:19–20). In the laws outlined above, we also notice that the brother and foreign worker receive the same protections (24:14–15; cf. Prov 12:10; 29:7). Here are three possible ways to expand on preaching about kindred in Deuteronomy.

Who is at your door?—God's love may be infinite, but man's is not: concern and solicitude perennially directed over the horizon diminishes what is available for the neighbor who stands in front of you (Mitchell 2013:58 in Storey and Silber Storey 2021:167).

This observation does not mean that we ignore the extraordinary needs and inequalities that exist around our world. Instead, we are meant to beware of a kind of overemphasis on the abstract needs of a global "humanity" that so often blinds us to the actual humans at our doorstep.

Here it is worth noticing the clever arrangement of the beginning and end of the law in 22:1–4.

v. 1   You shall not see your brother's ox or his sheep straying
       and ignore them.

v. 4   You shall not see your brother's donkey or ox fallen by the
way and ignore them.

This repetition sets the reader in the landscape of open fields, noticing
stray animals and lost property. It thus counters the natural inclination
look aside from those things and people that interrupt and inconvenience
our day. Further, by carefully tying the animal and property to "kin," the
reader cannot help but sympathize with the human need. Similar to the
law of paying wages and opening our land and crops to the needy, we are
to extend brotherhood, or kinship, beyond its normal confines of those
known to us (Nelson 2004:267). Kin is redefined as someone near you
in need.

In our cause-driven age, it is tempting to speak publicly and emotively
about abstract policies and issues—poverty, racism, abortion, criminal
justice, and climate change—but then do nothing for the people and en-
vironment in our community. The wandering ox, the lost property, and
the people within "your towns" in these laws open our eyes—and lift them
from our smart phones—to see and care for concrete people and things
next to me.

SOLIDARITY—These laws offer a related lesson about creating bonds
with others around us.

Not unlike adult life, the adolescent experience is one of finding community. It includes both the painful rejections of the in-group and the
comforting welcome of a few friends—someone who knows your name
and embraces you. One can easily illustrate this in a sermon with the way
children make friends and, at other times, find themselves excluded and
alone.

The biblical law is aware of these universal social dynamics. What may
be the most famous law in Leviticus plays upon the tension between one
who is a "neighbor" (near to me) and "brother" related to me:

You shall not hate your brother in your heart, but you shall reason
in earnest with your neighbor, lest you incur sin because of him.
You shall not take vengeance or bear a grudge against the sons of
your people, but you shall love your neighbor as yourself: I am
Yahweh. (Lev 19:17–18)

The law recognizes our tendency to let arguments turn into grudges,
division, and hatred. The remedy is not found in a kind of *getting along
with one another* or making the most of a hard situation. Rather, we hear
a divine command that goes deeper with a call for a devoted and sincere
love for the "brother" who lives near me, the one I may very well not like

and whose views I may stridently oppose. It is, in a word, self-denying attachment to, and care for, our fellow human beings who happen to share our community.

The idea of kinship ties these laws together. As Mark Glanville observes, "The unity of all of Israel as a family includes within its scope the vulnerable, namely, the fatherless, the widow, the slave, and the *gēr*" (2018:122). He also argues, based upon the text in Deuteronomy, that גֵּר is a legal term not simply for a foreigner, but for "people who have been displaced from their former kinship group and patrimony and from the protection that kinship and land affords and who seek sustenance in a new context" (2018:267).

We live in solidarity with every human being, all of us made in God's image. The law allows us to imagine spheres of this solidarity—caring for all but being especially mindful to welcome those around us who do not belong.

THE FAMILY OF CHRISTIAN DISCIPLESHIP—Finally, a preacher may link these laws to the spiritual reality of the church as a family. Our identity as the church begins with the doctrine of God, for we are together a reflection of the God we worship. That is, we do not worship three gods but one God whose name is the Father, the Son, and the Holy Spirit and who is bound together in mutual love. The name thus signifies the deep ties of filial relationships among the divine persons and among Christians who belong to God.

It is this love that Jesus shares with those who follow him (John 16:27), a point he emphasizes in his response to the crowds who tell him that his "mother and brothers" had come to see him: "My mother and my brothers are those who hear the word of God and do it" (Luke 8:19–21).

To be joined into this divine family of the Trinity leads us to love one another with the love we have from God. Peter writes, "Having purified your souls by your obedience to the truth for a sincere brotherly love, love one another earnestly from a pure heart" (1 Pet 1:22). The kinship we witness in the law is expanded and deepened by the work of the Spirit, uniting us to the Son, and bringing us together before our Father in heaven.

 ***What about the Animals?*** The Pentateuch approaches animal life with fascination and respect. "When," the first humans would have had to ask, "is an animal a unique thing? A new species?" "And what should we call it?" This particular work of naming the animals in Gen 2 adorns each creature with dignity and identity (Bauckham 2010:130).

The laws for clean and unclean foods in Leviticus and Deuteronomy (14:1–21) have a similar function. The reasons for these strange restrictions will continue to be debated as to whether they are symbolic, health-related, or something else altogether (14:1–21). There is an obscurity in the prescriptions that may never be resolved, yet perhaps one of the deeper implications for these laws is that they forced the people to carefully identify and appreciate the great diversity and interdependence of God's creatures. This tied the animals back to God's generous work of creating them in the beginning: herbivores, carnivores, and omnivores; divided hooves and undivided hooves; animals of air, land, and water, along with the fine distinctions between two related species.

This fascination with animal life appears memorably in biblical poetry too. The long reflection on sentient life in Ps 104 proclaims, "All of them look to you to give them their food in their time" (v. 27). The astute meditations on the small-but-wise beasts in Prov 30:24–28 invite a deep admiration for animal life.

While the Bible does not issue a modern list of animal rights, it does train the human eye and conscience to recognize the beauty of the natural order and God's divine providential hand that feeds them, as well as the cooperative balance between humans and other animals (Deut 22:6; Prov 12:10; 27:23–27). Further, as David Baker has observed, while returning a lost animal appears in comparative ancient law, helping to lift a sick or injured animal only appears in biblical law (2009:39).

In this way, Deuteronomy goes beyond abstract "rights" to narrow us in on the particulars of this animal in this ditch beside me; this bird and her young along my path (22:6); this ox of mine that works for me (25:4). It is an ethics of particularity over abstractions (Davis 2008:82). Deuteronomy will not let us get away with declarations of the "common good" and "rights of all creatures," unless we care for those in our own neighborhoods, cities, and local forests.

Dignity of Work and the Worker. We live in a culture with a distorted and incoherent relation to our work. Even in Christian circles, "vocation" has become romanticized, aimed at fulfilling my heartfelt dreams of happiness in work. For others, work exists in a dichotomy, separate from faith and religion. We are also prone to elevate retirement as the real goal of work: save up enough to settle down, do nothing, and spend time focused on me and my treasures.

In the laws above, work has a deeply religious nature, giving dignity to the worker and bringing unity and cooperation to members of the community. Notice first that the law in 24:19–21 is far more than a charitable handout. The statute puts the poor and needy to work for their food, which gives them honor, while the owner is released from working for what is given away (24:19–22). This cooperative aspect of laws for the poor is again unparalleled in the ancient Near East (Baker 2009:237).

Second, the law transforms standard assumptions about ownership. The repeated phrase, "It will be for the sojourner, the orphan, and the widow" transfers my claim to the crops on my land to the needs of others. The law does not outrightly reject the right to private ownership; rather, it creatively complicates our claim to such rights. The whole of the land thus becomes a public resource for common use not by legal mandate but by an appeal to compassion and generosity.

Third, the elderly come to need the young and the young find a calling in caring for widows and physically dependent people.

Finally, the phrase "the work of your hand(s)," מַעֲשֵׂה יָדֶ(י)ךָ, occurs six times in Deuteronomy, more than in any other Old Testament book (2:7; 14:29; 16:15; 24:19; 28:12; 30:9). The promised land thus becomes a place where humans may take up again the original design to subdue the good gifts of the land for the benefit of all (Gen 1:26–28).

This all culminates in a theological view of work that is based on the memory of God's generosity and a future hope for a generous and sharing community. We may ask our congregations what visions and virtues inspire the work of our hands.

A WARNING AND A PROMISE

As Deuteronomy ends, it seals God's covenant with Israel in a book that will be a repository for memory, prayer, worship, and repentance within the community. The short list of blessings in ch. 28 are followed by its much longer list of curses, strongly insinuating that the prospects for failure will be high. Chapter 30 reinforces that premonition, giving eerily detailed instructions for what will happen if (when!) Israel finds itself away from home, under foreign rule, and suffering the predicted fate of having rejected Yahweh. As sure as failure seems to be, God's promise to remember his covenant and redeem his people is surer still.

LARGER LITERARY CONTEXT ▸ 27:1–30:20

1a
וְהָיָה֩ כִֽי־יָבֹ֨אוּ עָלֶ֜יךָ כָּל־הַדְּבָרִ֣ים הָאֵ֗לֶּה
wəhāyâ kî-yāvō'û 'ālêkā kol-haddəvārîm 'ēlle

And it shall be that when these things come upon you,

1b
הַבְּרָכָה֙ וְהַקְּלָלָ֔ה אֲשֶׁ֥ר נָתַ֖תִּי לְפָנֶ֑יךָ
habbərākâ wəhaqqəlālâ 'ăšer nātattî ləfānêkā

the blessing and the curse that I am setting before you,

1c
וַהֲשֵׁבֹתָ֙ אֶל־לְבָבֶ֔ךָ בְּכָל־הַגּוֹיִ֔ם
wahăšēvōtā 'el-ləvāvkā bəkol-haggôyim
אֲשֶׁ֧ר הִדִּיחֲךָ֛ יְהוָ֥ה אֱלֹהֶ֖יךָ שָֽׁמָּה׃
'ăšer hiddîḥăkā YHWH 'ĕlōhêkā šāmmâ.

**and you take them to heart among all the nations
where Yahweh your God has scattered you,**

2a
וְשַׁבְתָּ֞ עַד־יְהוָ֣ה אֱלֹהֶ֗יךָ
wəšavtā 'ad-YHWH 'ĕlōhêkā

and you return to Yahweh your God,

2b
וְשָׁמַעְתָּ֣ בְקֹל֗וֹ כְּכֹ֤ל אֲשֶׁר־אָנֹכִ֛י מְצַוְּךָ֖ הַיּ֑וֹם
wəšāma'tā bəqōlô kəkōl 'ăšer-'ānōkî məṣawwəkā hayyôm

**and you obey his voice, according to all that
I am commanding you today,**

2c
אַתָּ֣ה וּבָנֶ֔יךָ בְּכָל־לְבָבְךָ֖ וּבְכָל־נַפְשֶֽׁךָ׃
'attâ ûvānêkā bəkol-ləvāvkā ûvəkol-nafšekā.

you and your children, with all your heart and with your whole life,

3a
וְשָׁ֨ב יְהוָ֧ה אֱלֹהֶ֛יךָ אֶת־שְׁבוּתְךָ֖ וְרִחֲמֶ֑ךָ
wəšāv YHWH 'ĕlōhêkā 'et-šəvûtəkā wərihămekā

**then Yahweh your God will restore your fortunes
and have compassion on you,**

3b   וְשָׁב וְקִבֶּצְךָ מִכָּל־הָעַמִּים אֲשֶׁר הֱפִיצְךָ יְהוָה אֱלֹהֶיךָ שָׁמָּה:

wəšāv wəqibbeṣkā mikkol-hā'ammîm 'ăšer hĕfîṣkā YHWH 'ĕlōhêkā šāmmâ.

and bring you back and gather you from among all the nations where Yahweh your God scattered you.

4a   אִם־יִהְיֶה נִדַּחֲךָ בִּקְצֵה הַשָּׁמָיִם

'im-yihye niddaḥăkā biqṣē haššāmāyim

Even if your banished one is at the ends of the heavens,

4b   מִשָּׁם יְקַבֶּצְךָ יְהוָה אֱלֹהֶיךָ וּמִשָּׁם יִקָּחֶךָ:

miššām yəqabbeṣkā YHWH 'ĕlōhêkā ûmiššām yiqqāḥekā.

from there Yahweh your God will gather you, and from there he will take you.

5a   וֶהֱבִיאֲךָ יְהוָה אֱלֹהֶיךָ אֶל־הָאָרֶץ אֲשֶׁר־יָרְשׁוּ אֲבֹתֶיךָ

wehĕvî'ăkā YHWH 'ĕlōhêkā 'el-hā'āreṣ 'ăšer yārəšû 'ăvōtêkā

And Yahweh your God will bring you to the land that your ancestors possessed,

5b   וִירִשְׁתָּהּ וְהֵיטִבְךָ וְהִרְבְּךָ מֵאֲבֹתֶיךָ:

wîrištāh wəhêṭivkā wəhirbəkā mē'ăvōtêkā.

and you will possess it, and he will prosper you and multiply you more than your ancestors.

6a   וּמָל יְהוָה אֱלֹהֶיךָ אֶת־לְבָבְךָ וְאֶת־לְבַב זַרְעֶךָ

ûmāl YHWH 'ĕlōhêkā bəkol-ləvāvkā wə'et-ləvav zar'ekā

And Yahweh your God will circumcise your heart and the heart of your offspring,

6b   לְאַהֲבָה אֶת־יְהוָה אֱלֹהֶיךָ

lə'ahăvâ 'et-YHWH 'ĕlōhêkā

so that you might love Yahweh your God

6c   בְּכָל־לְבָבְךָ וּבְכָל־נַפְשְׁךָ לְמַעַן חַיֶּיךָ:

bəkol-ləvāvkā ûvəkol-nafšəkā ləma'an ḥāyyêkā.

with all your heart and with all your life force so that you might live.

7a

וְנָתַן֙ יְהוָ֣ה אֱלֹהֶ֔יךָ אֵ֥ת כָּל־הָאָל֖וֹת הָאֵ֑לֶּה

wᵊnātan YHWH 'ĕlōhêḵā 'ēt kol-hā'ālôt hā'ēlle

And Yahweh your God will place all these curses

7b

עַל־אֹיְבֶ֥יךָ וְעַל־שֹׂנְאֶ֖יךָ אֲשֶׁ֥ר רְדָפֽוּךָ׃

'al-'ōyᵊvêḵā wᵊ'al-śōn'êḵā 'ăšer rᵊdāfûḵā.

upon your enemies and upon those who hated you and pursued you.

8a

וְאַתָּ֣ה תָשׁ֔וּב וְשָׁמַעְתָּ֖ בְּק֣וֹל יְהוָ֑ה

wᵊ'attâ tāšûv wᵊšāma'tā bᵊqôl YHWH

But you, you shall turn and obey the voice of Yahweh

8b

וְעָשִׂ֙יתָ֙ אֶת־כָּל־מִצְוֺתָ֔יו אֲשֶׁ֛ר אָנֹכִ֥י מְצַוְּךָ֖ הַיּֽוֹם׃

wᵊ'āśîtā 'et-kol-miṣwōtāyw 'ăšer 'ānōḵî mᵊṣawwᵊḵā hayyôm.

and do all the commandments that I am commanding you today.

9a

וְהוֹתִֽירְךָ֩ יְהוָ֨ה אֱלֹהֶ֜יךָ בְּכֹ֣ל ׀ מַעֲשֵׂ֣ה יָדֶ֗ךָ

wᵊhôtîrḵā YHWH 'ĕlōhêḵā bᵊkol ma'ăśē yādeḵā

**And Yahweh your God will make you prosper
in all the work of your hand,**

9b

בִּפְרִ֧י בִטְנְךָ֛

bifrî viṭnᵊḵā

in the fruit of your womb

9c

וּבִפְרִ֥י בְהֶמְתְּךָ֖

ûvifrî vᵊhemtᵊḵā

and in the fruit of your cattle

9d

וּבִפְרִ֥י אַדְמָתְךָ֖ לְטוֹבָ֑ה

ûvifrî 'admātᵊḵā lᵊṭôvâ

and in the fruit of your ground, for good.

9e

כִּ֣י ׀ יָשׁ֣וּב יְהוָ֗ה לָשׂ֤וּשׂ עָלֶ֙יךָ֙ לְט֔וֹב

kî yāśûv YHWH lāśûś 'ālêḵā lᵊṭôv

For Yahweh will turn to delight in you for good,

9f   כַּאֲשֶׁר־שָׂשׂ עַל־אֲבֹתֶיךָ׃

ka'ăšer-śāś 'al-'ăvōtêkā.

just as he delighted in your ancestors,

10a   כִּי תִשְׁמַע בְּקוֹל יְהוָה אֱלֹהֶיךָ

kî tišma' bəqôl YHWH 'ĕlōhêkā

if you obey the voice of Yahweh your God

10b   לִשְׁמֹר מִצְוֹתָיו וְחֻקֹּתָיו

lišmōr miṣwōtāyw wəḥuqqōtāyw

by keeping his commandments and his statutes—

10c   הַכְּתוּבָה בְּסֵפֶר הַתּוֹרָה הַזֶּה

hakkətûvâ bəsēfer hattôrâ hazze

all that is written in this book of the torah—

10d   כִּי תָשׁוּב אֶל־יְהוָה אֱלֹהֶיךָ בְּכָל־לְבָבְךָ וּבְכָל־נַפְשֶׁךָ׃

kî tāšûv 'el-YHWH 'ĕlōhêkā bəkol-ləvāvkā ûvəkol-nafšekā.

**if you return to Yahweh your God with all your heart
and with all your life force.**

1a   וְהָיָה כִי־יָבֹאוּ עָלֶיךָ כָּל־הַדְּבָרִים הָאֵלֶּה

And it shall be that when these things come upon you,

וְהָיָה היה	and it will be *wə·hā·yâ*	QAL WEQATAL 3MS	verb
כִּי־ כִּי	that/when *kî-*	---	conj
יָבֹאוּ בוא	they come *yā·vō·'û*	QAL IMPF 3MP	verb
עָלֶיךָ עַל	upon you *'ā·lê·kā*	--- W/ 2MS SX	prep

כָּל־	all	CST	noun
כֹּל	kol-		
הַדְּבָרִים	(the) things	ABS	noun
דָּבָר	had·də·vā·rîm	W/ DEF. ART.	
הָאֵלֶּה	(the) these	---	demonstr
אֵלֶּה	'ēl·le	W/ DEF. ART.	

This opening recalls the blessings and curses in the covenant provisions and ceremonies in chs. 27–29.

1b הַבְּרָכָה וְהַקְּלָלָה אֲשֶׁר נָתַתִּי לְפָנֶיךָ

the blessing and the curse that I am setting before you,

הַבְּרָכָה	the blessing	ABS	noun
בְּרָכָה	hab·bə·rā·kâ	W/ DEF. ART.	
וְהַקְּלָלָה	and the curse	ABS	noun
קְלָלָה	wə·haq·qə·lā·lâ	W/ CONJ וְ + DEF. ART.	
אֲשֶׁר	that/which	---	relative
אֲשֶׁר	'ă·šer		pron
נָתַתִּי	I give/set	QAL PF 1CS	verb
נתן	nā·tat·tî		
לְפָנֶיךָ	before you	---	prep
לְפָנֵי	lə·fā·nê·kā	W/ 2MS SX	

1c וַהֲשֵׁבֹתָ אֶל־לְבָבֶךָ בְּכָל־הַגּוֹיִם אֲשֶׁר הִדִּיחֲךָ יְהוָה אֱלֹהֶיךָ שָׁמָּה׃

and you take them to heart among all the nations where Yahweh your God has scattered you,

וַהֲשֵׁבֹתָ	and you return/bring	HIPH WEQATAL 2MS	verb
שׁוב	wa·hă·šē·vō·tā		
אֶל־	to	---	prep
אֶל	'el-		
לְבָבֶךָ	your heart	CST	noun
לְבָב	lə·vāv·kā	W/ 2MS SX	

Hebrew	Gloss	Parsing	POS
בְּכָל־ כֹּל *bə·ḵol-*	with/among all of	CST W/ PREP בְּ	noun
הַגּוֹיִם גּוֹי *hag·gô·yim*	the nations	ABS W/ DEF. ART.	noun
אֲשֶׁר אֲשֶׁר *ʾă·šer*	who/which	- - -	relative pron
הִדִּיחֲךָ נדח *hid·dî·ḥă·ḵā*	(he) scattered/spread you	HIPH PF 3MS W/ 2MS SX	verb
יְהֹוָה יהוה *YHWH*	Yahweh	ABS	noun
אֱלֹהֶיךָ אֱלֹהִים *ʾĕ·lō·hê·ḵā*	your God	CST W/ 2MS SX	noun
שָׁמָּה׃ שָׁם *šām·mâ*	(to) there	- - - W/ LOCATIVE ה	adv

<table>
<tr><td>2a</td><td colspan="3">וְשַׁבְתָּ עַד־יְהֹוָה אֱלֹהֶיךָ</td></tr>
<tr><td colspan="4">and you return to Yahweh your God,</td></tr>
</table>

Hebrew	Gloss	Parsing	POS
וְשַׁבְתָּ שׁוּב *wə·šav·tā*	and you turn/return	QAL WEQATAL 2MS	verb
עַד־ עַד *ʿad-*	to	- - -	prep
יְהֹוָה יהוה *YHWH*	Yahweh	ABS	noun
אֱלֹהֶיךָ אֱלֹהִים *ʾĕ·lō·hê·ḵā*	your God	CST W/ 2MS SX	noun

<table>
<tr><td>2b</td><td colspan="3">וְשָׁמַעְתָּ בְקֹלוֹ כְּכֹל אֲשֶׁר־אָנֹכִי מְצַוְּךָ הַיּוֹם</td></tr>
<tr><td colspan="4">and you obey his voice, according to all that
I am commanding you today,</td></tr>
</table>

Hebrew	Gloss	Parsing	POS
וְשָׁמַעְתָּ שׁמע *wə·šā·ma·tā*	and you listen/obey	QAL WEQATAL 2MS	verb

בְּקֹלוֹ קוֹל *bə·qō·lô*	to his voice	CST W/ PREP בְּ + 3MS SX	noun
כְּכֹל כֹּל *kə·ḵōl*	with/according to all	ABS W/ PREP כְּ	noun
אֲשֶׁר־ אֲשֶׁר *'ă·šer-*	that/which	---	relative pron
אָנֹכִי אָנֹכִי *'ā·nō·ḵî*	I	---	personal pron
מְצַוְּךָ צוה *mə·ṣaw·wə·ḵā*	(am) commanding you	PIEL PTCP MS W/ 2MS SX	verb
הַיּוֹם יוֹם *hay·yôm*	today	ABS W/ DEF. ART.	noun

As in the rest of Deuteronomy, שמע can mean "listen" or "obey."

<table><tr><td>2c</td><td style="text-align:center">אַתָּה וּבָנֶיךָ בְּכָל־לְבָבְךָ וּבְכָל־נַפְשֶׁךָ:</td></tr></table>

you and your children, with all your heart and with your whole life,

אַתָּה אַתָּה *'at·tâ*	you	---	personal pron
וּבָנֶיךָ בֵּן *û·vā·nê·ḵā*	and your children	CST W/ CONJ וּ + 2MS SX	noun
בְּכָל־ כֹּל *bə·ḵol-*	with all	CST W/ PREP בְּ	noun
לְבָבְךָ לֵבָב *lə·vāv·ḵā*	your heart	CST W/ 2MS SX	noun
וּבְכָל־ כֹּל *û·və·ḵol-*	and with all	CST W/ CONJ וּ + 2MS SX	noun
נַפְשֶׁךָ: נֶפֶשׁ *naf·še·ḵā*	your life/soul	CST W/ 2MS SX	noun

The Hebrew נֶפֶשׁ is a particularly difficult word to translate consistently since it is used to designate everything from the throat, to desire or appetite, to a person or life, and finally to the more abstract soul or life force (see the comments on 6:5 above).

The LXX omits "you and your children."

> then Yahweh your God will restore your fortunes
> and have compassion on you,

וְשָׁב שׁוב	and (he) will restore/return *wə·šāv*	QAL WEQATAL 3MS	verb
יְהוָה יהוה	Yahweh *YHWH*	ABS	noun
אֱלֹהֶיךָ אֱלֹהִים	your God *ʾĕ·lō·hê·ḵā*	CST W/ 2MS SX	noun
אֶת־ אֵת	(direct object marker) *ʾet-*	- - -	particle
שְׁבוּתְךָ שְׁבוּת	your fortunes *šə·vû·tə·ḵā*	CST W/ 2MS SX	noun
וְרִחֲמֶךָ רחם	and he will have compassion on you *wə·ri·ḥă·me·ḵā*	PI WEQATAL 3MS W/ 2MS SX	verb

The idiomatic pairing of the verb שׁוב with the noun שְׁבוּת is relatively common (25 times in the Old Testament; e.g., Jer 30:3), and its meaning has been a source of some debate. If שְׁבוּת comes from שׁבה ("to capture" or "lead away captive"), the natural translation would be "restore you from captivity" (NASB) or "turn thy captivity" (KJV). Taking שְׁבוּת as a nominal form of שׁוב, (thus, "return your returning"), meanwhile, leads to the translation "restore your fortunes" (NRSV, ESV).

> and bring you back and gather you from among all the nations
> where Yahweh your God scattered you.

וְשָׁב שׁוב	and he will restore/return/again *wə·šāv*	QAL WEQATAL 3MS	verb
וְקִבֶּצְךָ קבץ	and he will gather you *wə·qib·beṣ·ḵā*	PIEL WEQATAL 3MS W/ 2MS SX	verb
מִכָּל־ כֹּל	from all *mik·kol-*	CST W/ PREP מִן	noun
הָעַמִּים עַם	the peoples *hā·ʿam·mîm*	ABS W/ DEF. ART.	noun

אֲשֶׁר אֲשֶׁר	that/which *ʾă·šer*	---	relative pron
הֱפִיצְךָ פוץ	(he) scattered/spread you *hĕ·p̄îṣ·ḵā*	HIPH PF 3MS W/ 2MS SX	verb
יְהֹוָה יהוה	Yahweh *YHWH*	ABS	noun
אֱלֹהֶיךָ אֱלֹהִים	your God *ʾĕ·lō·hê·ḵā*	CST W/ 2MS SX	noun
שָׁמָּה: שָׁם	(to) there *šām·mâ*	--- W/ LOCATIVE ה	adv

וְשָׁב וְקִבֶּצְךָ could be translated "and will return and gather" or alterna-tively, "will again gather," if שָׁב is taken as an adverb (see *IBHS* 39.3.1b).

4a	אִם־יִהְיֶה נִדַּחֲךָ בִּקְצֵה הַשָּׁמָיִם

Even if your banished one is at the end of the heavens,

אִם־ אִם	if *ʾim-*	---	conj
יִהְיֶה היה	(it) is/will be *yih·ye*	QAL IMPF 3MS	verb
נִדַּחֲךָ נדח	your outcast one *nid·da·ḥă·ḵā*	NIPH PTCP MS W/ 2MS SX	verb
בִּקְצֵה קָצֶה	at the end/extremity of *biq·ṣē*	CST W/ PREP בְּ	noun
הַשָּׁמָיִם שָׁמַיִם	of the heavens *haš·šā·mā·yim*	ABS W/ DEF. ART.	noun

This singular Niphal participle נִדַּחֲךָ here is usually translated as a plural, "your banished ones."

מִשָּׁם יְקַבֶּצְךָ֙ יְהוָ֣ה אֱלֹהֶ֔יךָ וּמִשָּׁ֖ם יִקָּחֶֽךָ׃

from there Yahweh your God will gather you,
and from there he will take you.

מִשָּׁם	from there	---	adv
שָׁם	*miš·šām*	W/ PREP מִן	
יְקַבֶּצְךָ֙	(he) will gather you	PIEL IMPF 3MS	verb
קבץ	*yə·qab·beṣ·kā*	W/ 2MS SX	
יְהוָ֣ה	Yahweh	ABS	noun
יהוה	*YHWH*		
אֱלֹהֶ֔יךָ	your God	CST	noun
אֱלֹהִים	*ʾĕ·lō·hê·kā*	W/ 2MS SX	
וּמִשָּׁ֖ם	and from there	---	adv
שָׁם	*û·miš·šām*	W/ CONJ וְ + PREP מִן	
יִקָּחֶֽךָ׃	he will take/receive you	QAL IMPF 3MS	verb
לקח	*yiq·qā·ḥe·kā*	W/ 2MS SX	

וֶהֱבִֽיאֲךָ֞ יְהוָ֣ה אֱלֹהֶ֗יךָ אֶל־הָאָ֛רֶץ אֲשֶׁר־יָרְשׁ֥וּ אֲבֹתֶ֖יךָ

And Yahweh your God will bring you to the land
that your ancestors possessed,

וֶהֱבִֽיאֲךָ֞	and (he) will bring you	HIPH WEQATAL 3MS	verb
בוא	*we·hĕ·vî·ʾă·kā*	W/ 2MS SX	
יְהוָ֣ה	Yahweh	ABS	noun
יהוה	*YHWH*		
אֱלֹהֶ֗יךָ	your God	CST	noun
אֱלֹהִים	*ʾĕ·lō·hê·kā*	W/ 2MS SX	
אֶל־	to	---	prep
אֶל	*ʾel-*		
הָאָ֛רֶץ	the land	ABS	noun
אֶרֶץ	*hā·ʾā·reṣ*	W/ DEF. ART.	
אֲשֶׁר־	that/which	---	relative pron
אֲשֶׁר	*ʾă·šer*		
יָרְשׁ֥וּ	(they) possessed	QAL PF 3CP	verb
ירש	*yā·rə·šû*		

<table>
<tr><td>אֲבֹתֶיךָ
'ă·vō·**tê**·ḵā</td><td>your ancestors
אָב</td><td>CST
W/ 2MS SX</td><td>noun</td></tr>
</table>

<table>
<tr><td>5b</td><td colspan="3" align="center">וִירִשְׁתָּהּ וְהֵיטִבְךָ וְהִרְבְּךָ מֵאֲבֹתֶיךָ׃</td></tr>
<tr><td></td><td colspan="3" align="center">and you will possess it, and he will prosper you
and multiply you more than your ancestors.</td></tr>
</table>

וִירִשְׁתָּהּ יָרַשׁ *wî·riš·tāh*	and you will possess it	QAL WEQATAL 2MS W/ 3FS SX	verb
וְהֵיטִבְךָ יָטַב *wə·hê·ṭiv·ḵā*	and he will make you prosperous/successful	HIPH WEQATAL 3MS W/ 2MS SX	verb
וְהִרְבְּךָ רָבָה *wə·hir·bə·ḵā*	and make you increase	HIPH WEQATAL 3MS W/ 2MS SX	verb
מֵאֲבֹתֶיךָ׃ אָב *mē·'ă·vō·tê·ḵā*	more than your fathers	CST W/ PREP מִן + 2MS SX	noun

<table>
<tr><td>6a</td><td colspan="3" align="center">וּמָל יְהוָה אֱלֹהֶיךָ אֶת־לְבָבְךָ וְאֶת־לְבַב זַרְעֶךָ</td></tr>
<tr><td></td><td colspan="3" align="center">And Yahweh your God will circumcise your heart
and the heart of your offspring,</td></tr>
</table>

וּמָל מוּל *û·māl*	and (he) will circumcise	QAL WEQATAL 3MS	verb
יְהוָה יהוה *YHWH*	Yahweh	ABS	noun
אֱלֹהֶיךָ אֱלֹהִים *'ĕ·lō·hê·ḵā*	your God	CST W/ 2MS SX	noun
אֶת־ אֵת *'et-*	(direct object marker)	---	particle
לְבָבְךָ לֵבָב *lə·vāv·ḵā*	your heart	CST W/ 2MS SX	noun
וְאֶת־ אֵת *wə·'et-*	and (+ direct object marker)	--- W/ CONJ וְ	particle
לְבַב לֵבָב *lə·vav*	(the) heart of	CST	noun

זַרְעֶ֫ךָ	your seed/offspring	CST W/ 2MS SX	noun
זֶרַע *zar·'e·ḵā*			

so that you might love Yahweh your God

לְאַהֲבָ֤ה	to love	QAL INF CST W/ PREP לְ	verb
אהב *lə·'a·hă·vâ*			
אֶת־	(direct object marker)	---	particle
אֵת *'et-*			
יְהוָ֣ה	Yahweh	ABS	noun
יהוה *YHWH*			
אֱלֹהֶ֔יךָ	your God	CST W/ 2MS SX	noun
אֱלֹהִים *'ĕ·lō·hê·ḵā*			

with all your heart and with all your life force so that you might live.

בְּכָל־	with all	CST W/ PREP בְּ	noun
כֹּל *bə·ḵol-*			
לְבָבְךָ֥	your heart	CST W/ 2MS SX	noun
לֵבָב *lə·vāv·ḵā*			
וּבְכָל־	and with all	CST W/ CONJ וְ + PREP בְּ	noun
כֹּל *û·və·ḵol-*			
נַפְשְׁךָ֖	your soul/life	CST W/ 2MS SX	noun
נֶפֶשׁ *naf·šə·ḵā*			
לְמַ֥עַן	so that/in order that	---	prep
לְמַעַן *lə·ma·'an*			
חַיֶּֽיךָ׃	you will/may live	CST W/ 2MS SX	noun
חַיִּים *ḥāy·yê·ḵā*			

וְנָתַן יְהוָה אֱלֹהֶיךָ אֵת כָּל־הָאָלוֹת הָאֵלֶּה

And Yahweh your God will place all these curses

וְנָתַן נתן	and (he) will give/place *wə·nā·**tan***	QAL WEQATAL 3MS	verb
יְהוָה יהוה	Yahweh *YHWH*	ABS	noun
אֱלֹהֶיךָ אֱלֹהִים	your God *ĕ·lō·**hê**·kā*	CST W/ 2MS SX	noun
אֵת אֵת	(direct object marker) *'ēt*	---	particle
כָּל־ כֹּל	all *kol-*	CST	noun
הָאָלוֹת אָלָה	(the) curses/oaths *hā·'ā·**lôt***	ABS W/ DEF. ART.	noun
הָאֵלֶּה אֵלֶּה	(the) these *hā·'ēl·le*	---	demonstr W/ DEF. ART.

עַל־אֹיְבֶיךָ וְעַל־שֹׂנְאֶיךָ אֲשֶׁר רְדָפוּךָ׃

upon your enemies and upon those who hated you and pursued you.

עַל־ עַל	on/upon *'al-*	---	prep
אֹיְבֶיךָ איב	your enemies *'ō·yə·**vê**·kā*	QAL PTCP MP W/ 2MS SX	verb
וְעַל־ עַל	and on/upon *wə·'al-*	W/ CONJ וְ	prep
שֹׂנְאֶיךָ שׂנא	those hating you *śōn·'ê·kā*	QAL PTCP MP W/ 2MS SX	verb
אֲשֶׁר אֲשֶׁר	that/which *'ă·šer*	---	relative pron
רְדָפוּךָ׃ רדף	they chased/persecuted you *rə·dā·**fû**·kā*	QAL PF 3CP W/ 2MS SX	verb

וְאַתָּה תָשׁוּב וְשָׁמַעְתָּ בְּקוֹל יְהוָה

But you, you shall turn and obey the voice of Yahweh

וְאַתָּה אַתָּה	and/but you *wə·'at·tâ*	--- W/ CONJ וְ	personal pron
תָשׁוּב שׁוּב	you will return/again *tā·šûv*	QAL IMPF 2MS	verb
וְשָׁמַעְתָּ שׁמע	and you will listen *wə·šā·ma'·tā*	QAL WEQATAL 2MS	verb
בְּקוֹל קוֹל	to the voice of *bə·qôl*	CST W/ PREP בְּ	noun
יְהוָה יהוה	Yahweh *YHWH*	ABS	noun

As above, the word שׁוּב here is sometimes rendered "again."

וְעָשִׂיתָ אֶת־כָּל־מִצְוֺתָיו אֲשֶׁר אָנֹכִי מְצַוְּךָ הַיּוֹם:

and do all the commandments that I am commanding you today.

וְעָשִׂיתָ עשׂה	and you will do/keep *wə·'ā·śî·tā*	QAL WEQATAL 2MS	verb
אֶת־ אֵת	(direct object marker) *'et-*	---	particle
כָּל־ כֹּל	all *kol-*	CST	noun
מִצְוֺתָיו מִצְוָה	his commandments *miṣ·wō·tāyw*	CST W/ 3MS SX	noun
אֲשֶׁר אֲשֶׁר	that/which *'ă·šer*	---	relative pron
אָנֹכִי אָנֹכִי	I *'ā·nō·ḵî*	---	personal pron
מְצַוְּךָ צוה	command / am commanding you *mə·ṣaw·wə·ḵā*	QAL PTCP MS W/ 2MS SX	verb
הַיּוֹם: יוֹם	today/this day *hay·yôm*	ABS W/ DEF. ART.	noun

וְהוֹתִירְךָ֩ יְהֹוָ֨ה אֱלֹהֶ֜יךָ בְּכֹ֣ל ׀ מַעֲשֵׂ֣ה יָדֶ֗ךָ

And Yahweh your God will make you prosper
in all the work of your hand,

וְהוֹתִירְךָ֩	and (he) will make you prosperous/successful	HIPH WEQATAL 3MS	verb
יתר	wə·hô·tîr·**kā**	W/ 2MS SX	
יְהֹוָ֨ה	Yahweh	ABS	noun
יהוה	*YHWH*		
אֱלֹהֶ֜יךָ	your God	CST	noun
אֱלֹהִים	ʾĕ·lō·**hê**·kā	W/ 2MS SX	
בְּכֹ֣ל ׀	in all	CST	noun
כֹּל	bə·**kol**	W/ PREP בְּ	
מַעֲשֵׂ֣ה	(the) work of	CST	noun
מַעֲשֶׂה	ma·ʾă·**śē**		
יָדֶ֗ךָ	your hand	CST	noun
יָד	yā·**de**·kā	W/ 2MS SX	

בִּפְרִ֧י בִטְנְךָ֛

in the fruit of your womb

בִּפְרִ֧י	in (the) fruit of	CST	noun
פְּרִי	bif·**rî**	W/ PREP בְּ	
בִטְנְךָ֛	your womb	CST	noun
בֶּטֶן	viṭ·nə·**kā**	W/ 2MS SX	

וּבִפְרִ֥י בְהֶמְתְּךָ֖

and in the fruit of your cattle

וּבִפְרִ֥י	and in (the) fruit of	CST	noun
פְּרִי	û·vif·**rî**	W/ CONJ וְ + PREP בְּ	
בְהֶמְתְּךָ֖	your beast/cattle	CST	noun
בְּהֵמָה	və·hem·tə·**kā**	W/ 2MS SX	

וּבִפְרִי אַדְמָתְךָ לְטוֹבָה

and in the fruit of your ground, for good.

וּבִפְרִי פְּרִי	and in (the) fruit of *û·vif·rî*	CST W/ CONJ וְ + PREP בְּ	noun
אַדְמָתְךָ אֲדָמָה	your land *'ad·mā·tə·ḵā*	CST W/ 2MS SX	noun
לְטוֹבָה טוֹבָה	for good *lə·ṭô·vâ*	ABS W/ PREP לְ	noun

לְטוֹבָה may be taken as "well-being" or "prosperity" here and in v. 9e.

כִּי יָשׁוּב יְהוָה לָשׂוּשׂ עָלֶיךָ לְטוֹב

For Yahweh will turn to delight in you for good,

כִּי כִּי	for/when *kî*	---	conj
יָשׁוּב שׁוּב	(he) will return/again *yā·šûv*	QAL IMPF 3MS	verb
יְהוָה יהוה	Yahweh *YHWH*	ABS	noun
לָשׂוּשׂ שׂישׂ	to rejoice/delight *lā·śûś*	QAL INF CST W/ PREP לְ	verb
עָלֶיךָ עַל	over you *'ā·lê·ḵā*	--- W/ 2MS SX	prep
לְטוֹב טוֹב	for good *lə·ṭôv*	ABS W/ PREP לְ	noun

כַּאֲשֶׁר־שָׂשׂ עַל־אֲבֹתֶיךָ:

just as he delighted in your ancestors,

כַּאֲשֶׁר־ אֲשֶׁר	as *ka·'ă·šer-*	--- W/ PREP כְּ	relative pron
שָׂשׂ שׂישׂ	he rejoiced/delighted *śāś*	QAL PF 3MS	verb
עַל־ עַל	over *'al-*	---	prep

| אֲבֹתֶֽיךָ׃
אָב | your ancestors
ʾă·vō·tê·ḵā | CST
W/ 2MS SX | noun |

<table>
<tr><td>10a</td><td colspan="3" align="center">כִּי תִשְׁמַע בְּקוֹל יְהֹוָה אֱלֹהֶיךָ</td></tr>
<tr><td></td><td colspan="3" align="center">if you obey the voice of Yahweh your God</td></tr>
</table>

כִּי כִּי	for/when *kî*	---	conj
תִשְׁמַע שמע	you listen *tiš·maʿ*	QAL IMPF 2MS	verb
בְּקוֹל קוֹל	to (the) voice of *bə·qôl*	CST W/ PREP בְּ	noun
יְהֹוָה יהוה	Yahweh *YHWH*	ABS	noun
אֱלֹהֶיךָ אֱלֹהִים	your God *ʾĕ·lō·hê·ḵā*	CST W/ 2MS SX	noun

<table>
<tr><td>10b</td><td colspan="3" align="center">לִשְׁמֹר מִצְוֹתָיו וְחֻקֹּתָיו</td></tr>
<tr><td></td><td colspan="3" align="center">by keeping his commandments and his statutes—</td></tr>
</table>

לִשְׁמֹר שמר	to keep/guard *liš·mōr*	QAL INF CST W/ PREP לְ	verb
מִצְוֹתָיו מִצְוָה	his commandments *miṣ·wō·tāyw*	CST W/ 3MS SX	noun
וְחֻקֹּתָיו חֻקָּה	and his statutes/regulations *wə·ḥuq·qō·tāyw*	CST W/ CONJ וְ + 3MS SX	noun

<table>
<tr><td>10c</td><td colspan="3" align="center">הַכְּתוּבָה בְּסֵפֶר הַתּוֹרָה הַזֶּה</td></tr>
<tr><td></td><td colspan="3" align="center">all that is written in this book of the torah—</td></tr>
</table>

| הַכְּתוּבָה | the ones written
hak·kə·tû·vâ | QP PTCP FS
W/ DEF. ART. | verb |
| כתב | | | |

בְּסֵ֫פֶר	in (the) book of	CST		noun
סֵ֫פֶר	*bə·sē·fer*	W/ PREP בְּ		
הַתּוֹרָה	(the) torah/law	ABS		noun
תּוֹרָה	*hat·tô·râ*	W/ DEF. ART.		
הַזֶּה	(the) this	---		demonstr
זֶה	*haz·ze*	W/ DEF. ART.		pron

The Targums, Peshitta, 4QDeut[b], and LXX all render הַכְּתוּבָה in the plural, though that is not the only option, as shown in the translation above (literally, "that which is written," i.e., "all that is written").

10d כִּי תָשׁוּב אֶל־יְהוָה אֱלֹהֶיךָ בְּכָל־לְבָבְךָ וּבְכָל־נַפְשֶׁךָ:

if you return to Yahweh your God with all your heart
and with all your life force.

כִּי	for/when	---		conj
כִּי	*kî*			
תָשׁוּב	you turn/return	QAL IMPF 2MS		verb
שׁוּב	*tā·šûv*			
אֶל־	to	---		prep
אֶל	*'el-*			
יְהוָה	Yahweh	ABS		noun
יהוה	*YHWH*			
אֱלֹהֶיךָ	your God	CST		noun
אֱלֹהִים	*'ĕ·lō·hê·ḵā*	W/ 2MS SX		
בְּכָל־	with all	CST		noun
כֹּל	*bə·ḵol-*	W/ PREP בְּ		
לְבָבְךָ	your heart	CST		noun
לֵבָב	*lə·vāv·ḵā*	W/ 2MS SX		
וּבְכָל־	and with all	CST		noun
כֹּל	*û·və·ḵol-*	W/ CONJ וּ + PREP בְּ		
נַפְשֶׁךָ:	your soul/life	CST		noun
נֶפֶשׁ	*naf·še·ḵā*	W/ 2MS SX		

11a כִּי הַמִּצְוָה הַזֹּאת אֲשֶׁר אָנֹכִי מְצַוְּךָ הַיּוֹם

kî hammiṣwâ hazzō't 'ăšer 'ānōkî məṣawwəkā hayyôm

For this commandment that I am commanding you today

11b לֹא־נִפְלֵאת הִוא מִמְּךָ וְלֹא רְחֹקָה הִוא:

lō'-niflē't hī' mimməkā wəlō' rəḥōqâ hī'.

is not too difficult for you, and it is not far off.

12a לֹא בַשָּׁמַיִם הִוא

lō' vaššāmayim hī'

It is not in the heavens

12b לֵאמֹר מִי יַעֲלֶה־לָּנוּ הַשָּׁמַיְמָה וְיִקָּחֶהָ לָּנוּ

lē'mōr mî ya'ăle-lānû haššāmaymâ wəyiqqāḥekā lānû

that one should say, "Who will ascend for us to the heavens and get it for us,

12c וְיַשְׁמִעֵנוּ אֹתָהּ וְנַעֲשֶׂנָּה:

wəyašmi'ēnû 'ōtāh wəna'ăśennâ.

that we may hear and do it?"

13a וְלֹא־מֵעֵבֶר לַיָּם הִוא

wəlō' mē'ēver layyām hī'

It is not across the sea

13b לֵאמֹר מִי יַעֲבָר־לָנוּ אֶל־עֵבֶר הַיָּם וְיִקָּחֶהָ לָּנוּ

lē'mōr mî ya'ăvor-lānû 'el-'ēver hayyām wəyiqqāḥekā lānû

that one should say, "Who will cross over the sea for us and get it for us,

13c וְיַשְׁמִעֵנוּ אֹתָהּ וְנַעֲשֶׂנָּה:

wəyašmi'ēnû 'ōtāh wəna'ăśennâ.

that we might hear it and do it?"

14a   כִּי־קָר֥וֹב אֵלֶ֛יךָ הַדָּבָ֖ר מְאֹ֑ד

kî-qārôv 'ēlêḵā haddāvār mə'ōd

For this word is very near to you,

14b   בְּפִ֥יךָ וּבִלְבָבְךָ֖ לַעֲשֹׂתֽוֹ׃

bəfîḵā ûvilvāvḵā la'ăśōtô.

in your mouth and in your heart, so that you can do it.

11a   כִּ֚י הַמִּצְוָ֣ה הַזֹּ֔את אֲשֶׁ֛ר אָנֹכִ֥י מְצַוְּךָ֖ הַיּ֑וֹם

For this commandment that I am commanding you today

כִּ֚י	for	---	conj
כִּי	*kî*		
הַמִּצְוָ֣ה	(the) commandment	ABS	noun
מִצְוָה	*ham·miṣ·wâ*	W/ DEF. ART.	
הַזֹּ֔את	(the) this	---	demonstr
זֹאת	*haz·zōʾt*	W/ DEF. ART.	pron
אֲשֶׁ֛ר	that/which	---	relative
אֲשֶׁר	*ă·šer*		pron
אָנֹכִ֥י	I	---	personal
אָנֹכִי	*ʾā·nō·ḵî*		pron
מְצַוְּךָ֖	(am) commanding you	PIEL PTCP MS	verb
צוה	*mə·ṣaw·wə·ḵā*	W/ 2MS SX	
הַיּ֑וֹם	today/this day	ABS	noun
יוֹם	*hay·yôm*	W/ DEF. ART.	

11b   לֹֽא־נִפְלֵ֥את הִוא֙ מִמְּךָ֔ וְלֹ֥א רְחֹקָ֖ה הִֽוא׃

is not too difficult for you, and it is not far off.

לֹא־	no/not	---	particle
לֹא	*lō·ʾ-*		

נִפְלֵאת פלא *nif·lē't*	(too) difficult	NIPH PTCP FS	verb
הוּא היא *hī'*	it	---	personal pron
מִמְּךָ מן *mim·mə·kā*	for you	--- W/ 2MS SX	prep
וְלֹא לֹא *wə·lō'*	and no/not	--- W/ CONJ וְ	particle
רְחֹקָה רָחוֹק *rə·ḥō·qâ*	distant/far off	FS PRED	adj
הוּא׃ היא *hī'*	it	---	personal pron

12a

לֹא בַשָּׁמַיִם הִוא

It is not in the heavens

לֹא לֹא *lō'*	no/not	---	particle
בַשָּׁמַיִם שָׁמַיִם *vaš·šā·ma·yim*	in the heavens	ABS W/ PREP בְּ + DEF. ART.	noun
הִוא היא *hī'*	it/that	---	personal pron

12b

לֵאמֹר מִי יַעֲלֶה־לָּנוּ הַשָּׁמַיְמָה וְיִקָּחֶהָ לָּנוּ

that one should say, "Who will ascend for us to the heavens and get it for us,

לֵאמֹר אמר *lē·mōr*	to say/saying	QAL INF CST W/ PREP לְ	verb
מִי מִי *mî*	who	---	interr pron
יַעֲלֶה־ עלה *ya·'ă·le-*	(he) will go up	QAL IMPF 3MS	verb

לָ֫נוּ לְ	for us *lā·nû*	--- W/ 1CP SX	prep
הַשָּׁמַ֫יְמָה֙ שָׁמַ֫יִם	to the heavens *haš·šā·may·mâ*	ABS W/ DEF. ART. + LOCATIVE ה	noun
וְיִקָּחֶ֫הָ לקח	and get it *wə·yiq·qā·he·ḵā*	QAL IMPF 3MS W/ CONJ וְ + 3FS SX	verb
לָ֫נוּ לְ	for us *lā·nû*	--- W/ 1CP SX	prep

12c וְיַשְׁמִעֵ֫נוּ אֹתָהּ וְנַעֲשֶֽׂנָּה׃

that we may hear and do it?”

וְיַשְׁמִעֵ֫נוּ שמע	and (he) will make us hear *wə·yaš·mi·ē·nû*	HIPH IMPF 3MS W/ CONJ וְ + 1CP SX	verb
אֹתָהּ אֵת	it *ʾō·tāh*	--- W/ 3FS SX	particle
וְנַעֲשֶֽׂנָּה׃ עשה	and we will do it *wə·na·ʾă·śen·nâ*	QAL IMPF 1CP W/ CONJ וְ + 3FS SX	verb

13a וְלֹא־מֵעֵ֫בֶר לַיָּ֥ם הִ֑וא

It is not across the sea

וְלֹא־ לֹא	and no/not *wə·lō·*	--- W/ CONJ וְ	particle
מֵעֵ֫בֶר עֵ֫בֶר	beyond/across *mē·ʾē·ver*	ABS W/ PREP מִן	noun
לַיָּ֥ם יָם	(to) the sea *lay·yām*	ABS W/ PREP לְ + DEF. ART.	noun
הִ֑וא הִיא	it *hī·*	---	personal pron

לֵאמֹר מִי יַעֲבָר־לָנוּ אֶל־עֵבֶר הַיָּם וְיִקָּחֶהָ לָּנוּ

that one should say, "Who will cross over the sea for us
and get it for us,

לֵאמֹר אמר	to say/saying *lē·mōr*	QAL INF CST W/ PREP לְ	verb
מִי מִי	who *mî*	---	interr pron
יַעֲבָר־ עבר	(he) will go across *ya·ʾă·vor-*	QAL IMPF 3MS	verb
לָנוּ לְ	for us *lā·nû*	--- W/ 1CP SX	prep
אֶל־ אֶל	to *ʾel-*	---	prep
עֵבֶר עֵבֶר	across *ʿē·ver*	CST	noun
הַיָּם יָם	the sea *hay·yām*	ABS W/ DEF. ART.	noun
וְיִקָּחֶהָ לקח	and get it *wə·yiq·qā·he·ḵā*	QAL IMPF 3MS W/ CONJ וְ + 3FS SX	verb
לָּנוּ לְ	for us *lā·nû*	--- W/ 1CP SX	prep

וְיַשְׁמִעֵנוּ אֹתָהּ וְנַעֲשֶׂנָּה:

that we might hear it and do it?"

וְיַשְׁמִעֵנוּ שמע	and (he) will make us hear *wə·yaš·mi·ʿē·nû*	HIPH IMPF 3MS W/ CONJ וְ + 1CP SX	verb
אֹתָהּ אֵת	it *ʾō·tāh*	--- W/ 3FS SX	particle
וְנַעֲשֶׂנָּה: עשה	and we will do it *wə·na·ʿă·śen·nâ*	QAL IMPF 1CP W/ CONJ וְ + 3FS SX	verb

כִּי־קָרוֹב אֵלֶיךָ הַדָּבָר מְאֹד

For this word is very near to you,

כִּי־	when/for	---	conj
כִּי	*kî-*		
קָרוֹב	near	MS PRED	adj
קָרוֹב	*qā·rôv*		
אֵלֶיךָ	to you	---	prep
אֶל	*'ē·lê·ḵā*	W/ 2MS SX	
הַדָּבָר	the word/matter	ABS	noun
דָּבָר	*had·dā·vār*	W/ DEF. ART.	
מְאֹד	very	---	adv
מְאֹד	*mə·'ōd*		

בְּפִיךָ וּבִלְבָבְךָ לַעֲשֹׂתוֹ׃

in your mouth and in your heart, so that you can do it.

בְּפִיךָ	in your mouth	CST	noun
פֶּה	*bə·fî·ḵā*	W/ PREP בְּ + 2MS SX	
וּבִלְבָבְךָ	and in your heart	CST	noun
לֵבָב	*û·vil·vāv·ḵā*	W/ CONJ וְ + PREP בְּ + 2MS SX	
לַעֲשֹׂתוֹ׃	to do it	QAL INF CST	verb
עָשָׂה	*la·'ă·śō·tô*	W/ PREP לְ + 3MS SX	

15a

רְאֵ֨ה נָתַ֤תִּי לְפָנֶ֙יךָ֙ הַיּ֔וֹם

rə'ē nātattî ləfānêkā hayyôm

Look, I am setting before you today

15b

אֶת־הַֽחַיִּ֥ים וְאֶת־הַטֹּ֖וב וְאֶת־הַמָּ֥וֶת וְאֶת־הָרָֽע׃

'et-haḥāyîm wə'et-haṭṭôv wə'et-hammāwet wə'et-hārā'.

life and prosperity and death and calamity,

16a

אֲשֶׁ֨ר אָנֹכִ֤י מְצַוְּךָ֙ הַיּ֔וֹם

'ăšer 'ānōkî məṣawwəkā hayyôm

which I am commanding you today,

16b

לְאַהֲבָ֞ה אֶת־יְהוָ֤ה אֱלֹהֶ֙יךָ֙

lə'ahăvâ 'et-YHWH 'ĕlōhêkā

to love Yahweh your God,

16c

לָלֶ֣כֶת בִּדְרָכָ֗יו

lāleket bidrākāyw

to walk in his ways,

16d

וְלִשְׁמֹ֧ר מִצְוֹתָ֛יו וְחֻקֹּתָ֖יו וּמִשְׁפָּטָ֑יו

wəlišmōr miṣwōtāyw wəḥuqqōtāyw ûmišpāṭāyw

to keep his commands and statutes and judgments,

16e

וְחָיִ֣יתָ וְרָבִ֔יתָ וּבֵֽרַכְךָ֙ יְהוָ֣ה אֱלֹהֶ֔יךָ

wəḥāyîtā wərāvîtā ûvērakəkā YHWH 'ĕlōhêkā

בָּאָ֕רֶץ אֲשֶׁר־אַתָּ֥ה בָא־שָׁ֖מָּה לְרִשְׁתָּֽהּ׃

bā'āreṣ 'ăšer-'attâ vā' šāmmâ lərištāh.

that you may live and increase, and that Yahweh your God
may bless you in the land that you are going in to possess.

וְאִם־יִפְנֶה לְבָבְךָ וְלֹא תִשְׁמָע

wə'im-yifne ləvāvḵā wəlō' tišma'

But if your heart turns, and you do not obey,

17b

וְנִדַּחְתָּ וְהִשְׁתַּחֲוִיתָ לֵאלֹהִים אֲחֵרִים וַעֲבַדְתָּם:

wəniddaḥtā wəhištaḥăwîtā lē'lōhîm 'ăḥērîm wa'ăvadtām.

and you allow yourself to be scattered,
and you worship other gods and serve them,

18a

הִגַּדְתִּי לָכֶם הַיּוֹם כִּי אָבֹד תֹּאבֵדוּן

higgadtî lāḵem hayyôm kî 'āvōd tō'vēdûn

I declare to you today that you will surely perish;

18b

לֹא־תַאֲרִיכֻן יָמִים עַל־הָאֲדָמָה

lō'-ta'ărîḵun yāmîm 'al-hā'ădāmâ

you will not prolong your days upon the land

18c

אֲשֶׁר אַתָּה עֹבֵר אֶת־הַיַּרְדֵּן לָבֹא שָׁמָּה לְרִשְׁתָּהּ:

'ăšer 'attâ 'ōvēr 'et-hayyardēn lāvō' šāmmâ lərištāh.

that you are crossing over the Jordan to go in and possess.

19a

הַעִידֹתִי בָכֶם הַיּוֹם אֶת־הַשָּׁמַיִם וְאֶת־הָאָרֶץ

ha'îdōtî vāḵem hayyôm 'et-haššāmayim wə'et-hā'āreṣ

I call the heavens and the earth as witnesses against you this day.

19b

הַחַיִּים וְהַמָּוֶת נָתַתִּי לְפָנֶיךָ הַבְּרָכָה וְהַקְּלָלָה

haḥāyîm wəhammāwet nātattî ləfānêḵā habbərāḵâ wəhaqqəlālâ

I set before you life and death, blessing and curse.

19c

וּבָחַרְתָּ בַּחַיִּים לְמַעַן תִּחְיֶה אַתָּה וְזַרְעֶךָ:

ûvāḥartā baḥāyîm ləma'an tiḥyê 'attâ zar'eḵā.

So choose life, so that you may live, you and your offspring,

20a

לְאַהֲבָה אֶת־יְהוָה אֱלֹהֶיךָ לִשְׁמֹעַ בְּקֹלוֹ וּלְדָבְקָה־בוֹ

lə'ahăvâ 'et-YHWH 'ĕlōhêḵā lišmōa' bəqōlô lədovqâ-vô

to love Yahweh your God, to obey his voice and to cling to him.

20b

כִּי הוּא חַיֶּיךָ וְאֹרֶךְ יָמֶיךָ לָשֶׁבֶת עַל־הָאֲדָמָה

kî hû' ḥayêḵā wə'ōreḵ yāmêḵā lāševet 'al-ha'ăḏāmâ

For he is your life and your length of days
that you may dwell on the land

20c

אֲשֶׁר נִשְׁבַּע יְהוָה לַאֲבֹתֶיךָ

'ăšer nišba' YHWH la'ăvōtêḵā

that Yahweh swore to your ancestors—

20d

לְאַבְרָהָם לְיִצְחָק וּלְיַעֲקֹב לָתֵת לָהֶם:

lə'avrāhām ləyiṣḥāq ûləya'ăqōv lātēt lāhem.

to Abraham, to Isaac, and to Jacob—to give to you.”

15a	רְאֵה נָתַתִּי לְפָנֶיךָ הַיּוֹם		

Look, I am setting before you today

רְאֵה ראה	See/look *rə·'ē*	QAL IMPV MS	verb
נָתַתִּי נתן	I give/set *nā·**tat**·tî*	QAL PF 1CS	verb
לְפָנֶיךָ לִפְנֵי	before you *lə·fā·**nê**·ḵā*	--- W/ 2MS SX	prep
הַיּוֹם יוֹם	today/this day *hay·**yôm***	ABS W/ DEF. ART.	noun

15b	אֶת־הַחַיִּים וְאֶת־הַטּוֹב וְאֶת־הַמָּוֶת וְאֶת־הָרָע:		

life and prosperity and death and calamity,

אֶת־ אֵת	*(direct object marker)* *'et-*	---	particle

הַֽחַיִּים֙ חַיִּים *ha·ḥā·yîm*	the life/lives	ABS W/ DEF. ART.	noun
וְאֶת־ אֵת *wə·'et-*	and (+ *direct object marker*)	--- W/ CONJ וְ	particle
הַטּ֔וֹב טוֹב *haṭ·ṭôv*	the good	ABS W/ DEF. ART.	noun
וְאֶת־ אֵת *wə·'et-*	and (+ *direct object marker*)	--- W/ CONJ וְ	particle
הַמָּ֖וֶת מָוֶת *ham·mā·wet*	the death	ABS W/ DEF. ART.	noun
וְאֶת־ אֵת *wə·'et-*	and (+ *direct object marker*)	--- W/ CONJ וְ	particle
הָרָֽע: רַע *hā·rā'*	the evil	ABS W/ DEF. ART.	noun

One should think both of the moral polarity of טוֹב ("good") and רַע ("evil") in Gen 2–3 and of the two sets of consequences in the blessings and the curses in Deut 27–28.

	אֲשֶׁ֧ר אָנֹכִ֛י מְצַוְּךָ֖ הַיּֽוֹם֙
16a	
	which I am commanding you today,

אֲשֶׁ֧ר אֲשֶׁר *'ă·šer*	that/which	---	relative pron
אָנֹכִ֛י אָנֹכִי *'ā·nō·ḵî*	I	---	personal pron
מְצַוְּךָ֖ צוה *mə·ṣaw·wə·ḵā*	(am) commanding	PIEL PTCP MS W/ 2MS SX	verb
הַיּֽוֹם֙ יוֹם *hay·yôm*	today/this day	ABS W/ DEF. ART.	noun

The scribes who copied the MT appear to have changed the wording that was used earlier in 11:27. But it seems more likely that, in copying the text, their eyes accidentally jumped from the first אֲשֶׁר to the second אֲשֶׁר, losing the introductory clause, "If you obey . . ." Most translations believe the LXX has correctly preserved the introductory clause that is missing in the MT of this verse.

לְאַהֲבָ֖ה אֶת־יְהוָ֣ה אֱלֹהֶ֔יךָ

to love Yahweh your God,

לְאַהֲבָ֖ה אהב	to love *lə·'a·hă·vâ*	QAL INF CST W/ PREP לְ	verb
אֶת־ אֵת	(direct object marker) *'et-*	---	particle
יְהוָ֣ה יהוה	Yahweh *YHWH*	ABS	noun
אֱלֹהֶ֔יךָ אֱלֹהִים	your God *'ĕ·lō·hê·ḵā*	CST W/ 2MS SX	noun

לָלֶ֖כֶת בִּדְרָכָ֑יו

to walk in his ways,

לָלֶ֖כֶת הלך	to walk *lā·le·ḵet*	QAL INF CST W/ PREP לְ	verb
בִּדְרָכָ֑יו דֶּרֶךְ	in his ways *bid·rā·ḵāyw*	CST W/ PREP בְּ + 3MS SX	noun

וְלִשְׁמֹ֛ר מִצְוֺתָ֥יו וְחֻקֹּתָ֖יו וּמִשְׁפָּטָ֑יו

to keep his commands and statutes and judgments,

וְלִשְׁמֹ֛ר שמר	and to keep/observe *wə·liš·mōr*	QAL INF CST W/ CONJ וְ + PREP לְ	verb
מִצְוֺתָ֥יו מִצְוָה	his commandments *miṣ·wō·tāyw*	CST W/ 3MS SX	noun
וְחֻקֹּתָ֖יו חֻקָּה	and his statutes/regulations *wə·ḥuq·qō·tāyw*	CST W/ CONJ וְ + 3MS SX	noun
וּמִשְׁפָּטָ֑יו מִשְׁפָּט	and his judgments *û·miš·pā·ṭāyw*	CST W/ CONJ וְ + 3MS SX	noun

וְחָיִיתָ וְרָבִיתָ וּבֵרַכְךָ יְהוָה אֱלֹהֶיךָ
בָּאָרֶץ אֲשֶׁר־אַתָּה בָא־שָׁמָּה לְרִשְׁתָּהּ׃

that you may live and increase, and that Yahweh your God may bless you in the land that you are going in to possess.

וְחָיִיתָ חיה	and/then you will live *wə·ḥā·yî·tā*	QAL WEQATAL 2MS	verb
וְרָבִיתָ רבה	and you will increase/multiply *wə·rā·vî·tā*	QAL WEQATAL 2MS	verb
וּבֵרַכְךָ ברך	and (he) will bless you *û·vē·ra·kə·kā*	PIEL WEQATAL 3MS W/ 2MS SX	verb
יְהוָה יהוה	Yahweh *YHWH*	ABS	noun
אֱלֹהֶיךָ אלהים	your God *ʾĕ·lō·hɛ̂·kā*	CST W/ 2MS SX	noun
בָּאָרֶץ אֶרֶץ	in the land *bā·ʾā·reṣ*	ABS W/ PREP בְּ + DEF. ART.	noun
אֲשֶׁר־ אֲשֶׁר	that/which *ʾă·šer-*	---	relative pron
אַתָּה אַתָּה	you *ʾat·tâ*	---	personal pron
בָא־ בוא	go/going *vā·ʾ*	QAL PTCP MS	verb
שָׁמָּה שָׁם	(to) there *šām·mâ*	--- W/ LOCATIVE ה	adv
לְרִשְׁתָּהּ׃ ירש	to possess/dispossess it *lə·riš·tāh*	QAL INF CST W/ PREP לְ + 3FS SX	verb

וְאִם־יִפְנֶה לְבָבְךָ וְלֹא תִשְׁמָע

But if your heart turns, and you do not obey,

וְאִם־ אם	and/but if *wə·ʾim-*	--- W/ CONJ וְ	conj
יִפְנֶה פנה	(it) turns *yif·ne*	QAL IMPF 3MS	verb

לְבָבְךָ לֵבָב	your heart *lə·vāv·kā*	CST W/ 2MS SX	noun
וְלֹא לֹא	and no/not *wə·lō'*	--- W/ CONJ וְ	particle
תִשְׁמָע שמע	you hear/obey *tiš·ma'*	QAL IMPF 2MS	verb

17b

וְנִדַּחְתָּ וְהִשְׁתַּחֲוִיתָ לֵאלֹהִים אֲחֵרִים וַעֲבַדְתָּם׃

and you allow yourself to be scattered,
and you worship other gods and serve them,

וְנִדַּחְתָּ נדח	and/but you are banished/ led astray *wə·nid·daḥ·tā*	NIPH WEQATAL 2MS	verb
וְהִשְׁתַּחֲוִיתָ שחה	and you bow down/worship *wə·hiš·ta·ḥă·wî·tā*	HITHPALEL WEQATAL 2MS	verb
לֵאלֹהִים אֱלֹהִים	to gods *lē'·lō·hîm*	ABS W/ PREP לְ	noun
אֲחֵרִים אַחֵר	others *'ă·ḥē·rîm*	MP ATTR	adj
וַעֲבַדְתָּם׃ עבד	and you serve them *wa·'ă·vad·tām*	QAL WEQATAL 2MS W/ 3MP SX	verb

On the translation of the Niphal of נדח as "*allow yourself* to be scattered,"
see *HALOT* s.v. נדח and *IBHS* 23.4f.

18a

הִגַּדְתִּי לָכֶם הַיּוֹם כִּי אָבֹד תֹּאבֵדוּן

I declare to you today that you will surely perish;

הִגַּדְתִּי נגד	I make known/declare *hig·gad·tî*	HIPH PF 1CS	verb
לָכֶם לְ	to you *lā·kem*	--- W/ 2MP SX	prep
הַיּוֹם יוֹם	today/this day *hay·yôm*	ABS W/ DEF. ART.	noun

כִּי	that	---	conj
כִּי	*kî*		
אָבֹד	perishing/going astray	QAL INF ABS	verb
אבד	*'ā·vōd*		
תֹּאבֵדוּן	you will perish/go astray	QAL IMPF 2MP W/ PARAGOGIC נ	verb
אבד	*tō'·vē·dûn*		

18b — לֹא־תַאֲרִיכֻן יָמִים֙ עַל־הָאֲדָמָ֔ה

you will not prolong your days upon the land

לֹא־	no/not	---	particle
לֹא	*lō'-*		
תַאֲרִיכֻן	you (all) will prolong	HIPH IMPF 2MP W/ PARAGOGIC נ	verb
ארך	*ta·'ă·rî·ḵun*		
יָמִים֙	your days	ABS	noun
יוֹם	*yā·mîm*		
עַל־	on/upon	---	prep
עַל	*'al-*		
הָאֲדָמָה	the land	ABS W/ DEF. ART	noun
אֲדָמָה	*hā·'ă·dā·mâ*		

18c — אֲשֶׁר אַתָּה עֹבֵר אֶת־הַיַּרְדֵּן לָבֹא שָׁמָּה לְרִשְׁתָּהּ׃

that you are crossing over the Jordan to go in and possess.

אֲשֶׁר	that/which	---	relative pron
אֲשֶׁר	*'ă·šer*		
אַתָּה	you	---	personal pron
אַתָּה	*'at·tâ*		
עֹבֵר	are going across	QAL PTCP MS	verb
עבר	*'ō·vēr*		
אֶת־	(direct object marker)	---	particle
אֶת	*'et-*		
הַיַּרְדֵּן	the Jordan	ABS W/ DEF. ART.	noun
יַרְדֵּן	*hay·yar·dēn*		

לָבֹא	to go/come	QAL INF CST	verb
בוא	*lā·vōʾ*	W/ PREP לְ	
שָׁמָּה	(to) there	---	adv
שָׁם	*šām·mâ*	W/ LOCATIVE ה	
לְרִשְׁתָּהּ׃	to possess/dispossess (it)	QAL INF CST	verb
ירשׁ	*lə·riš·tāh*	W/ PREP לְ + 3FS SX	

19a הַעִידֹתִי בָכֶם הַיּוֹם אֶת־הַשָּׁמַיִם וְאֶת־הָאָרֶץ

I call the heavens and the earth as witnesses against you this day.

הַעִידֹתִי	I call/invoke	HIPH PF 1CS	verb
עוד	*ha·ʾî·dō·tî*		
בָכֶם	with/against you	---	prep
בְּ	*vā·ḵem*	W/ 2MP SX	
הַיּוֹם	today/this day	ABS	noun
יוֹם	*hay·yôm*	W/ DEF. ART.	
אֶת־	(direct object marker)	---	particle
אֵת	*ʾet-*		
הַשָּׁמַיִם	the heavens/skies	ABS	noun
שָׁמַיִם	*haš·šā·ma·yim*	W/ DEF. ART.	
וְאֶת־	and (+ direct object marker)	---	particle
אֵת	*wə·ʾet-*	W/ CONJ וְ	
הָאָרֶץ	the earth	ABS	noun
אֶרֶץ	*hā·ʾā·reṣ*	W/ DEF. ART.	

The invocation of heaven and earth as witnesses in 4:26; 31:28; and 32:1 reflects a common practice in ancient Near Eastern treaties.

19b הַחַיִּים וְהַמָּוֶת נָתַתִּי לְפָנֶיךָ הַבְּרָכָה וְהַקְּלָלָה

I set before you life and death, blessing and curse.

הַחַיִּים	the life/lives	ABS	noun
חַיִּים	*ha·ḥā·yîm*	W/ DEF. ART.	
וְהַמָּוֶת	and the death	ABS	noun
מָוֶת	*wə·ham·mā·wet*	W/ CONJ וְ + DEF. ART.	

נָתַ֫תִּי נתן	I give/set *nā·**tat**·tî*	QAL PF 1CS	verb
לְפָנֶ֫יךָ לִפְנֵי	before you *lə·fā·**nê**·ḵā*	--- W/ 2MS SX	prep
הַבְּרָכָה בְּרָכָה	the blessing *hab·bə·rā·**ḵâ***	ABS W/ DEF. ART.	noun
וְהַקְּלָלָ֑ה קְלָלָה	and the curse *wə·haq·qə·lā·**lâ***	ABS W/ CONJ וְ + DEF. ART.	noun

וּבָחַרְתָּ֙ בַּֽחַיִּ֔ים לְמַ֥עַן תִּֽחְיֶ֖ה אַתָּ֥ה וְזַרְעֶֽךָ׃

So choose life, so that you may live, you and your offspring,

וּבָחַרְתָּ֙ בחר	and you choose *û·vā·har·**tā***	QAL WEQATAL 2MS	verb
בַּֽחַיִּ֔ים חַיִּים	the life/lives *ba·ḥā·**yîm***	ABS W/ PREP בַּ + DEF. ART.	noun
לְמַ֥עַן לְמַ֫עַן	so that/in order that *lə·**ma**·ʿan*	---	prep
תִּֽחְיֶ֖ה חיה	you will/may live *tih·**yê***	QAL IMPF 2MS	verb
אַתָּ֥ה אַתָּה	you *ʾat·**tâ***	--- PRON	personal
וְזַרְעֶֽךָ׃ זֶ֫רַע	and your seed/offspring *zar·ʿe·**ḵā***	CST W/ CONJ וְ + 2MS SX	noun

לְאַהֲבָה֙ אֶת־יְהוָ֣ה אֱלֹהֶ֔יךָ לִשְׁמֹ֥עַ בְּקֹל֖וֹ וּלְדָבְקָה־בֽוֹ

to love Yahweh your God, to obey his voice and to cling to him.

לְאַהֲבָה֙ אהב	to love *lə·ʾa·hă·**vâ***	QAL INF CST W/ PREP לְ	verb
אֶת־ אֵת	(direct object marker) *ʾet-*	---	particle
יְהוָ֣ה יהוה	Yahweh *YHWH*	ABS	noun

אֱלֹהֶיךָ אֱלֹהִים *ĕ·lō·hê·ḵā*	your God	CST W/ 2MS SX	noun
לִשְׁמֹעַ שמע *liš·mō·a'*	to listen/obey	QAL INF CST W/ PREP לְ	verb
בְּקֹלוֹ קוֹל *bə·qō·lô*	to his voice	CST W/ PREP בְּ + 3MS SX	noun
וּלְדָבְקָה־ דבק *lə·dov·qâ-*	and to cling to/grasp	QAL INF CST W/ CONJ וְ + PREP לְ	verb
בוֹ בְּ *vô*	him	--- W/ 3MS SX	prep

20b   כִּי הוּא חַיֶּיךָ וְאֹרֶךְ יָמֶיךָ לָשֶׁבֶת עַל־הָאֲדָמָה

For he is your life and your length of days
that you may dwell on the land

כִּי כִּי *kî*	for	---	conj
הוּא הוּא *hû'*	he	---	personal pron
חַיֶּיךָ חַיִּים *ḥa·yê·ḵā*	(is) your life	CST W/ 2MS SX	noun
וְאֹרֶךְ אֹרֶךְ *wə·'ō·reḵ*	and length of	CST W/ CONJ וְ	noun
יָמֶיךָ יוֹם *yā·mê·ḵā*	your days	CST W/ 2MS SX	noun
לָשֶׁבֶת ישב *lā·še·vet*	to dwell	QAL INF CST W/ PREP לְ	verb
עַל־ עַל *'al-*	on/upon	---	prep
הָאֲדָמָה אֲדָמָה *ha·'ă·dā·mâ*	the land	ABS W/ DEF. ART.	noun

אֲשֶׁר נִשְׁבַּע יְהוָה לַאֲבֹתֶיךָ

that Yahweh swore to your ancestors—

אֲשֶׁר	that/which	---	relative
אשר	*ʾă·šer*		pron
נִשְׁבַּע	(he) swore	NIPH PF 3MS	verb
שבע	*niš·baʿ*		
יְהוָה	Yahweh	ABS	noun
יהוה	*YHWH*		
לַאֲבֹתֶיךָ	to your ancestors	CST	noun
אָב	*la·ʾă·vō·t̂ê·ḵā*	W/ PREP לְ + 2MS SX	

לְאַבְרָהָם לְיִצְחָק וּלְיַעֲקֹב לָתֵת לָהֶם:

to Abraham, to Isaac, and to Jacob—to give to you."

לְאַבְרָהָם	to Abraham	ABS	noun
אַבְרָהָם	*lə·ʾav·rā·hām*	W/ PREP לְ	
לְיִצְחָק	to Isaac	ABS	noun
יִצְחָק	*lə·yiṣ·ḥāq*	W/ PREP לְ	
וּלְיַעֲקֹב	and to Jacob	ABS	noun
יַעֲקֹב	*û·lə·ya·ʿă·qōv*	W/ CONJ וְ + PREP לְ	
לָתֵת	to give	QAL INF CST	verb
נתן	*lā·tēt*	W/ PREP לְ	
לָהֶם:	to them	---	prep
לְ	*lā·hem*	W/ 3MP SX	

Turning and Gathering for Prospering. These three powerful metaphors usher this chapter along from Israel's future dispersion and exile to a distant, later return to life in the land. Israel imagines their future selves becoming a flock of wandering sheep forgetful of their good shepherd who always remembers them. *Turning* in the Old Testament is the stock and trade metaphor of the wisdom literature, depicting our departure from the simplicity and folly of youth to pursue the wisdom and prosperity of the mature (Prov 1:23; 9:4). Wisdom themes are always close at hand in Deuteronomy, for both wisdom and law direct us to God's moral ordering of the world wherein we find life and promise (4:5–8).

The chapter's metaphors also convey the sublime mystery of God's sovereignty working alongside human freedom. Notice how the verb שׁוּב appears seven times in the first half of the chapter (vv. 1, 2, 3 [twice], 8, 9, 10), uniting God's work of "turning" and "restoring" Israel with Israel's need to repent (turn) and return to God.

As we will see in the next preaching section, God initiates the grace that leads the people back to him. Repentance emerges not as human effort but as God's gift to us. Yet it is also a gift that assumes a corresponding responsibility, not to earn forgiveness but to receive it with gratitude and cooperate as he works within our "heart" and "soul/life" to turn and grow and be fruitful (vv. 2, 6, 10). The pattern of repentance and bearing new fruit appears again powerfully in the prophecies in Jer 31 and Ezek 36.

One might profitably connect this image to Jesus' declaration that "the harvest is plentiful, but the workers are few" (Luke 10:2) and his commission to go out teaching, baptizing, and making disciples (Matt 28:19–20). The new and fuller repentance brought about by Jesus' death and resurrection initiates a new form of fruitfulness—not fruit in the land but fruit among the nations. To turn to him in repentance for our sins is to begin our work as laborers in his harvest.

The Circumcising of our Hearts. Chapters 1–27 of Deuteronomy remain mostly optimistic about future life in the land. Israel will dwell and bear fruit as they "hear," "keep," and "do" all this law. Coming at the end of a long and hopeful collection of sermons, the covenant ceremony in ch. 27 feels like the starting gun at the beginning of a race.

But then things change. We meet a prolonged list of curses in ch. 28 followed by the promise that God will need to circumcise Israel's hearts.

Despite the confidence in Moses' earlier message, there is now news of the need for God to heal disordered humans at their very center. McConville observes the important way ch. 30 turns a hopeful book to its regrettable end: the circumcision of heart by Israel commanded in 10:16 will now have to be accomplished by God (30:6) and the blessing and curse set before Israel in 11:26 comes to Israel three emphatic and final times (30:1, 15, 19) (2002:423). In the end, the blessing is on offer, but the curse is suddenly all the more likely.

When we pause to look at circumcision as a metaphor (Rom 2:28–29), we see just how invasive God's reach will have to be into the deepest fiber of the human life. What we need is a divine act to cut away what has become malignant, twisted, and evil.

The latter prophets renew and recast Deuteronomy's vision in the message of a new covenant in which the law once written in Moses' "book," "tablets," and "stones" will one day be on each person's heart (Jer 31:31–34). They will be renewed from a "heart of stone" to a "heart of flesh" (Ezek 36:26).

Paul's call to moral awakening in Rom 8 likewise advances Deuteronomy's vision. Our life in the "flesh" is transformed by faith in Jesus as we come into union with him in his resurrection and enter into life in the Spirit (8:9–16). Now in Christ we are empowered to live not without law (7:14) but led by the Spirit that inspired the law. No longer led by mere rules and commands, we are lifted into God's own life by prayer and indwelling of his Spirit.

 ***Near and Not Too Difficult.*** We have already mentioned that ancient laws like those of Hammurabi in the eighteenth century BC were rarely promulgated publicly or accessible to the people. This distance of law put the masses who lived on the margins of society at a clear disadvantage as compared to the smaller group of elites, leaving a wide gap between the haves and have-nots.

One might start a sermon with the story of Solon the Lawgiver in Ancient Greece (630–560 BC). Solon, remembered as one of the seven sages of ancient Greece, was elected to be lawgiver for a year during a politically tumultuous time of rising tensions between rich and poor classes. Solon issued laws that forced the rich to negotiate with the poor, quelling an uprising. To ensure enforcement of the laws, Solon placed them prominently around Athens for all to see. It was a law that was *brought near* so that citizens of every class might be represented.

Israel's law may be the first example of such a law intended for every individual in society. In Deuteronomy, the rich and poor, foreigner and citizen, and male and female came as equals before God and his divine legislation. Even the king was subject to divine law (see 17:14–20).

The nearness of the law is tied to its simplicity: "This commandment . . . is not too difficult for you" (30:11b). Such a claim may strike us as contradictory. If chs. 28–32 deliver a foreboding warning of future failure, how could the law be something Israel can do without difficulty (30:14)?

This *do-ableness* and *simplicity* are in its being near—right there in a book and on stones, readable, and not very difficult to understand. The law was near in the way it was written and spoken often in the family, in religious liturgies, and the gathering of the community. The failure to keep the law, then, can only be explained by Israel's hardness of heart. For as ch. 30 demonstrates, law-keeping requires the full application of humility, gratitude, and conformity of our will to a sense of order that is not our own. This is too much to ask of fallen, sinful human beings.

For Christians, these dynamics of Deuteronomy's law take center stage in Romans. Paul tells us that Deuteronomy's inspiring vision for the law turned out to be insufficient for what lay ahead for Israel. In Paul's mind, the law always pointed to something deeper than what we read on the surface of the scrolls. It was the "law of the spirit of life" deep in the commandments—and revealed to us in Jesus—that was necessary to set us free from the "law of sin and death" (Rom 8:1; cf. 3:21–22).

As evidenced in the life of Abraham, drawing near to God comes by faith, not by the exertion of the flesh in anxious striving to keep the law (Rom 9:30–32). Picking up on the vision in Deut 30, Paul tells us that that now, in the gospel message of faith in Christ, God has come near in a way always envisioned in the law (Rom 10:6). In Jesus, God has come near to reveal the way to renewed moral agency. That is, Jesus does not simply save, but he illumines the world again so that we may walk wisely and righteously before him in the Spirit.

This stands in tension with the common and mistaken prejudice that Old Testament law was a regrettable or dispensable piece of God's revelation. For Paul, the law was good and a treasure among the rich bounties of Israel's inheritance (Rom 7:13–14; 9:4). It guided them with sure moral principles that directed their actions in a complex and changing world— so well that it attracted the praise of the nations (Deut 4:5–8).

The problem in Deut 30 and Romans is not with the law itself, but with its proper use. While Jesus engages legal experts on many fine points of the law, he speaks not primarily as a scribe but as a prophet who seeks to bring the law near to the people (see O'Donovan 1996:100–101). And he does so in two major ways. First, drawing on Deuteronomy, Jesus summarizes the law into its two great imperatives: love God and love your neighbor

(Matt 22:34–39; Deut 6:5; 10:12, 19; Lev 19:18). Second, under the burden of Pharisaic legal scrupulosity, Jesus raises the torah's "weightier things of the law" in order to prioritize mercy over sacrifice (Matt 23:23–24) (1996:102–3). The legal authorities had made the law more difficult. Jesus simplifies it, reminds us of its central vision, and brings it near.

Israel's future failure to obey hangs hauntingly over the end of a comparatively hopeful book. The failure is buffered by God's promise to return them to the land and the anticipation of a prophet like Moses, the latter of which we turn to in our final section.

THE DEATH OF MOSES THE PROPHET

These last four chapters make up the final section of the book, each with its own purpose:

ch. 31   The commissioning of Joshua, writing "this book" (31:34), and anticipating a final song

ch. 32   Moses' song

ch. 33   Blessings of the tribes of Israel

ch. 34   The death of Moses

Scholars have long debated whether Deuteronomy is more optimistic or pessimistic about Israel's future. The near future offers the promise of a new land, a concrete book of laws, equal individual standing before the law, wisdom and understanding among the nations, a coming prophet like Moses, and the nearness of God in his law. All of these stand alongside a more distant future where forgetfulness and hard-hearted rebellion derail the covenant and when no prophet like Moses has arisen. It might be best to let the various perspectives stand together without trying to resolve them or reduce the book to a single point. The future is open, not determined, and so we must take our moral agency seriously and "choose life" (30:19).

The final law book in these chapters appears again memorably in the reign of Josiah when Hilkiah the high priest found "the book of the law in the house of the LORD" (2 Kgs 22:8). The event echoes the king's public reading of the law in Deuteronomy (17:18–20; 31:11) as Josiah had the book read aloud and instituted a reform of Israel's worship and a return to honor Yahweh their God (2 Kgs 22:19). At the center of this story, Yahweh commends Josiah for his contrition and repentance, a reminder that Deuteronomy holds out grace in the end (McConville 1993).

LARGER LITERARY CONTEXT   ▸   31:1–34:12

1a

וַיַּעַל מֹשֶׁה

wayyaʿal mōše

And Moses went up

1b

מֵעַרְבֹת מוֹאָב אֶל־הַר נְבוֹ רֹאשׁ הַפִּסְגָּה

mēʿarvōt môʾāv ʾel-har nəvô rōʾš happisgâ

from the plains of Moab to Mount Nebo, at the peak of Pisgah,

1c

אֲשֶׁר עַל־פְּנֵי יְרֵחוֹ

ʾăšer ʿal-pənê yərēḥô

which is before Jericho.

1d

וַיַּרְאֵהוּ יְהוָה אֶת־כָּל־הָאָרֶץ

wayyarʾēhû YHWH ʾet-kol-hāʾāreṣ

And Yahweh showed him all the land:

1e

אֶת־הַגִּלְעָד עַד־דָּן׃

ʾet-haggilʿād ʿad-dān.

Gilead as far as Dan,

2a

וְאֵת כָּל־נַפְתָּלִי

wəʾēt kol-naftālî

and all Naphtali,

2b

וְאֶת־אֶרֶץ אֶפְרַיִם וּמְנַשֶּׁה

wəʾet-ʾereṣ ʾefrayim ûmənašše

and the land of Ephraim and Manasseh,

2c

וְאֵת כָּל־אֶרֶץ יְהוּדָה

wəʾēt kol-ʾereṣ yəhûdâ

and all the land of Judah,

2d עַד הַיָּם הָאַחֲרֽוֹן׃
'ad hayyām hā'aḥărôn.

to the western sea,

3a וְאֶת־הַנֶּגֶב וְאֶת־הַכִּכָּ֡ר
wə'et-hannegev wə'et-hakkikkār

and the Negeb, the plain,

3b בִּקְעַת יְרֵחֽוֹ
biq'at yərēḥô

the valley of Jericho,

3c עִיר הַתְּמָרִים
'îr hattəmārîm

the city of palms,

3d עַד־צֹֽעַר׃
'ad-ṣō'ar.

to Zoar.

4a וַיֹּאמֶר יְהוָה אֵלָיו זֹאת הָאָרֶץ
wayyō'mer YHWH 'ēlāyw zō't hā'āreṣ

And Yahweh said to him, "This is the land

4b אֲשֶׁר נִשְׁבַּעְתִּי לְאַבְרָהָם לְיִצְחָק וּלְיַעֲקֹב
'ăšer nišba'tî lə'avrāhām ləyiṣḥāq ûləya'ăqōv

that I swore to Abraham, Isaac, and Jacob,

4c לֵאמֹר לְזַרְעֲךָ אֶתְּנֶנָּה
lē'mōr ləzar'ăkā 'ettənennâ

saying, 'To your seed I will give it.'

4d הֶרְאִיתִיךָ בְעֵינֶיךָ וְשָׁמָּה לֹא תַעֲבֹֽר׃
her'îtîkā və'ênêkā wəšāmmâ lō' ta'ăvōr.

**I have let you see it with your eyes,
but you shall not cross over there."**

5a | וַיָּ֣מָת שָׁ֣ם

wayyāmot šām

And he died there—

5b | מֹשֶׁ֥ה עֶֽבֶד־יְהֹוָ֖ה

mōše ʿeved YHWH

Moses, the servant of Yahweh—

5c | בְּאֶ֥רֶץ מוֹאָ֖ב עַל־פִּ֥י יְהֹוָֽה׃

bəʾereṣ môʾāv ʿal-pî YHWH.

in the land of Moab, according to the mouth of Yahweh.

6a | וַיִּקְבֹּ֨ר אֹת֤וֹ בַגַּי֙

wayyiqbōr ʾōtô vaggay

And he buried him in the valley

6b | בְּאֶ֣רֶץ מוֹאָ֔ב מ֖וּל בֵּ֣ית פְּעֽוֹר

bəʾereṣ môʾāv mûl bêt pəʿōr

in the land of Moab opposite Beth Peor.

6c | וְלֹא־יָדַ֥ע אִישׁ֙ אֶת־קְבֻ֣רָת֔וֹ

wəlō-yādaʿ ʾîš ʾet-qəvurātô

And no one knows his burial place,

6d | עַ֖ד הַיּ֥וֹם הַזֶּֽה׃

ʿad hayyôm hazze.

even to this day.

7a | וּמֹשֶׁ֗ה בֶּן־מֵאָ֧ה וְעֶשְׂרִ֛ים שָׁנָ֖ה בְּמֹת֑וֹ

ûmōše ben-mēʾâ wəʿeśərîm šānâ bəmōtô

And Moses was 120 years old when he died,

7b | לֹא־כָהֲתָ֥ה עֵינ֖וֹ

lō-kāhătâ ʿênô

and his eye did not grow dim

7c

וְלֹא־נָס לֵחֹה׃

wəlō'-nās lēḥō.

and his vitality did not fade.

8a

וַיִּבְכּוּ בְנֵי יִשְׂרָאֵל

wayyivkû vənê yiśrā'ēl

And the children of Israel wept

8b

אֶת־מֹשֶׁה

'et-mōše

for Moses

8c

בְּעַרְבֹת מוֹאָב שְׁלֹשִׁים יֹום

bə'arvōt mô'āv šəlōšîm yôm

in the plains of Moab for thirty days.

8d

וַיִּתְּמוּ יְמֵי בְכִי אֵבֶל מֹשֶׁה׃

wayyitmû yəmê vəkî 'ēvel mōše.

Then the days of mourning for Moses were completed.

9a

וִיהוֹשֻׁעַ בִּן־נוּן מָלֵא רוּחַ חָכְמָה

wîhôšuaʿ bin-nûn mālē' rûaḥ ḥokmâ

And Joshua, son of Nun, was filled with a spirit of wisdom,

9b

כִּי־סָמַךְ מֹשֶׁה אֶת־יָדָיו עָלָיו

kî-sāmak mōše 'et-yādāyw 'ālāyw

for Moses had laid his hands on him.

9c

וַיִּשְׁמְעוּ אֵלָיו בְּנֵי־יִשְׂרָאֵל

wayyišməʿû 'ēlāyw bənê-yiśrā'ēl

And the children of Israel listened to him

9d

וַיַּעֲשׂוּ כַּאֲשֶׁר צִוָּה יְהוָה אֶת־מֹשֶׁה׃

wayyaʿăśû ka'ăšer ṣiwwâ YHWH 'et-mōše.

and they did as Yahweh had commanded Moses.

10a   וְלֹא־קָ֨ם נָבִ֥יא ע֛וֹד בְּיִשְׂרָאֵ֖ל כְּמֹשֶׁ֑ה

wəlō-qām nāvî ʾôd bəyiśrāʾēl kəmōše

There has not arisen a prophet again in Israel like Moses—

10b   אֲשֶׁר֙ יְדָע֣וֹ יְהוָ֔ה פָּנִ֖ים אֶל־פָּנִֽים׃

ʾăšer yədāʿû YHWH pānîm ʾel-pānîm.

who knew Yahweh face to face—

11a   לְכָל־הָ֨אֹת֜וֹת וְהַמּוֹפְתִ֗ים אֲשֶׁ֤ר שְׁלָחוֹ֙ יְהוָ֔ה

ləkol-hāʾōtôt wəhammôfətîm ʾăšer šəlāḥô YHWH

with regard to all the signs and wonders that Yahweh sent him

11b   לַעֲשׂ֖וֹת בְּאֶ֣רֶץ מִצְרָ֑יִם

laʿăśôt bəʾereṣ miṣrāyim

to do in the land of Egypt

11c   לְפַרְעֹ֥ה וּלְכָל־עֲבָדָ֖יו וּלְכָל־אַרְצֽוֹ׃

ləfarʿō ûləkol-ʿăvādāyw ûləkol-ʾarṣô.

against Pharoah and against all his servants and against all the land,

12a   וּלְכֹל֙ הַיָּ֣ד הַחֲזָקָ֔ה וּלְכֹ֖ל הַמּוֹרָ֣א הַגָּד֑וֹל

ûləkōl hayyād haḥăzāqâ ûləkōl hammôrāʾ haggādôl

and with regard to his mighty hand and all the awesome deeds

12b   אֲשֶׁר֙ עָשָׂ֣ה מֹשֶׁ֔ה לְעֵינֵ֖י כָּל־יִשְׂרָאֵֽל׃

ʾăšer ʿāśâ mōše ʿênêkā kol-yiśrāʾēl.

that Moses did in the sight of all Israel.

❧❦❧

<table>
<tr><td>1a</td><td align="center">וַיַּעַל מֹשֶׁה</td></tr>
</table>

And Moses went up

וַיַּעַל	and (he) went up/arose	QAL WAYY 3MS	verb
עלה	*way·ya·ʿal*		
מֹשֶׁה	Moses	ABS	noun
מֹשֶׁה	*mō·še*		

As commanded in 3:27.

<table>
<tr><td>1b</td><td align="center">מֵעַרְבֹת מוֹאָב אֶל־הַר נְבוֹ רֹאשׁ הַפִּסְגָּה</td></tr>
</table>

from the plains of Moab to Mount Nebo, at the peak of Pisgah,

מֵעַרְבֹת	from (the) desert plains/steppes of	CST	noun
עֲרָבָה	*mē·ʾar·vōt*	W/ PREP מִן	
מוֹאָב	Moab	ABS	noun
מוֹאָב	*mô·ʾāv*		
אֶל־	to	---	prep
אֶל	*ʾel-*		
הַר	mount/mountain	CST	noun
הַר	*har*		
נְבוֹ	Nebo	ABS	noun
נְבוֹ	*nə·vô*		
רֹאשׁ	(the) head/first/top of	CST	noun
רֹאשׁ	*rō·š*		
הַפִּסְגָּה	(the) Pisgah	ABS	noun
פִּסְגָּה	*hap·pis·gâ*	W/ DEF. ART.	

Notice the narrator's voice again, returning to the place where the book began: Moab (see 1:7). This long geographical journey from Moab to Egypt and back to Moab in Deuteronomy brings readers back to the place where we stand today. Here and now we must act based upon what we have heard and seen.

Given the naming of פִּסְגָּה in 3:27 and פִּסְגָּה and נְבוֹ in 32:48–52, it is unclear whether נְבוֹ and פִּסְגָּה are two names for the same mountain (like Horeb and Sinai) or parts of the same mountain. It may be that Nebo is the highest peak of the mountain called Pisgah.

<table>
<tr><td>1c</td><td colspan="3" align="center">אֲשֶׁר עַל־פְּנֵי יְרֵחֹו</td></tr>
<tr><td></td><td colspan="3" align="center">which is before Jericho.</td></tr>
<tr><td></td><td>אֲשֶׁר
אֲשֶׁר
ʾă·šer</td><td>that/which</td><td>---</td><td>relative pron</td></tr>
<tr><td></td><td>עַל־
עַל
ʿal-</td><td>on/upon</td><td>---</td><td>prep</td></tr>
<tr><td></td><td>פְּנֵי
פָּנֶה
pə·nê</td><td>(the) face of</td><td>CST</td><td>noun</td></tr>
<tr><td></td><td>יְרֵחֹו
יְרִיחֹו
yə·rē·ḥô</td><td>Jericho</td><td>ABS</td><td>noun</td></tr>
</table>

<table>
<tr><td>1d</td><td colspan="3" align="center">וַיַּרְאֵהוּ יְהוָה אֶת־כָּל־הָאָרֶץ</td></tr>
<tr><td></td><td colspan="3" align="center">And Yahweh showed him all the land:</td></tr>
<tr><td></td><td>וַיַּרְאֵהוּ
רָאָה
way·yar·ʾē·hû</td><td>and (he) showed him</td><td>HIPH WAYY 3MS
W/ 3MS SX</td><td>verb</td></tr>
<tr><td></td><td>יְהוָה
יהוה
YHWH</td><td>Yahweh</td><td>ABS</td><td>noun</td></tr>
<tr><td></td><td>אֶת־
אֵת
ʾet-</td><td>(direct object marker)</td><td>---</td><td>particle</td></tr>
<tr><td></td><td>כָּל־
כֹּל
kol-</td><td>all</td><td>CST</td><td>noun</td></tr>
<tr><td></td><td>הָאָרֶץ
אֶרֶץ
hā·ʾā·reṣ</td><td>the land</td><td>ABS
W/ DEF. ART.</td><td>noun</td></tr>
</table>

<table>
<tr><td>1e</td><td colspan="3" align="center">אֶת־הַגִּלְעָד עַד־דָּן:</td></tr>
<tr><td></td><td colspan="3" align="center">Gilead as far as Dan,</td></tr>
<tr><td></td><td>אֶת־
אֵת
ʾet-</td><td>(direct object marker)</td><td>---</td><td>particle</td></tr>
<tr><td></td><td>הַגִּלְעָד
גִּלְעָד
hag·gil·ʿād</td><td>(the) Gilead</td><td>ABS
W/ DEF. ART.</td><td>noun</td></tr>
</table>

עַד־	to/until/as far as	---	prep
עַד *'ad-*			
דָּן׃	Dan	ABS	noun
דָּן *dān*			

2a   וְאֵת כָּל־נַפְתָּלִי

and all Naphtali,

וְאֵת	and (+ *direct object marker*)	---	particle
אֵת *wə·'ēt*		W/ CONJ וְ	
כָּל־	all	CST	noun
כֹּל *kol-*			
נַפְתָּלִי	Naphtali	ABS	noun
נַפְתָּלִי *naf·tā·lî*			

2b   וְאֶת־אֶרֶץ אֶפְרַיִם וּמְנַשֶּׁה

and the land of Ephraim and Manasseh,

וְאֶת־	and (+ *direct object marker*)	---	particle
אֵת *wə·'et-*		W/ CONJ וְ	
אֶרֶץ	(the) land of	CST	noun
אֶרֶץ *'e·reṣ*			
אֶפְרַיִם	Ephraim	ABS	noun
אֶפְרַיִם *'ef·ra·yim*			
וּמְנַשֶּׁה	and Manasseh	ABS	noun
מְנַשֶּׁה *û·mə·naš·še*		W/ CONJ וְ	

2c   וְאֵת כָּל־אֶרֶץ יְהוּדָה

and all the land of Judah,

| וְאֵת | and (+ *direct object marker*) | --- | particle |
| אֵת
 wə·'ēt | | W/ CONJ וְ | |

כָּל־ כֹּל	all *kol-*	CST	noun
אֶרֶץ אֶרֶץ	(the) land of *'e·reṣ*	CST	noun
יְהוּדָה יְהוּדָה	Judah *yə·hû·dâ*	ABS	noun

<table>
<tr><td>2d</td><td colspan="3" align="center">עַד הַיָּם הָאַחֲרוֹן:</td></tr>
<tr><td colspan="4" align="center">to the western sea,</td></tr>
</table>

עַד עַד	to/until/as far as *'ad*	---	prep
הַיָּם יָם	the sea *hay·yām*	ABS W/ DEF. ART.	noun
הָאַחֲרוֹן: אַחֲרוֹן	the back/behind/west *hā·'a·ḥă·rôn*	MS ATTR W/ DEF. ART.	adj

Beginning with Gilead and Gad, Moses' view starts in the north and appears to sweep the land circularly following the command in 3:27.

<table>
<tr><td>3a</td><td colspan="3" align="center">וְאֶת־הַנֶּגֶב וְאֶת־הַכִּכָּר</td></tr>
<tr><td colspan="4" align="center">and the Negeb, the plain,</td></tr>
</table>

וְאֶת־ אֵת	and (+ *direct object marker*) *wə·'et-*	--- W/ CONJ וְ	particle
הַנֶּגֶב נֶגֶב	the Negeb *han·ne·gev*	ABS W/ DEF. ART.	noun
וְאֶת־ אֵת	and (+ *direct object marker*) *wə·'et-*	--- W/ CONJ וְ	particle
הַכִּכָּר כִּכָּר	the round/plain *hak·kik·kār*	ABS W/ DEF. ART.	noun

כִּכָּר literally means "round" or "round loaf" (*HALOT*). The ESV, RSV, and NRSV translate this as a proper name: "the Plain." In this case, the name may have started as a metaphor, in the same way that Mesa Verde ("green table") in Colorado, or Sandia ("watermelon") in New Mexico, inherited their names.

<table>
<tr><td>3b</td><td colspan="4" align="center">בִּקְעַת יְרֵחוֹ</td></tr>
<tr><td></td><td colspan="4" align="center">the valley of Jericho,</td></tr>
<tr><td></td><td>בִּקְעַת
בִּקְעָה</td><td>(the) valley/plain of
biq·ʿat</td><td>CST
W/ PREP בְּ</td><td>noun</td></tr>
<tr><td></td><td>יְרֵחוֹ
יְרִיחוֹ</td><td>Jericho
yə·rē·ḥô</td><td>ABS</td><td>noun</td></tr>
</table>

Verse 3b describes v. 3a.

<table>
<tr><td>3c</td><td colspan="4" align="center">עִיר הַתְּמָרִים</td></tr>
<tr><td></td><td colspan="4" align="center">the city of palms,</td></tr>
<tr><td></td><td>עִיר
עִיר</td><td>(the) city of
ʿîr</td><td>CST</td><td>noun</td></tr>
<tr><td></td><td>הַתְּמָרִים
תָּמָר</td><td>(the) palm trees/date palms
hat·tə·mā·rîm</td><td>ABS
W/ DEF. ART.</td><td>noun</td></tr>
</table>

<table>
<tr><td>3d</td><td colspan="4" align="center">עַד־צֹעַר:</td></tr>
<tr><td></td><td colspan="4" align="center">to Zoar.</td></tr>
<tr><td></td><td>עַד־
עַד</td><td>to/until/as far as
ʿad-</td><td>---</td><td>prep</td></tr>
<tr><td></td><td>צֹעַר:
צֹעַר</td><td>Zoar
ṣō·ʿar</td><td>ABS</td><td>noun</td></tr>
</table>

<table>
<tr><td>4a</td><td colspan="4" align="center">וַיֹּ֤אמֶר יְהוָה֙ אֵלָ֔יו זֹ֣את הָאָ֔רֶץ</td></tr>
<tr><td></td><td colspan="4" align="center">And Yahweh said to him, "This is the land</td></tr>
<tr><td></td><td>וַיֹּ֤אמֶר
אמר</td><td>and (he) said
way·yō'·mer</td><td>QAL WAYY 3MS</td><td>verb</td></tr>
<tr><td></td><td>יְהוָה֙
יהוה</td><td>Yahweh
YHWH</td><td>ABS</td><td>noun</td></tr>
<tr><td></td><td>אֵלָ֔יו
אֶל</td><td>to him
'ē·lāyw</td><td>---
W/ 3MS SX</td><td>prep</td></tr>
<tr><td></td><td>זֹ֣את
זֹאת</td><td>this (is)
zō't</td><td>---</td><td>demonstr
pron</td></tr>
<tr><td></td><td>הָאָ֔רֶץ
אֶרֶץ</td><td>the land
hā·'ā·reṣ</td><td>ABS
W/ DEF. ART.</td><td>noun</td></tr>
</table>

<table>
<tr><td>4b</td><td colspan="4" align="center">אֲשֶׁ֣ר נִשְׁבַּ֗עְתִּי לְאַבְרָהָ֛ם לְיִצְחָ֥ק וּֽלְיַעֲקֹב֙</td></tr>
<tr><td></td><td colspan="4" align="center">that I swore to Abraham, Isaac, and Jacob,</td></tr>
<tr><td></td><td>אֲשֶׁ֣ר
אֲשֶׁר</td><td>that/which
'ă·šer</td><td>---</td><td>relative
pron</td></tr>
<tr><td></td><td>נִשְׁבַּ֗עְתִּי
שׁבע</td><td>I swore
niš·ba'·tî</td><td>NIPH PF 1CS</td><td>verb</td></tr>
<tr><td></td><td>לְאַבְרָהָ֛ם
אַבְרָהָם</td><td>to Abraham
lə·'av·rā·hām</td><td>ABS
W/ PREP לְ</td><td>noun</td></tr>
<tr><td></td><td>לְיִצְחָ֥ק
יִצְחָק</td><td>to Isaac
lə·yiṣ·ḥāq</td><td>ABS
W/ PREP לְ</td><td>noun</td></tr>
<tr><td></td><td>וּֽלְיַעֲקֹב֙
יַעֲקֹב</td><td>and to Jacob
û·lə·ya·'ă·qōv</td><td>ABS
W/ CONJ וְ + PREP לְ</td><td>noun</td></tr>
</table>

<table>
<tr><td>4c</td><td colspan="4" align="center">לֵאמֹ֔ר לְזַרְעֲךָ֖ אֶתְּנֶ֑נָּה</td></tr>
<tr><td></td><td colspan="4" align="center">saying, 'To your seed I will give it.'</td></tr>
<tr><td></td><td>לֵאמֹ֔ר
אמר</td><td>saying
lē·mōr</td><td>QAL INF CST
W/ PREP לְ</td><td>verb</td></tr>
</table>

<table>
<tr><td>לְזַרְעֶךָ
זֶרַע
lə·zar·ʿă·ḵā</td><td>to your seed/offspring</td><td>CST
W/ PREP לְ + 2MS SX</td><td>noun</td></tr>
<tr><td>אֶתְּנֶנָּה
נתן
ʾet·tə·nen·nâ</td><td>I will give it</td><td>QAL IMPF 1CS
W/ 3FS SX</td><td>verb</td></tr>
</table>

4d הֶרְאִיתִיךָ בְעֵינֶיךָ וְשָׁמָּה לֹא תַעֲבֹר׃

I have let you see it with your eyes,
but you shall not cross over there."

<table>
<tr><td>הֶרְאִיתִיךָ
ראה
her·ʾî·tî·ḵā</td><td>I have shown you</td><td>HIPH PF 1CS
W/ 2MS SX</td><td>verb</td></tr>
<tr><td>בְעֵינֶיךָ
עַיִן
və·ʿê·nê·ḵā</td><td>with your eyes</td><td>CST
W/ PREP בְּ + 2MS SX</td><td>noun</td></tr>
<tr><td>וְשָׁמָּה
שָׁם
wə·šām·mâ</td><td>and/but there</td><td>---
W/ CONJ וְ + LOCATIVE ה</td><td>adv</td></tr>
<tr><td>לֹא
לֹא
lō'</td><td>no/not</td><td>---</td><td>particle</td></tr>
<tr><td>תַעֲבֹר׃
עבר
ta·ʿă·vōr</td><td>you will go over/cross</td><td>QAL IMPF 2MS</td><td>verb</td></tr>
</table>

Verse 4 brings us back to the first reminder of God's promise in 1:8 and the judgment against Moses in 1:37 and 3:26–27.

5a וַיָּמָת שָׁם

And he died there—

<table>
<tr><td>וַיָּמָת
מות
way·yā·mot</td><td>and he died</td><td>QAL WAYY 3MS</td><td>verb</td></tr>
<tr><td>שָׁם
שָׁם
šām</td><td>there</td><td>---</td><td>adv</td></tr>
</table>

Moses, the servant of Yahweh—

מֹשֶׁה מֹשֶׁה	Moses *mô·še*	ABS	noun
עֶבֶד־ עֶבֶד	(the) servant of *'e·ved*	CST	noun
יְהֹוָה יהוה	Yahweh *YHWH*	ABS	noun

I render עֶבֶד as "servant" here, recognizing that I use "slave" throughout the rest of my translation. While the word עֶבֶד is not uncommon and is used to describe a wide range of work and service, its formulation here is rare: Moses is called עֶבֶד־יהוה, "the servant of Yahweh," a rare honorific title that is reserved for special biblical figures (cf. Josh 24:9; Judg 2:8; 2 Sam 3:18; 5:7–8, etc.).

in the land of Moab, according to the mouth of Yahweh.

בְּאֶרֶץ אֶרֶץ	in (the) land of *ba·'e·reṣ*	CST W/ PREP בְּ	noun
מוֹאָב מוֹאָב	Moab *mô·'āv*	ABS	noun
עַל־ עַל	according to *'al-*	---	prep
פִּי פֶּה	(the) mouth of *pî*	CST	noun
יְהֹוָה: יהוה	Yahweh *YHWH*	ABS	noun

עַל־פִּי יְהֹוָה could also be translated "according to the command of Yahweh," signaling God's authoritative and definitive word that stands over the prophet who heard God speak face to face. We sense some irony in the fact that this Moses, who so faithfully pleads with Israel to heed God's commands, finds his own life judged by those commands.

<table>
<tr><td>6a</td><td colspan="3" align="center">וַיִּקְבֹּר אֹתוֹ בַגַּיְ</td></tr>
<tr><td></td><td colspan="3" align="center">And he buried him in the valley</td></tr>
<tr><td></td><td>וַיִּקְבֹּר
קבר</td><td>and he buried
way·yiq·bōr</td><td>QAL WAYY 3MS   verb</td></tr>
<tr><td></td><td>אֹתוֹ
אֵת</td><td>(direct object marker +) him
ʾō·tô</td><td>---   particle
W/ 3MS SX</td></tr>
<tr><td></td><td>בַגַּיְ
גַּיְא</td><td>in the valley
vag·gay</td><td>ABS   noun
W/ PREP בְּ + DEF. ART.</td></tr>
</table>

The verb וַיִּקְבֹּר is singular, indicating that Yahweh buried him. The LXX and Samaritan Pentateuch, perhaps to avoid the anthropomorphism or implication that Yahweh became impure through contact with a corpse, have the plural here: "they buried." English translations vary as to who buried Moses. The fact that no one knows where he is buried (v. 6c) supports the singular reading in the MT.

<table>
<tr><td>6b</td><td colspan="3" align="center">בְּאֶרֶץ מוֹאָב מוּל בֵּית פְּעוֹר</td></tr>
<tr><td></td><td colspan="3" align="center">in the land of Moab opposite Beth Peor.</td></tr>
<tr><td></td><td>בְּאֶרֶץ
אֶרֶץ</td><td>in (the) land of
bə·ʾe·reṣ</td><td>CST   noun
W/ PREP בְּ</td></tr>
<tr><td></td><td>מוֹאָב
מוֹאָב</td><td>Moab
mô·ʾāv</td><td>ABS   noun</td></tr>
<tr><td></td><td>מוּל
מוּל</td><td>across/opposite
mûl</td><td>---   prep</td></tr>
<tr><td></td><td>בֵּית פְּעוֹר
בֵּית פְּעוֹר</td><td>Beth Peor
bêt pə·ʿôr</td><td>ABS   noun</td></tr>
</table>

<table>
<tr><td>6c</td><td colspan="3" align="center">וְלֹא־יָדַע אִישׁ אֶת־קְבֻרָתוֹ</td></tr>
<tr><td></td><td colspan="3" align="center">And no one knows his burial place,</td></tr>
<tr><td></td><td>וְלֹא־
לֹא</td><td>and no/not
wə·lō'-</td><td>---   particle
W/ CONJ וְ</td></tr>
<tr><td></td><td>יָדַע
ידע</td><td>(he) knows
yā·daʿ</td><td>QAL PF 3MS   verb</td></tr>
</table>

אִישׁ	man/one	ABS	noun
אִישׁ	*ʾîš*		
אֶת־	*(direct object marker)*	---	particle
אֶת	*ʾet-*		
קְבֻרָתוֹ	his grave/burial place	CST	noun
קְבֻרָה	*qə·vu·rā·tô*	W/ 3MS SX	

עַד הַיּוֹם הַזֶּה׃

even to this day.

עַד	to/until/as far as	---	prep
עַד	*ʿad*		
הַיּוֹם	(the) day	ABS	noun
יוֹם	*hay·yôm*	W/ DEF. ART.	
הַזֶּה׃	(the) this	---	demonstr
זֶה	*haz·ze*	W/ DEF. ART.	pron

וּמֹשֶׁה בֶּן־מֵאָה וְעֶשְׂרִים שָׁנָה בְּמֹתוֹ

And Moses was 120 years old when he died,

וּמֹשֶׁה	and Moses	ABS	noun
מֹשֶׁה	*û·mō·še*	W/ CONJ וְ	
בֶּן־	son of	CST	noun
בֵּן	*ben-*		
מֵאָה	hundred	ABS	cardinal number
מֵאָה	*mē·ʾâ*		
וְעֶשְׂרִים	and twenty	ABS	cardinal number
עֶשְׂרִים	*wə·ʿeś·rîm*	W/ CONJ וְ	
שָׁנָה	year(s)	ABS	noun
שָׁנָה	*šā·nâ*		
בְּמֹתוֹ	when he died	QAL INF CST	verb
מוּת	*bə·mō·tô*	W/ PREP בְּ + 3MS SX	

This is a shorter life span than those given for Abraham, Jacob, Isaac, and Joseph, but it is clearly a full life. Egyptian thought considered 110 years to be the perfect lifespan, so it is possible the narrators want to emphasize Moses' superiority to the Egyptians and their Pharaohs. Tigay highlights two other points of significance for the number 120. It is the full life span for humans in Gen 6:3 and in ancient Sumerian literature. Second, the Mesopotamians had a sexagesimal numbering system based on sixty rather than ten (1996:338). In this case, Moses' long life has a kind of doubled sense of fullness or perfection. Moses' death, therefore, both represents a reminder of our common human sinfulness and serves as an example of a full and faithful life.

7b	לֹא־כָהֲתָה עֵינוֹ		
	and his eye did not grow dim		
	לֹא־ לֹא	and no/not lō'-	---	particle
	כָהֲתָה כהה	it faded/became faint kā·hă·tâ	QAL PF 3FS	verb
	עֵינוֹ עַיִן	his eye 'ê·nô	CST W/ 3MS SX	noun

Notice singular עַיִן, perhaps best translated "sight." Some translate this as plural ("eyes").

7c	וְלֹא־נָס לֵחֹה:		
	and his vitality did not fade.		
	וְלֹא־ לֹא	and no/not wə·lō'-	W/ CONJ וְ	particle
	נָס נוס	it fled/escaped nās	QAL PF 3MS	verb
	לֵחֹה: לֵחַ	his vitality/strength lē·hō	CST W/ 3MS SX	noun

לֵחַ denotes "moistness," "freshness," or "vigor," which is a striking contrast to the report of his weakness and old age in 31:2. We raise the point in the "From Text to Sermon" section below.

<table>
<tr><td>8a</td><td colspan="3" align="center">וַיִּבְכּ֤וּ בְנֵ֣י יִשְׂרָאֵ֖ל</td></tr>
<tr><td></td><td colspan="3" align="center">And the children of Israel wept</td></tr>
<tr><td></td><td>וַיִּבְכּ֤וּ
בכה</td><td>and they wept
way·yiv·kû</td><td>QAL WAYY 3MP</td><td>verb</td></tr>
<tr><td></td><td>בְנֵ֣י
בֵּן</td><td>(the) sons of
və·nê</td><td>CST</td><td>noun</td></tr>
<tr><td></td><td>יִשְׂרָאֵ֖ל
יִשְׂרָאֵל</td><td>Israel
yiś·rā·ʾēl</td><td>ABS</td><td>noun</td></tr>
</table>

<table>
<tr><td>8b</td><td colspan="3" align="center">אֶת־מֹשֶׁ֛ה</td></tr>
<tr><td></td><td colspan="3" align="center">for Moses</td></tr>
<tr><td></td><td>אֶת־
אֵת</td><td>(direct object marker)
ʾet-</td><td>---</td><td>particle</td></tr>
<tr><td></td><td>מֹשֶׁ֛ה
מֹשֶׁה</td><td>Moses
mō·še</td><td>ABS</td><td>noun</td></tr>
</table>

<table>
<tr><td>8c</td><td colspan="3" align="center">בְּעַֽרְבֹ֥ת מוֹאָ֖ב שְׁלֹשִׁ֥ים יֹֽום</td></tr>
<tr><td></td><td colspan="3" align="center">in the plains of Moab for thirty days.</td></tr>
<tr><td></td><td>בְּעַֽרְבֹ֥ת
עֲרָבָה</td><td>in/from (the) desert plains/
steppes of
bə·ʿar·vōt</td><td>CST
W/ PREP בְּ</td><td>noun</td></tr>
<tr><td></td><td>מוֹאָ֖ב
מוֹאָב</td><td>Moab
mô·ʾāv</td><td>ABS</td><td>noun</td></tr>
<tr><td></td><td>שְׁלֹשִׁ֥ים
שְׁלֹשִׁים</td><td>thirty
šə·lō·šîm</td><td>ABS</td><td>cardinal
number</td></tr>
<tr><td></td><td>יֹֽום
יוֹם</td><td>day(s)
yôm</td><td>ABS</td><td>noun</td></tr>
</table>

<table>
<tr><td>8d</td><td colspan="4" align="right">וַיִּתְּמֹוּ יְמֵי בְכִי אֵבֶל מֹשֶׁה:</td></tr>
</table>

Then the days of mourning for Moses were completed.

וַיִּתְּמֹוּ תמם	and they were complete/ended *way·yit·mû*	QAL WAYY 3MP	verb
יְמֵי יוֹם	(the) days of *yə·mê*	CST	noun
בְכִי בְּכִי	weeping *və·ḵî*	CST	noun
אֵבֶל אֵבֶל	(and) mourning *ʾē·vel*	CST	noun
מֹשֶׁה: מֹשֶׁה	Moses *mō·še*	ABS	noun

<table>
<tr><td>9a</td><td colspan="4" align="right">וִיהוֹשֻׁעַ בִּן־נוּן מָלֵא רוּחַ חָכְמָה</td></tr>
</table>

And Joshua, son of Nun, was filled with a spirit of wisdom,

וִיהוֹשֻׁעַ יְהוֹשֻׁעַ	and Joshua *wî·hô·šu·aʿ*	ABS W/ CONJ וְ	noun
בִּן־ בֵּן	son of *bin-*	CST	noun
נוּן נוּן	Nun *nûn*	ABS	noun
מָלֵא מלא	was full of *mā·lēʾ*	QAL PF 3MS	verb
רוּחַ רוּחַ	spirit of *rû·aḥ*	CST	noun
חָכְמָה חָכְמָה	wisdom *ḥoḵ·mâ*	ABS	noun

כִּי־סָמַ֨ךְ מֹשֶׁ֤ה אֶת־יָדָיו֙ עָלָ֔יו

for Moses had laid his hands on him.

כִּי־	for/that/which	---	conj
כִּי	*kî-*		
סָמַ֨ךְ	(he) lay/rest	QAL PF 3MS	verb
סמך	*sā·mak*		
מֹשֶׁ֤ה	Moses	ABS	noun
מֹשֶׁה	*mō·še*		
אֶת־	*(direct object marker)*	---	particle
אֶת	*'et-*		
יָדָיו֙	his hands	CST	noun
יָד	*yā·dāyw*	W/ 3MS SX	
עָלָ֔יו	on/upon him	---	prep
עַל	*'ā·lāyw*	W/ 3MS SX	

וַיִּשְׁמְע֥וּ אֵלָ֖יו בְּנֵי־יִשְׂרָאֵ֑ל

And the children of Israel listened to him

וַיִּשְׁמְע֥וּ	and (they) heard/listened/ obeyed	QAL WAYY 3MP	verb
שמע	*way·yiš·mə·'û*		
אֵלָ֖יו	(to) him	---	prep
אֶל	*'ē·lāyw*	W/ 3MS SX	
בְּנֵי־	(the) children of	CST	noun
בֵּן	*bə·nê-*		
יִשְׂרָאֵ֑ל	Israel	ABS	noun
יִשְׂרָאֵל	*yiś·rā·'ēl*		

וַיַּעֲשׂ֕וּ כַּאֲשֶׁ֛ר צִוָּ֥ה יְהוָ֖ה אֶת־מֹשֶֽׁה׃

and they did as Yahweh had commanded Moses.

| וַיַּעֲשׂ֕וּ | and they did | QAL WAYY 3MP | verb |
| עשה | *way·ya·'ă·śû* | | |

כַּאֲשֶׁר	according to/just as	---	relative
אֲשֶׁר	*ka·'ă·šer*	W/ PREP כְּ	pron
צִוָּה	(he) commanded	PIEL PF 3MS	verb
צוה	*ṣiw·wâ*		
יְהוָה	Yahweh	ABS	noun
יהוה	*YHWH*		
אֶת־	*(direct object marker)*	---	particle
אֵת	*'et-*		
מֹשֶׁה:	Moses	ABS	noun
מֹשֶׁה	*mō·še*		

10a — וְלֹא־קָם נָבִיא עוֹד בְּיִשְׂרָאֵל כְּמֹשֶׁה

There has not arisen a prophet again in Israel like Moses—

וְלֹא־	and no/not	---	particle
לֹא	*wə·lō'-*	W/ CONJ וְ	
קָם	he/it arise	QAL PF 3MS	verb
קום	*qām*		
נָבִיא	prophet	ABS	noun
נָבִיא	*nā·vî'*		
עוֹד	another	---	adv
עוֹד	*'ôd*		
בְּיִשְׂרָאֵל	in Israel	ABS	noun
יִשְׂרָאֵל	*bə·yiś·rā·'ēl*	W/ PREP בְּ	
כְּמֹשֶׁה	like Moses	ABS	noun
מֹשֶׁה	*kə·mō·še*	W/ PREP כְּ	

If we read this verse alongside the promise in 18:15 of a future "prophet like [Moses]," we sense a promise that remains unfulfilled. The narrator's phrase "has not arisen" has an air of antiquity to it, evoking feelings of longing and waiting. We hear a similar comparison made of Josiah: "Before him there was no king like him who turned to Yahweh with all his heart . . . according to all the law of Moses, and afterwards no one has arisen like him" (2 Kgs 23:25). The reference to Moses and his law here only serves to elevate Moses as the paradigm for great kings and great prophets and especially for that great priest, prophet, and king who would one day be greater than both Solomon and Moses (Matt 12:42; Heb 3:1–6).

10b	אֲשֶׁר יָדְעוֹ יְהוָה פָּנִים אֶל־פָּנִים:
	who knew Yahweh face to face—

אֲשֶׁר	that/who	---	relative
אֲשֶׁר	ʾă·šer		pron
יָדְעוֹ	he knew	QAL PF 3MS	verb
ידע	yə·dā·ʿô	W/ 3MS SX	
יְהוָה	Yahweh	ABS	noun
יהוה	YHWH		
פָּנִים	face	ABS	noun
פָּנִים	pā·nîm		
אֶל־	to	---	prep
אֶל	ʾel-		
פָּנִים	face	ABS	noun
פָּנִים	pā·nîm		

11a	לְכָל־הָאֹתֹות וְהַמּוֹפְתִים אֲשֶׁר שְׁלָחוֹ יְהוָה
	with regard to all the signs and wonders that Yahweh sent him

לְכָל־	with regard to all	CST	noun
כֹּל	lə·ḵol-	W/ PREP לְ	
הָאֹתֹות	the signs	ABS	noun
אֹות	hā·ʾō·tôt	W/ DEF. ART.	
וְהַמּוֹפְתִים	and the wonders	ABS	noun
מוֹפֵת	wə·ham·mô·fə·tîm	W/ CONJ וְ + DEF. ART.	
אֲשֶׁר	that/which	---	relative
אֲשֶׁר	ʾă·šer		pron
שְׁלָחוֹ	(he) sent him	QAL PF 3MS	verb
שלח	šə·lā·ḥô	W/ 3MS SX	
יְהוָה	Yahweh	ABS	noun
יהוה	YHWH		

לַעֲשׂוֹת בְּאֶרֶץ מִצְרָיִם

to do in the land of Egypt

לַעֲשׂוֹת עשׂה	to do *la·ʿă·śôt*	QAL INF CST W/ PREP לְ	verb
בְּאֶרֶץ אֶרֶץ	in (the) land of *bə·ʾe·reṣ*	CST W/ PREP בְּ	noun
מִצְרָיִם מִצְרַיִם	Egypt *miṣ·rā·yim*	ABS	noun

לְפַרְעֹה וּלְכָל־עֲבָדָיו וּלְכָל־אַרְצוֹ׃

against Pharoah and against all his servants and against all the land,

לְפַרְעֹה פַּרְעֹה	to/against Pharaoh *lə·far·ʿō*	ABS W/ PREP לְ	noun
וּלְכָל־ כֹּל	and to/against all *û·lə·ḵol-*	CST W/ CONJ וְ + PREP לְ	noun
עֲבָדָיו עֶבֶד	his servants *ʿă·vā·dāyw*	CST W/ 3MS SX	noun
וּלְכָל־ כֹּל	and to/against all *û·lə·ḵol-*	CST W/ CONJ וְ + PREP לְ	noun
אַרְצוֹ׃ אֶרֶץ	his land *ʾar·ṣô*	CST W/ 3MS SX	noun

As in v. 5, I render עבד "servant" rather than "slave." The lexical breadth of עבד is difficult to render consistently in English.

וּלְכֹל הַיָּד הַחֲזָקָה וּלְכֹל הַמּוֹרָא הַגָּדוֹל

and with regard to his mighty hand and all the awesome deeds

וּלְכֹל כֹּל	and with regard to all *û·lə·ḵōl*	CST W/ CONJ וְ + PREP לְ	noun
הַיָּד יָד	the hand *hay·yād*	ABS W/ DEF. ART.	noun

הַחֲזָקָה	(the) strong/mighty	FS ATTR	adj
חָזָק	ha·ḥă·zā·qâ	W/ DEF. ART.	
וּלְכֹל	and with regard to all	CST	noun
כֹּל	û·lə·ḵōl	W/ CONJ וְ + PREP לְ	
הַמּוֹרָא	(the) fearful/awesome deed(s)	ABS	noun
מוֹרָא	ham·mô·rā'	W/ DEF. ART.	
הַגָּדוֹל	the great	MS ATTR	adj
גָּדוֹל	hag·gā·dôl	W/ DEF. ART.	

Elsewhere in Deuteronomy, the phrases יָד הַחֲזָקָה ("mighty hand") and הַמּוֹרָא הַגָּדוֹל ("awesome deeds") are applied only to Yahweh (4:34; 6:22; 7:19; 11:3; 26:8; 29:2–3). In the context of the law in 13:2, Moses' successful signs and wonders authenticate him as a true prophet whose message is to be obeyed (Olson 1994:169).

12b	אֲשֶׁר עָשָׂה מֹשֶׁה לְעֵינֵי כָּל־יִשְׂרָאֵל:

that Moses did in the sight of all Israel.

אֲשֶׁר	that/which	- - -	relative
אֲשֶׁר	'ă·šer		pron
עָשָׂה	(he) did	QAL PF 3MS	verb
עָשָׂה	'ā·śâ		
מֹשֶׁה	Moses	ABS	noun
מֹשֶׁה	mō·še		
לְעֵינֵי	to/before (the) eyes of	CST	noun
עַיִן	'ê·nê·ḵā	W/ PREP לְ	
כָּל־	all	CST	noun
כֹּל	kol-		
יִשְׂרָאֵל:	Israel	ABS	noun
יִשְׂרָאֵל	yiś·rā·'ēl		

And Moses died there. (Deut 34:5)

Israel's greatest prophet is gone. When we look far off in the distance to Jesus' transfiguration, it is only Moses and Elijah who appear with Jesus (Matt 17:3; Mark 9:3; Luke 9:30). Elijah is, arguably, a manifestation of the line of prophetic lineage promised to begin with Moses. Elijah's story is only a few chapters long, whereas Moses dominates four long books and appears in more than a dozen others.

Further, in the way Deuteronomy records Moses' final words and final days, it lays down the major pillars for the unfolding story in Scripture, giving us the past and a proleptic view of what is to come: the beginning with the good creation and the fall of humanity; divine grace; the promise to Abraham; the nation of Israel and the law; the fall of the Jews; and a shadowy anticipation of a future day of grace in the Messiah, the true prophet who is both like and unlike Moses. This final chapter offers several overlapping ways to approach one or more sermons.

 *A Prophet Like and Not Like Moses.* As Deuteronomy ends, it leaves behind an unresolved tension: God promises that he will send a "prophet like [Moses]" (18:15). And yet, in language that beckons from a time long after Moses' death, "there has not arisen a prophet . . . like Moses" (34:10). The paradox points us back to compare other prophets to Moses and forward to the eschatological horizon as we long for the promised and final prophet. In several ways Moses is both a standard for present judgment and a beacon for what is to come.

First, as noted in the comment on 34:12a above, the mighty acts that were attributed to Yahweh's hand (4:34; 6:22; 7:19; 11:3; 26:8; 29:2–3) are now depicted as the works of Moses. Given the narrator's awareness of other prophets, we can infer that God will speak and work by other prophets (cf. Heb 1:1). God has, does, and will do mighty deeds through his people.

Second, Moses is the bearer of God's word. Deuteronomy begins distinctly with, "These are the words of Moses" (1:1) in sharp contrast to the earlier books: "And the Lord spoke" (Lev 1:1); "And the Lord said" (Num 1:1). For Deuteronomy, a prophet is one who conveys God's word truthfully to the people (13:1–5).

And third, Moses stands in Israel's memory as one who prays contritely. We take this up again in the next section.

Above all, the surprising statement that "no prophet has yet arisen" strikes a chord of anticipation that will resound throughout the Hebrew scriptures (Miller 1987:249). In the servant songs in Isa 40–55, the chord rises to its peak with images of a praying prophet and a servant who will be stricken for his people (Isa 53:3–6).

And that prophet finally arrives in Jesus. Citing Deut 18:15–22, Peter definitively names Jesus as the "servant" (Acts 3:22, 26) who has succeeded the "servant" Moses (cf. Deut 34:5). John's gospel picks up the Deuteronomic promise with allusions to the possibility that John the Baptist is "the prophet" (John 1:21, 25). Self-aware, John points our eyes to the one after him who is Moses' true successor (6:14; 7:40). We now turn to two more themes that expand on this succession of prophets.

 ***Knowing God Face to Face.***

> *And Yahweh spoke to Moses face to face,*
> *as one man speaks to his friend. (Exod 33:11)*

The end of Deuteronomy replays the memory of Moses meeting with God "face to face" (34:10), recalling his unequalled intimacy with Yahweh. The narrator hastens to remind us that Moses' burial place remains unknown. Much might be said about this strange ending, but one thing we should grasp is that there is something about this prophet that *cannot be grasped*. We cannot build a temple over his bones. And we can never know what it was like to see the living God.

And yet we may also conclude that God's presence was mediated through Moses in his day. In the new era of the torah and community tradition, God's presence will be at one remove. On the one hand, this leaves us always anticipating the return of God's fiery presence mediated through another expected prophet. On the other hand, it leads us to cling to the words of this torah that the prophet spoke, wrote, and left behind in a book. In its own way, this book brings us face to face with Yahweh.

Finally, we should not lose sight of Moses' intercession as central to his knowledge of God. Deut 9–10 very carefully weaves together Moses' two extended stays on the mountain to receive the law (9:9, 11; 10:10) and the two incidents of Israel's rebellion when Moses petitioned God on Israel's behalf for forty days and nights (9:18, 25). In his intimacy with God, Moses receives not only a law to guide moral order but also, more importantly, a deep sense of God's gracious and compassionate character that can be called upon in times of failure. It makes perfect sense for the editors of the Psalter, then, to place Ps 90, a psalm of Moses, after the story of David's broken covenant in Ps 89. God, "our dwelling place" can be called on in each new day to bring grace in time of deepest need (90:1).

Likewise, Jesus' intercession on behalf of the rebellious and the ignorant reveals his identity as the long-awaited prophet who prays for the forgiveness of others, that they may return to the presence of the Father (Luke 23:34).

 ***The Succession of Tradition: From Moses to Joshua and the Book.*** Notice that near the end of his address, Moses says to Israel, "I am no longer able to go out and come in" (31:2), seeming to signal his failing health. But then the narrator contradicts this with the report that Moses' "sight" and "vigor" were strong to the day of his death. How do we resolve these?

Here Olson recognizes that these passages uphold two facts: one, that Moses was mortal, but two, that this was not a natural death (1994:168). Such unnaturalness inevitably recalls Moses' three prominent declarations to Israel that it was "for your sake" that he was prohibited from entering the land (1:37; 3:26; 4:21). It is not difficult to see that this death is in some way vicarious (McConville 2002:478–79): Moses dies *for his people*. Or, as Patrick Miller observes, the end of the book gives us Moses the "intercessor" who is also the "suffering servant of God" (1987:251). This is perhaps the first indication in Scripture of how a future servant would save his people.

And yet, while Moses' death is vicarious in a way, it is also limited, for Moses also dies for his own sins (32:48–52). Servant or not, this is not the Son of God whose death will vanquish the sin of the whole world and bring God near once and for all.

We attend at last to the succession of Moses. In his death, Moses leaves behind two things that will sustain the Israelite faith in the future.

First, Joshua is raised up to take Moses' place as the servant and leader of Israel. In Deut 34:9, Joshua had been "filled with a spirit of wisdom, *for Moses had laid his hands on him* [כִּי־סָמַךְ מֹשֶׁה אֶת־יָדָיו עָלָיו]" (cf. Num 27:18, 23). (It is interesting to note in this light that rabbinic ordination, *semikhah*, "laying on [of hands]," is based upon this verb סמך [Tigay 1996:339].) The "spirit of wisdom," is always a sign of those called to act in pivotal moments in the history of redemption (cf. Exod 28:3; 31:3–6; 1 Kgs 4:29; 5:12; 7:14; 2 Chr 1:10–12; Isa 11:2; Acts 6:3; Eph 1:17). And it is the same Spirit we receive in our baptism.

But second, Moses also leaves behind the torah along with family and liturgical practices of teaching and remembering. As discussed in the material on ch. 4, Deuteronomy is the only book in the Pentateuch to employ the verb למד, "teach" (Piel). In some way or fashion, Moses' knowledge of

God will carry on, not in political authorities but in homes, at community gates, and in prayer at festivals as these words are read and repeated day after day, year after year. That practice was continued in the early church and should issue a challenge to our intake of Scripture in each new day.

When we look back at Joshua's anointing in Numbers, we see that only some of Moses' authority is passed on (Num 27:18–23). Joshua also does not meet face to face with Yahweh as Moses did. In other words, Moses had a degree of access to the divine that will not continue with Joshua and Israel's leaders. God's full presence and authority end in a pause, awaiting the future prophet and Son who will finally show us the Father.

WORKS CITED

Altmann, Peter. 2001. *Festive Meals in Ancient Israel*. Beihefte zur Zeitschrift für die alttestamentliche Wissenschaft. Berlin: de Gruyter.

Anderson, Eugene N. 2005. *Everyone Eats: Understanding Food and Culture*. New York: New York University Press.

Augustine. 1997. *On Christian Teaching*. Translated by R. P. H. Green. Oxford: Oxford University Press.

Baker, David L. 2009. *Tight Fists or Open Hands? Wealth and Poverty in Old Testament Law*. Grand Rapids: Eerdmans.

Bartholomew, Craig G. 2009. *Ecclesiastes*. Grand Rapids: Baker Academic.

Bauckham, Richard. 2010. *The Bible and Ecology: Rediscovering the Community of Creation*. Waco: Baylor University Press.

Black, C. Clifton. 2018. *The Lord's Prayer*. Louisville: Westminster John Knox.

Block, Daniel I. 2012. "The Decalogue in the Hebrew Scriptures." Pages 1–27 in *The Decalogue through the Centuries: From the Hebrew Scriptures to Benedict XVI*. Edited by Jeffrey P. Greenman and Timothy Larsen. Louisville: Westminster John Knox.

Braaten, Carl E., and Christopher R. Seitz, eds. 2005. *I Am the Lord Your God: Christian Reflections on the Ten Commandments*. Grand Rapids: Eerdmans.

Braulik, Georg. 1994a. "Wisdom, Divine Presence and Law: Reflections on the Kerygma of Deut 4:5–8." Pages 1–25 *The Theology of Deuteronomy: Collected Essays of Georg Braulik*. North Richland Hills, TX: BIBAL Press.

———. 1994b. "The Joy of the Feast." Pages 27–65 in *The Theology of Deuteronomy: Collected Essays of Georg Braulik*. North Richland Hills, TX: BIBAL Press.

———. 1994c. "Deuteronomy and Human Rights." Pages 131–50 in *The Theology of Deuteronomy: Collected Essays of Georg Braulik*. North Richland Hills, TX: BIBAL Press.

———. 2003. "The Sequence of the Laws in Deuteronomy 12–26 and in the Decalogue." Pages 313–34 in *A Song of Power and the Power of Song: Essays on the Book of Deuteronomy*. Edited by Duane L. Christensen. Winona Lake, IN: Eisenbrauns.

———. 2006. "Die Sieben Säulen der Weisheit im Buch Deuteronomium." Pp 77–109 in *Studien zu den Methoden der Deuteronomiumsexegese*. Stuttgarter biblische Aufsatzbände 42. Stuttgart: Katholisches Bibelwerk.

———. 2019. "Das Ende eine Karrier: Zum Dekalog in Deuteronomium 5 und der revidierten Einheitsübersetzungen." Pages 82–99 in *Tora und Fest: Aufsätze zum Deuteronomium und zur Liturgie*. Stuttgarter biblische Aufsatzbände 69. Stuttgart: Katholisches Bibelwerk.

Brueggemann, Walter. 2001. *Deuteronomy*. Abingdon Old Testament Commentaries. Nashville: Abingdon.

Carr, Nicholas. 2010. *The Shallows: What the Internet Is Doing to Our Brains*. New York: Norton.

Casey, Edward S. 1993. *Getting Back into Place: Toward a Renewed Understanding of the Place-World*. Bloomington: Indiana University Press.

Cumming, G. J. 1969. *A History of Anglican Liturgy*. London: MacMillan/St. Martin's.

Davies, W. D., and D. C. Allison. 1997. *Matthew 19–28*. International Critical Commentary. New York: T&T Clark.

Davis, Ellen F. 2008. *Scripture, Culture, and Agriculture: An Agrarian Reading of the Bible*. Cambridge: Cambridge University Press.

Dinesen, Isak. 2010. *Babette's Feast*. McClean, VA: Trinity Forum.

Evans, Craig A. 2012. "The Decalogue in the New Testament." Pages 29–46 in *The Decalogue through the Centuries*.

Ford, David F. 1999. *Self and Salvation: Being Transformed*. Cambridge: Cambridge University Press.

Glanville, Mark R. 2018. *Adopting the Stranger as Kindred in Deuteronomy*. Atlanta: SBL Press.

Glatzer, Nahum N., ed. 1981. *The Schocken Passover Haggadah*. New York: Schocken.

Grant, Jamie A. 2004. *The King as Exemplar: The Function of Deuteronomy's Kingship Law in the Shaping of the Book of Psalms*. Academia Biblica 17. Atlanta: Society of Biblical Literature.

Green, Joel B. 1997. *The Gospel of Luke*. New International Commentary on the New Testament. Grand Rapids: Eerdmans.

Hamilton, Jeffries M. 1992. *Social Justice and Deuteronomy: The Case of Deuteronomy 15*. Society of Biblical Literature Dissertation Series 136. Atlanta: Scholars Press.

Hirschfeld, Mary L. 2019. "Rethinking Economic Inequality: A Theological Perspective." *Journal of Religious Ethics* 47.2: 259–82.

Holmstedt, Robert D., and Andrew R. Jones. 2017. "Apposition in Biblical Hebrew: Structure and Function." *KUSATU* 22: 21–51.

Hopkins, Gerard Manley. 1918. "34 [As kingfishers catch fire, dragonflies dráw fláme]." Page 54 in *Poems of Gerard Manley Hopkins*. London. Accessed at https://www.proquest.com/books/34-as-kingfishers-catch-fire-dragonflies-dráw/docview/2147748522/se-2.

Houston, Walter J. 2009. "Rejoicing Before the Lord: The Function of the Festal Gathering in Deuteronomy." Pages 1–14 in *Contributions to Biblical Exegesis and Theology*. Edited by C. Tuckett. Leuven: Peeters.

Imes, Carmen Joy. 2018. *Bearing YHWH's Name at Sinai: A Reexamination of the Name Command of the Decalogue*. University Park, PA: Eisenbrauns.

Jackson, Bernard S. 2006. *Wisdom-Laws: A Study of the Mishpatim of Exodus 21:1–22:16*. Oxford: Oxford University Press.

Johnson, Dru. 2016. *Knowledge by Ritual: A Biblical Prolegomenon to Sacramental Theology*. Winona Lake: Eisenbrauns.

Kass, Leon R. 1999. *The Hungry Soul: Eating and the Perfecting of our Nature*. Chicago: University of Chicago Press.

Kline, Meredith G. 1960. "The Two Tables of the Covenant." *WTJ* 22: 133–46.

Leithart, Peter J. 2014. *Gratitude: An Intellectual History*. Waco: Baylor University Press.

Levenson, Jon D. 2016. *The Love of God: Divine Gift, Human Gratitude, and Mutual Faithfulness in Judaism*. Princeton: Princeton University Press.

MacDonald, Nathan. 2003. *Deuteronomy and the Meaning of Monotheism*. Tübingen: Mohr Siebeck.

May, Simon. 2011. *Love: A History*. New Haven: Yale University Press.

McBride, S. Dean, Jr. 1993. "Polity of the Covenant People: The Book of Deuteronomy." Pages 62–77 in *A Song of Power and the Power of Song: Essays on the Book of Deuteronomy*. Edited by Duane L. Christensen. Winona Lake: Eisenbrauns.

McCann, J. Clinton, Jr. 1993. *A Theological Introduction to the Book of Psalms: The Psalms as Torah*. Nashville: Abingdon.

McConville, J. Gordon. 1993. *Grace in the End: A Study of Deuteronomic Theology*. Grand Rapids: Zondervan.

———. 2002. *Deuteronomy*. Apollos Old Testament Commentary. Downers Grove, IL: InterVarsity Press.

McConville, J. Gordon, and J. G. Millar. 1994. *Time and Place in Deuteronomy*. Journal for the Study of the Old Testament Supplement Series 179. Sheffield: Sheffield Academic.

Meilander, Gilbert. 2020. *Thy Will be Done: The Ten Commandments and the Christian Life*. Grand Rapids: Baker Academic.

Merton, Thomas. 1955. *No Man Is an Island*. New York: Harvest.

Miller, Patrick D. 1987. "'Moses My Servant': The Deuteronomic Portrait of Moses." *Interpretation* 41.3: 245–55.

———. *Deuteronomy*. 1990. Interpretation. Louisville: John Knox.

———. 1999. "Deuteronomy and Psalms: Evoking a Biblical Conversation." *Journal of Biblical Literature* 118:1: 3–18.

———. 2004a. "The Place of the Decalogue in the Old Testament." Pages 3–16 in *The Way of the Lord: Essays in Old Testament Theology*. Grand Rapids: Eerdmans.

———. 2004b. "The Sufficiency and Insufficiency of the Commandments." Pages 17–36 in *The Way of the Lord: Essays in Old Testament Theology*. Grand Rapids: Eerdmans.

———. 2018. *The Ten Commandments*. Interpretation. Louisville: Westminster John Knox.

Mitchell, Joshua. 2013. *Tocqueville in Arabia: Dilemmas in a Democratic Age*. Chicago: University of Chicago Press.

Morrow, William S. 2017. *An Introduction to Biblical Law*. Grand Rapids: Eerdmans.

Nelson, Richard D. 2004. *Deuteronomy*. Old Testament Library. Louisville: Westminster John Knox.

O'Donovan, Oliver. 1996. *Desire of the Nations: Rediscovering the Roots of Political Theology*. Cambridge: Cambridge University Press.

————. 2004. "The Loss of the Sense of Place." Pages 296–320 in Oliver O'Donovan and Joan Lockwood O'Donovan, *Bonds of Imperfection: Christian Polities, Past and Present*. Grand Rapids: Eerdmans.

Oden, Thomas C. 2005. "No Other Gods." Pages 41–54 in *I Am the Lord Your God: Christian Reflections on the Ten Commandments*. Edited by Carl E. Braaten and Christopher R. Seitz. Grand Rapids: Eerdmans.

Olson, Dennis T. 1994. *Deuteronomy and the Death of Moses: A Theological Reading*. Minneapolis: Fortress.

Pinches, Charles. 2014. "On Hope." Pages 349–68 in *Virtues and Their Vices*. Edited by Kevin Timpe and Craig A. Boyd. Oxford: Oxford University Press.

Radner, Ephraim. 2016. *A Time to Keep: Theology, Mortality, and the Shape of a Human Life*. Waco, TX: Baylor University Press.

Richter, Sandra L. 2007. "The Place of the Name in Deuteronomy." *Vetus Testamentum* 57: 342–66.

Sandel, Michael J. 2021. *The Tyranny of Merit: What's Become of the Common Good?* New York: Penguin.

Schipper, Bernd U. 2019. *Proverbs 1–15: A Commentary*. Hermeneia. Minneapolis: Fortress.

Schipper, Bernd U., and Andrew D. Teeter, eds. 2013. *Wisdom and Torah: The Reception of 'Torah' in the Wisdom Literature of the Second Temple Period*. Leiden: Brill.

Schmitz, Kenneth L. 1982. *The Gift: Creation*. Milwaukee: Marquette University Press.

Seneca, Lucius Annaeus. *On Benefits* [*De beneficiis*]. Translated by Aubrey Stewart. London: George Bell and Sons, 1911. Accessed at https://onemorelibrary.com/index.php/en/?option=com_djclassifieds&format=raw&view=download&task=download&fid=27871.

Shepherd, Massey H., Jr. 1952. *The Worship of the Church*. New York: Seabury.

Sonnet, Jean-Pierre. 1997. *The Book within the Book: Writing in Deuteronomy*. Leiden: Brill.

Storey, Benjamin, and Jenna Silber Storey. 2021. *Why We are So Restless: On the Modern Quest for Contentment*. Princeton: Princeton University Press.

Strawn, Brent A. 2003. "Keep/Observe/Do—Carefully—Today! The Rhetoric of Repetition in Deuteronomy." Pages 215–40 in *A God*

So Near: Essays on Old Testament Theology in Honor of Patrick D. Miller. Edited by Brent A. Strawn and Nancy R. Bowen. Winona Lake, IN: Eisenbrauns.

Tigay, Jeffrey H. 1996. *The JPS Torah Commentary: Deuteronomy*. Philadelphia: Jewish Publication Society.

Toulmin, Steven. 1958. *The Uses of Argument*. Cambridge: Cambridge University Press.

Tran, Jonathan. 2022. *Asian Americans and the Spirit of Racial Capitalism*. Oxford: Oxford University Press.

Visser, Margaret. 2015. *The Rituals of Dinner: The Origins, Evolution, Eccentricities, and Meaning of Table Manners*. Toronto: Harper Perennial.

Walton, John H. 2012. "The Decalogic Structure of the Deuteronomic Law." Pages 93–117 in *Interpreting Deuteronomy: Issues and Approaches*. Downers Grove, IL: IVP Academic.

Weil, Louis. 2013. *Liturgical Sense: The Logic of Rite*. New York: Seabury.

Weil, Simone. 1952. *The Need for Roots: Prelude to a Declaration of Duties towards Mankind*. London: Routledge.

Weinfeld, Moshe. 1972. *Deuteronomy and the Deuteronomic School*. Oxford: Clarendon. Repr., Winona Lake, IN: Eisenbrauns, 1992.

———. 1991. *Deuteronomy 1–11*. Anchor Bible 5. New York: Doubleday.

———. 1995. *Social Justice in Ancient Israel and the Ancient Near East*. Jerusalem: Magnes.

Williams, Rowan 2007. "God in Company." Pages 104–33 in *Tokens of Trust: An Introduction to Christian Belief*. Louisville: Westminster John Knox.

Wright, Christopher J. H. 1990. *God's People in God's Land: Family, Land, and Property in the Old Testament*. Grand Rapids: Eerdmans.

Wright, Christopher J. H. 1996. *Deuteronomy*. New International Biblical Commentary. Peabody, MA: Hendrickson.

Yerushalmi, Yosef Hayim. 1982. *Zakhor: Jewish History and Jewish Memory*. Seattle: University of Washington Press.

12:18–28   208
12:21   189
12:26   72
12:32   14, 25
13–14   69, 100
13:1–5   382
13:2   381
13:17   103
14   190
14–16   62, 185, 214, 240, 281
14:1–21   214, 313
14:2   210
14:22–16:17   103, 214
14:22–27   207, 209, 243
14:22–29   65, 72, 207, 239
14:23   189, 190, 196, 208–9,
   250
14:24   189, 195
14:26   210, 277
14:28–29   207, 209, 220, 239
14:29   179, 209–10, 314
15   215, 223, 241
15–16   69, 100
15:1   213
15:1–11   213, 310
15:1–18   65, 72, 186
15:1–19   23
15:2   239–40
15:2–3   213
15:3   240
15:4   223, 236, 237
15:4–6   213, 238
15:4–11   210
15:7   240
15:7–11   213, 229
15:8   232
15:9   240, 293
15:9–10   215
15:11   213, 238, 240
15:12   65, 81, 213, 215, 240
15:12–18   96, 213, 215, 238
15:12–26   214
15:13–14   213
15:15   81, 140, 213
15:16   213, 238
15:16–18   213, 241
15:17   81
16   243, 276
16–18   70
16:1–17   23, 207
16:2   189
16:3   140, 269
16:4   275
16:5–6   275
16:6   189
16:7   275
16:8   269

16:9   269
16:9–15   243
16:11   179, 189, 277
16:12   140, 269
16:13   269
16:14   178–79, 277
16:14–15   277
16:15   206, 277, 314
16:16–17   23
16:17–18:22   68
16:18–18:22   102, 214, 281
16:18–20   101–2
16:19   65, 177
16:20   93
17   126
17:14   93
17:14–20   102, 208
17:15   310
17:18   7, 14, 126
17:18–20   24, 358
17:19   196, 208
18:9   93
18:9–14   102
18:15   378, 382
18:15–22   383
19–21   70
19:1–13   65
19:14   26
19:15–21   94
21:11   174
22   310
22–23   70
22–25   281
22:1   289
22:1–4   310
22:2   310
22:6   313
22:13–19   65
23–25   70
23:19–20   310
24   185, 310
24–25   70
24–26   70
24:9   140
24:12–15   210
24:14–15   310
24:14–20   179
24:15   234
24:17   178
24:17–22   65
24:18   140
24:19   206, 314
24:19–21   313
24:19–22   23, 72, 314
24:22   140
25   70
25:4   313

25:13   306
25:17   140
26   207
26:1–15   207
26:2   23, 189
26:8   381–82
26:10   33
26:11   277
26:12   23
26:16   33, 62
26:19   66, 107
27   189, 352
27–28   343
27–29   320
27–34   105
27:3   126
27:8   126
27:17   26
27:25   177
28   315, 352
28–32   354
28:12   206, 314
28:13   226
28:15–68   215
28:58   126
28:61   126
29   181
29:2–3   381–82
29:5   140, 145
29:19   126
29:20   126
29:26   126
30   315, 353–54
30:1   352–53
30:2   352
30:3   352
30:6   175, 352–53
30:8   352
30:9   206, 314, 352
30:10   7, 126, 352
30:11   354
30:11–14   37
30:14   354
30:15   353
30:16   138
30:19   353, 358
31   357
31:2   374, 384
31:9   71, 126
31:9–13   7
31:11   358
31:13   196
31:19   33, 126
31:20   206
31:22   126
31:24   7, 126
31:28   348

31:34   14
32   357
32:1   348
32:4   65
32:6   65
32:7   140
32:9   65
32:39   33, 107, 119
32:47   14
32:48–52   364, 384
33   357
33:4   118
34   357
34:1–12   14
34:5   10, 380, 382, 383
34:9   65
34:10   382–83
34:12   382

Joshua
1:7–8   24
24:9   371

Judges
2:8   371

Ruth
2:14   206

1 Samuel
8:10–18   207, 211

2 Samuel
3:13   273
3:18   371
5:7–8   371
9:1–13   211
14:28   273
14:32   273

1 Kings
3–10   66
4:29   384
5:12   384
7:14   384
9:3   189
10:20   258
11:36   189
14:21   189

2 Kings
21:4   189
21:7   189
22:8   358
22:19   358
23:25   378

2 Chronicles
1:10–12   384
19:7   177

Ezra
6:12   189

Nehemiah
1:9   189
9:25   206

Esther
6:1   163

Job
34:19   177

Psalms
1   24, 63, 123, 129
1–2   25
1:2   14
6:6–9   24
19   63
19:4   7
19:4–5   63
19:7–8   63
24   173
25:1   293
50   162
51:16–19   276
68   108
78:29   206
89   384
90   383
90:1   384
95   89, 162
95:7   9, 26
104:27   313
106   163
106:7   163
106:13   163
106:21   163
106:45   163
115:4–7   107
116:4   97
119   63
119:9   7
119:16   7
119:17   7
119:98   108
119:105   108
135:15–18   107
143:8   293

Proverbs
1:1   65
1:8   14

1:23   352
3:11–12   146
3:12   185
6:22   123, 129
8:17   101
9:1   65
9:4   352
10:1   65
12:10   310, 313
20:10   306
22:17   65
24:23   65
25:1   65
27:6   186
27:10   310
27:23–27   313
29:7   310
30:1   65
30:7–9   71
30:24–28   313
31:1   65
31:10–31   209
31:13   209
31:16   209
31:19   209
31:20   209, 231
31:30   209
31:31   209

Ecclesiastes
12:1   277

Isaiah
1:13   258
11:1–9   66
11:2   384
40–55   383
45:5   107
45:18   107
46:9   109
46:11   109
53:3–6   383

Jeremiah
4:4   175
7:12   189
22:27   293
30:3   323
31   352
31:31–34   353
31:33   126
44:14   293

Ezekiel
22:6–8   102
36   352
36:26   353

Ryan O'Dowd (PhD, University of Liverpool) serves as Academic Director and Senior Chaplain at Chesterton House, a center for Christian study at Cornell University. From 2010 to 2023, he was the founding rector of Bread of Life Anglican Church in Ithaca, NY, where he now continues ministry as an assisting priest. In his scholarly work, Ryan is interested in moral theology, particularly through the study of biblical law and wisdom literature. He has published several books, including *Proverbs* in the Story of God Biblical Commentary series (Zondervan, 2017) and *Old Testament Wisdom Literature: A Theological Introduction*, with Craig Bartholomew (IVP Academic, 2011).

Ryan is also a graduate of the US Air Force Academy and served for thirty years in the US Air Force on Active Duty and Reserve status, until his retirement in 2020. He and his wife, Amy, have three grown children serving in the military and live with their youngest daughter amidst the glorious hills and gorges surrounding Ithaca. In his free time, Ryan loves to bake, garden, cycle, run, and swim.